To Bill —

with beox wishes

Thomas H. O'Connor

Boston Catholics

Northeastern University   1898–1998

Boston Catholics

*A History of
the Church
and Its
People*

Thomas H. O'Connor

Northeastern University Press
Boston

Northeastern University Press

Library of Congress Cataloging-in-Publication Data
O'Connor, Thomas H., 1922–
     Boston Catholics : a history of the church and its people / Thomas H.
O'Connor
          p. cm.
     Includes bibliographical references and index.
     ISBN 1-55553-359-0 (hardcover : alk. paper)
     1. Catholic Church. Archdiocese of Boston (Mass.)—History.   2. Boston
(Mass.)—Church history.   I. Title.
   BX1417.B6036   1998
   282'.744—dc21   98-18996

Designed by Virginia Evans

Composed in Horley Oldstyle by Graphic Composition, Inc., Athens,
Georgia. Printed and bound by Maple Press, York, Pennsylvania. The paper
is Maple Antique, an acid-free sheet.

MANUFACTURED IN THE UNITED STATES OF AMERICA

02   01   00   99   98   5   4   3   2   1

Ad maiorem Dei gloriam

Contents

⚶

Illustrations ix

Introduction xi

1 *No Catholics Need Apply* 3

2 *Strangers in the Land* 41

3 *The Famine Years* 79

4 *Growth and Assimilation* 119

5 *A Changing Church* 158

6 *A Sense of Solidarity* 193

7 *Winds of Change* 239

8 *Meeting the Future* 283

Conclusion 331

Index 339

Illustrations

Jean Lefebvre de Cheverus, first bishop of Boston   **20**

Holy Cross Church on Franklin Street   **25**

Painting of Mother Elizabeth Ann Bayley Seton   **27**

Benedict Joseph Fenwick, second bishop of Boston   **44**

Sister Ann Alexis   **50**

Patrick Donahoe, editor of the Pilot   **60**

The burning of the Ursuline convent, 1834   **65**

John Bernard Fitzpatrick, third bishop of Boston   **81**

Anti-Catholic cartoon   **94**

James Augustine Healy, first chancellor of Boston   **102**

An Irish regiment with its chaplain during the Civil War   **107**

John Joseph Williams, fourth bishop of Boston   **124**

The Cathedral of the Holy Cross in the South End   **131**

John Boyle O'Reilly, editor of the Pilot   **144**

Katherine Eleanor Conway, editor of the Pilot   **146**

Anti-Catholic cartoon by Thomas Nast   **152**

An Italian religious festival in Boston's North End   **167**

Celebrating six hundred years of Lithuanian Christianity   **172**

Young basketball players from the South End   **176**

Daughters of Charity of St. Vincent de Paul leaving the cathedral   **182**

William Henry O'Connell, fifth bishop of Boston   **196**

A procession of priests in Roxbury   210

John F. Fitzgerald and his daughter, Rose   216

Cardinal O'Connell admonishing the faithful   229

Members of the League of Catholic Women convene   250

Cardinal Cushing meets with Dr. Billy Graham   257

Cardinal Cushing with some of his "special children"   260

President Kennedy and Cardinal Cushing at Boston College   278

Cardinal Medeiros greets Mother Teresa of Calcutta   286

Pope John Paul II arrives in Boston   297

Court-ordered busing in South Boston   302

Bernard Francis Law, archbishop of Boston   308

Cardinal Law and some young, recent immigrants   311

Introduction

⚜

BOSTON IS A TOWN WHERE PEOPLE HAVE ALWAYS
taken their religion seriously. From the very beginnings of the so-called Bible Commonwealth in the Massachusetts
Bay Colony, the questions of the nature of God, the sinfulness of human beings, and the prospects of eternal salvation were uppermost in
the minds of all citizens. It would be impossible to write the history
of colonial Boston without seriously examining the origins of Puritanism, the structure of the congregational system, and the impact
of spiritual influences on the everyday lives of men, women, and
children.

Throughout the eighteenth century, and well into the nineteenth,
theological precepts and moral convictions helped shape the public
character of the city and the personal lives of its people. The rise of
Unitarianism in the early 1800s provided an optimistic response to
old-time Calvinism, and the new religious movement was so closely
identified with the Northeastern community that many persons referred to it as "the Boston religion." It replaced the fierce God of judgment and punishment with a more beneficent God of love and protection; it rejected the idea that all people were born sinful, in favor of

a belief that all persons were born basically good and potentially perfectible; and it held out the prospect of salvation, not just for the "saints" and the "elect," but for all who lived their lives in a spirit of brotherhood under the fatherhood of God. These new religious ideals became an integral part of the spirit of Boston during the early 1800s as many citizens worked to build a new, better, and more equitable community.

Later on, during the 1830s and 1840s, the Transcendental movement that grew out of the literary and philosophical ideas of Ralph Waldo Emerson and his disciples up at Concord also took on definite religious implications that were influential in shaping the social character of the city. By emphasizing the importance of individuals in determining for themselves what was true and false, moral and immoral, just and unjust, without necessarily referring to the doctrines of any particular church or any sort of divine revelation, the Transcendentalists advanced the concept of a "higher law." This notion became influential in supporting the ideals of the abolition movement during the ante-bellum period, as well as the activities of those who passively resisted established statutory and constitutional law.

The subject of religion, then, particulary where the history of Boston is concerned, is absolutely central to a proper understanding of the community and the people. Over the course of three hundred years, religious beliefs have been instrumental in shaping the moral values, the social behavior, the economic views, and the political philosophy of those who led and those who followed. And so, when large numbers of Roman Catholic immigrants began arriving in Boston during the middle of the nineteenth century, it was almost inevitable that the differences between their religious beliefs and those of the native-born leaders of the city would generate the misunderstandings, tensions, and even episodes of violence that characterized an often difficult but always fascinating history.

As Catholics slowly began to emerge from their immigrant status (in which they had no power and little influence) in the years following the Civil War, they, too, began changing the form and character of

Boston society. The spires of their churches dotted the landscape, the sight of their black-robed priests became more familiar and less threatening, the habits of their nuns could be seen in classrooms and hospitals throughout the city. The Catholic Christmas soon began to take its place alongside the Pilgrim Thanksgiving, the Irish arranged to celebrate St. Patrick's Day in conjunction with the Yankee Evacuation Day, and the faithful Irish domestics brought home stories about how the Brahmins lived their lives on Beacon Hill.

Catholic political leaders introduced a new and more compassionate view of public life that called for the government to take greater responsibility for the poor, the aged, the disabled, and those who could not care for themselves. They also urged a view of the legal system that emphasized the morality of justice as well as the letter of the law. And Catholic religious leaders felt free to use the constitutional benefits of a pluralist society to speak out on moral and ethical issues they regarded as unique to the character of their Church and essential to the faith of their people. Well into the twentieth century, therefore, it was apparent that religion continued to play an important part in the life of Boston, as new philosophies merged with old practices to produce a constantly changing community. As in Puritan times, Bostonians continued to take their religion seriously.

Boston Catholics is a short history of the archdiocese of Boston, designed for the general reader. It examines the almost two-hundred-year history of the Catholic Church in the city within the various historical periods in which its remarkable growth and development took place. It is the work of a professional historian who is a Roman Catholic, but who is neither a priest nor a theologian. The approach taken in this book is to describe the activities, the successes, and the failures of the leaders of the Church and the people of the Church as objectively as possible, and also to compare, from time to time, various positions on theological and philosophical issues without necessarily subscribing to any one point of view. The approach of this historian is basically descriptive and analytical; it is not theological.

This brief study is not to be regarded as a catalogue of churches or an encyclopedia of factual information. There are many excellent reference sources that can provide detailed information regarding the dates of the founding of churches, the names of the various pastors, the number of communicants, the enrollment of schools, and similar topics. The archdiocese of Boston publishes the *Boston Catholic Directory* each year, and the annual volumes of the *Official Catholic Directory* provide statistical data on every diocese in the United States.

Boston Catholics, by contrast, is designed to paint, in very broad strokes, a recognizable picture of the major trends and developments of the Catholic Church in the archdiocese of Boston over the course of nearly two centuries. It is an effort to see what general patterns have emerged by which the past history of the Church can be assessed, its present activities analyzed, and its future prospects explored. My main effort is not so much to engage in original archival research as to synthesize and bring together the results of the collective thinking and scholarly conclusions that have already been formulated. To assist general readers in expanding their knowledge about a particular person or event, I have included at the end of each chapter a list of books that I have consulted. I have tried to select works that are accurate, informative, and readable and that are also available to both general readers and scholars in most public libraries.

Writing a work of historical synthesis such as this requires a great dependency upon the scholarship of historians, social scientists, theologians, and philosophers who studied the history of the Catholic Church from a distance. It also requires, especially in dealing with the events of more recent years, relying upon the memories and recollections of those who were often active participants in various ecclesiastical and institutional events.

From the very beginning of my work on this history of the Archdiocese of Boston, His Eminence Bernard Cardinal Law has been most encouraging and supportive, generously offering the resources of the archdiocese and its splendid archives without reservation or condition. I found Bishop William F. Murphy, Vicar General of the archdiocese and Moderator of the Curia, to be both a close friend and an invaluable colleague; he shared with me a clear understanding of ecclesiastical procedures and an incredibly accurate knowledge of history. I am greatly indebted to Bishop Lawrence J. Riley, S.T.D., who read the entire manuscript with consummate care and whose keen editorial judgment saved me from any number of factual errors and interpretive oversights. On a number of topics dealing with more recent history where written accounts are not yet available, the contributions of Monsignor Peter Conley, pastor of Infant Jesus Church, Brookline, and editor of the *Pilot*, of Monsignor William Helmick, pastor of St. Theresa's, West Roxbury, and former secretary to Cardinal Medeiros, and of Father William T. Schmidt, pastor of St. Patrick's, Stoneham, and former secretary of pastoral services, were extremely enlightening. In informal discussions and interviews, friends and colleagues among the local clergy were always ready to provide me with personal views and recollections, as well as suggestions for topics and issues to explore.

Several fellow historians generously shared the results of their current work in the history of the Catholic Church. Dr. Ronald Patkus, archivist at the Burns Library at Boston College, provided me with insights from his own research into the changing nature of the Church in Boston during the episcopacies of Bishop Cheverus and Bishop Fenwick. I never failed to learn something valuable about the history of European immigration from Father William Wolkovich, pastor of St. George's, Norwood, who was always generous with his extensive learning. Conversations with Dr. James M. O'Toole, associate professor of history at the University of Massachusetts at Boston, about the history of the Church under Cardinal O'Connell during the first half of the twentieth century were always productive and informative. I am very grateful to William C. Leonard, currently a doctoral candidate at Boston College, for sharing with me some of the results of his continuing work on the history of African Americans in the archdiocese of Boston. And my sincere thanks go to Gregory Liegel, an undergraduate research assistant at Boston College, who greatly assisted me in seeking out statistical data and graphic information. To Robert Johnson-Lally and Sandra Sudak of the Archdiocesan Archives and to Father Robert O'Grady and Stephen Gawlik of the *Pilot* goes my gratitude for assistance in providing photographs and illustrations.

Once again, I am indebted to William Frohlich, director at Northeastern University Press, for encouraging the preparation of this work and for accepting it for publication. John Weingartner, senior editor at the Press, and by this time a good friend as well as a professional associate, has worked closely with me in guiding the study through its various preliminary stages with care and efficiency. And Ann Twombly, production director at Northeastern University Press, has again used her editorial skills and organizational talents to bring forth a book that is both meaningful to the mind and attractive to the eye.

Chestnut Hill, Massachusetts
February 10, 1998

Boston Catholics

I · No Catholics Need Apply

I F THE ENGLISH PURITANS WHO FOLLOWED JOHN
Winthrop to the Shawmut Peninsula had their way,
there never would have been a Roman Catholic Church in Massachusetts.

The English people who came across the Atlantic with Winthrop
during the summer of 1630 were members of a Protestant religious
group known as Puritans. Ever since King Henry VIII had broken
away from the Church of Rome over the question of the dissolution
of his marriage, open hostility had grown between the followers of the
King and the supporters of the Church. The eventual establishment
of a national church with its own set of doctrines and its own hierarch-
ical structure—the Church of England, or the Anglican Church—by
Queen Elizabeth I completed the final break between England and
Rome. At this point, English Protestants viewed Roman Catholics
not only as members of a pagan and blasphemous religion but also as
subversive enemies committed to the downfall of the monarchy.

This hostile view of Catholicism was reflected in the thinking of
most English Protestants, and it was especially strong among the Puritans. "For the Puritan, Catholicism was a corruption of the Christian

message," writes Father James Hennesey in his study *American Catholics*. "Rome was Babylon, the pope the anti-Christ of the Apocalypse." Puritans, however, not only wanted to erase any and all traces of Roman Catholicism but also criticized the Anglican Church for keeping too many external practices and ecclesiastical rituals they felt were similar to those of the Catholic Church. Although most Puritans agreed to obey the law and join the Anglican Church, they announced that they would work from within to "purify" it of what they perceived to be "Papist" practices and rituals. More extreme Puritans, called Separatists, refused to join the official church at all.

For their outspoken anti-Anglican views, the Puritans suffered considerable harassment and persecution at the hands of English authorities who viewed their stubborn opposition as unpatriotic and disloyal. In 1620, a group of Separatists left England and landed at Cape Cod, where they started a small settlement of their own at Plymouth Plantation. Ten years later John Winthrop led a number of Puritan dissenters to the shores of Massachusetts Bay, where they eventually settled on the Shawmut Peninsula. Winthrop and the Puritans brought with them to America their violent opposition to the Roman Catholic Church. Now that they had their own City on a Hill in the town they named Boston, they were free to construct the type of religious worship they had wanted back in England. They organized their churches on the congregational model, with each congregation virtually an independent unit managing its own affairs and selecting its own pastor. Unlike such traditional denominations as the Catholic, the Lutheran, and the Anglican, the Puritans had no bishops and no hierarchy of any kind, except for periodic meetings of ministers and elders sitting in synods. Their places of worship were unadorned meeting houses, stripped of every outward sign of Catholicism or Anglicanism. There were no stained-glass windows, holy-water fonts, statues, candles, or crucifixes; no vestments, robes, or surplices to remind them of earlier Catholic practices. The Puritan leaders made it abundantly clear that they did not really welcome into Massachusetts

Bay Colony anyone who did not accept their religious views or subscribe to the congregational form of worship. Newcomers who did not become congregationalists, therefore, were permitted to reside in the Bay Colony only as long as they did not cause any disturbance and agreed to submit to the authority of the established church. Nor were they allowed to take an active role in the governance of the colony. This was a responsibility that was carefully reserved to members in good standing of the Congregational church.

Despite a certain degree of toleration, however, under no circumstances were Roman Catholics to be allowed to reside in the Massachusetts Bay Colony, much less participate in any of its activities. The traditional anti-Catholic spirit of the Puritans was particularly directed against immigrants from Ireland, against whom they bore a strong hatred that combined the zealousness of religious conviction with the ferocity of national pride. There had been centuries of savage military struggles between the Irish and the English, under Henry VIII and Elizabeth I during the sixteenth century, and especially under the Puritan Oliver Cromwell during the seventeenth century. Replete with indescribable slaughters, massacres, and brutality on both sides, the fighting created the kind of barrier between two peoples that even the passage of time could not breach. As a result of such pitiless encounters, the English came to view the Irish not only as members of an immoral and sacrilegious religion but also as an ignorant and barbarous race, incapable of being governed, who were set upon the overthrow of lawful authority and the destruction of the English government. The unsuccessful attempt in 1605 by a group of disgruntled Catholics, among them Guy Fawkes, to blow up King, Lords, and Commons in one spectacular explosion—the so-called Gunpowder Plot—only made the English more certain than ever that Catholics were engaged in a Papist conspiracy of cosmic proportions.

Reports concerning the virulent hatred and open hostility of Puritans toward Roman Catholics in general, and the "St. Patrick's Vermin" from Ireland in particular, caused most Catholics who emigrated to America from the British Isles during the eighteenth century to avoid New England and settle in other colonies. Certainly the example of what the Puritans did to a woman named Ann Glover was enough to frighten most prospective newcomers away from the Puritan capital. In 1688, shortly before the famous witchcraft trials in nearby Salem, Goodwife Glover was hanged as a witch on Boston Common after allegedly reciting for Cotton Mather the Lord's Prayer in Latin, Irish, and English. Glover died forgiving her enemies and her executioner, but announced to the magistrates: "I die a Catholic." If even Protestants from northern Ireland felt it necessary to head for the comparative safety of frontier settlements like Belfast in Maine, Londonderry in New Hampshire, or Orange County in Vermont, then the tragedy of Goody Glover made it quite clear why those few Irish Catholics from the southern counties who decided to come to New England stayed well clear of the Boston area.

In light of this Puritan anti-Catholicism, French people, too, became an object of considerable fear and intimidation throughout colonial New England. Not only were they Roman Catholics but they also posed a more direct and immediate menace to the safety and security of the region. At exactly the same time the English were establishing the first outposts of their colonial empire at places like Jamestown (1607), Plymouth (1620), and Boston (1630) along the mid-Atlantic coast, the French were setting up trading posts at Quebec (1608) and Montreal (1642) in the northern regions. These settlements of "New France" provided the basis for part of a colonial empire that extended from the northern banks of the St. Lawrence River westward to the Great Lakes. This French region that was now called Canada lay uncomfortably close to the northern borders of the English colonies of Maine, New Hampshire, and New York, thereby posing a definite military threat to the whole future of the English colonial system.

Beginning with the accession of William and Mary to the throne of England in 1688, England and France became involved in a series of four great European wars that lasted until 1763. Each of these imperial struggles had its counterpart in North America, where English and French colonists, along with their Indian allies, fought for the interests of their respective mother countries. With much of the fighting taking place along the exposed frontier from Maine to Massachusetts, these colonial conflicts quickly transformed what had been essentially religious differences into more serious issues of national survival. In the English colonies the French, as an alien people, speaking a foreign language, and committed to the Papist religion, now took on an additional role as a dangerous colonial rival. "The Frenchman" became a sinister and almost demonic creature, complete with horns and cloven hooves, that English parents used to frighten naughty children. French Jesuits, especially, were seen by the Puritans as a dangerous menace, a particularly subversive brand of secret agents doing the bidding of the Vatican. Maine was still a wilderness frontier, with the Kennebec River separating Protestant New England from Catholic New France. On the Canadian side, the Jesuits worked among the Hurons and the Algonquins, who were allies of the French and friendly to the "Black Robes." The Iroquois, however, had been pushed south into the Mohawk Valley of present-day New York, where they became allies of the English and implacable enemies of the French and their Jesuit missionaries. The people in Boston were very disturbed to learn that French Jesuits like Father Sebastian Râle were also actively working among the Abenakis and other Indian tribes along the Kennebec River in Maine; they feared that if the priests converted the Native Americans to Catholicism the Indians would also become political allies of the French.* Convinced that the Jesuits would "debauch, seduce, and withdraw the Indians from their due obedience unto his Majesty and stir them up to sedition, rebellions, and open hostility against his Majestie's government," the Massachusetts General Court in June 1700 passed a law forbidding any

* Father Râle lost his life, and his Indians lost their ancestral lands, when the Puritans destroyed the Abenaki settlement on the Kennebec River in 1724.

Catholic priest to be present in Massachusetts territory under penalty of life imprisonment. And, if he escaped and was recaptured, he would be subject to death.

There are times, however, when common sense can overcome the narrow strictures of bureaucracy, and the story of Father Gabriel Druillettes, SJ, is a case in point. Having come to New France in 1643 to work among the Montagnais of Quebec and the Abenaki of Maine, Father Druillettes was sent to create an alliance between the French and English colonists against the Iroquois (who were hostile to the French). Traveling south from Quebec, Father Druillettes reached Boston in December 1650 and met with Governor Thomas Dudley at his Roxbury home. After presenting his credentials, the Jesuit made his appeal for an alliance between New France and New England. Despite the longstanding antipathy of Puritans toward Catholic priests in general, and Jesuits in particular, the fact that Father Druillettes was serving as an ambassador exempted him from prosecution. The governor listened to the priest politely, and then promised to arrange a council meeting to arrive at a decision. A short time later, Govenor Dudley and the members of his council invited Father Druillettes to dinner, where they listened to his appeal for an alliance. He was informed, however, that the Massachusetts Bay Colony could not act alone. Since the Abenaki were located in territory under the jurisdiction of Plymouth, he would have to address the authorities there as well.

On December 21, Father Druillettes left Boston on the forty-mile journey to Plymouth Colony, where he was received courteously by Governor William Bradford and granted an audience the next day. Despite his personal aversion to Catholicism, and his view that such things as "Popish fasts" were "wicked and damnable," Bradford was sensitive enough to serve a fish dinner to the Jesuit so that he would not have to eat meat on Friday. As a result of the subsequent meeting with Plymouth leaders, Father Druillettes felt certain that his mission would produce positive results. Leaving Plymouth on December 24, he stopped at the Roxbury home of Reverend John Eliot, called the Puritan "Apostle to the Indians" because of his missionary efforts in Massachusetts and his success in translating the entire Bible into the Algonkian language. "He treated me with respect and kindness," the priest later wrote, "and begged me to spend the winter with him." Father Druillettes declined the offer, however, and went on to Boston for a final interview with Governor Dudley. Although he returned to Quebec with a favorable report to his superiors, the New England colonies eventually rejected the proposed alliance against the Iroquois.

The civil and courteous treatment accorded the Jesuit priest, however, proved to be the rare exception rather than the general rule. New Englanders maintained their traditional fear of the Catholic menace. During the winter of 1731–32, Boston was thrown into a minor panic when the rumor circulated that there was a Roman Catholic priest in town who was planning to celebrate a Mass for the local Papists on March 17—it being "what they call St. Patrick's Day." Governor Jonathan Belcher immediately prepared to put into force the Massachusetts anti-priest law, and issued a warrant to the sheriff, the deputy sheriff, and the constables of Suffolk County authorizing them to break into dwelling houses, shops, or any other "Places or apartments" in tracking down and apprehending any "Popish Priest and other Papists of his Faith and Perswasion."

Although no such priest was ever found, an almost paranoid fear of the Catholics, the French, and their Indian allies continued to permeate the town of Boston. When residents became aware that there were several persons living among them who were identified as "Roman Catholicks," they decided it was very hazardous to have such persons walking around unsupervised and unguarded, "in Case we should be attack'd by an Enemy." At a town meeting on September 22, 1746, they voted that a three-man committee be appointed to make "strict Search and enquiry" into the activities of these local Catholics in order to prevent any possible danger to the town. This type of hostility and suspicion continued undiminished over the years.

In 1772, Boston's leaders voted to extend "liberty of conscience" to most Christian denominations. They specifically excluded "Catholics or Papists" from such toleration, however, because their doctrines were considered "subversive of society." Besides recognizing the pope in "an absolute manner," Catholics, they reminded the townspeople, also taught that heads of state who were excommunicated could be deposed and that persons they called "Hereticks" could be destroyed without mercy. The spectre of the papal conspiracy and the stereotype of every Catholic as a potential terrorist continued to inflame Puritan emotions, and for generations on Guy Fawkes Day, November 5, the people of Boston took part in a public demonstration called "Pope's Night." Marked by processions of floats, wagons, tableaux, and other forms of anti-Popery exhibits, this annual celebration climaxed with the burning of the pope in effigy. Often the night ended in a pitched battle, fought with clubs, staves, bricks, and cobblestones, between rival gangs from the North End and the South End of the town.

England's defeat of France in the Seven Years' War in 1763 finally brought to a close the lengthy series of imperial conflicts between the two countries. It signaled the end, once and for all, of any prospects of French domination in North America. The victory of the English was so complete and so overwhelming, in fact, that the government of Great Britain decided to relax its official anti-Catholic policies regarding its newly acquired French-Catholic population in what had now become British Canada. Indeed, the British king assured his new Roman Catholic subjects in the former French colony that they would be allowed to profess their religion "according to the rites of the Romish Church, as far as the laws of Great Britain allowed."

In Massachusetts, however, it was clear that Congregational leaders had no idea of letting down their guard against foreign enemies, or of changing their traditional anti-Papist attitudes. Delivering a Dudleian lecture "against popery" in the chapel of Harvard College on May 8, 1765, Reverend Jonathan Mayhew, pastor of West Church and champion of old-time Puritanism, expressed his regrets that persons who called themselves Protestants (obviously a reference to the king and his Anglican supporters) were now looking upon Popery as "a harmless and indifferent thing."* Referring scornfully to members of the Church of England as "half-Papists" who conducted "Masses" instead of holding "Meetings," he seriously questioned where this new type of liberal and reckless thinking would eventually lead. "May this seminary of learning, may the people, ministers, and churches of New England," he pleaded, "ever be preserved from popish and all other pernicious errors." John Adams, a thirty-year-old lawyer from Braintree, also expressed the belief that Popery was incompatible with liberty, and agreed with Mayhew that Catholicism had no right to recognition or toleration. After all, he asserted, it was the "Roman system" that had kept human nature in chains "for ages, in a cruel, shameful, and deplorable servitude." Only three years later John's cousin, Sam Adams, went so far as to express the opinion that the American colonies had more to fear from "the growth of Popery" than from the infamous Stamp Act. Despite a growing degree of toleration toward Catholics in certain parts of the English colonies after the French and Indian War, therefore, it was clear that the leaders of Boston were still determined not to make any allowances for a religion they despised and a people they mistrusted.

It was the coming of the American Revolution that brought about some remarkable and totally unexpected changes in the traditional attitude of Bostonians toward Roman Catholics. In the early stages of the Revolution, the American rebels saw the strategic advantages of developing good relations with the French inhabitants of neighboring Canada, not only as a convenient source of provisions and matériel but also as a potential military ally in their war against Britain. This concern for friendship and alliance with the French Canadians was one of the main reasons General George Washington, when he arrived

* Harvard College offered the Dudleian lectures; the fourth in each series was devoted to "detecting, convicting, and exposing the idolatry, error, and superstitions of the Romish church."

in Cambridge in November 1775 to take command of the Continental army, issued an order prohibiting his officers and men from taking part in that "ridiculous and childish" custom known as "Pope's Night." He pointed out the "impropriety" of insulting the religious beliefs of their French-Canadian allies in such a "monstrous" and inexcusable fashion.

These were days, too, when the business of organizing the war caused many Bostonians to leave their parochial surroundings and travel to other cities and other parts of the country; there, they began encountering people with whom they had never before been associated. After meeting Charles Carroll of Carrollton, for example, a prominent citizen of Maryland who had served on Committees of Correspondence, was a member of the Continental Congress, and subsequently signed the Declaration of Independence, John Adams was greatly impressed not only by the gentleman's liberal education and his ability to speak French but also by the fact that although he was a dedicated Roman Catholic he also appeared to be a patriotic American. Adams went so far as to approve the sending of Carroll's cousin John, "a Roman Catholic Priest and a Jesuit," to work among the people of Canada—a remarkable stretch of Yankee tolerance. Although there was no doubt a great deal of pragmatic posturing in these wartime associations, the various rounds of dinners, conferences, and meetings went a long way toward gradually reducing many old stereotypes.

In the spring of 1778, religious attitudes in Boston showed signs of even greater toleration when news arrived that France had agreed to conclude a major military and commercial alliance with the newly formed United States of America following the Colonial army's victory over the English at Saratoga the previous fall. This treaty was of such "extraordinary importance," according to Rev. John E. Sexton in the first volume of the *History of the Archdiocese of Boston*, "that it rightfully dominates the whole history of that time." The Puritan city's traditional antipathy to things French and Catholic was now further subordinated to the necessity of securing aid in its life-and-death struggle for independence. Local dignitaries became downright fulsome in their praise for the French and in their hospitality to their officers and men, whose vessels were now tied up in Boston harbor. On a visit in 1778, a French admiral, Comte Charles Henri d'Estaing, and members of his staff were graciously received by leading citizens of the town and later invited to dine at the Beacon Hill home of John Hancock. Abbé Robin, a French army chaplain, reported that during the summer of 1781 he was continually receiving "new civilities" from members of several of the "best families" in town, but he was also careful to note that "the people in general retain their old prejudices." Unfortunately, he was not mistaken in this assessment. There was still a nasty undercurrent of distrust and resentment among local residents against the "odious" French. One unfortunate example of this prejudice occurred when one of the admiral's young officers, Chevalier de St. Sauveur, was beaten and killed by some local rowdies when he and a group of sailors came ashore to get provisions for the French ships. The Massachusetts House of Representatives, fearing an international incident, immediately voted to erect a monument in honor of the young French officer and even suggested that a public Mass might be held in his memory. Anxious to avoid creating a further incident, Comte d'Estaing declined the offer, but agreed to a private religious service.

At ten o'clock on the night of September 15, a Franciscan priest said a funeral Mass in secret in the basement of King's Chapel, in a crypt known as the "Stranger's Vault." "Eight sailors of the *Tonnant* bore the coffin on their shoulders, preceded by the sexton and the grave diggers," recorded the secretary of the French fleet. "We started in that order at 10 o'clock and arriving at King's Chapel found the basement illuminated with many candles." Under these unusual circumstances took place the first Mass ever conducted in a Boston church. Beyond official formalities and occasional meetings, there was not a great deal of socializing between the Bostonians and their French visitors. The presence of so many foreigners in town did, however, give curious local Puritans an opportunity to witness at first hand some of the "dreadful" religious rituals they had heard so much about. French chaplains celebrated Mass in public on many occasions and in many different settings—aboard ships, in barracks, in military hospitals—undoubtedly helping to reduce the fear and apprehension with which such practices were traditionally viewed in Boston.

These various changes in the local religious climate help explain why, when Massachusetts delegates met in September 1779 to draw up the draft of a constitution for their newly organized state, they composed a bill of rights that guaranteed "equal protection of the law" to all religious denominations and stated that no one denomination would be subordinate to any other. On the surface, this new constitution appeared to put Catholics on an equal footing with all other believers. In fact, however, few were under the delusion that Catholics would receive any such equal treatment, especially as the new constitution required all state officials to swear that they were not subject to the jurisdiction or authority of any "foreign prince, person, prelate, state, or potentate." Since all Protestants assumed that Catholics were subject to both pope and prelate, this clause automatically excluded them from holding public office in Massachusetts.

Despite the continued existence of political limitations, however, the general religious climate in the town had definitely improved. In view of the good will created by the wartime alliance with France, and the presence of so many of their fellow countrymen in town, the French residents of Boston were the first to react to the new climate of toleration, and began practicing their religion openly. There were not very many Catholics in town, only a handful of French and Irish, but when a French naval chaplain, l'Abbé Claude de la Poterie, stayed behind to organize a small congregation, they held services in a former Huguenot church on School Street. On Sunday, November 2, 1788, they celebrated what is recorded as the first public Mass in Boston. The chaplain remained about a year before leaving for other parts; he was followed by another French priest, Father Louis de Rousselet, who tried to hold the small congregation together despite his heavy accent and the growing indifference of many of his Irish parishioners, who were hoping for the arrival of an American priest reported to be on his way to Boston.

On January 2, 1790, the long-awaited American priest finally arrived, paid his respects to Father Rousselet, and said his first public Mass on January 10. John Thayer had been born in Boston of staunch Congregational parents, attended Yale College, traveled to France, and then spent time in Italy, where in 1783 he was converted to Catholicism. After his ordination in 1787, he decided to return to America as a missionary following extensive preparation in London and Paris. The final arrival of Father Thayer brought an almost immediate increase in the size of the small congregation of some fifty to sixty men and women. The Irish, especially, were pleased finally to have an English-speaking curate at their disposal; they began to attend church services in greater numbers, brought their children (many of them six, seven, ten, and even sixteen years old) to be baptized, and had their earlier Protestant marriages solemnized in the Catholic Church.

According to the Boston directories for 1789 and 1796, there were Callahans, Cavanaghs, Dohertys, Doyles, Driscolls, Duggans, Fitzpatricks, Kennys, Lynches, Mahoneys, McCarthys, O'Briens, O'Donnells, Ryans, Sullivans, and Walshes living in the town during the 1780s. One of the first and most active members of Father Thayer's little congregation was Mrs. Mary Lobb (née Mary Connell), widow of a sea captain, who in 1779 had married a propertied resident of the town named George Lobb. John Magner, from County Waterford, was a local blacksmith who was also active in parish affairs, as was Patrick Campbell, a blacksmith and veterinarian who became one of the church's first wardens. Joseph Harrington worked as a cooper; Michael Mellony made his living as a chimney sweep. Francis Mulligan and Daniel Hay owned rental property in Boston; Joshua Farrington was a merchant. John Boyle and his sons were booksellers; Anna McClure was a schoolteacher; Patrick Duggan and his brother John were lemon dealers; John Larkin sold tea; and Michael Burns was a liquor dealer.

Most of these Irish Catholics were not fresh off the boat; they had been residents of the town for many years, living unobtrusively among their neighbors, following local customs, and passing easily as northerners from Ulster. Lacking churches and priests of their own in this faraway country, they had married young Congregational women, recorded the births of their children in the town register, and as often as possible on the Sabbath attended the more familiar Anglican liturgies, where, as the Reverend Mayhew had sourly observed, they held "Masses" instead of "Meetings." Sensing the warm air of change, these Irish Catholics slowly lifted their heads, cautiously sniffed the breeze, and tentatively came out in public to declare themselves members of the previously outlawed sect. During the early years, the local Catholics practiced their religion in a quiet and reserved manner, generally reflecting the Congregational style of worship with which most of them were familiar. There were few public demonstrations, and most religious devotions were conducted in private homes or in small groups. Following the traditional Protestant model, laymen were elected as wardens, served as trustees, and assumed responsibility for the finances of the church and the maintenance of the property.

The total number of Catholics living in Boston, though very small by later standards, showed definite signs of increasing after the Revolution, reaching nearly five hundred by 1790.* The number of Irish parishioners, especially, reflected circumstances in the home country that caused them to make the difficult decision to emigrate to America. Suffering under continued British oppression that deprived them of their rights and stripped them of their livelihood, many of the

* According to one report, there were 1,368 persons of Irish descent in Boston in 1770. Most of these were from northern Ireland, and only a small number were Roman Catholics.

Irish looked to the outbreak of the French Revolution in 1789 as an expression of the same hopes of personal liberties and political freedom they wanted for themselves. Efforts by Irish revolutionary groups to join with French expeditionary forces and rise up against British rule, however, were put down by the British military with a ruthless efficiency that ended all hope for political freedom. In 1800 the British government followed up its military advantage by passing the Act of Union, which absorbed Ireland into the United Kingdom and eliminated any further semblance of Irish independence. Deprived of political self-determination, subject to oppressive penal laws, and laboring under a heavy burden of taxation, an increasing number of Irish Catholics saw little chance for an independent future and began emigrating to America during the late 1790s and early 1800s.

As many of the newcomers made their way to Boston, it soon became evident that the new American priest, Father Thayer, was having difficulty dealing with the growing size of his parish and, especially, reconciling the interests of his French parishioners with those of the Irish. Despite high hopes at the start, Father Thayer proved to be a disappointment. His constant bickering with Father Rousselet alienated the French members of the parish, while his provocative theological disputes with local Protestants threatened to turn public opinion against the small Catholic community.

The dangerous implications of the situation in Boston came to the attention of Bishop John Carroll in Baltimore, giving him an opportunity to demonstrate his personal diplomatic skill and administrative judgment. One result of the American Revolution had been the decision of various religious groups to cut their ties with English and European denominations and create their own American churches. Groups affiliated with the Anglican Church, for example, established the Protestant Episcopal Church and proceeded to consecrate their own American bishops. In 1784 the Methodists met at Baltimore to create the Methodist Episcopal Church, and the American Presbyterians established themselves as an independent body the next year. In 1792 the Lutherans adopted a new constitution, and the following year the Dutch and Reformed Churches separated from the mother church in Holland. Catholics in America, too, had national aspirations, and Father John Carroll, cousin of Charles Carroll of Carrollton (the highly respected patriot and a Maryland signer of the Declaration of Independence), petitioned the pope to form a separate American Catholic Church under the direction of a native American bishop. As a result, directly after the Revolution Father Carroll was appointed as head of American missions. In 1790 he was appointed bishop of Baltimore, thus helping to dispel the prevailing notion that American Catholics were totally under the contol of a foreign and "alien" power. Less than two years later, then, the new bishop was faced with a potentially dangerous conflict of interests in Boston. He wisely resolved it by reassigning both priests to posts in other parts of the country, with the wish that more people would work toward developing "not Irish, or English, or French Congregations & Churches" but ones that were "Catholic-American." A short time later, Bishop Carroll sent to Boston a new French priest, François Matignon, aged thirty-eight, who had recently fled the revolutionary government in his native country. A kind, gentle, personable man who made friends easily and listened to both sides of an issue, Matignon slowly brought order out of chaos, mended the rift between the French and the Irish, began making some needed repairs on the old church, and gradually earned the respect and affection of his parishioners.

In October 1796, Bishop Carroll made a perhaps even wiser decision when he assigned to Boston Jean-Louis de Cheverus, twenty-eight, a friend and former student of Father Matignon. Born January 28, 1768, in the parish of Notre Dame de Mayenne, Jean-Louis-Anne-Madelaine Lefebvre de Cheverus was the eldest of six children. His high school performance was so outstanding that in 1779 the bishop of Le Mans awarded him a diocesan scholarship to the prestigious Collège de Louis-le-Grand in Paris. After graduation Cheverus went on to the seminary conducted by the Fathers of the Oratory, Saint Magloire; following his ordination to the priesthood in December 1790, he returned home to celebrate his first Mass. But even as the newly ordained priest was assuming his initial duties, the French Revolution had taken a distinctly anticlerical turn, and in 1791 the new National Assembly decreed that all priests were public officials and would be required to take an oath to uphold the Civil Constitution of the Clergy. As a devout Catholic and a loyal monarchist, young Cheverus refused to take such an oath. As his scholarly biographer, Annabelle Melville, expressed it: "The altar and the throne were objects of his devotion to the day he died." As a result, the newly ordained priest was subsequently hounded out of his native city by supporters of the new revolutionary regime. By the summer of 1792 he had gone into hiding during an outbreak of violence; by autumn he was forced to leave France in fear for his life.

Traveling alone, disguised as a merchant, Cheverus crossed the Channel and arrived in England as one of a number of French émigrés. This was at the moment when the British government had decided to improve conditions for Roman Catholics with the Relief Act of 1791. In a more tolerant climate, Cheverus was able to find work teaching French and mathematics at a boarding school while he learned to read and write English. In 1794 he was assigned to the village of Tottenham, just outside London, where he set up a small chapel, a modest rectory, and a school that also provided shelter for other émigré priests. It is quite possible that this brief interlude, during which he encountered English-speaking people and experienced a diversity of non-Catholic denominations, helped the young Frenchman adjust to the distinct culture shock of an Anglo-Saxon society. In 1796 Cheverus received an appeal from Father François Matignon, his former professor in Paris, to come to Boston. The older priest needed help in administering a mission territory that he had discovered extended from Buzzards Bay and Nantucket Sound in the south all the way to Maine and the Canadian border. With the approval of

Jean Lefebvre de Cheverus was twenty-eight years old when he decided to leave the revolutionary terrors of his native France and make America his new home. Joining Father François Matignon in Boston, Cheverus supervised the construction of the first Cathedral of the Holy Cross on Franklin Street, and in 1808 was named first bishop of the diocese of Boston, which originally encompassed practically all of New England. (Courtesy of the Archdiocese of Boston.)

his local bishop and the final authorization of Bishop John Carroll, Cheverus set sail for America.*

On October 3, 1796, Father Jean Cheverus arrived in the town of Boston; the next day he met with his former teacher, Father Matignon, who was now pastor of a small Catholic community composed largely of French and Irish immigrants. After settling in during the winter and spring, by the following summer young Cheverus was on his way north to the wilderness of Maine to minister to the American Indians of the region. A Passamaquoddy settlement was located at Pleasant Point, south of the town of Belfast; a small tribe of Penobscots was located farther south, on the Penobscot River, near the village of Old Town. These tribes had originally been converted to Catholicism during the seventeenth century by French missionaries from Canada who worked among the Native Americans in the New England territory claimed by both France and England. Although the entire region came under English rule after the defeat of France in 1763, the English were unable to persuade the Indians to abandon their faith and convert to Protestantism. The Maine Indians clung to the rudiments of their Catholic faith as best they could over the years, and after learning that the Church had begun to function publicly in Boston they sent frequent requests to Father Matignon for a resident priest. After Father Cheverus came to Boston in 1796, one of the first things Matignon did was to send his younger and more vigorous assistant on the long journey to the two tribes that so eagerly awaited his arrival. Cheverus said Mass, heard confessions, prepared children to receive their first Holy Communion, administered the sacraments (although he had to withhold communion from a number of persons because of their drinking), and prepared a rudimentary six-page catechism to help the Indians sustain their faith.

After this visit, the young priest traveled south by canoe to Bristol,

* Maine was originally a proprietary colony, but in 1691 it was annexed by Massachusetts. Maine remained part of the commonwealth until 1820, when it became a separate state under the terms of the Missouri Compromise.

where he met the members of the Hanly family. Patrick and Roger Hanly had emigrated from Ireland in the 1770s, and between them they had fathered fifteen children. From Bristol, Cheverus took the post road to Newcastle, where he received a warm welcome from the Kavanagh and Cottrill families. James Kavanagh and Matthew Cottrill were two immigrants from County Wexford who had landed at the port of Boston in 1781 and then made their way north to settle in Newcastle, Maine, on the banks of the Damariscotta River.* Here they became business partners, investing in lumber, building sailing vessels, and then profiting in the West Indies trade. In a region dominated by Congregationalists, with a generous sprinkling of Presbyterians and Baptists, the Kavanagh and Cottrill households became the focal point of a small but devout group of Roman Catholics. In addition to his visits with the Penobscot and Passamaquoddy Indians and with immigrant families, Father Cheverus traveled to the towns of Bedford and Portsmouth while he was in New Hampshire. Returning to Massachusetts, he made missionary visits to small Catholic congregations in the towns of Newburyport and Salem on the North Shore, and then traveled down to Wrentham, Carver, Plymouth, and Scituate on the South Shore.

Although Cheverus always retained a deep affection and serious concern for his Indian converts ("his children," as he called them) and visited as often as possible with them and with the Kavanaghs and the Cottrills in Maine, the greater portion of his time was necessarily spent back in Boston working closely with his friend Father Matignon and the small congregation that was fast becoming predominantly Irish. The cheerful and cooperative spirit of the two French priests, and especially their heroic work during a virulent outbreak of yellow fever in 1798, did much to reduce the strong anti-Catholic prejudice of the Puritan town. In February 1801, after Napoleon Bonaparte had

---

* In 1808 Newcastle became the site of St. Patrick's Church, the oldest Catholic church still standing in New England.

overthrown the Directory, Cheverus was urged by his father and by his ecclesiastical superior to return to France. But after consulting with Bishop Carroll, Cheverus informed the members of his congregation at Mass on Easter Sunday, 1803, that his mission was in America and that he would remain in Boston.

As the number of Catholics continued to increase, there was clearly a need to construct a larger place of worship than the former Huguenot chapel they had been using on School Street. On March 31, 1799, members of the congregation met to consider raising money to purchase a piece of land for the construction of a new church. John Magner, Patrick Campbell, and Michael Burns, the three wardens of the group, assumed leadership of the enterprise, and were joined by Edmund Connor, John Duggan, and Owen Callahan. The names of all these men were clearly Irish, tangible evidence that by this time most of the French parishioners had moved away and that the great majority of the Boston congregation was now Irish. Considering that the number of communicants had grown from a mere handful to nearly one thousand, a committee was formed to organize plans for raising money, purchasing a plot of land, and constructing a church. After Sunday Mass on April 7, the committee's plans for fundraising were approved by "an universal show of hands," and the subscription process was under way. In October 1799, Father Matignon was able to report to the committee that a site had been chosen on Franklin Street and that it was available for the sum of $2,500. The committee decided to proceed with the purchase, and the announcement was made to the entire congregation following high Mass on Christmas Day.

Having decided upon the site, the committee was pleased to accept an architectural design drawn up by young Charles Bulfinch, who had only recently designed the new State House on Beacon Hill. Raising money for the project was a difficult and time-consuming task, and construction work often had to be delayed while more funds were acquired through monthly collections, special collections, sales of pews, and general appeals to the public. On August 28, 1800, a subscription was started among "the inhabitants of the town of Boston and other gentlemen"; the name of "The President of the United States," John Adams, was at the top of the list with a donation of $100. For nearly a year, however, no new names were added, leading Father Matignon to complain that "hardly anything" came in from outside sources during that time. Beginning in August 1802, the number of non-Catholic contributors increased rapidly, with names of such prominent Bostonians as Nathan Fellows, Thomas and James Perkins, Stephen Higginson, Joseph Coolidge, Rufus Amory, David Sears, Theodore Lyman, Samuel Tuckerman, and Gardiner Greene added to the subscription list, which also recorded gifts from persons named Dexter, Hunnewell, Otis, Peabody, Quincy, Sturgis, and Weld. Thanks to the increase in the size and number of contributions, construction of the new church was completed in the fall of 1803. Bishop John Carroll came up from Baltimore for the occasion, and on Thursday, September 29, the feast of St. Michael the Archangel, he formally dedicated the Church of the Holy Cross with a pontifical high Mass attended by an overflow crowd of parishioners, members of Boston society, and visiting clergy from neighboring states. Looking around him at the gathering, Father John Tisserant, up from Connecticut, observed that the parishioners were largely Irish people "who were drawn here by the miserable conditions that existed in their native country." It was in this church that Father Cheverus continued to share the labors with Father Matignon, tending to the needs of the parishioners, traveling to northern Maine to serve his Indian converts, and, in the spring of 1805, helping to persuade Elizabeth Bayley Seton, a recent widow and the mother of five children, to become a Roman Catholic. With the constant friendship and advice of Cheverus, Mother Seton went on to become the founder of the Sisters of Charity, the first American sisterhood.

Meanwhile, Bishop John Carroll let it be known that he was planning to make Boston a separate diocese, with Father Matignon as its first bishop. Pleading old age and ill health, Matignon strongly urged

The plans for Boston's first Holy Cross Church on Franklin Street were donated free of charge to Boston Catholics by the famed architect Charles Bulfinch. In gratitide for his assistance, local Catholics gave him a silver coffee urn on which was engraved: "To Charles Bulfinch, Esquire. Presented by the Catholics of Boston, January 1, 1800." The urn is now in Boston's Museum of Fine Arts. (Courtesy of the Archdiocese of Boston.)

that his younger assistant be named to the post. Bishop Carroll agreed, and on April 8, 1808, Pope Pius VII appointed Jean Lefebvre de Cheverus the first bishop of Boston, much to the delight of the town's citizens, Catholic and Protestant alike. This appointment took place at the same time that the pontiff named John Carroll the first American archbishop and created the four new American dioceses of

Boston, New York, Philadelphia, and Bardstown, Kentucky. Anxious to establish a strong American church that would be loyal to the pope and in communion with Rome, yet responsive to the unique challenges of a vast new continent, Archbishop Carroll scheduled a meeting with the members of his new hierarchy in mid-November. They were to discuss the current state of the Catholic Church, the captivity of Pope Pius VII, the conditions of their respective dioceses, ecclesiastical procedures, the administration of the sacraments, and the use of the vernacular in the Mass. The agreement of the bishops on such matters, according to Cheverus's biographer Annabelle Melville, constituted the earliest code of canon law in the American Church. It was clear that, even at this early date, the Catholic Church in the United States was already beginning to take shape.

Bishop Cheverus and Father Matignon continued to be fondly regarded and kindly treated in a non-Catholic town where, not too much earlier, a Roman Catholic priest could be jailed and executed. The two French priests occupied modest quarters near the newly designated Cathedral of the Holy Cross, on Leveret's Lane, just off King Street (later State Street), and were a source of inspiration to their neighbors. "Those who witnessed the manner in which they lived together," observed the *Boston Monthly Magazine*, "will never forget the refinement and elevation of their friendship." Cheverus had to do most of the work himself, since there were few others to help him carry the load. Reverend William Ellery Channing, the well-known Unitarian clergyman, later recalled with sincere admiration "this good man, bent on his errands of mercy," hurrying through the crooked streets of Boston "under the burning sun of summer or the fiercest storms of winter, as if armed against the elements by the power of charity."

Even when he engaged in public debates over religious issues, the civility of the bishop's responses and the clarity of his arguments were enough to suppress any angry retorts. In commenting on a sermon the Catholic bishop delivered in a Presbyterian church, one Protestant journal commented on the "moderation" and even "affection" with

This painting hung over the central door in St. Peter's Basilica in Rome during the beatification ceremonies of Mother Elizabeth Ann Bayley Seton. The scene depicts the various religious communities that stemmed from her work, all of which are Sisters of Charity, with headquarters in (from left to right) Emmitsburg, Md.; Halifax, Nova Scotia; Greensburg, Pa.; Convent Station, N.J.; Cincinnati; and New York. Mother Seton was canonized in 1975. (Courtesy of NC Photo.)

which he spoke about men "of different belief from his own." Such an approach, noted the journal, formed a striking contrast to the "violent and angry language that sometimes dishonors Protestant pulpits." In this small colonial walking-town where everyone knew everyone else and met frequently on the streets, Cheverus earned the respect and friendship of prominent Bostonians, who regarded him as a cultivated gentleman. "He was friendly to our literary associations," commented the *Boston Monthly Magazine*, observing that when the Boston Athenaeum was being organized the bishop assisted in the enterprise "by liberal donations from his extensive library." A charming conversationalist and a delightful dinner companion, the bishop was always included in the town's social and cultural activities, even in an era when changing times and emerging political issues caused strains and tensions among even the closest of friends.

Although originally no provisions had been made for political parties in the United States, the controversies between President George Washington's secretary of the treasury, Alexander Hamilton of New York, and his secretary of state, Thomas Jefferson of Virginia, by 1794 had produced two political factions. Favoring a centralized system of government with an active program of financial enterprises, Hamilton and his followers preferred the stability of an English parliamentary system and looked with horror at the excesses of the French Revolution. Jefferson and his supporters, on the other hand, supported a states-rights system based on the ideal of a small nation of yeoman farmers and sympathized with the French Revolution, whose Declaration of the Rights of Man they found reminiscent of the Declaration of Independence. In Boston, both political groups vied for the favor and support of the small but growing number of Irish voters. Upper-class Federalists urged the immigrants not to listen to the hypocritical appeals of the Jeffersonian Democrats, whereas the Jeffersonians presented themselves as the only true friends of the immigrants in America.

Bishop Cheverus and Father Matignon had both fled for their lives from the excesses of a revolutionary and "republican" regime in France, one that had secularized their church and executed members of the clergy. Not suprisingly, they supported the conservative principles and pro-English policies of Hamilton and his Federalist supporters, while opposing the liberal views and pro-revolutionary pronouncements of the Jeffersonians. In this respect, the sentiments of Cheverus and Matignon were very much in line with the thinking of leading members of Boston society who were backing John Adams as the exemplar of sound Federalist principles. For the most part, however, Bishop Cheverus carefully avoided political disputes and partisan issues that did not directly involve church matters, generally accepting the constitutional parameters of the new American republic. This adjustment could not have been either easy or natural for a cleric raised in the rigidly prescribed monarchical system of eighteenth-century France and trained in the strict religious conservatism of the European Church. But he saw clearly the limitations imposed upon Catholics in America over the years by traditional Anglo-Saxon prejudices, and he worked with Gallic realism within these limitations in the expectation that in time they would gradually lessen. In 1801, although he had been in Boston only five years, he wrote to Bishop John Carroll summing up the prevailing situation sadly but philosophically: "Papists are only tolerated," he told the bishop. "As long as our ministers behave, we will not disturb them, but let us expect no more than that." In 1820, however, when Maine was separated from Massachusetts and had written its own state constitution, Cheverus rejoiced that the Massachusetts clause preventing Catholics from holding public office was absent from Maine's constitution. "Now," said the bishop with clear satisfaction, "Catholics, Jews, and Moslems can hold office here."

By and large, the rank and file of the Irish-Catholic parishioners in Boston were staunch supporters of the Jeffersonian Democrats. The homespun image of Jefferson, the perception of the party as of the common people, the chance to give moral support to the French rebels, and the opportunity to strike a blow at Great Britain were all factors that appealed to the immigrant voters. As a result, in a pattern that would last well into the twentieth century, the political ideals of the common people were often at variance with those of the members of the hierarchy. Fortunately for all concerned, the American principle of separation of church and state made it possible for parishioners to hold political views that were different from (and sometimes in conflict with) those of their bishops, while continuing to submit loyally and obediently to their ecclesiastical authority in religious matters. This was something a famous French visitor, Alexis de Tocqueville, observed in his travels around the United States during the early 1830s. American Catholics, he noted, appeared very "faithful to the observances of their religion . . . fervent and zealous in the belief of their doctrines." And yet, he wrote, they constituted "the most republican and most democratic class in the United States."

The split between the Federalist elite and the more democratic Irish Americans broadened considerably after John Adams was elected president of the United States in 1796; it widened even further as the maritime conflict between England and France brought the United States to the brink of war with the French. Anticipating a full-scale conflict, Hamilton and some other Federalist leaders used the "quasi-war" as a chance to stop Irish, French, and German immigrants from coming to America and joining the rival Democratic-Republican party of Jefferson and Madison. In 1798, the Federalist-dominated Congress passed the Alien and Sedition Acts, which increased residency requirements for citizenship, allowed the president to banish "dangerous" aliens, and threatened punishment for anyone who publicly criticized members of the federal government. Although the Alien and Sedition Acts were intended to help the Federalist cause by cutting down on the expanding size of the Democratic-Republican party, they boomeranged. The major political attacks came from the pens of Thomas Jefferson and his colleague James Madison.

They drafted protests, which became known as the Kentucky and Virginia Resolutions, denouncing the acts as dictatorial, unconstitutional, and a violation of states' rights. On the grass-roots level, too, opposition to the Alien and Sedition Acts produced exactly the kind of growth the Federalists had sought to thwart. Their mean-spirited stand against immigrants and foreign-born citizens, and especially the unwarranted increase in the residency requirements for naturalization, brought strong reaction from the Irish, moving them toward the Democratic-Republicans in even greater numbers. Despite the efforts of the Federalists to forestall the inevitable, they lost the election of 1800. The victory of Thomas Jefferson, and his inauguration in March 1801, were greeted by Irish Catholics with great joy, especially when the new administration changed the naturalization act to reduce the residency period for immigrants from fourteen to only five years. This was clear evidence to the Irish that they had made the right political decision in casting their lot with the Democratic-Republicans.

Although President Jefferson had stated in his inaugural address that he intended to focus primarily on domestic issues, he was forced by circumstances to deal with complicated international affairs. During his first administration he was preoccupied with negotiations with Napoleonic France that eventually led in 1803 to the purchase of the vast Louisiana Territory. During his second administration he was forced to confront the consequences of naval warfare between the British and the French, whose warships were attacking neutral American vessels on the high seas. At first, in 1807, Jefferson tried to neutralize the problem with an embargo that prevented American vessels from sailing into foreign ports. As a strategy, however, this proved extremely unpopular and clearly ineffective, since the United States suffered heavy commercial losses, whereas England and France found other nations with which to conduct essential trade. On March 1, 1809, only a few days before retiring from office, Jefferson repealed the embargo and allowed for the reopening of international trade.

After 1809, the balance of power shifted. With the French navy growing increasingly weak and ineffective, Great Britain emerged as the villain of the piece. The Royal Navy was capturing American ships, impressing American sailors, and confiscating American cargoes at an even greater rate than before. Public opinion in the United States quickly forgot about the French and turned decidedly against the English. After 1810, new congressional representatives from the South and the West, known collectively as the "War Hawks," clamored for an all-out war to avenge the numerous British insults against the nation's honor. Massachusetts (and New England) Federalists, with their pro-English leanings, strongly opposed a war with Great Britain because of the damage it would do to the Bay State's mercantile economy. Many Irish immigrants, however, supported those national policies they viewed as appropriate responses to the depredations of an arrogant foreign power they hated. They were delighted at anything that would cause problems for the British and upset relations between the two countries. At a later date, August John Foster, the young British minister to Washington during the crisis, testified before Parliament that Irish "exiles" had been the ones who kindled the fires that inflamed Americans against the British people.

On June 1, 1812, President James Madison finally gave in to public pressure and sent a message to Congress demanding a war with Great Britain to avenge the impressment of American seamen, the violation of neutral rights, the blockade of American ports, and the inciting of hostile Indians on the frontier. Within three days, the House of Representatives voted in favor of war; on June 18 the Senate followed suit. With that, America's second war for independence was on. Although Massachusetts troops did not enter the service of the federal government, and assumed they would not be required to serve outside their own borders, Bay Staters were always conscious of the possibility of naval attacks along their coastline. Inhabitants of Boston, especially, were in constant fear of invasion, and a wave of panic swept through the town whenever a British ship was sighted in New England waters. Local troops were drilled every morning and afternoon, and sentries were stationed at intervals along the stretch of unprotected beach running along the peninsula from Dorchester Neck (South Boston) to Dorchester. When reports filtered down in September 1814 that British troops out of Canada would be advancing southward along the Maine coast, Boston selectmen issued appeals for help in fortifying the harbor. In response, a number of volunteer organizations representing various civic, fraternal, and religious groups worked from the middle of September to the middle of October at different military installations in and around the town. Even the popular Catholic bishop, Jean Cheverus, accompanied a group of 250 of his predominantly Irish parishioners as they marched in a body over to Dorchester Heights, the site of the British army's evacuation of Boston, to rebuild and reinforce the old Revolutionary fortifications. They constructed a new powderhouse near the redoubts and erected platforms to hold a number of cannon if they were needed to repulse British warships coming into Boston harbor.

Fortunately, these elaborate defenses did not prove necessary. By the closing months of 1814, British and American negotiators were conducting serious peace talks in the little Belgian town of Ghent. Early in 1815, even while they were celebrating the news of General Andrew Jackson's dramatic victory over the British at New Orleans, the American people learned that a peace treaty had been concluded some six weeks earlier. The war with England was over, and the United States was now about to embark upon a new and decidedly different phase of its national history.

Cheverus was greatly saddened when he learned of the death of Archbishop John Carroll in December 1815. Although there was a strong movement among some American bishops to have Cheverus himself succeed Carroll, the bishop of Boston was greatly relieved when Ambrose Maréchal was named archbishop of Baltimore. Cheverus was perfectly content to remain in Boston, and he was pleased to see his congregation expanding and the number of his priests increasing every year. To accommodate the needs of the growing number of parishioners, as early as June 1802 he had shown an interest in the peninsula across the channel called South Boston, after Abraham Gould and his wife, the former Susanna Foster, sold him a piece of land there for four hundred dollars. According to the original deed, the property was located between lower Fifth and Sixth Streets "on or near Nook Hill lying in South Boston." Just what Father Cheverus planned to do with this land is not at all clear, although one historian suggests he may have wanted to construct another small school similar to the one he put up for the Ursuline nuns next to the church on Franklin Street.

When Father Matignon died unexpectedly in September 1818, Cheverus had his friend's body placed in the Old Granary Burying Ground on Tremont Street in a tomb belonging to one of the congregation's most active members, John Magner. Up to this time, Catholics were buried alongside their Protestant neighbors in such downtown cemeteries as the Granary Burying Ground, Copp's Hill in the North End, or the Central Burying Ground on Boston Common. Bishop Cheverus, however, took steps to move Father Matignon's body to what he regarded as a more appropriate site. In November 1815, the Board of Health of the Town of Boston gave permission to "that group of Christians known as Roman Catholics" to erect a cemetery of their own in the South Boston peninsula. Father Philip Lariscy, an energetic Irish Augustinian who had come down to Boston from the Canadian provinces, launched a fundraising campaign that netted $680 for the purchase of a piece of land at the corner of Dorchester Street and Sixth Street. More than two hundred parishioners of Boston's Cathedral of the Holy Cross subscribed to the new cemetery and made arrangements to transfer the bodies of a number of Catholic relatives and friends from local cemeteries to the new Catholic burial ground in South Boston.

Almost three months to the day of his death, the body of Father Matignon was removed from the Old Granary Burying Ground and taken to its final resting place in South Boston. A procession of more than a thousand persons attended the cortege as it made its way down Tremont Street, through the south end of town, and then crossed over the South Bridge at Dover Street into South Boston. The remains of the French priest were placed in a large vault standing above ground, covered with a heavy marble slab, and then consecrated by Bishop Cheverus. "The services, in the open air, were very impressive," wrote the *Columbian Centinel* approvingly, "and the assemblage of members of the church and citizens large." The successful fundraising activities of Father Lariscy enabled Bishop Cheverus also to build a small mortuary chapel in the cemetery the following year. It was located just behind Father Matignon's tomb, and Bishop Cheverus blessed it and named it in honor of St. Augustine. Constructed of hard-burned brick, cruciform in shape, with a slate roof and high Gothic windows, the chapel is believed to be the oldest Gothic-style building in New England. As the Irish population in South Boston gradually increased, the little chapel was used more and more as a place to hold Sunday Mass whenever a priest could be spared from his duties at the intown church on Franklin Street, where the bishop spent most of his time now. The little church had become a cathedral by virtue of Father Cheverus's elevation as bishop, and in order to accommodate more parishioners he was forced to enlarge the structure considerably, while also constructing an Ursuline convent and school adjoining the church.

By the 1820s, Cheverus could see that the Catholic Church in the United States was facing new problems and challenges. First was the nation's rapid geographical expansion, with the acquisition of the Louisiana Territory, being followed by a burst of proud nationalism after the War of 1812. This caused bishops in various parts of the United States to confront unanticipated conditions and to come up with unprecedented solutions. Unfortunately, since the size of the country was expanding so rapidly, bishops found it increasingly difficult to meet together and discuss related issues and difficulties. As a result, there was a serious lack of unity and rapport among the members of the American hierarchy. A second problem facing the Church was the great distance between Europe and America, which meant that communications with Rome itself were most unsatisfactory. Many American bishops feared that the Vatican was so preoccupied with the numerous and complex problems of post-Napoleonic Europe that it was not interested in issues involving America and not acquainted with the country's enormous size and unique characteristics. A final problem was that changing immigration patterns were producing strains and tensions between older local congregations that were increasingly Irish and newly appointed bishops who were predominantly French.

But it would not be Bishop Cheverus who would have to confront most of these American problems; early in 1823, Bostonians were distraught to learn that King Louis XVIII had named him to be bishop of Montauban. They pleaded that the beloved bishop be allowed to remain in Boston. A letter signed by two hundred of the town's leading Protestants attempted to explain to French authorities how much they loved and admired the prelate. "We hold him to be a blessing and a treasure in our social community, which we cannot part with," they wrote, "and if withdrawn from us, can never be replaced." But it was to no avail. Persuaded by the appeals of his family, his religious superior, and finally the king himself, Cheverus bowed to the inevitable and agreed to return to France. On September 26, 1823, Cheverus departed Boston for the last time, leaving behind a legacy of enormous hard work and incredible goodwill. His efforts on behalf of the poor and the needy quickly made him one of the most popular prelates in France, leading King Charles X to name him archbishop of Bordeaux. In 1836, at the end of his career, and only three months before the end of his life, Cheverus was named to the college of cardinals by Pope Gregory XVI.

+═══ ADDITIONAL READING

There are several studies of the Catholic Church in the United States that provide a background for a more localized examination of the

Church in New England. John Gilmary Shea, *History of the Catholic Church in the United States* (4 v., New York, 1886–92), covers the history of the Church in great detail. Thomas J. McAvoy, *History of the Catholic Church in the United States* (Notre Dame, Ind., 1969), is a valuable one-volume institutional history. Jay Dolan, *The American Catholic Experience: A History from Colonial Times to the Present* (Garden City, N.Y., 1985), and James Hennesey, *American Catholics: A History of the Roman Catholic Community in the United States* (New York, 1981), are readable and informative histories that incorporate more information from the Catholic community itself. Charles R. Morris, *American Catholic: The Saints and Sinners Who Built America's Most Powerful Church* (New York, 1997), is a general historical survey that analyzes the problems and challenges faced by the Catholic Church on the eve of the twenty-first century. Gerald Shaughnessy, *Has the Immigrant Kept Faith?* (New York, 1925), offers important statistics regarding the nature of the Catholic population. John Tracy Ellis, ed., *Documents of American Catholic History* (rev. ed., Chicago, 1967), provides essential documents for historical researchers. William Byrne et al., *History of the Catholic Church in the New England States* (2 v., Boston, 1899), establishes a general account of Catholic expansion in the region.

To write a history of the archdiocese of Boston would be impossible without consulting Robert H. Lord, Edward T. Harrington, and John E. Sexton, *History of the Archdiocese of Boston* (3 v., New York, 1944). These three priests of the archdiocese were trained historians and recognized scholars. The first volume, written by Father Sexton, is a detailed and documented study of the origins of the Catholic Church in New England that ranges from earliest colonial times to the establishment of the diocese of Boston. Two collections of historical essays by archdiocesan archivists also provide valuable insights into various aspects of Church history by drawing upon documents and records in the archives of the archdiocese: James M. O'Toole, *From Generation to Generation* (Boston, 1983), and Ronald D. Patkus, *From Generation* to *Generation II* (Boston, 1992), contain reprints of essays that originally appeared in the *Pilot*.

Since the first bishop's responsibilities included the Native-American peoples of Maine, a general background in the work of the early French missionaries in Canada and New England is helpful. Serious scholars must consult the series *Jesuit Relations and Allied Documents* (73 v., ed. Reuben G. Thwaites, Cleveland, 1896), which contains firsthand accounts by French Jesuits concerning their missionary labors in North America. A more general treatment of the Jesuits can be found in W. J. Eules, *France in America* (New York, 1973). Francis Parkman, *The Jesuits in North America* (Boston, 1867), remains a brilliant piece of literature and history by a Unitarian scholar from Boston who admired the courage and devotion of the Catholic missionaries even though he disapproved of their religious objectives. A larger picture of the hostile relations between two rival imperial powers is provided in Allan Forbes and Paul Cadman, *France and New England* (2 v., Boston, 1927). Francis X. Talbot, *Saint among Savages* (New York, 1935), offers a moving portrayal of the Jesuit missionary and martyr Isaac Jogues; John Francis Sprague, *Sebastian Râle: A Maine Tragedy of the Eighteenth Century* (Boston, 1906), describes the missionary work of a later French Jesuit in New England. The story of Father Druillettes's visit to Boston and Plymouth can be found in Rev. Gabriel Druillettes, "Narre du Voyage," in Thwaites, *Jesuit Relations*, XXXVI, pp. 82–111. A letter from Druillettes to John Winthrop, "Epistola Patris Gabrielis Druillettes ad Joannem Winthrop, Scutarium," is printed in *The Winthrop Papers* (ed. Malcolm Freiburg, Boston, 1992), VI.

Mary Celeste Leger, *The Catholic Indian Missions in Maine, 1611–1820* (Washington, 1929), brings the story of the Native Americans in Maine into the nineteenth century; William Leo Lucey, *Edward Kavanagh* (Francestown, N.H., 1946), is an impressive biography of a statesman and diplomat whose family helped establish a Catholic community in Maine. James Sullivan, *The History of the District of*

Maine (Boston, 1795), endures as an original history by the son of an Irish immigrant who later became governor of Massachusetts.

In focusing on the origins of the Church in Boston itself, the work of John Tracy Ellis, *Catholics in Colonial America* (Baltimore, 1975), is extremely helpful in providing a general account of the position of Roman Catholics in English North America. Mary A. Ray, *American Opinion of Roman Catholicism in the Eighteenth Century* (New York, 1936), is essential for understanding the prevailing attitudes toward Roman Catholics in the English colonies; Carl Bridenbaugh, *Mitre and Sceptre* (New York, 1962), analyzes the relationship between church and state in colonial America. George F. Donovan, *The Pre-Revolutionary Irish in Massachusetts, 1620–1775* (Menasha, Wisc., 1908), focuses on the numbers, distribution, and status of the early Irish in the Massachusetts Bay Colony. Martin Griffin, *Catholics and the American Revolution* (3 v., Philadelphia, 1907–1911), James Haltigan, *The Irish in the American Revolution* (Washington, 1908), and Charles H. Metzger, *Catholics and the American Revolution: A Study in Religious Climate* (Chicago, 1962), investigate the role Catholics played in the War for Independence; Arthur J. Riley, *Catholicism in New England to 1788* (Washington, 1936), brings the story into the post-Revolutionary era. Michael J. O'Brien, *The Irish at Bunker Hill* (Shannon, Ireland, 1968), focuses on the participation of local Irishmen in the rebellion. James B. Cullen, *The Story of the Irish in Boston* (Boston, 1893), traces the course of the city's Irish from colonial times through the Revolution to the Civil War era.

The beginnings of a new life for the Catholic Church in the independent United States can be traced through such works as John Gilmary Shea, *The Life and Times of the Most Rev. John Carroll, Bishop and First Archbishop of Baltimore* (New York, 1888), and Peter Guilday, *The Life and Times of John Carroll, Archbishop of Baltimore, 1735–1815* (New York, 1922). Arthur T. Connolly, *An Appreciation of the Life and Labors of Rev. Francis Matignon, D.D.* (Boston, 1908), is an early tribute to Boston's first permanent curate. Annabelle M. Melville, *Jean Lefebvre de Cheverus, 1768–1836* (Milwaukee, 1958), is a scholarly and readable account of the French émigré who served as Boston's first bishop. Walter Muir Whitehill, *A Memorial to Bishop Cheverus* (Boston, 1951), is a modern tribute to his scholarly attainments; it includes a full listing of the books in Cheverus's library that he gave to the Boston Athenaeum. Leo Ruskowski, *French Emigré Priests in the United States, 1791–1815* (Washington, 1940), and S. J. Connolly, *Priests and People in Pre-Famine Ireland, 1780–1845* (New York, 1980), provide informative backgrounds for understanding the influence of French and Irish priests in early America. Annabelle Melville, *Elizabeth Bayley Seton, 1774–1821* (New York, 1951), has supplied a splendid biography of Bishop Cheverus's friend and spiritual daughter, who became Mother Seton as founder in 1809 of America's first order of nuns, the Sisters of Charity of Emmitsburg (later incorporated into the Daughters of Charity of St. Vincent de Paul, founded in France in 1633). An earlier work by Sister Anna B. McGill, *The Sisters of Charity of Nazareth, Kentucky* (New York, 1917), has been supplemented by Sister Daniel Hannefin, *Daughters of the Church: A Popular History of the Daughters of Charity in the United States, 1908–1987* (New York, 1989).

2 Strangers in the Land

WITH THE DEPARTURE OF BISHOP CHEVERUS IN 1823 to assume his episcopacy in France, and after the death of his friend Father François Matignon five years earlier, the diocese of Boston was badly in need of the kind of clerical leadership that could build upon the remarkable beginning the two popular French priests had made in the old Yankee town. Cheverus's first choice as his successor was Father William Taylor, a young Irish priest who had moved from New York to Boston, where he was eventually appointed vicar-general. Cheverus was perfectly content, however, when he was informed that Rome had named Benedict Fenwick, a Jesuit from Maryland, as the new bishop of Boston. During various visits to New York, Cheverus had been impressed by the efforts of the Jesuits in that city; he singled out for special mention the work of Father Fenwick, who was already among those being considered for an American bishopric and whom he found to be "the object of universal respect and love." "His zeal, piety & talents need not my praise," Cheverus said in a letter to his mother. "His praise is in the hearts of all who know him. He is I sincerely believe *dilectus Deo & hominibus*"—beloved by God and by men.

In Benedict Joseph Fenwick, aged forty-three, Boston got a native-born American, a dedicated Jesuit, an experienced administrator, a recognized educator, and a widely traveled observer of the Catholic Church in America. Fenwick was born September 3, 1782, in St. Mary's County, Maryland, of a family that could trace its origins as far back as 1633, when the *Ark* and the *Dove* arrived on the shores of America. Established as a proprietary colony under Sir George Calvert, the first Lord Baltimore, Maryland was originally designed to be a haven for English Catholics, but before long it was taken over by Puritans who reshaped it into another Protestant colony. Despite occasional harassment, the original Catholic families, like the Carrolls and the Fenwicks, lived mostly in St. Mary's and Charles Counties and formed part of the colony's political and social elite. Fenwick's father, George Fenwick II, was a planter and surveyor; his mother, the former Margaret Medley, was known as a very devout woman. After the Fenwicks moved to Georgetown, Benedict was enrolled at Georgetown Academy, staffed by former members of the Society of Jesus (which had been officially suppressed in 1773). By 1801 he had begun ecclesiastic training, and from then until the summer of 1805 he also taught at the school. By that time the Jesuits had been given permission to reorganize their society in the United States.

Benedict and his brother Enoch spent a brief period at St. Mary's Seminary at Baltimore, and returned there as postulants in the fall of 1806; on June 11, 1808, Benedict and his brother were ordained as Jesuits in Trinity Church, Georgetown, by Bishop Leonard Neale. Father Benedict Fenwick was then assigned to New York, where he remained for nine years as rector of St. Peter's Church and as vicar-general. He was recalled to Georgetown College in April 1817 to serve as its president, in addition to serving as pastor of the adjacent Trinity Church. The following year he was sent to Charleston, South Carolina, where he settled a troublesome trustee controversy with such dispatch that he was appointed vicar-general for the two Carolinas and Georgia. In 1822 he published *The Laity's Directory to the Church*

Service, which remains an essential primary source for Church historians, and in May of that year he returned to Georgetown College for a brief period of rest before being sent to serve for two years as chaplain for religious orders in southern Maryland. In January 1825, he was recalled to Georgetown College for another brief term as president. Father Fenwick was then elevated to the rank of bishop and sent to Boston to assume "the great and awfully responsible charge" of the diocese.

Benedict Joseph Fenwick was consecrated the second bishop of Boston on November 1, 1825, in the cathedral at Baltimore by Archbishop Ambrose Maréchal. On assuming his duties he found himself in charge of the smallest and weakest of the nine dioceses that existed in the United States at that time. In all New England there were only eight churches, "all of which, with the exception of the Cathedral [on Franklin Street] scarcely deserve the name," he confided to his journal. The Catholic population, he further observed, lived mainly in Boston, and were few in number, "though latterly they are, from various circumstances, beginning to become somewhat more numerous." During the first few years of his episcopacy, Fenwick remained in Boston and concentrated his attention on the local parish, expanding the small church structure to nearly double its original size and providing some extra rooms in the basement for the instruction of children. In May 1826 he also moved the small community of teaching Ursuline nuns from their original "confined location" adjoining the Franklin Street church, where "their declining health creates much uneasiness," to a plot of land he had purchased across the Charles River in Charlestown. The nuns named their new site "Mount Benedict" in the bishop's honor, but they were destined to face problems in a location where the residents were almost entirely Protestant, with a penchant for anti-Catholic violence.

Education was always uppermost in the mind of Fenwick, and so in addition to the usual catechetical instruction he sought new ways to prepare promising young men for the priesthood. Within a year, he

Benedict Joseph Fenwick, SJ, succeeded Jean Cheverus as bishop of Boston in 1825. A descendant of one of Maryland's oldest Catholic families, Fenwick was a pastor of churches in New York and Charleston before arriving in Boston. He had also served as the president of Georgetown University in Washington, D.C. Although the burning of the Ursuline Convent in 1834 was his greatest heart-ache, the construction of the College of the Holy Cross was perhaps his greatest delight. (Photo by Sister Rita Murray.)

picked up the practice Cheverus had started of taking a few young men into his own lodgings to instruct them in the basics of theology and to provide personal advice and guidance in their vocation. By means of this makeshift arrangement, he soon ordained three young men to assist him in the Boston parish: James Fitton, son of an immigrant wheelwright; William Wiley, a zealous convert from New York; and William Tyler, who came down from Vermont to study at Fenwick's "house seminary." In a short time, Fenwick saw that he also had to provide facilities for those parishioners who were beginning to move out of the center of town into the waterfront areas. In 1831, therefore, he enlarged the little cemetery chapel of St. Augustine in South Boston; in 1836 he dedicated St. Mary's Church in the North End; and in the same year he consecrated St. Patrick's Church in the South End. But numbers were growing faster than churches, and when the bishop later returned to South Boston he found St. Augustine's chapel already "crowded to suffocation." He constructed an impressive Gothic structure on west Broadway in honor of Saints Peter and Paul to accommodate the growing number of Irish newcomers who were moving into the lower end of the peninsula district in search of work.

Most Irish immigrants lived close to the sights and sounds and smells of the city's docks, packed together in dilapidated brick buildings and tumbled-down wooden houses long abandoned by their original occupants. Straggling along the waterfront, from the old Fort Hill district on the south side to the expanding North End, on either side of the bustling market district, the area was what foreign visitors and native Yankees contemptuously referred to as the "Irish quarter"—the appalling slum where the despised "Paddies" lived. And yet a small trickle of Catholic immigrants was already beginning to move out of the waterfront areas of downtown Boston. They headed for various inland parts of the state where land was more plentiful and opportunities for work more readily available, especially with the growth of new textile-factory towns all the way from the Blackstone Valley up to the falls of the Merrimack River.

During the War of 1812, while Cheverus was still bishop, a number of Boston businessmen had experimented with the manufacture of textile products after the British blockade made it impossible for them to invest their capital in maritime enterprises. What started out as an expedient became a permanent part of the Bay State's economy when the resulting profits demonstrated a huge consumer market for textile goods. By the early 1820s, a group of local investors, known collectively as the Boston Associates, had discovered the immense water-power generated by the falls of the Merrimack River, some forty-five miles north of Boston. In a short time the associates created a network of canals, built a complex of cotton-textile factories, constructed a series of boarding houses, and created what became famous as the mill village of Lowell. Word quickly spread to Boston that unskilled laborers were needed to dig the canals and construct the buildings at the new site, and by the spring of 1822 immigrants were eagerly applying to Lowell's agents for work. Irishmen from the Boston area, together with a number of their brethren who came down from Canada, soon made up a sizeable portion of the region's unskilled-labor market. By the early 1830s, there were over five hundred Irish people living in the Lowell district, scattered about in so-called Paddy Camps on stretches of open land beyond the boundaries of the mill village itself. A larger camp, the Acre, lay west of the Western Canal and was inhabited by immigrants from southwestern Ireland; a smaller camp, the Half-Acre, lay to the northwest and was made up of "West County" Irish people from Connaught.

The presence of a small but growing community of Irish Catholics only forty-five miles north of Boston caused Bishop Fenwick to send Father Patrick Byrne, an Irish missionary, on sporadic visits to Lowell from 1822 to 1827, after which he sent Father John Mahoney, another Irish missionary, to divide his time between Lowell and Salem. Meanwhile, Fenwick worked quietly with several members of the Boston

Associates to get their approval for a church and to persuade them to donate a plot of land for that purpose. Fenwick was well aware of the influence of families like the Lowells, the Lawrences, the Appletons, and other leading members of the city's business community. He cultivated their friendship, and whenever possible operated with their approval and support. The Yankee businessmen, for their part, recognized that their Irish-Catholic workers would be much happier, easier to deal with, and much less inclined to move away if they had convenient access to their own priests and their own church. The associates, therefore, agreed to the idea of a Catholic church in the area and donated to Bishop Fenwick an eight-hundred-square-foot lot near the Western Canal. Work on the project was begun during the winter and spring of 1830–31, and on July 3, 1831, the bishop formally dedicated St. Patrick's Church as further evidence of the growth and expansion of the Catholic community.

With the movement of many Catholics away from the Boston waterfront into many other parts of New England, Bishop Fenwick was forced to spend more and more of his time traveling to other sections of his far-flung diocese in order to say Mass, administer the sacraments, renovate old churches, create new parishes, and build new churches in places where no previous structures existed. His first building projects were modest ones, putting up a church in Salem, another in Lowell, and one in Charlestown, which also served East Cambridge. A versatile man, Fenwick sometimes designed the buildings himself and even borrowed from his father's talents and actually surveyed the land the churches were to occupy.

Fenwick also took a special interest in ministering to the substantial Native-American population of Maine. Some four hundred Penobscot Indians still lived in the settlement at Old Town, about twenty miles north of Bangor; a second community of about the same number of Passamaquoddy Indians was located farther east, near Eastport. Surrounded by expanding white settlements that threatened their hunting grounds and their fishing rights, the Indians found themselves trapped between the desires of Catholic authorities to hold on to their ancient loyalties and the vigorous efforts of local Protestant missionaries to win them over. Although Fenwick scraped together enough money to build a small church for the Penobscots in 1828, he could not afford to leave a permanent pastor with either group, despite their constant requests. Rhode Island, southeastern Massachusetts, and Connecticut, as "mission territory," also constituted an important part of Bishop Fenwick's responsibilities, and between 1828 and 1830 he supervised the dedication of churches in Newport, Pawtucket, and New Bedford. To serve seventy Irish glassworkers who had moved into the town of Sandwich, the bishop had a small frame church constructed in Boston and shipped by water to the Cape Cod town. On June 17, 1830, he dedicated Holy Trinity, the first Catholic church in Connecticut.

In his continuing interest in education, Bishop Fenwick was especially concerned about the welfare of immigrant children. He searched for ways to have "the poor Catholic children of Boston placed under the superintendence and institution of some Religious association, the better to form their morals and train them up to habits of Virtue." In February 1832 he wrote to the Sisters of Charity of Emmitsburg, Maryland, asking the community to send four nuns to Boston to undertake this task. The sisters were no strangers to such work. Founded in 1809 by Mother Elizabeth Seton, to whom Bishop Cheverus had extended his personal friendship and spiritual guidance, the order was anxious to accomplish what Bishop Fenwick described as "all the good in their power."

When Fenwick received word that three sisters would come to Boston for the purpose he had in mind, he called a public meeting for Sunday afternoon, March 18, 1832, for "all who felt interested in their success." A large group of people, "principally ladies," came to the meeting not only to demonstrate their moral support but also to form an association that would take care of such practical matters as renting a house for the sisters, acquiring the necessary furniture, and purchasing books and school supplies for the children. Almost immediately the women began a fundraising program, offering to list anyone who contributed at least one dollar as a "Benefactor" in the Book of the Association. More than four hundred benefactors stepped forward, handed over a dollar, and promised another one in the future.

Eleanor Whelan, Ellen Connell, and Bridget Ryan were among several women who contributed the generous sum of $3; an unnamed clergyman (Fenwick?) gave $5; and the Charitable Irish Society donated a corporate gift of $25. The meeting adjourned with the formation of the Female Charitable Society, which continued to meet regularly. Even at this comparatively early stage in its history, the diocese of Boston could boast of having a congregation of women who were active and energetic in support of Catholic education.

The institution started by the Sisters of Charity became known as St. Vincent's Orphan Asylum, and it had a long and distinguished history until it finally closed its doors in 1949. Perhaps the most important reason for its success and longevity was the indefatigable direction of one of its first three nuns. Arriving from Emmitsburg in May 1832, she took up residence in a house in Boston's Fort Hill section, where many of the early Irish immigrants settled. Sister Ann Alexis, the daughter of a prominent Pennsylvania family named Shorb, had joined Mother Seton's order of nuns in 1825, and she was only twenty-eight years old when she took charge of the Boston orphanage. Through good times and bad, Sister Ann Alexis skillfully managed the meager resources of her institution for more than forty years until her death in 1875. She was "a lady of noticeable refinement and education," recalled Father James Healy in his eulogy, and "she charmed all who met her" as she won the respect and admiration of the Boston community.

All too often, however, Fenwick's ecclesiastical routines of preaching the Gospel, administering the sacraments, building new churches, and organizing charitable institutions were rudely interrupted. A number of more mundane preoccupations were generated by the

Sister Ann Alexis was one of the first members of the Daughters of Charity in Emmitsburg, Maryland, the order founded by Mother Elizabeth Seton. With three other nuns, Sister Ann Alexis came to Boston in 1832 to begin St. Vincent's Orphan Asylum for destitute children. Later, as a Daughter of Charity, St. Vincent de Paul, she gained an outstanding reputation for the manner in which she managed and maintained the Carney Hospital. (Courtesy of the Archdiocese of Boston.)

enormous expanse of the diocese for which he was responsible, as well as by the incredibly diverse character of its population. When John Carroll became bishop of Baltimore in 1790, he faced the task of ministering to the spiritual needs of some three hundred thousand Catholics widely dispersed throughout the United States. Since there were only thirty priests on hand to accomplish this work, he had to rely upon priests brought over from various parts of Europe—especially from France. After Carroll's death in 1815, the leading dignitary of the Church in America was the French archbishop Ambrose Maréchal, and prominent French bishops were placed at the head of the country's other major dioceses. Jean Lefebvre de Cheverus had been assigned to Boston, Jean DuBois to New York, Louis DuBourg to New Orleans, and Benedict Flaget to Kentucky.

In the years following Andrew Jackson's celebrated victory at New Orleans and the end of the War of 1812, when nationalism was clearly on the rise and when Catholics were trying hard to establish their Americanism, the prominence of so many "foreign" bishops and priests was deeply resented in many quarters. Irish Americans in Boston and New York, for example, grew annoyed at the strange customs and faulty English of the French priests and began demanding English-speaking clergy of their own background. German Catholics in Pennsylvania and Maryland, on the other hand, wanted neither French nor Irish priests; they called for German priests. The situation became so critical that Catholics in Virginia and South Carolina actually contemplated establishing an "Independent Catholic Church of America" until the Vatican quickly stepped in and set up new bishoprics—this time under Irish or American bishops. In 1820, Bishop Patrick Kelly was sent to Richmond, Virginia; Bishop John England was assigned to Charleston, South Carolina; and Bishop Fenwick, as we have seen, was sent to Boston to replace Cheverus. The timing of these appointments was certainly no coincidence.

But conflict over nationalities was not the only problem the Catholic Church faced during the early part of the nineteenth century. Even the new Irish bishops encountered serious difficulties as they sought to bring some measure of unity and organization to their far-flung dioceses. Because of the serious lack of priests during the early 1800s, the traditional legal structures that were carried over from the colonial period, and the familiar traditions of most Protestant church bodies in America, Bishop John Carroll had accommodated himself to the prevailing practice of placing Church property in the hands of boards of lay trustees, who were responsible for administering it and representing the congregation before the courts of law. In Boston, too, it would appear that Bishop Cheverus went along with the prevailing custom of using prominent members of the laity to assist him in raising funds, directing construction efforts, and managing the financial affairs of the congregation.

As the spirit of Jacksonian democracy spread throughout the land during the 1820s and 1830s, emphasizing the virtues of egalitarian participation, many Catholic laymen came to feel that the Church in America should operate in an even more democratic manner. Members of numerous congregations felt they should have a much greater say in the conduct of parish affairs, in the appointment of pastors, and especially in the management of financial matters and property ownership. It was customary in rural areas for prosperous landowners and prominent political figures to hold significant leadership roles in Catholic parishes; in urban communities, successful lawyers and businessmen usually served as lay trustees and property administrators. This not only continued traditional local practices but also reflected what many people regarded as the constitutional provision of the separation of church and state. "Here [in the United States] no Church, Catholic or Protestant, can possess temporal goods or income to its name," Bishop Connolly of New York had written to Rome in 1818, explaining the unique legalities of the American process. "If it is built by public money the congregation must yearly elect trustees to administer the property, and priests as such have no right to interfere with this property." The Vatican, as we have seen, was occasionally willing to make adjustments where a conflict was over a matter of national preference. The pope sent the Irish bishops John England and Patrick Kelly, for example, to head up new dioceses in South Carolina and Virginia to placate angry Irish parishioners who were dissatisfied with French pastors. The Holy See was much less willing, however, to make concessions in matters involving diocesan authority. Neither Rome, nor an increasing number of American bishops who had been trained in the seminaries of Europe and educated in the doctrines of central-ized episcopal authority, found the congregational model of lay in-volvement acceptable as a permanent arrangement for the Catholic Church in the United States.

After 1815, with the defeat of Napoleon Bonaparte, the restoration of the traditional boundaries of Europe, and the trauma of the French Revolution a thing of the past, Vatican authorities were freed of diffi-cult political restraints. They were in a much better position to move the American church away from the decentralized process of what was called "lay trusteeism" and more in the centralized direction of episcopal authority. The result was a period of strain and tension that often broke out into bitter recrimination and occasional violence. And there was hardly a parish or a diocese in the United States that did not feel the effects of these conflicts. In New York City, for example, bitter strife went on for many years between the lay trustees of St. Peter's Church and the irascible Bishop John Hughes ("Dagger John"), who eventually formed his own administrative board and brought the church under his control. "Episcopal authority comes from above and not from below," he announced in no uncertain terms. "Catholics do their duty when they obey their bishop." Philadelphia also experienced all kinds of divisions between German priests and Irish parishioners, Irish bishops and native trustees, and the hierarchy and an eccentric priest named William Hogan, whose offensive antics frustrated Church authorities and delighted his loyal supporters. When Bishop Conwell finally excommunicated Hogan in 1821, a wholesale brawl broke out on the steps of St. Mary's Church that had to be put down by the city police. In Charleston, South Carolina, and Norfolk, Virginia, national differences also played a role in causing Irish boards of trustees not only to oppose French pastors but also eventually to engage in a confrontation with the French archbishop of Baltimore. It was in 1818, as a young Jesuit, that Benedict Fenwick had been sent to resolve the complicated dispute in South Carolina. Now, as bishop of Boston, he found himself with his own local controversy. Shortly after it had been founded, St. Mary's Church in the North End of the city had become the scene of an unsavory dispute between its copastors. Father Patrick O'Beirne and Father Thomas O'Flaherty had each built up his own coterie of loyal supporters, and each priest now wanted to exercise primary control over the parish. Despite repeated meetings between Bishop Fenwick and representatives of the two factions, neither side would give in, and a compromise solution proved impossible. The distasteful tug-of-war would drag on for several more years.

In addition to the troublesome issue of lay trustees, Bishop Fenwick was also forced to confront even more distressing problems with the majority Protestant population of the town. These related to the rapid influx of Irish-Catholic immigrants into Boston. In the period following the War for Independence, Father Matignon and Bishop Cheverus had been able to capitalize upon a temporary but welcome tolerance by native residents of Roman Catholics. The wartime alliance with France and the invaluable assistance of French military and naval forces caused most Bostonians to moderate their traditional hostility toward foreigners. Moreover, the number of French and Irish immigrants during the post-Revolutionary decade was comparatively small, the newcomers were quietly dispersed, and they were valuable to the local economy in performing tasks not usually taken by native workers. All of this allowed them to become a tolerated minority in early Boston.

By the time Fenwick arrived to succeed Cheverus as bishop of Boston in 1825, however, the situation had begun to change dramatically. The number of Catholics emigrating from the southern counties of

Ireland was increasing at a remarkable rate. The end of the Napoleonic Wars in 1815 had forced the government of Great Britain to adopt drastic new measures to fill up its empty treasury and manage its colossal war debt. The passage of corn laws that forced up grain prices, trade laws that gave special protection to English tradesmen and artisans, and enclosure acts that drove small farmers and cottagers off the land created havoc throughout Ireland. Despairing of their prospects of making a decent living in the future, large numbers of Irish craftsmen and small businessmen abandoned their workrooms and shops and moved with their families to America. Joining their countrymen were many emigrants from the farming areas in the southern counties of Ireland, many of them young, most of them Roman Catholic. These were generally disillusioned and dispossessed families who could see no future in a country that could no longer offer them either land or opportunity.

The first of the new wave of Irish immigrants began to arrive in Boston in sizeable numbers during the 1820s, when the town was in the process of transforming itself into a substantial metropolis. Charles Bulfinch had erected the new State House on the crest of Beacon Hill in the late 1790s, providing the stimulus for a vigorous wave of construction in the decades that followed. It was a time when alert real-estate developers were busy putting up public buildings, constructing warehouses, designing churches, building new private residences, filling in coves, leveling off hills, laying out a fashionable residential district on Beacon Hill, and filling in the south side of Boston Neck to create the South End. Raw labor was desperately needed to complete these numerous construction projects. Irish laborers, therefore, were in great demand as long as their numbers were manageable and they did not take jobs away from local workmen. From only a few hundred, when the first official congregation was formed, the number of Irish Catholics in Boston rose to some two thousand by 1820, and to more than five thousand by 1825. By 1830, the numbers had passed the seven thousand mark.

The sudden growth in the city's number of Irish Catholics began to bring back the old sense of fear and foreboding among native Bostonians, whose traditional Puritan suspicions concerning the dangerous and subversive character of "Papists" had never completely disappeared. A welcome source of labor only a few years earlier, the foreigners were now increasingly viewed as a danger to the livelihood of American workers as local construction projects neared completion. There had already been sporadic outbreaks of violence against persons and property along Ann Street and Broad Street, and in other Irish-Catholic sections of the city near the waterfront. Throughout the hot July and August of 1825, for example, the *Boston Daily Advertiser* reported that "disgraceful riots" were taking place almost every night involving gangs of marauding toughs who broke windows, damaged furniture, and actually destroyed "several small houses." Things got so bad that the mayor and aldermen finally had to station six constables in the Irish district from ten o'clock at night until early in the morning in an attempt to keep the peace.

By the 1830s, however, prejudice against Catholics, directed by a number of conservative Protestant groups in the area, began to take a broader and more systematized form called "nativism." Energized by the geographical expansion of the United States into the vast regions of the trans-Mississippi West, as well as by the commercial enterprise that brought Yankee skippers across the Pacific Ocean to the Far East, Protestant groups saw new worlds for Christian conversion. For this reason, they organized a variety of "foreign missions"; these were intended not only to work among the American Indians and the peoples of Mexico but also to preach the Gospel in the Far East and the Hawaiian Islands. But "home missions" also attracted the concern of those Protestant leaders who had become alarmed by what they regarded as the liberal teachings and secularist views of such new sects as the Unitarians and the Universalists. Determined to restore the true and literal teachings of the Scriptures, many Presbyterians and Congregationalists, joined by Methodists and Baptists, banded together to form a series of powerful national associations designed to promote the reading of the Bible, preserve the basic Anglo-Saxon virtues, and safeguard fundamental Protestant teachings.* In addition to their mission of fostering Protestant moral values at home and promoting the Christian religion abroad, the new Protestant organizations also assumed responsibility for protecting the United States from all kinds of dangerous ideologies and alien influences. They saw Freemasonry, for example, as a movement that had incorporated atheistic ideas and radical foreign doctrines from the French Enlightenment. During the early 1800s, they helped forge the Anti-Masonic movement into a full-fledged political party in order to counteract what they saw as the unusual powers and privileges being exercised by members of the Masonic Order.

The Protestant associations struck out at Roman Catholics in their communities with even greater determination. They ascribed their rapid growth in numbers and influence less to adverse economic conditions than to a deliberate, worldwide papal conspiracy to reestablish the menacing power of the Roman Catholic Church in the New World. Local weekly publications, like the *Boston Recorder* and the *Christian Watchman*, working in close association with a variety of New York–based newspapers and magazines such as *The Protestant*, the *New York Observer*, the *Christian Spectator*, and the *Home Missionary*, launched an all-out assault against what they saw as the insidious ideologies and alien influences of "Popery." By the late 1820s and early 1830s, a regular campaign of vituperation was being carried out in religious newspapers and journals, as well as in sermons, lecture programs, and public speeches. So-called native Americans denounced the "blasphemy" of Catholic doctrines, the "immorality" of the Roman religion, the "idolatry" of the sacraments, the "cruelty" of the priests, and the "subversive" nature of papal machinations emanating from the Vatican.

* The five major interdenominational societies were the American Education Society, the American Home Missionary Society, the American Bible Society, the American Tract Society, and the American Sunday School Society.

Catholic leaders in different parts of the country tried in various ways to answer the attacks made on their religious beliefs and practices. They established newspapers of their own, set up tract societies to publish pamphlets explaining their beliefs, and organized public lectures to demonstrate the false, malicious, and often ridiculous nature of the charges being brought against them. In Boston, the assaults against Roman Catholics reached a point where some type of organized response could not be avoided. As a guest in an "adopted land," Bishop Cheverus might have been gentle in his approach and diplomatic in his controversies, but as a native-born American Bishop Fenwick had no intention of having his loyalty questioned or his patriotism impugned. Unlike his predecessor, Bishop Cheverus, who was a small and even delicate man, Fenwick at age forty-three was nearly six feet tall, heavy-set, and weighed well over 250 pounds. Although he was known among his friends for his easygoing disposition and ready wit, he could also be stern and commanding when the situation called for it. On one occasion, for example, the bishop wrote an angry letter to Boston's mayor, Martin Brimmer, protesting the use in the city's public schools of a particular history book that contained a number of overtly anti-Catholic passages. "It is not such a book as should be put in the hands of any denomination," he told Brimmer in no uncertain terms. Fenwick closed with an explicit threat to pull Catholic children out of the public schools. Recognizing what they were up against, Brimmer and the Boston school committee agreed to withdraw the offensive textbook.

It was in this forthright spirit that Bishop Fenwick decided to meet the wide-ranging attacks against Catholics head-on, and not allow undocumented charges and innuendos to rest unchallenged. He authorized a weekly newspaper called *The Jesuit,* or *Catholic Sentinel,* as a means by which he could "explain, diffuse, and defend the principles of the One, Holy, Catholic, and Apostolic Church." In the first issue, dated September 5, 1829, Fenwick announced that in defending the doctrines of the Catholic Church he and his editors would not "seek battle," but would never shrink from it "when forced upon us." For the most part, however, most of these new undertakings were too few in number and too weakly funded to compete effectively with the large-scale efforts of the anti-Catholic press. In many cases, too, their methods and techniques proved counterproductive. Too often their newspaper articles adopted the same shrill and argumentative tone as those of their adversaries. Only a month after *The Jesuit*'s first appearance, for example, its editor, Father Thomas J. O'Flaherty, was referring to Protestants as "mercenary Bible-mongers" and "modern Pharisees," while excoriating "foul libelers" and "scurrilous scribblers" who exhausted "the armory of falsehood" in their efforts to injure the Catholic Church. The influence of their publications was pretty much confined to their own readers, and their lecture programs all too often degenerated into raucous shouting matches. Even Fenwick's choice of a title for his newspaper proved a serious tactical error, since the very word "Jesuit" symbolized to most native Bostonians the very worst excesses they associated with the Catholic Church. Most nativists of the period usually singled out Jesuits as wily secret agents, "prowling about" in all parts of the country "in every possible disguise," looking for effective ways in which to carry out the conspiracies of the Vatican and to concoct new schemes to "disseminate Popery."

Fenwick eventually decided to change the name of his newspaper. For a while it was called the *United States Catholic Intelligencer*, and later became the *Literary and Catholic Sentinel*. Unhappy with the paper's progress, in 1834 Bishop Fenwick transferred ownership to two laymen, Henry L. Devereux, his publisher, and Patrick Donahoe, one of the employees, who soon became sole proprietor and editor. At the end of 1836, Donahoe announced that the name of the paper would be the *Boston Pilot*, in honor of "one of the most popular and patriotic journals in Dublin." In changing the title, however, Donahoe assured his readers that they would find no change in the company's principles, "which are decidedly and inherently Catholic and Irish." The *Boston Pilot* went on to become one of the longest-running publica-

The Boston Pilot *was established in 1829 by Bishop Fenwick, who later sold it to Patrick Donahoe of the editorial staff. Donahoe was an energetic entrepreneur who acted as banker, bookseller, and travel agent, in addition to publishing a newspaper that from the 1830s to well into the twentieth century became popularly known as "the Irishman's Bible." Except for a brief period in the mid-1870s, the paper remained in lay hands until it was purchased in 1908 by Cardinal O'Connell. (Courtesy of the Print Department, Boston Public Library.)*

tions in the United States, catering to a predominantly Catholic readership and providing a permanent and invaluable record of Boston's Irish-Catholic community.

Besides its role of defending the Catholic faith against attackers, Bishop Fenwick also intended the *Pilot* to serve as an effective teaching instrument for members of the diocese. In addition to reports on current news about events in America and in Ireland, the early issues of the newspaper also featured essays on philosophical truths and Christian doctrines, as well as sections containing reflections and poetry. Readers were encouraged to save the weekly issues of the newspaper because, when gathered together, they would be able to provide "a complete demonstration of the truths of religion."

Fenwick was clearly conscious of the printed word as a teaching tool, and supported other periodicals for that purpose. From 1830 to 1831, for example, he oversaw the production of *Expostulator*, a publication aimed at the Catholic youth of Boston. In language reminiscent of *The Jesuit*, it was explained that the purpose of the newspaper was "to explain to children in simple language the principles of the Church's doctrine—as foundations on which the edifice of a firm and lasting Catholicism may stand." Each issue included articles on morality and the Catholic faith, as well as stories or "edifying narratives," reflections, and occasional book reports. Here, too, the fullness of the faith was to be presented over the course of twelve months. In later years, articles directed at children appeared in the *Pilot*, and during part of 1840 a juvenile magazine, the *Young Catholic's Friend*, appeared in Boston under the editorship of Dr. Henry B. C. Greene.

In addition to periodicals, several catechetical works were published by and for Boston Catholics. In 1828, the new edition of Fleury's catechism, originally made available in English by Bishop Cheverus, was printed for the use of the Catholic Sunday School. Although this work apparently served the community for a number of years, a new and fuller explanation of the Catholic faith was considered necessary, and in 1843 Bishop Fenwick approved the publication of *A Short*

Abridgment of the Christian Doctrine. Organized in question-and-answer form, the book's first part offered an overview of Catholic doctrines; the second provided instruction for preparing for the sacraments of Penance, Confirmation, and Communion; and the third gave an explanation of the Church calendar. With these publications, catechism classes were more effectively organized for children in Boston. A small number of girls and boys attended Catholic schools during these years, where they naturally received instruction in Church doctrine. The majority of youngsters, however, received religious training through catechism classes in the Sunday School, which was administered through the cathedral, and by receiving further catechetical instruction two evenings during the week. Learning the doctrines of the Church was regarded as particularly important for children who were preparing for the sacraments of Communion and Confirmation. Their knowledge of specific topics was tested by their teachers and their elders—and sometimes by Bishop Fenwick himself.

The relative merits of newspaper publication and catechetical instruction, however, were rapidly being overshadowed by the aggressive assaults of the nativist crusade, which spread quickly beyond the printed page and the lecture platform to more open and public areas. Rhetoric was quickly replaced by innuendo, as critics moved from condemning the doctrinal dangers of the Catholic Church to questioning those ecclesiastical practices they claimed promoted all sorts of personal vice and immoral behavior. During the 1830s, several American publishing houses revived a series of older anti-Catholic polemics, most originally published in Europe a century earlier and many focusing on bizarre stories about the Spanish Inquisition. The suggestive titles and subtitles of these books pointed up a more subtle and even more vicious trend in the nativist crusade. Although most of these works purported to expose the hidden rituals, the secret rites, and the elaborate intrigues of the "Popish religion," many of them actually made a special point of elaborating on the supposedly licentious character of convents and nunneries, where "lecherous" priests and "compliant" nuns were engaged in almost continuous sexual depravity. "Escaped nuns" like Maria Monk, who published a totally fabricated story called *Awful Disclosures* describing the terrible things that supposedly happened to her at the Hôtel Dieu Nunnery at Montreal, found a ready-made market among those readers who were prepared to believe the worst about Roman Catholics.

Boston saw its own version of this type of lurid fiction when a woman named Rebecca Reed went about claiming that she had "escaped" from the Ursuline convent in nearby Charlestown, a building where a small group of nuns lived and conducted a rather fashionable school for girls. Miss Reed's harrowing tales of convent life provoked such outrage in the community that a group of enterprising citizens immediately exploited the situation. They put the young woman's fantasies between the covers of a book, *Six Months in a Convent;* some two hundred thousand copies of the novel were sold within the first month of publication. Late in July 1834 one of the regular Ursuline nuns suffered a nervous breakdown, wandered away from the Charlestown convent in a confused state, and had to be returned. When local anti-Catholic groups heard about this, they became more certain than ever that Rebecca Reed's hysterical charges were true. Despite attempts by Bishop Fenwick to clarify the situation, wild rumors circulated throughout Boston that helpless women were being held behind convent walls against their will. To those who had been brought up on a traditional Anglo-Saxon diet of Spanish inquisitions, Jesuit threats, Irish uprisings, gunpowder plots, and papal schemes, all these sensational stories seemed plausible and terrifying.

By the first week of August, anti-Catholic feelings in Boston and Charlestown were running dangerously high. In the midst of this excitement, Reverend Lyman Beecher, a well-known Protestant preacher who had recently left his post at the Hanover Street Church to accept the presidency of Lane Theological Seminary in Ohio, returned to Boston on a fundraising tour. On Sunday night, August 10, Beecher delivered a series of thunderous anti-Catholic sermons in three different Protestant churches, repeating his earlier denunciations of Catholicism and calling upon his listeners to take decisive action against the resurgence of Popery in America. Given the general anti-Catholic sentiment of the times, the prolonged newspaper campaign, the hate-mongering sermons of Reverend Beecher, the rash of shocking exposé literature, the dreadful stories of Rebecca Reed, and the persistent rumors about what was going on behind the walls of the nearby convent, the situation in Boston was primed for an explosion of violence. It came on the night of Monday, August 11, 1834, when a mob of about forty or fifty laborers and truckmen stormed the gates of the Ursuline Convent on Mount Benedict, broke through the doors, pilfered the property of nuns and students, and smashed pianos, harps, and other musical instruments. After allowing the nuns time to evacuate their students to the comparative safety of a nearby mausoleum where the convent buried its dead, the intruders set fire to the building while Yankee fire companies and a large crowd stood and watched the entire structure become engulfed in flames. By dawn, the three-story brick convent building lay in ruins.*

Prominent Bostonians publicly denounced the burning of the Ursuline Convent, and leading Protestant journals officially protested against the use of violence in the anti-Catholic crusade. A committee of respected citizens, headed by former U.S. senator Harrison Gray Otis, subsequently cleared the Ursulines of all the unfounded rumors, and provided evidence leading to the arrest of thirteen men. But there was little indication that such sentiments of regret reflected any basic change of attitude on the part of those who were obviously glad to see the offensive convent gone. Although eight of the ringleaders were eventually brought to trial for the capital offense of arson, all of them were found not guilty—a verdict greeted with cheers of delight by their friends and neighbors who had packed the courtroom.

* Today, all that remains of the original Ursuline Convent are the bricks that form the arch of the front vestibule of the Cathedral of the Holy Cross in Boston's South End.

As the number of Roman Catholics became greater, so did the fears and anxieties of local Bostonians. On the night of August 11, 1834, a band of disgruntled workers set fire to the building housing the convent and boarding school in Charlestown operated by the Ursuline nuns. Fortunately, the nuns and the children escaped unharmed. Despite nearly twenty years of petitions, all attempts to indemnify the Ursulines failed. (Courtesy of the Archdiocese of Boston.)

It was not members of Boston's upper classes who had attacked the Ursuline Convent. Physicians, lawyers, merchants, and bankers might have found the growing influx of foreigners decidedly distasteful, but they certainly did not see them as a danger to their businesses or their incomes. It was, rather, members of the local working classes who had vented their anger at the immigrants. Day laborers, street sweepers, lamp lighters, stablemen, gardeners, truckmen—workingmen who made a meager living—could easily see Irishmen as potential rivals. Their depressed standard of living would make it possible for them to take away from the native worker his job and his livelihood. Even members of the police department and the fire department, whose uniformed ranks were jealously reserved exclusively for able-bodied

"American" candidates, could see the obvious economic consequences when immigrants moved up the social ladder and eventually demanded their rightful place on the city payroll. Men confronted with such frightening possibilities were only too ready to lash out at any tangible evidence of growth, prosperity, and stature among the immigrant population. The fact that most of the newcomers were members of the hated Roman Catholic Church only added to the nativist determination to keep them in their place.

Most educated Protestants in the city were shocked and outraged by the unprovoked attack on helpless nuns and children, and for many years many prominent Bostonians tried to persuade the state legislature to provide an indemnification. The first petition for such an action, organized by the poet John Greenleaf Whittier, was presented in 1841, but it failed to receive any positive response. Two years later, the textile magnate Abbott Lawrence led another petition drive, which was supported by such distinguished figures as Harrison Gray Otis, Charles Sumner, James Russell Lowell, Charles Francis Adams, and William Lloyd Garrison; once again, the effort came to naught. Fair-minded citizens of Boston continued to protest the failure of city and state authorities to provide compensation to help rebuild the ruined convent. And upon his death Dr. George Cheyne Shattuck, president of the Massachusetts Medical Society, left a substantial bequest to the Roman Catholic bishop of Boston as an apology for the "unindemnified destruction of the Ursuline Convent."

Formal apologies and expressions of regret may have been well-meaning, but at the time they were relatively scarce, and they did little to change the general air of fear and suspicion that permeated Boston and its environs. In the weeks and months that followed the burning of the convent, Irish Catholics in the city continued to be subjected to a relentless campaign of verbal abuse and physical harassment. Nativist attacks on Catholic property, not only in Boston but throughout Massachusetts, became so frequent that many congregations were forced to place armed guards around their churches. There were even several unsuccessful attempts to torch the small Catholic cathedral on Franklin Street in Boston. And the first anniversary of the burning of the convent was commemorated by local residents with several public celebrations in the city reminiscent of the Pope's Night of colonial days. The level of hatred between Catholics and Protestants remained extremely high, and before long it broke out into an incident of mob violence that for a moment threatened to engulf the city.

On June 11, 1837, a hot Sunday afternoon, a company of Yankee firemen returning from a call clashed at a downtown intersection with a Catholic funeral procession that was moving along Broad Street in the opposite direction. In a matter of minutes what started out as a fistfight had mushroomed into a full-scale riot. Nearly all the fire-engine companies in Boston rushed to assist their comrades as fire bells sounded the alarm, while friends and relatives of the Irish mourners spilled out of their lodgings onto the streets in order to help their own fighters. For more than two hours the battled raged up and down the streets of the lower part of the city where the immigrants lived, with literally thousands of people standing around watching some eight hundred men fighting it out with sticks and stones, bricks and cudgels. The so-called Broad Street Riot was finally brought to a halt only when Mayor Samuel Eliot brought in the National Lancers, followed by some eight hundred of the state militia, with fixed bayonets, to disperse the rioters and restore order. Although a total of fourteen Irishmen and four native Bostonians were eventually brought to trial, not a single Yankee was found guilty, whereas three of the fourteen Irishmen were given jail sentences for their part in the riot. It was a dramatic example of how religion and ethnicity had become combustible elements in Boston.

In addition to what they perceived as religious, social, and economic problems caused by the increasing number of Roman Catholics in their midst, native Bostonians were also troubled by what appeared to be the immigrants' growing influence in local and national politics. As old-time supporters of Thomas Jefferson and his principles, most

Irish Catholics had quickly joined behind the new Democratic party of Andrew Jackson when it was formed after the new candidate from the West failed to defeat John Quincy Adams in 1824. The Boston Irish hailed Jackson's entrance into national politics, not only because he seemed to represent many of Jefferson's simple rustic virtues but also because he appealed to the "real people" of the nation—planters, farmers, mechanics, laborers—"the bone and sinew of the country" with whom immigrants could easily relate. And for Old Hickory to be a self-proclaimed Irishman enhanced his following in the Irish community even further—a fact that was quickly observed by the Republican followers of John Quincy Adams, who commented unfavorably about the way in which the new Democratic party had moved into town and was welcoming immigrant voters with open arms. Noting that Democratic organizers were busy registering voters in the Irish-Catholic sections of town near the waterfront, one critic commented that the Jackson campaign managers had come into town looking for new recruits "in the kennels and the gutters." Proclaiming Old Hickory to be an Irishman, the writer observed, his Irish followers had marched through the downtown streets waving their shillelaghs as "hickory sticks" and planting their flag in "the menage of Broad Street" where the tenants of "poor houses and penitentiaries" made their homes.

When it became known that Jackson had defeated the Bay State's own John Quincy Adams for the presidency in 1828, the complaints of his supporters became even louder as they bemoaned the hordes of ill-bred followers the uncouth westerner would bring into his administration. After the first of the year, one disgruntled Adams backer remarked that "all Broad Street" (the Irish-Catholic section of Boston) had been invited to come to Washington to attend the presidential inauguration, since they were the "peculiar favorites of the *Irish* President." Pro-Adams newspapers declared it to be a "curse" that foreigners who were "naturally and morally alien to our feelings, manners, and institutions" should not only be allowed to vote but actually have the right to be elected to public office. As far as one writer was concerned, he would not want to see any foreign-born person in any office "above that of door-keeper in a public building."

The perception that Roman Catholics were moving into positions of political power and influence in the Democratic party gave native-born Americans one more reason to fear the threat that Roman Catholicism posed to the freedom of Anglo-Saxon traditions and the safety of American democratic institutions. The artist-inventor Samuel F. B. Morse took up the pen in hopes of saving his country from what he perceived as an insidious Papist conspiracy, insisting that every Catholic immigrant was a potential secret agent of a papal plot to take over America. The only way to prevent this catastrophe, he wrote, was to put an end to immigration itself. "Awake! To your posts! Place your guards . . . shut your gates!" he cried in alarm. The Reverend Lyman Beecher, who had stirred up so much anti-Catholic hatred in Boston in 1834, published a new collection of his explosive sermons in which he elaborated upon the warnings of Morse and pointed to the Mississippi Valley as the immediate danger zone involving the aggressive Catholic conspiracy. Protestants everywhere must be constantly on guard against such alien plots, he warned, and should be especially determined to offset the subversive influence of the growing number of Catholic schools in the United States.

Nothing could convince many local Protestants that Irish Catholics could ever become fully assimilated into the American culture or become truly loyal and dependable citizens of the United States. It was the conviction otherwise that led directly to an insulting blow directed at Irish-Catholic citizens of Boston who had formed their own militia company. In keeping with what similar Irish-Catholic groups had done in many other American cities, in January 1837 a number of local Irish Americans received permission from the Governor's Council to form an Irish militia company in Boston. It was named the Tenth Company of Light Infantry, Regiment of Light Infantry, Third Brigade, First Division, Massachusetts Volunteer Guards—better known as the Montgomery Guards.* The new organization was greeted with approval by most city officials; Governor Edward Everett himself reviewed their first parade; and the *Boston Morning Post* reported that their ranks were full, their discipline good, and their maneuvering "excellent."

When the new Irish company showed up to participate for the first time at the annual Fall Muster on Boston Common on September 12, 1837, however, the Yankee military units openly displayed their resentment and pent-up anger that Irish immigrants had been admitted to their ranks. Just as the Montgomery Guards had marched onto the Common and taken their place in the Brigade Line, the other units began marching off the field. The Irish soldiers, left all alone, went through their maneuvers to the taunts and jeers of the onlookers, who obviously enjoyed the humiliating spectacle. And when the men of the Montgomery Guards were finally dismissed and began marching across town to their armory, they were subjected to verbal insults and physical attacks by hostile crowds who lined the streets. Although many newspapers and public officials expressed outrage at this incident, no official action was taken until Governor Everett finally disbanded *all* the militia companies—the mutinous ones because they had deserted their duties, the Irish company because it might cause further "outrages of a dangerous character." Within six months, all the Yankee companies had reassembled with the same officers in charge; the Montgomery Guards made no such reappearance. The citizens of Boston had made it quite clear that they would not have a "foreign" militia group in their city.

Quarrels between priests, feuds among parishioners, conflicts with trustees, violence against immigrants, attacks on churches, the burning of a convent, riots in the streets, bigotry on parade—all these things created a continual series of worries, distractions, and frustra-

---

* Richard Montgomery was an Irish-born brigadier general in the Continental Army who had died leading an attack against English forces at Quebec.

tions for Bishop Fenwick, who was working around the clock to administer a diocese that extended from the frontier of northern Maine to the shore of Narragansett Bay. Fortunately, some measure of relief came with the arrival from France of Father John Fitzpatrick, a newly ordained priest. Born in Boston on November 15, 1812, he was the son of a hard-working tailor and a mother whose father had fought with a Massachusetts regiment in the Revolutionary War. Fitzpatrick was a bright and studious lad, a graduate of the Boston Latin School, whom Fenwick had taken under his wing when he indicated a vocation for the priesthood. Seeing the young man's intellectual potential, the bishop sent him to be trained at the minor seminary of St. Sulpice in Montreal, and then to the major seminary in Paris, where he was ordained in June 1840.

Returning home to Boston, Fitzpatrick offered his talents and energies to Bishop Fenwick, his mentor and his friend. Wasting no time, Fenwick put the young curate to work, at first in routine assignments saying Mass, preaching sermons, and giving retreats, and then in more complicated matters like helping resolve the troublesome controversy that was still going on at St. Mary's Church in the North End. After repeated attempts to resolve the difficulties between the two feuding pastors, Fenwick decided to end the stalemate by transferring Father O'Beirne to Providence and by assigning young Father Fitzpatrick to assist Father O'Flaherty. O'Beirne's supporters were furious at this decision, and some four hundred of them signed a petition calling for Bishop Fenwick to remove O'Flaherty and bring back O'Beirne. When the bishop showed no signs of complying with this demand, the frustrated parishioners turned to more aggressive tactics. As Father O'Flaherty was saying Mass on Sunday, February 20, 1842, a group of O'Beirne supporters, positioned in various parts of the congregation, interrupted the proceedings by suddenly jumping to their feet and shouting: "We won't have you!" "Pull him down!" "Down with the tyrant!" Father Fitzpatrick, who had been assisting Father O'Flaherty at Mass, immediately crossed to the pulpit, confronted the troublemakers, and called for silence. Expressing his astonishment at such "scandalous" and "disgraceful" conduct, he ordered everyone to leave the church at once. When he reported the episode to Fenwick, the bishop locked the doors of the church and placed St. Mary's under interdict. Transferring Father O'Flaherty to a parish in Salem, he put Father Fitzpatrick in charge. Although O'Flaherty's supporters continued to agitate for several years for the restoration of their pastor, no more public disturbances were ever recorded at the church—an indication that the thirty-year-old curate must have brought some measure of order and discipline to the troubled parish. Later that year, Fitzpatrick was transferred to East Cambridge. He was appointed pastor of the newly constructed St. John's Church, which one local newspaper described as "the largest and finest church in the town of Cambridge."

Despite the welcome assistance from his young curate, however, Bishop Fenwick himself was constantly on the go, traveling in a rickety stagecoach over unpaved roads in the heat of summer and the cold of winter, keeping a pace that was taking a serious toll on his health. In July 1840, for example, he administered the sacrament of Confirmation in Lowell; the next month he was down in Fall River to dedicate the new church of St. John the Baptist; in October he dedicated St. Peter's Church in Burlington, Vermont. In July 1842 he traveled to Providence, Rhode Island, to dedicate St. Patrick's Church; later that same month he was in Bridgeport, Connecticut, to dedicate another church; in September he was back in Boston to dedicate St. Mary's Church in Quincy; the following month it was back out to Lowell to dedicate St. Peter's Church. In the midst of these incessant duties, Fenwick also spent a great deal of time in Aroostook County, Maine, on eleven thousand acres of land he had purchased as a site for an ambitious utopian enterprise he called the "Benedicta Community."

During the 1830s and 1840s, a combination of religious perfectionism and Jacksonian democracy brought forth many ideas about improving and perfecting American society. "We are all a little mad here with numberless projects of social reform," wrote Ralph Waldo Emerson in 1840. "Not a reading man but has a draft of a new community in his pocket." And new communities were, indeed, one of the major expressions of the reformist spirit; there, people of similar backgrounds and interests could come together and live in harmonious cooperation. Some, like the Shakers and the Quakers, were inspired by religious motives; others, like the Oneida Community in New York, were organized along economic lines; still others, like Robert Owen's New Harmony, were based on communalist social principles. In West Roxbury, just outside Boston, Brook Farm was one of the most celebrated utopian communities, largely because it had the support or involvement of such well-known literary personalities as Emerson, Nathaniel Hawthorne, and George Ripley.

Bishop Fenwick, too, had an idea for a utopian community that would reflect the spirit of the exciting age in which he lived. His proposal was designed to take poor Irish-Catholic immigrants out of the squalid slums of the Boston waterfront, away from the scourge of tuberculosis and the spectre of cholera, and bring them into the fresh air of rural Maine. There, they could become revived and refreshed and learn constructive trades and useful skills. The bishop personally supervised the dredging of a canal, the building of a saw mill, and the designing of his most cherished dream—a Catholic college and seminary for his own diocese. Truly, it would be a paradise for a people who had come to America in search of a new world and a better life.

For the most part, however, the gregarious immigrants from Ireland failed to display any enthusiasm for moving to the solitude of northern Maine and becoming farmers. They preferred, instead, to remain in Boston, close to their families, their priests, and their friends. As a people, they had already lost so much by uprooting themselves from their native soil and by leaving behind them their beloved Irish traditions that they were determined not to give up any more. In the unity of togetherness, there was not only the strength and security they desperately needed in a hostile environment but also the last opportunity to preserve whatever remained of their Catholic faith and their Celtic identity. The small piece of turf they had carved out along the shabby waterfront of the city might be unsightly and unsanitary, but it was *theirs*, and they did not intend to give it up.

Bishop Fenwick was eventually forced to concede that his original plan for a utopian community in the wilderness of Aroostook County would not succeed. But he was still determined to create a college where young men could receive a Catholic education. He decided, therefore, to build his college at Worcester, Massachusetts, about forty miles west of Boston, where Father James Fitton had purchased fifty-two acres of land known as Mount St. James. Father Fitton had originally been a student at Fenwick's little "house seminary" in Boston, and after being ordained to the priesthood by Fenwick in 1827 he had served on the cathedral staff before going off to Connecticut for several years. In 1836, Fitton was transferred to Worcester, where he worked among the Irish immigrant laborers who were laying track for the expanding network of railroad lines radiating outward from the city. Hoping to prepare Catholic boys for future careers as businessmen and merchants, Fitton bought "60 acres of good land" for a boarding school. In 1842, Bishop Fenwick purchased the property and the buildings from Father Fitton to use as the site for the college he had always dreamed of—the College of the Holy Cross, named after the original church in Boston.

In May 1843, Fenwick left Boston to attend the Fifth Provincial Council of Baltimore, where he presented two major proposals for consideration. First, he recommended that the states of Rhode Island and Connecticut (now containing nearly ten thousand Catholics) be separated into an independent diocese with its own bishop. Second, he requested that his curate, Father John Fitzpatrick, then thirty-one, be appointed as a coadjutor, to assist him in his administrative duties and to succeed him when he died. Fenwick's fellow bishops accepted his recommendations, and Rome soon gave its approval. Father William Tyler, another former student at Fenwick's "house seminary," was named bishop of the new Hartford diocese, and John Bernard Fitzpatrick was appointed coadjutor bishop of Boston with the right of succession. Almost immediately, Fitzpatrick took over most of his ailing friend's more demanding chores. He administered the sacrament of Confirmation throughout the diocese, carried out regular episcopal visitations, conducted investigations into parish affairs, said Mass, and preached regularly at the cathedral. With only a handful of priests to care for the needs of some thirty thousand parishioners, even the new bishop had to pitch in and carry out all kinds of routine tasks. As Fitzpatrick himself jokingly remarked, he did everything at the small Franklin Street church from the duties of the "portership" (answering bells and opening doors) "to those of the Episcopacy."

It was evident that Bishop Fenwick had made his arrangements none too soon. Before a year had passed, shortly after his sixty-fourth birthday, the old man's health began to deteriorate badly, and it fell to Father Fitzpatrick to keep the daily journal, take the ailing bishop for carriage rides in the country, read to him in the evenings, and make his last days comfortable. Death came to Benedict Fenwick on Tuesday morning, August 11, 1846, on the anniversary of the burning of the Ursuline Convent—the very day, observed the *Boston Pilot*, "on which he had drank the bitterest chalice of affliction during the whole course of his apostolic labors." For two days the body of the bishop of Boston lay in state, as an estimated sixty thousand people filed through the little church on Franklin Street and paid their last respects. After a pontifical high Mass on Friday, August 14, celebrated by Bishop Fitzpatrick, a procession accompanied the coffin through the streets of Boston to the railroad station, whence a special train carried the prelate's remains to Worcester for burial at his beloved Holy Cross College. John Bernard Fitzpatrick returned to Boston, and on Sunday, August 16, 1846, he formally assumed his responsibilities as the third Roman Catholic bishop of Boston.

✝ ADDITIONAL READING

In the absence of a full-scale biography of Bishop Benedict Joseph Fenwick, the second volume of the *History of the Archdiocese of Boston* is indispensable for facts about the life of the Jesuit from Maryland who succeeded Bishop Cheverus to become the second bishop of Boston. Because of his previous experience as an ecclesiastical administrator and a college president, however, Fenwick was conscious of recording historical facts. He started the *Bishop's Journal*, a daily log of events that is an invaluable source of information; it is available in the archdiocesan archives for scholars of Church history. Fenwick also compiled a great deal of contemporary material in anticipation of writing his own history of his life and times. This work has been edited by Joseph M. McCarthy and published under the title *Memoirs to Serve for the Future* (Yonkers, N.Y., 1978).

Loven P. Beth, *The American Theory of Church and State* (Miami, 1958), and Evarts B. Greene, *Religion and the State* (Ithaca, N.Y., 1959), provide general backgrounds on the issue of religion in a democratic republic; Peter Guilday, *Trusteeism* (New York, 1928), and Jerome Kerwin, *The Catholic Viewpoint on Church and State* (Garden City, N.Y., 1960), focus on Catholic issues. Patrick W. Casey, *People, Priests, and Prelates: Ecclesiastical Democracy and the Tensions of Trusteeism* (Notre Dame, Ind., 1987), compares American attitudes toward democracy in the Church with those of European-trained bishops. Francis E. Tourcher, *The Hogan Schism and Trustee Troubles in St. Mary's Church, Philadelphia, 1820–1829* (Philadelphia, 1930), describes one of the more complex struggles over trusteeism in the early nineteenth century. Dealing with more spiritual matters, Ann Taves, in *The Household of Faith: Roman Catholic Devotions in Mid–Nineteenth Century America* (Notre Dame, Ind., 1986), analyzes the various forms of Catholic liturgy and worship that were distinctive during the Fenwick period.

Henry Ward Beecher, *A Plea for the West* (Cincinnati, 1835), and Samuel F. B. Morse, *Foreign Conspiracy Against the Liberties of the United States* (New York, 1836), are two prominent contemporary works warning of the dangers of the Catholic Church to American institutions. Rebecca Theresa Reed, *Six Months in a Convent* (Boston, 1835), is perhaps the most infamous example of the many scurrilous attacks on convent life during the Fenwick period. A modern and more accurate picture of early Catholic sisterhoods is provided by Mary Ewens, *The Role of the Nun in Nineteenth-Century America* (New York, 1978). Jenny Franchot, *Roads to Rome: The Antebellum Protestant Encounter with Catholicism* (Berkeley, Calif., 1944), discusses the attractions that persuaded many American Protestants to convert. Ray Allen Billington, *The Protestant Crusade, 1800–1860* (Chicago, 1938), is a pioneering study of nativism in the United States. Carleton Beals, *The Brass-Knuckle Crusade* (New York, 1960), tells how the early stages of nativism eventually shaped the dimensions of the Know-Nothing movement. Richard Hofstadter, *The Paranoid Style in American Politics* (Chicago, 1979), traces the impact of various paranoid conspiracies in American history. The second volume of *The History of the Archdiocese of Boston* gives a thorough account of the burning of the Ursuline convent; a compilation of the original documents may be found in *The Charlestown Convent: Its Destruction by a Mob on the Night of August 11, 1834, with a History of the Excitement before the Burning . . .* (Boston, 1870).

Francis R. Walsh, "The Boston Pilot: A Newspaper for the Irish Immigrant, 1829–1908" (Ph.D. diss., Boston University, 1960), provides a general history of the Catholic weekly. Mary Alphonsine Frawley, *Patrick Donahoe* (Washington, 1946), is a well-written biography of the *Pilot*'s publisher. Oscar Handlin, *Boston's Immigrants* (Cambridge, 1941), is a classic study of the social, economic, and political adjustments of the Irish immigrants in nineteenth-century Boston. Jay Dolan, *The Immigrant and the Church* (Baltimore, 1975), deals with the early history of Irish and German Catholics in New York City before the Civil War; Thomas H. O'Connor, *The Boston Irish: A Political History* (Boston, 1995), focuses on the lives of the city's Irish Catholics. Sister Marie of the Visitation Nicknair, *Bishop Benedict J. Fenwick and the Origins of the Benedicta, Maine, Community* (Augusta, Me., 1992), observes Fenwick's cherished community against the background of contemporary utopian ideals. Walter J. Meagher and William Grattan, *The Spires of Fenwick* (New York, 1966), provide a scholarly and readable history of the College of the Holy Cross from its founding in 1843 by Bishop Fenwick.

 The
Famine
Years

AS JOHN FITZPATRICK SETTLED INTO HIS NEW position as bishop of Boston, it seemed to most people that the tall, dignified, well-built, and apparently robust young prelate was almost guaranteed a tenure that would be long, successful, and eminently peaceful. He took over a diocese that was organizationally sound; Fenwick had been a thoughtful manager who had planned carefully. His friend had steadily increased the number of priests and churches to keep pace with the growing Catholic population; he had kept most of the lay-trustee disputes under control; and he had reduced the size of the diocese to more manageable proportions by detaching Connecticut and Rhode Island. All in all, it was generally agreed that there were no serious fiscal or administrative problems facing the new bishop.

Equally important was the warm and enthusiastic manner in which "Bishop John," as he was popularly known, was received. This was the response not only of his parishioners but also of the members of Boston's leading families, who accepted him as a native son, a graduate of the Boston Latin School, and a cultivated gentleman of refinement and good taste. "Although two-thirds of the City are still Protestant," reported a visiting French prelate in some surprise, "Boston cheerfully hailed the arrival of its new Bishop, whom the Bostonians are proud to designate a countryman of their own." Fitzpatrick was on good terms with judges and lawyers, industrialists and bankers, educational leaders and patrons of the arts. Because of his own wide-ranging interests in literature, music, and other fine arts, as well as theology, philosophy, and science, he was invited to become a charter member of the exclusive Thursday Evening Club, designed as a weekly gathering "of gentlemen for social and scientific conversation." These were simple and uncomplicated days, when the bishop lived in a small house near the church and there was no bureaucracy to complicate his time and no administrative organization to restrict his travels. He strolled casually through all parts of Boston, visited with his parishioners in their homes, attended meetings of the club, and dined at the residences of his friends on Beacon Hill—the last Roman Catholic bishop, according to one writer, to be seen "in ordinary society."

One of the first matters to which Fitzpatrick turned his attention was creating more churches. Despite the efforts of Bishop Fenwick in expanding the number of churches throughout the diocese, there were still not enough. Even though the Boston diocese had lost some ten thousand Catholics when Fenwick detached Connecticut and Rhode Island in 1844, there were still nearly seventy thousand left in the remaining four states that Fitzpatrick took over in 1846. Massachusetts alone contained over fifty thousand Catholics, with nearly thirty-five thousand just in the capital. "In Boston, we are sadly off for want of churches," complained the *Boston Pilot* in June 1845. "There is not half enough room for the people." The new bishop agreed, and a short time after he assumed office he began adding to the number of churches in the diocese. In August 1846, he dedicated St. Joseph's Church in the Roxbury area, and about the same time saw the completion of Holy Trinity Church, which pious German immigrants had built on Shawmut Avenue in the South End. A year later, he authorized the acquisition of an old Unitarian church downtown on Pur-

John Bernard Fitzpatrick, a native of Boston and a graduate of the Boston Latin School, succeeded Benedict Fenwick to become the third bishop of Boston. Fitzpatrick presided over the critical years of the Great Famine, the Know-Nothing movement, and the Civil War. The love of Irish Catholics for their "Bishop John," and the great respect of Yankee leaders for an intelligent churchman, made it possible for Fitzpatrick to bring Boston Catholics through this crucial period without bloodshed or violence. (Courtesy of the Archdiocese of Boston.)

chase Street, near Pearl Street, just south of the Fort Hill section. Here, on May 14, 1848, St. Vincent's Church was officially opened to serve the many Irish immigrants who lived close to the waterfront.

It was at this time that Bishop Fitzpatrick also began thinking about the future of Catholic education. Just before his death, Bishop Fenwick had been pleased to see the beginnings of Holy Cross as a residential college in Worcester, but Fitzpatrick felt that a day college for immigrant boys in the heart of Boston itself might serve an even greater purpose. When he was installed as bishop, Fitzpatrick realized that he could no longer continue to serve as pastor of St. Mary's Church in the North End, and so he offered that divided and troublesome parish to the Jesuit fathers. In August 1847 the Jesuits accepted the offer, and recommended as pastor Father John McElroy, SJ, a well-known retreat master who had just completed a tour of duty as a chaplain in the Mexican War. Fitzpatrick was more than satisfied with the arrangement. It not only put the parish in good hands but also marked a giant step toward realizing his plans for a "College in the City."

For the moment, however, there were more pressing issues to be resolved. Cities in other parts of Massachusetts were also experiencing a rapid growth of Catholic populations that demanded the bishop's immediate attention. On the north shore, new pastors were sent in to take charge of expanding Catholic populations in Chelsea and Lynn; St. Mary's Church in Salem was made responsible for mission stations in Marblehead, Gloucester, and Ipswich. On the south shore, Fenwick had already built several new churches, with an additional network of mission stations as satellites to service outlying areas. St. Mary's Church in West Quincy provided a focal point for people in Quincy, Braintree, Weymouth, and Milton, for residents of Randolph and Stoughton, for those in Hingham and Cohasset, and for communities as far south as Plymouth. Because of the increase in textile manufacturing, Fall River was the only mission in the southeastern part of the state to show any appreciable growth, and in August 1840 the Church of St. John the Baptist was constructed to serve the estimated one thousand Catholics in that area. Otherwise, the prospects of expansion at this time in such Cape and island communities as Wareham, Sandwich, and Nantucket were not regarded as very encouraging.

To the west of Boston, things were much different. Before 1840 there had not been a single church or chapel west of Worcester. By 1846, however, there were brand new churches at Cabotville, Pittsfield, Northampton, and Springfield. The number of Catholics in the city of Worcester alone had risen to nearly two thousand persons, and in June 1846 Fitzpatrick, in one of his first functions as Fenwick's coadjutor, dedicated the impressive new Church of St. John the Evangelist. But it was the region along the Merrimack River, some forty miles north of Boston, that had the most dramatic increase in the number of Catholics. The expanding textile center was attracting many Irish immigrants who were eager for work, and by 1841 the Catholic population of the city of Lowell was estimated to have reached four thousand, already outgrowing St. Patrick's Church, which Bishop Fenwick had dedicated only ten years earlier. Even though he authorized the construction of St. Peter's Church in 1842, three years later he had to purchase a large Methodist meeting house and convert it into St. Mary's Church to accommodate the rapidly growing numbers. The nearby textile city of Lawrence, too, experienced a population explosion, going from fewer than two hundred Catholics in 1845 to over six thousand by 1848, demonstrating the dimensions of the problem with which Bishop Fitzpatrick would have to cope.

At this time, the jurisdiction of the bishop of Boston included not only the commonwealth of Massachusetts but also the states of Vermont, New Hampshire, and Maine. Vermont was clearly the most populous of the three, but its five thousand Catholics were widely dispersed, with few churches and only a handful of priests. Most parishioners were concentrated in the extreme northwestern part of the state, near the town of Burlington, where Fenwick had dedicated St. Peter's Church in 1841. In next-door New Hampshire, the number of

Catholics had always been small and therefore had never required much attention until the Amoskeag Manufacturing Company began its textile operations at Manchester in 1839. After that, it was necessary for an itinerant priest to say Mass on a regular basis while the bishop of Boston figured out how to provide for New Hampshire's expanding Catholic communities. With well over forty-five hundred Catholics, Maine ranked second to Vermont in northern New England. During the 1830s, the slow but steady growth of the population was marked by a series of churches that went up along the southern coast at Dover, at Portland, and then at Eastport. As a result of the sale of valuable timber land, the town of Bangor experienced a speculative boom that attracted about a thousand new Catholics; St. Michael's Church was built for them in 1839. There was a small Catholic community at Ellsworth; there were communities at West Machias and Lubec; and a small church at Houlton met the needs of those who lived close to the Canadian border. In addition to white Catholics of Yankee stock or of Irish and Scotch-Irish parentage, Fitzpatrick continued to have responsibility for the Penobscot and Passamaquoddy Indians in the region, about whom Bishop Fenwick had been so concerned. During the summer of 1847, less than a year after his installation, Bishop Fitzpatrick decided to take a two-month journey through Maine. Despite the many other administrative demands that required his attention, he felt it essential to become more acquainted with the full scope and extent of his diocesan responsibilities. Starting out on July 23, he traveled all the way to the Canadian border, then made his way down the state's east coast, visited congregations at Machias, Lubec, and several other towns, and finally returned to Boston on September 10, ready to deal with more routine matters.

But Fitzpatrick's future was to be anything but routine. All the bishop's hopes for a slow, gradual, and orderly process of growth and development for his New England diocese were doomed to bitter disappointment due to catastrophic events taking place across the Atlantic Ocean. Late in 1845, newspapers reported that a strange disease had attacked the Irish potato crop, the mainstay of the working people's diet. At first, few appreciated the seriousness of the disaster, and in light of a warm spring many publications assured their readers that there would be an "abundant" crop and a "luxuriant" harvest. But early in 1846 the deadly fungus broke out again, and by the end of the summer it had ruined Ireland's entire crop of potatoes. By the end of September, many Irish towns had not a single loaf of bread or pound of meal to feed their hungry people. Deprived of work, firewood, and shelter by one of the worst winters in recorded history, the poor people of Ireland began to die by the tens of thousands of starvation, exposure, typhus, dysentery, and scurvy. Dead bodies were found lying in the streets, on the roads, in alleyways, and in ditches. Men and women wandered around aimlessly, like living skeletons; children were a pitiful sight with their distended bellies and matchstick limbs.

Americans were stunned at the enormity of the disaster that had overtaken Ireland, and citizens from all walks of life and every religious persuasion responded to the desperate plight of a starving people. The city of Boston, with its large Irish-Catholic population, reacted immediately to the emergency. From the pulpit, Bishop Fitzpatrick made an eloquent plea for assistance to a people "consumed by the fever's fire, frantic, mad with pangs of hunger"—a people whose "wild shrieks of famine and despair" could be heard across the Atlantic. Speaking in the name of humanity, he demanded an extraordinary outpouring of generosity that would actually reach heroic proportions. "Apathy and indifference, on an occasion like this," he warned his parishioners, "are inseparable from crime!" That very evening he organized his diocese into districts in order to begin collecting money, and as early as March 1 he was able to send $20,000 directly to the primate of Ireland for the relief of all those in dire need, regardless of their religious affiliation. "This sum," he wrote, "is the united offering of the Catholic Clergy and Laity scattered in little flocks over the vast surface of the Diocese of Boston."

Non-Catholic Bostonians, too, expressed their deep concern over the sufferings of the Irish people. Protestant churches throughout the state provided generous contributions to the victims of the famine, and so-called Donation Parties were held without respect to religious denomination. About two weeks after the meeting of the bishop's relief committee, prominent Bostonians organized a public meeting of their own at Faneuil Hall to consider "what Boston should do for Ireland." Addressed by such dignitaries as Mayor Josiah Quincy, Jr., President Edward Everett of Harvard College, and Dr. Samuel Gridley Howe, the noted humanitarian, the meeting established a committee to begin a fundraising drive immediately.

Meanwhile, Boston merchants persuaded the United States Congress to let them use the U.S.S. *Jamestown*, a sloop of war berthed at the Charlestown Navy Yard, to bring the provisions to Ireland. The vessel was assigned to Captain Robert Bennet Forbes, an experienced sailor, and on March 27, 1847, the *Jamestown*, carrying eight hundred tons of grain, meal, potatoes, other foodstuffs, and clothing, set sail from Boston harbor. After only fifteen days, it put into the harbor of Cork, Ireland, to the cheers and shouts of assembled throngs who turned out to greet their American benefactors.

Despite efforts to halt the famine and save the people, however, the aftereffects of the terrible disaster persisted. To many of the poor people of Ireland there seemed to be no future at all. Their land was ruined; food was unobtainable; work was unavailable; and eviction from their cottages was inescapable. All they could do was to run away—escape from the accursed land. Scraping together what little money they could, they booked passage to America in unprecedented numbers. Reports told of 11,000 people leaving from Sligo; 9,000 from Dublin; 4,000 from Waterford; 700 from Mayo; and smaller numbers from Ballimore, Ballina, Westport, Tralee, Killala—many leaving in vessels so poorly constructed they were called "coffin ships."

Although Americans must have expected some increase in Irish immigration as a result of the famine, they did not anticipate the tidal wave that now threatened to engulf them. In 1847, for example—in a single year—the city of Boston, which had been absorbing immigrants at the rate of four or five thousand a year, was inundated by thirty-seven thousand new arrivals. "This transfer of immense bodies of people, " wrote Edward Everett Hale, "is the most remarkable social phenomenon of our times." Bostonians had always found it difficult to accept foreign immigrants, especially the Irish, but at least those who had arrived during the 1830s and early 1840s had been robust and sturdy—strong enough to level the hills, dredge the canals, fill in the coves, and build the roads. Most of the "famine Irish," however, came ashore pallid and weak, half-starved, disease ridden, and impoverished. Few had any skills at all, and the fact that Boston's capital had been invested in mills at Lowell and Lawrence meant that there were few opportunities in the city for unskilled laborers. Most of the newcomers moved in with friends and relatives in congested districts along the waterfront, close to the docks and the wharves, where unskilled men might find occasional work and extra scraps of food while their wives and sisters worked as domestics in nearby homes and hotels.

As their numbers increased, the Irish were forced to find new and even more depressing forms of shelter. Abandoned old houses were subdivided to accommodate multiple families; deserted warehouses were partitioned and crammed with people; makeshift huts were thrown up in alleyways; and even cellars, without light, air, or drainage, were used to house impoverished immigrant families. Within a short time, violence and crime flourished, alcoholism was rampant, the water was not fit to drink, and tuberculosis was a constant menace. During the hot months of 1849 an epidemic of Asiatic cholera took the lives of over five hundred of Fitzpatrick's parishioners. Sickness and disease always took a terrible toll among the children. In his report on the Boston census, Lemuel Shattuck observed that between 1840 and 1845 nearly 62 percent of the Irish Catholics who died in

Boston were under the age of five. "Children in the Irish district," he commented sadly in his official report, seemed "literally born to die."

Native Bostonians might have been willing to send money and food to aid the starving Irish as long as they remained in Ireland, but they certainly did not want them coming to America. They were appalled at their unsanitary living conditions, and complained that the new-comers were turning Massachusetts into a "moral cesspool." And they objected to the demands immigrants were making on the city's social and charitable institutions, hospitals and asylums, and police and fire departments, as well as blaming them for forcing tax rates up and bringing property values down. In addition, there was the matter of religion. Boston had retained much of its distinctive Anglo-Saxon–Protestant character, and many of the residents still regarded Catholicism as both a political menace and a religious heresy. They were convinced that few of the Irish-Catholic immigrants would ever be able to escape the influence of their foreign church leaders and become responsible members of a democratic society. Already there were groups calling themselves native Americans who were opposed to any public funds being used to assist immigrants. They were also spoiling for a fight. Early in June 1847, some nativists distributed handbills calling for the destruction of the hospital facilities on Deer Island that were being used to treat incoming "FOREIGN PAUPERS." They called upon "AMERICAN CITIZENS" to be "IN AT THE DEATH" when they provoked another uprising like the one that had led to the burning of the Ursuline Convent thirteen years earlier.

The question for Bishop Fitzpatrick was how to respond to such provocative and dangerous activities. By personal temperament and religious conviction, the bishop was opposed to violence as a solution to prejudice and bigotry. As a Boston-born American citizen, he decided that if it were necessary to protect the rights of his Church and the liberties of his people, he would rely upon those freedoms guaranteed by the Constitution of the United States. Furthermore, he saw that if Catholics did resort to violence or retaliation they would be playing into the hands of the nativists, who would be only too glad to use such a response as further evidence of the immigrants' lack of discipline and self-control. Fitzpatrick hoped that by establishing himself as a human bridge between his own Irish immigrants who loved him, and his Yankee friends who respected him, he would be able to promote a spirit of tolerance and understanding between the groups. For this reason, he called upon his parishioners to adopt the ways of American culture as soon as possible. Immigrants should become naturalized citizens at the earliest opportunity and exercise the right of suffrage in every election. As new citizens they should make a total and unreserved commitment to their adopted country. "This is our country now," he stated in the pages of the *Boston Pilot*. The Irish should march "shoulder to shoulder" with the Germans, the French, and the other new-immigrant nationalities so that native-born people would not sneer at the Irish for being apathetic and careless.

It was due in great part to his own sense of patriotic pride, as well as to a natural strain of financial conservatism, that Fitzpatrick decided that neither the time nor the circumstances were right for him to allocate Church funds for social, medical, or educational institutions. First of all, he felt that such expenditures would be a needless waste of his impoverished parishioners' meager savings in a city that boasted of having such fine public schools and hospitals. Furthermore, it would be an outright denial of his insistence on the rights of immigrants as legitimate American citizens. He feared that if Catholics started out by operating their own separate schools, hospitals, asylums, and poorhouses it might well buttress the arguments of many Bostonians that the newcomers were persisting in their separate, "foreign" ways and were refusing to become assimilated into the mainstream of American life and society.

With the very limited funds available to him, the bishop's first priority was to build churches for his rapidly growing Catholic population. Not just small, makeshift structures, but impressive churches that would rival the famous cathedrals of Europe. And indeed, in the twenty years of his episcopacy, Fitzpatrick would oversee the construction of at least seventy new churches in the diocese—triple the number standing when he became bishop in 1846. These structures would minister to the spiritual needs of the members of his flock while he devoted his own time, talents, and energies to making sure the government extended to them the same level of economic care and social welfare it offered to all other American citizens—no more, but no less. When he learned, for example, that his priests were being denied regular admittance to Catholic patients in the Deer Island hospital and in the almshouse at South Boston, he paid personal visits to Mayor Josiah Quincy, Jr., to protest such discriminatory practices. Although his complaints produced no immediate changes, the authorities eventually assured him that a priest would be notified whenever a Catholic inmate was dying. After several more years of agitation, in 1850 Mayor John P. Bigelow finally gave orders that a priest appointed by the bishop would be allowed to minister to Catholic patients at Deer Island.

Even in the matter of burying those who died, Fitzpatrick ran into continual problems with the municipal bureaucracy. At one point the Church had to go through a long and costly lawsuit just to get permission to take bodies out of the city for burial elsewhere; on another occasion it was forced to pay an extra tax for every corpse buried at a Catholic cemetery in Charlestown. Authorities in Malden refused to allow Catholics to purchase a plot of land to use as a cemetery; Roxbury claimed that Catholics were violating the law concerning the depth of graves; and city officials ordered historic St. Augustine's cemetery in South Boston closed, on the pretext that the graves had not been sunk deep enough. Fitzpatrick was furious at these petty annoyances. He showed up in person to testify before a senate committee at the statehouse, and he fired off an indignant letter to the grand jury, complaining that city authorities were acting in an unconstitutional manner. He put the mayor and the members of the city council on notice that he would use all his powers as bishop of Boston to protect Catholics from any more illegal harassment.

Fitzpatrick's anger at the unfair treatment of his people was further inflamed when he learned that Catholic children in several of Boston's orphanages, poorhouses, and other public institutions were being deliberately subverted to Protestantism. This was done either directly, by proselytizing the children in the institutions, or indirectly, by sending the children out to work and live in Protestant homes. Despite the limited funds at his disposal, the bishop enlarged the modest facilities of St. Vincent's Orphan Asylum on Purchase Street (which had been founded by Bishop Fenwick for Catholic girls). In addition, he encouraged Father George Foxcroft Haskins to provide a similar facility for neglected and homeless boys. A Harvard graduate, a former Episcopalian minister, and a convert to Catholicism, Father Haskins was denied funding by city officials, but went ahead on his own. Using his personal funds and donations from his fellow priests, he set up the House of the Angel Guardian in the North End to provide a Catholic setting for needy boys.

The plight of Catholic children in the city's public schools was a particular source of concern to Bishop Fitzpatrick during the late 1840s and early 1850s. In 1829, the First Plenary Council of Baltimore had insisted that parochial schools be established to teach young people "the principles of faith and morality." Although he readily acknowledged that in theory parochial schools were superior, and certainly a goal for the future, Bishop Fitzpatrick remained convinced that for the time being a good working relationship between Boston's fine existing schools and a strong Church was a more sensible and practical solution. Being a product of the public schools himself, he thought that for the time being there was "no great danger" if Catholic children attended such schools while Church leaders provided effective programs of catechetical instruction and protected the youngsters from discriminatory practices. By 1848 it was estimated that of the ten thousand pupils enrolled in the primary grades of the city's schools, over five thousand were the sons and daughters of immigrant families.

Although the state's new public school system had done away with the denominationalism that had characterized the early church-owned academies, Boston's public schools were still imbued with a strong Protestant flavor. Protestant hymns were sung in the classrooms; Protestant prayers were said regularly; the King James Version of the Bible was read daily. Textbooks presented a Protestant view of world history that was decidedly anti-Catholic; readers and primers were critical of "Papist" ideas and practices; geography books made disparaging remarks about Catholic countries; literary works almost always portrayed Catholics in disrespectful terms. Parents and clergymen protested that Catholic children were forced to participate in prayers and practices they found harmful to their faith and prejudicial to their culture. The school issue came to a head in March 1850, when the submaster of Boston's Eliot School was brought to trial on the charge of having "maliciously assaulted" a Catholic pupil named Thomas Wall because he had refused to recite the Protestant version of the Ten Commandments. For his disobedience, the boy was beaten across the hands with a rattan until his palms were cut and bleeding; he subsequently required medical attention.

With Catholic parents up in arms over this outrageous event, Bishop Fitzpatrick took it upon himself to prevent any further incidents of such a nature. He encouraged the parents of Thomas Wall to secure legal advice and bring legal charges against the submaster, and he himself drew up a strong letter for the Boston School Committee explaining clearly the ways in which the King James Version of the Bible, the Protestant sequence of the Ten Commandments, and the Protestant form of the Lord's Prayer conflicted with the traditional teachings of the Roman Catholic Church. Not only were such practices personally offensive to Catholics, he pointed out, but they also constituted a serious matter of conscience since they violated the fundamental doctrines of the Catholic faith. Although the school committee never formally acknowledged guilt in the case of Thomas Wall, it did quietly clamp down on the administration of the Eliot School. A short time later it also changed the regulations so that in the future only the teacher was required to read the Bible and to recite the Lord's Prayer.

Despite what was clearly an abrasive climate of prejudice, Fitzpatrick refused to order Catholic parents to take their children out of the public schools. That would only allow "the bigots" to win by default, he argued; it would not change the existing system or protect the constitutional rights of American Catholics. Although he urged the children themselves to obey the law, attend the schools, and get the kind of education that would help them succeed in their adopted country, he also advised them to assume a position of nonviolent resistance toward Protestant prayers and ceremonies, even if it meant submitting to punishment by school authorities. In the meantime, in his capacity as bishop of Boston, he promised to seek out proper redress through the courts and the legislature in order to change a system he clearly regarded as un-American and unconstitutional.

The continued influx of foreigners into the United States during the late 1840s and early 1850s, and the success of Catholic prelates like John Fitzpatrick in gaining some measure of social and economic benefits for their parishioners, convinced native-born Americans that more drastic steps were necessary to stem the immigrant tide. A number of local nativist societies with such patriotic names as "The Sons of Sires," "The Sons of '76," "The Order of the Star Spangled Banner," and "The Order of United Americans" came together to form a new political party—the American Party—a national political organization designed to protect the nation from "the insidious wiles of foreigners." With membership restricted to "native-born" Americans of Protestant parentage, the new party was so secret that its members were instructed to respond "I know nothing" when asked about its organization, membership, finances, or activities. As a result, it be-

THE FIERY CROSS!

This anti-Catholic cartoon of the early nineteenth century shows how Nativists saw the Catholic hierarchy moving aggressively across the Atlantic from the various counties in southern Ireland. Fearing a papal conspiracy to establish the power of the Catholic Church in the United States, Protestants organized various patriotic organizations to defend the nation against the inroads of foreigners.

came popularly known as the Know-Nothing party. When they had taken power at the state and then the national levels, party leaders planned to pass legislation that would restrict further immigration, delay the naturalization process, and keep immigrants as a permanent, subservient underclass.

What began as a loose coalition of nativist groups suddenly mushroomed into a political organization of national proportions. Sparked by religious bigotry and ethnic prejudice, the Know-Nothing party also offered opportunities for politicians who sought to escape the disruptive effects slavery was having on both the Democratic and Whig parties. Almost overnight, political power in such East Coast cities as Boston, New York, Philadelphia, and Baltimore began to swing to the new party. In the spring of 1854, Know-Nothings swept to power in Pennsylvania, and by that fall New York was estimated to have at least seventy-thousand registered "American" voters. In Massachusetts, the newly formed party ran away with the entire commonwealth, filling every one of the forty seats in the state senate and capturing all but four seats in the house. Henry J. Gardner, a former Whig who had gone over to the Know-Nothings, was elected governor of Massachusetts, and Jerome Van Crowninshield Smith, a longtime nativist, became mayor of Boston

The Know-Nothing legislature lost little time in seeking to suppress the growing immigrant influence. In addition to passing the so-called Twenty-One-Year Law, which prevented any immigrant from voting until he had been a resident for twenty-one years, the commonwealth also dissolved all Irish militia companies, occupied their armories, and confiscated all their military equipment. One law made the reading of the Protestant version of the Bible compulsory in all public schools; another deprived diocesan officials of all control over Church property. Some members wanted a law denying public office to anyone who owed spiritual allegiance to a "foreign prince" (such as the pope); others wanted Catholic schools to be inspected by authorities from the public schools.

In February 1855 a committee of both houses of the state legislature was formed to inquire into "certain practices" alleged to be taking place in nunneries and in Catholic schools. The so-called Nunnery Committee undertook three separate investigations—one at Holy Cross College in Worcester, another at a school run by the Sisters of Notre Dame in Lowell, and a third at a school in Roxbury operated by nuns of the same order. The investigation at Roxbury was especially offensive, as some two dozen men suddenly appeared at the school, announced they were on state business, and proceeded to tramp through the building. They poked into closets, searched cellars, intimidated nuns, frightened the children—and found absolutely nothing incriminating. As Bishop Fitzpatrick fumed with rage at how Know-Nothings were violating the civil rights of defenseless nuns and innocent schoolchildren, he found welcome allies in a number of decent and fair-minded native Bostonians who were also disgusted at how the Nunnery Committee was exceeding its authority. When local newspapers began publicizing the unsavory personal conduct of members of the committee, as well as the outrageous manner in which they were invading the privacy of citizens without proper search warrants, the committee lost all credibility and was quickly dissolved.

The political power of the Know-Nothing party in Massachusetts in 1854 was so overwhelming that a number of Catholic leaders suggested that Irish immigrants might do better to adopt a low profile for the time being, stay away from the polls, and act in a more subordinate manner—like "guests" in someone else's home. Bishop Fitzpatrick would have none of it. He called upon the new citizens to go on exercising their constitutional right to vote, regardless of the outcome at the polls. By all means use prudence and caution, he wrote in the *Boston Pilot*. Go to the polls singly rather than in groups; cause no commotion; keep the peace; don't get into fights. But by all means vote in the November elections so that everyone can see that you are ready to exercise your rights as American citizens. Failure to vote, he insisted, would actually work to the advantage of the Know-Nothings by creating a pernicious "wall of separation"—this time between naturalized citizens and members of the native population.

Fortunately for the newcomers, the Know-Nothing movement, on both the national and the state levels, collapsed almost as suddenly as it had begun. In addition to the powerful attraction of the slavery issue and the political ineptness of local American party leaders, the steady, patient work of Bishop Fitzpatrick must be credited for the party's breakup. The city of Boston, with its unusually large Irish-Catholic population and its anti-Catholic heritage, was a powder keg ready to explode at any moment. In other American cities during the mid-1850s, tensions between nativists and immigrants often resulted in violent confrontations. In Baltimore there were pitched battles at the polling places; in New Orleans at least four persons were killed in religious clashes; in St. Louis the election of 1854 brought on a major riot in which ten persons were killed; in Louisville, a series of bloody conflicts left some twenty persons dead and several hundred wounded. No such violence occurred in Boston.* Bishop Fitzpatrick restrained the volatile emotions of his parishioners, warned them to avoid even the hint of trouble, refused to sanction violence in any form, patiently resorted to the law, and steadfastly appealed to the courts. His success in holding the passions of his people in check helped undermine the Know-Nothing cause in Boston by depriving it of those combustible materials so necessary to fuel the flames of hatred and prejudice.

On the national scene, violence and bloodshed on the plains of Kansas Territory during 1855–56 brought the controversial issue of slavery back into national prominence with such dramatic force that

---

* There was a tragic exception in the case of Rev. John Bapst, SJ, whom Bishop Fitzpatrick had sent to work among the Penobscot Indians. In October 1854, a Know-Nothing mob in Ellsworth, Maine, brutally beat the priest, tarred and feathered him, and rode him out of town on a rail. After serving for a time at Holy Cross College, in 1864 Father Bapst became president of Boston College, where he remained until his death in 1887.

all other considerations were practically forgotten. The fact that the American party candidate for president of the United States in 1856, Millard Fillmore, received the electoral votes of only a single state was clear indication that almost everyone regarded the divisive slavery question a much greater menace to the future of the Union than something as vague and contrived as the "Catholic Menace." But in Boston, the question of slavery provided one more complex issue that served to create further emotional divisions between the city's Irish-Catholic community and its traditional Yankee-Protestant majority.

Ever since 1831, when William Lloyd Garrison ran off the first issue of his antislavery newspaper, *The Liberator*, Boston had been the storm center of an emotionally charged abolition movement that regarded slavery as a moral evil and called for the immediate and total emancipation of all slaves. Although in the early years the reach of the movement was small and the number of its supporters was few, the growing controversy during the 1840s over whether slavery should expand into the new western territories caused more and more people to join the abolition crusade. Well-educated sons and daughters of the Brahmin establishment became zealous members of the cause. They held meetings, wrote pamphlets, organized demonstrations, and pressured public officials, demanding that the major political parties adopt an antislavery platform.

Escaping from the horrors of their devastated homeland during the mid-1840s, the "famine Irish" paid little attention to an institution that had been firmly established in the American South for some two hundred years. Stangers in a new land and a hostile environment, preoccupied with their own survival, most immigrants gave little thought to the country's "peculiar institution." Although they showed no indication of wanting such an institution for themselves, they generally conceded the rights of citizens in other parts of the country to hold their slave property until some way could be found to eliminate the institution in a peaceful and gradual manner. Most Irish Catholics rejected the militant approach of Garrison and his abolitionist followers, especially when the reformers denounced the Constitution of the United States as "a covenant with death and an agreement with hell" because it sanctioned slavery. Irish Americans had transferred their allegiance to the government of their adopted country, and they were shocked that any movement would place a "higher law" above the authority of a constitution they regarded as a sacred guarantee of their liberties. Furthermore, seeing that a number of abolitionist leaders were active supporters of the Know-Nothing party, Catholics regarded the antislavery reformers as hypocrites who preached liberty and equality for black people while they worked to take basic rights away from poor white immigrants.

There was hardly a major institution in the United States—political, social, or economic—that was not seriously affected by the controversy over slavery. Organized religion was no exception. When serious moral and ethical arguments were put forth, it became almost impossible for religious leaders of any denomination to avoid taking a stand. Despite efforts to reconcile differences, violent disputes often caused deep divisions within established churches. Baptists in the South, for example, withdrew from the national body and formed their own Southern Baptist Convention. Among Methodists and Presbyterians, too, members from the slave states broke with their northern brethren and formed separate branches in their own region. Conscious of the weak position of their young and highly vulnerable immigrant church, Catholic leaders made a conscious effort to avoid having the explosive issue of slavery divide their church and splinter their congregations. They avoided the subject as much as possible in private conversation, and in public regarded it as a matter of private conscience best left to the decision of leaders at the state and local levels. It was certainly not an issue in which they wanted to see American Catholics become involved.

In the Boston area, this hands-off policy reflected the attitude of the immigrant congregations. Their members generally believed that African Americans were much better off under the paternalism of slavery, and they feared that, if emancipated, slaves would move north and take away the menial jobs they had worked so hard to obtain. In November 1850, the editor of the *Boston Pilot*, Father John Roddan, drew upon the writings of Pope Gregory XVI to spell out for his readers the Catholic Church's official position regarding the morality of slavery. Roddan insisted that the institution of slavery, in itself and by itself, was neither a moral evil nor a sinful practice. It was, rather, something like war or pestilence—a thing to be deplored, but impossible to avoid—and Catholics who tried to reform things of that nature were only deluding themselves. In 1854, the *Pilot* came out in support of the Democratic senator Stephen A. Douglas and his Kansas-Nebraska Act, which made it possible for slavery to expand north into the Kansas territory. Later that same year, the Irish militia regiment, the Columbian Artillery, was among the numerous Massachusetts units deployed to prevent any attempt to rescue a fugitive slave, Anthony Burns, as he was marched through Boston on his way back to slavery. And in 1857, when Chief Justice Roger B. Taney handed down the Supreme Court's decision in the case of Dred Scott, declaring that black people were "beings of an inferior order" who possessed no rights that "the white man was bound to respect," the *Pilot* took great satisfaction in pointing out that the decision justified its own position and that of Catholic theologians. Although the *Pilot* was still technically an independent publication, there can be little doubt that its stated views regarding slavery reflected the prevailing opinion of Bishop Fitzpatrick and most other leaders of the Catholic Church at the time.

Even though Bishop Fitzpatrick accepted the unwritten code of gentlemanly silence concerning slavery, made no effort to curb the racist statements of the *Boston Pilot*, and continued to criticize what he regarded as the illegal and antisocial tactics of radical abolitionists, in June 1855 he took a step that distinguished his personal attitude regarding racial equality from his acceptance of public policy. He appointed a young African-American priest the first chancellor of the diocese of Boston.

Exactly ten years earlier, while traveling to Georgetown for his consecration as Fenwick's coadjutor, Fitzpatrick had encountered a prosperous planter named Michael Morris Healy. An Irish immigrant who had moved to Georgia and eventually amassed three thousand acres of cotton land, he had married a slave woman and produced a close-knit family of ten children. According to the slave codes of the antebellum South, all the boys and girls were officially classified as Negroes, and consequently not allowed to receive an education. Mr. Healy, therefore, was on his way north to find a college for his two oldest sons, James and Hugh, when he met the new bishop from Boston. Fitzpatrick persuaded the planter to send his sons to Holy Cross College in Worcester, promising that he and his own family would look after them carefully. Out of this chance meeting at a Baltimore railroad station came a steady procession northward of bright young African-American boys and girls who were destined to become important figures in the life of the nation and the history of the Catholic Church.*

James, the oldest Healy boy, became especially attached to Bishop Fitzpatrick, who visited him at the college, took him on tours of Boston, and talked with him about his future. When the young man indicated his desire to become a priest after he graduated from Holy Cross in 1849, the bishop helped him enter the Sulpician minor seminary at Montreal, and after that the major seminary at Paris, where he himself had studied. After his ordination in 1854, James returned to Boston. Fitzpatrick first assigned him to work with Father George Foxcroft Haskins at the House of the Angel Guardian, and later moved him into the rectory on Franklin Street to serve as a secretary and adminis-

---

* In 1875, James Healy was named bishop of Portland, Maine, the first African American to hold such a position. His brother Patrick became a Jesuit; his other brother, Alexander Sherwood Healy, became a diocesan priest who was eventually stationed at St. James Church on Harrison Avenue until his untimely death in 1875. James's two sisters, Josephine and Eliza, both became nuns. Josephine entered the order of the Good Shepherd to work with homeless girls; Eliza went to Montreal to join the Congregation of Notre Dame, where she eventually became a superior.

James Augustine Healy was the son of an Irish immigrant who became a successful Georgia planter and an African-American woman who was a slave. Healy received his college education at Holy Cross College in Worcester, Massachusetts. After his ordination to the priesthood, in 1855 he became the first chancellor of the diocese of Boston. After a long career in Boston, in 1875 Healy was made bishop of Portland, Maine, the first African American to be named a bishop in the Catholic Church. (Courtesy of the Archdiocese of Boston.)

trative assistant. Then, in June 1855, the bishop named Father James Healy chancellor of the diocese, a new position designed to monitor the diocesan account books, supervise expenditures, and handle such canonical matters as marriage dispensations.

The appointment came none too soon. The bishop's health was beginning to deteriorate, and in March 1855 he suffered some kind of collapse or stroke. Despite his hearty and robust appearance, John Fitzpatrick was not a well man. Although he was only in his early forties, he was already showing the signs of dangerously high blood pressure, aggravated by long hours, hard work, and incessant worry. In addition to easing the administrative load, young Healy also became the ailing Fitzpatrick's constant companion and confidant. They made an incongruous pair—the big, heavy bishop and the small, slender priest—making their way slowly through the streets of the city. For more important episcopal matters and policy decisions, Fitzpatrick relied substantially upon his longtime friend, Father John J. Williams, whom he appointed rector of the cathedral. It was clear that the bishop had great faith in the abilities of the tall, spare, tight-lipped priest he was already grooming to be his successor. Increasingly, Healy and Williams were called upon to assume more and more diocesan responsibilities during the late 1850s as the bishop suffered increasing spells of dizziness, splitting headaches, and bouts of temporary paralysis.

In spite of his worsening condition, or perhaps because of it, Fitzpatrick threw himself into his episcopal duties, saw to the construction of more churches, and occupied himself with projects he obviously wanted to bring to completion. Although he had helped create a separate diocese for Vermont and another incorporating Maine and New Hampshire, he was still responsible for a diocese that encompassed the whole of Massachusetts, with a Catholic population as large as the original four-state diocese he first took over as bishop in 1846. He had to travel from one part of the state to another, visiting Holy Cross College in Worcester, administering the sacrament of Confirmation in Fall River and New Bedford, dedicating new churches in the mill towns of Lowell and Lawrence, visiting congregations in Bridgewater and Sandwich south of Boston, setting out for Salem on the north shore. In May 1859, he dedicated St. Patrick's Church in Brockton; a week later he traveled all the way to Chicopee to dedicate the Church of the Holy Name of Jesus. In September he laid the cornerstone for St. Francis de Sales Church in Charlestown; in December he was present at the dedication of St. Francis Xavier Church in Weymouth.

It was in the late 1850s, too, that Fitzpatrick began to give serious thought to building a new and more spacious cathedral for Boston. The simple old brick church on Franklin Street, constructed back in 1803, was clearly no longer large enough to accommodate Boston's expanding Catholic population. Observing that many of the city's well-to-do residents were already moving into the fashionable town houses of the recently developed South End, he and his advisors felt that this site had the best prospects for the future. The South End location had the added attraction of being fairly close to where his friend Father John McElroy and his fellow Jesuits were planning to build their own Immaculate Conception Church, as well as being the place where the building housing their new men's college—Fitzpatrick's "College in the City"—would eventually rise. With the reluctant consent of the downtown congregation, the bishop sold the Franklin Street property, and on September 16, 1860, celebrated a sad and final service in the old Cathedral of the Holy Cross. After that, Sunday Masses were conducted at various locations throughout the city until a permanent replacement could be built.

Plans for Boston's new cathedral had to be put aside indefinitely, however, as the controversy over slavery moved toward the terrible crisis of disunion and civil war. The election of the northern Republican, Abraham Lincoln, to the presidency in November 1860 provoked hostile and almost immediate reaction. The secession of South Carolina from the Union in December was the signal for six more southern states to follow. By February 1861, Mississippi, Florida, Alabama,

Georgia, Louisiana, and Texas had also seceded; with South Carolina, they formed the Confederate States of America. Although many Americans hoped that eleventh-hour efforts at compromise might prove successful, such hopes were dashed early on April 12, 1861, when Confederate shore batteries opened fire on United States forces at Fort Sumter in Charleston Harbor.

As longtime Democrats, the Irish Catholics of Boston had loyally supported Stephen A. Douglas in the 1860 campaign and had steadfastly opposed Lincoln and the Republican party. They maintained their hostility toward African Americans, refused to support emancipation in any form, and often expressed sympathy for the plight of white Southerners. With the outbreak of war, however, the Irish rushed to join the colors. They might not be willing to fight for the freedom of the slave, but they would give their lives for the Constitution and the Union. "We have hoisted the American Stars and Stripes over THE PILOT Establishment," wrote the editor of the diocesan weekly, "and there they shall wave till the 'star of peace' returns." Bishop Fitzpatrick made it clear that he supported President Lincoln and the Union, and he assured Governor John Andrew that he was willing to render any service he could to Massachusetts during the crisis.

Boston's Catholics followed their bishop's lead. Thomas Cass, former commander of the Columbian Artillery (which the Know-Nothings had forced to disband seven years earlier), offered to organize a regiment of Irishmen. With Governor Andrew's enthusiastic permission, during the spring of 1861 Cass used the nucleus of his old unit to recruit the Ninth Regiment, Massachusetts Volunteer Infantry. Patrick Donahoe, publisher of the *Pilot*, also took an active role in recruiting volunteers for Cass's Ninth Regiment, as well as serving as treasurer of a citizens' committee raising funds to provide equipment for the "Fighting Ninth," as the Irish regiment came to be called. On June 24, 1861, the newly formed unit paraded through the streets of Boston and marched to the statehouse; there, it was reviewed by Governor Andrew, who praised "this splendid regiment." A few weeks later, at the annual Fourth of July festivities on Boston Common, the Irish flag was raised among the flags of all nations. This marked the first time in Boston's history that the flag of Ireland was honored by city authorities; they also ordered that the Irish national anthem be played along with those of other nations.

After consulting with Bishop Fitzpatrick and other prominent Catholic representatives, Governor Andrew asked President Lincoln's permission to raise additional regiments—including another one of Irishmen. When the president authorized ten additional regiments from Massachusetts, the governor informed Patrick Donahoe that he could begin recruiting a second Irish regiment immediately. Here was another opportunity, said the *Pilot*, for the Irish to show their love for "the country of their adoption" and their concern for the "safety and protection of the Union." The second Irish unit—designated the Twenty-Eighth Regiment—was sworn into service on December 13, 1861, at a ceremony attended by the governor and other state officials, who formally presented the national and state flags.

Throughout these activities Bishop Fitzpatrick was constantly on the watch to see that Catholic troops were given the opportunity to practice their faith. Whenever he learned that these soldiers or sailors were not being allowed to attend Catholic services or were being required to attend Protestant ones, he wrote directly to the military and naval officials in Washington or to Governor Andrew and local authorities at the statehouse. On one occasion he traveled to Virginia to visit the Massachusetts Ninth Regiment at its encampment near Fairfax Court House. After witnessing a military review staged in his honor, he met with the officers personally and then gave his episcopal blessing to the men as they prepared to go into battle. Although he made a special effort to provide Catholic chaplains for the Massachusetts regiments, he also called upon the federal government to expand greatly the number of Catholic chaplains throughout the armed forces in response to the increasing number of Catholics in the services.

Nearly 150,000 Irish fought to preserve the Union during the Civil War. Boston's Bishop Fitzpatrick exerted pressure on the government to make sure that Catholic soldiers in Irish regiments had their own chaplains. "Nothing can make me feel happier than to hear that we have the sacrifice of the Mass every Saturday," Edward O'Brien of the Ninth Regiment wrote home to his father in South Boston. "We take our prayer books and read every Sunday." (Courtesy of the Print Department, Boston Public Library.)

The various Catholic sisterhoods also made an impressive showing during the Civil War, and in many ways helped create in the public mind a more positive image of the Catholic nun. When President Lincoln issued his call for seventy-five thousand volunteers on April 15, 1861, there was no organized medical corps and no army nurse corps to deal with the casualties of war or the victims of disease. More than six hundred nuns, representing as many as twelve different religious orders, promptly volunteered to nurse ill and wounded soldiers in hospitals, first-aid stations, and on the battlefield itself. Although many of the first hospitals were often little more than empty barns or vacant warehouses, in the hands of the sisters, according to one commentator, "they became finally a model for European military sanitation." President Lincoln gave the nuns permission to purchase all the supplies they needed for the Union cause, and at the end of the fighting he paid public tribute to the sacrifice and devotion of such nursing orders as the Sisters of Charity, the Sisters of Mercy, and the Holy Cross Sisters.

The impressive outpouring of patriotism on the part of Boston's Catholic population, and the growing reports of the gallantry displayed by Irish troops on the battlefields (as regularly passed along in the columns of the *Pilot*), produced an increase of tolerance throughout the city and brought unusual honors for the Catholic bishop. In July 1861 Fitzpatrick was informed that Harvard College had voted to confer upon him the honorary degree of doctor of divinity as an expression of respect for his "character and learning." Observing that this was the first time Harvard had ever bestowed such an honor on a Roman Catholic cleric, Amos A. Lawrence, a member of the Harvard Corporation, admitted that it probably would not have been done had it not been for "the loyalty shown by him [the bishop] and by the Irish who offered themselves freely for the army."

In the spring of 1862, with little advance notice, Bishop Fitzpatrick left Boston for a visit to Europe. Landing in Italy, he traveled through France and then ended up in Belgium, where he stayed at the United States legation in Brussels. Although the bishop insisted that the trip was entirely for "reasons of health," his modern biographer suggests he was also helping the Lincoln administration build up better relations with those Catholic nations of Europe that were sympathetic to the Confederacy. With Archbishop John Hughes of New York working unofficially in France for the Union cause, it seems likely that the bishop of Boston was doing the same thing in Belgium. Certainly that was how most Southerners saw it. A. Dudley Mann, the Confederate ambassador to Belgium, informed his government that Fitzpatrick had been sent by "the Lincoln cabinet" to win the country's population over to the side of "the Abolitionists." The United States consul,

Henry Sanford, reported to Secretary of State William Seward that Fitzpatrick had "strengthened our cause" and had done a great deal to project a much more favorable image of the Union point of view.

While Bishop Fitzpatrick was in Belgium, back in Boston things were taking an ugly turn in reaction to two recent decisions of the Lincoln administration. The first concerned the institution of slavery. As Union forces suffered one defeat after another during the winter and spring of 1861–62, President Lincoln decided to issue a proclamation freeing the slaves. Such a move, he hoped, would not only disrupt the Confederate economy and cripple its system of labor but also neutralize the efforts of Confederate sympathizers in Great Britain and Europe. Using the Union victory at the Battle of Antietam as an appropriate opportunity, on September 22, 1862, Lincoln issued a preliminary announcement that unless the seceded states had returned to the United States by January 1, 1863, all slaves in the Confederacy would be "then, thenceforward, and forever free." Although many in the North hailed the Emancipation Proclamation with great joy and celebration, there were others who saw it as an out-and-out disaster. Immigrants, in particular, feared that hordes of freed slaves would flood northward, take away their jobs, and reduce their pitiful incomes. Irish-Catholic workers in Boston were typical of those who announced they were no longer supporting Lincoln or his administration.

Fuming over the implications of the Emancipation Proclamation, immigrant groups were further enraged by the conscription law that Congress passed early in 1863. Working people felt the new law was unfair from the very start, since it allowed rich young men either to hire substitutes or to purchase outright exemption for $300. Immigrants saw this as further evidence of how the Lincoln administration discriminated against the working classes. The poor man, they complained, was being asked to fight a "rich man's war." In cities throughout the North—in Ohio, New York, New Jersey, Pennsylvania, Wisconsin, Indiana, Illinois—there were demonstrations, disturbances, and riots. During July 1863 in New York City, a mob of predominantly Irish workingmen went on a bloody three-day rampage during which they attacked the police, looted stores and houses, and lynched a number of innocent black people by hanging them from lamp posts. Authorities had to bring United States Army troops up from the Gettysburg campaign to put down the rioting and restore order in the city.

Boston, with an Irish-Catholic population now totaling well over fifty-thousand, seemed a likely prospect for a similar outburst of violence, especially with Bishop Fitzpatrick still in Belgium. These fears were quickly realized when trouble broke out in the working-class district of the North End late in the afternoon of July 14—only one day after the beginning of the New York riot. When two provost marshals showed up to serve draft papers on some local Irish boys, they were set upon by angry men and women in the neighborhood. The arrival of Boston policemen produced more fighting, and within a short time what had begun as a series of fistfights had turned into a wholesale riot. Fearing for the safety of the city, the mayor called out state militia companies, which were soon augmented by regular troops from outside the city. By nightfall, combinations of police, militia, and soldiers had cleared most of the streets, but everyone feared what might happen the next day. Rumors that the Irish were planning new and more violent disturbances caused nativist vigilante groups from nearby communities to offer their services to local authorities.

Fortunately, however, there was no further trouble; the "Boston riot" was nothing like the murderous rampage that had devastated parts of New York City. Several reasons have been cited for the absence of serious violence on this occasion. The alert response of Mayor Frederic Lincoln, the prompt action of the city police, and the effective deployment of local militia groups certainly did much to contain the initial outbreak of violence. But considerable credit, too, must be given to Catholic Church authorities and local pastors for their determined efforts to keep the trouble from getting out of hand. In the bishop's absence, Father James Healy took immediate countermeasures, knowing that his superior would never countenance violence in any form. Bishop Fitzpatrick had regularly counseled his clergy to avoid scenes of confrontation, and he had conditioned his parishioners to refrain from all acts of public disorder. Even during the worst periods of Know-Nothing provocation, Fitzpatrick's recourse had always been to legal and constitutional remedies.

Acting in his capacity as chancellor of the diocese, Father Healy composed a letter calling upon the Boston clergy to take an active part in suppressing trouble wherever it appeared and to persuade their people to avoid all forms of "fractious assemblies." As they had done so many times before, priests patrolled the streets of their parishes, advised people to stay indoors, made sure residents were off the streets at night, and broke up small groups of men and boys before they could grow into mobs. Father Healy recorded that Father Robert W. Brady, SJ, of St. Mary's Church had dispersed a gathering in the North End by a "well-timed admonition," and the *Boston Journal* commended Father James Fitton of St. Nicholas Church for his efforts in advising his East Boston parishioners to stay in their homes and avoid trouble. "And like good citizens," said the paper, "they complied with the order almost to a man." The *Pilot*, too, came out against public violence, and praised the mayor and city authorities for putting down the trouble in the North End so swiftly. The weekly newspaper noted with satisfaction that in thanking those who helped suppress the rioting Mayor Lincoln had included a number of the Catholic clergy, "who labored to preserve quiet among their congregations." For the remainder of that troublesome week, the priests continued to walk the streets, talk to the people, reprimand unruly teenagers, and generally keep the peace until tempers had cooled and tensions had eased. Bishop Fitzpatrick might have been far away in Europe, but his influence was very much in evidence in the way his people responded to calls for peace and avoided the kind of violence that might well have added a tragic page to the city's illustrious history.

In August 1864, Bishop Fitzpatrick returned to Boston in time to witness the closing scenes of the Civil War. After the critical Confederate defeats at Gettysburg and Vicksburg in the summer of 1863, the tide of war had shifted for the first time in favor of the Union. Once General Ulysses S. Grant had assumed overall command, the war began to bring total devastation to the South. By the summer of 1864, General Sherman's army was making its way across Georgia; General Sheridan's cavalry was ripping up the Shenandoah Valley; and General Grant's Army of the Potomac was inching its way toward Richmond. By the time Abraham Lincoln was elected to his second term in November 1864, it was obvious that the total collapse of the Confederacy was only a matter of time. Like most other Bostonians, Fitzpatrick read the newspapers with great interest, followed the latest reports of the advancing Union armies, and on April 10, 1865, rejoiced over the news that the previous day General Lee had surrendered to General Grant at Appomattox Courthouse. "Boston participates in the joy that pervades the whole country," said the *Pilot*.

The great celebrations that were still taking place in Northern cities came to an abrupt halt on Saturday morning, April 15, when citizens heard the terrible news that President Lincoln had been assassinated the night before. Although the next day was Easter Sunday, there was none of the joy and excitement usually associated with the day of resurrection. Men and women dressed in mourning clothes crowded the Boston churches; altars were draped in black; and the bishop ordered that the joyous *Te Deum*, celebrating the close of Lent and the start of the Easter season, be omitted from the liturgy. After Sunday services, the streets of Boston were thronged with people who moved along slowly, silently, and without expression. "As one passes along the street," observed the *Boston Journal*, "strong men are met with their eyes dimmed with tears."

With the end of the Civil War and the death of President Lincoln, Bishop Fitzpatrick lost more of his strength and stamina as his constitution steadily deteriorated. Recognizing the seriousness of his condition, he took steps to have a coadjutor appointed—the same position he himself had filled for Bishop Fenwick twenty years earlier. For this post as his successor he suggested his good and trusted friend, Father John J. Williams, a recommendation that was finally confirmed by Pope Pius IX on January 8, 1866. After that arrangement was completed, the end came quickly. By the last days of the month the bishop had lapsed into a coma, and on the morning of Tuesday, February 13, 1866, John Bernard Fitzpatrick quietly passed away. The death of the bishop of Boston produced an outpouring of grief and mourning from citizens representing all walks of life. The solemn High Mass of Requiem was attended by priests and prelates from all over New England and by the governor of the commonwealth, Alexander H. Bullock, along with his entire staff. This was the first time in history that such officials had ever attended the funeral services of a Roman Catholic bishop. Mayor Frederic W. Lincoln, former mayor Joseph M. Wightman, the honorable Robert C. Winthrop, members of the Boston Common Council, and representatives of the city's political and religious establishment were also present to demonstrate their respect and affection for a fine churchman and an honorable gentleman. He was, after all, as one of Fitzpatrick's curates had once remarked, "a true patriot of the Yankee sort."

The end of the Civil War and the passing of Bishop Fitzpatrick marked an important milestone in the history of the Catholic Church in Boston. The forty years from 1825 to 1865, from the time when Benedict Joseph Fenwick became the second bishop of Boston to the death of its third bishop, John Bernard Fitzpatrick, had been one of the most complex, disruptive, and dangerous periods in the early life of the Roman Catholic Church in the United States. Starting with the devastating famine that brought hundreds of thousands of impoverished Irish immigrants to Boston, Fitzpatrick had to confront angry taxpayers, frustrated Protestants, and outraged nativists who were convinced that the newcomers were a serious threat to the nation's democratic institutions. With limited funds and a handful of clergy, the bishop faced the rise of the Know-Nothing movement, an organized political party that endangered the future of the Catholic Church at the very time when the conflict over slavery was leading the nation to the brink of civil war. The absence of catastrophic explosions during those two anxious decades is far less an indication that there were no combustible issues at hand than a tribute to the alert and determined way in which Fitzpatrick anticipated problems and defused them before they reached the explosive stage.

Throughout the course of his twenty years as bishop of Boston, Fitzpatrick worked to prevent the outbreak of violence between hostile nativist groups and hot-tempered immigrants, in a city whose religious traditions appeared to make such conflicts unavoidable. But the bishop refused to accept such a depressing prospect. He was determined to use every means at his disposal to head off the kind of ethnic and religious violence that would prevent the gradual and peaceful melding of the two opposing cultures. And only he could do it. There was no other representative of the Catholic faith in the entire region at the time, layman or clergyman, who was accepted by the Brahmin establishment of the city with such sincere respect and genuine affection as Bishop John.

Without ever compromising his own religious convictions or his personal loyalties to the Roman Catholic Church, Fitzpatrick effectively pioneered a policy of social and political accommodation that balanced off the rights of his immigrant parishioners with the sensitivities of native-born residents. As a Boston-born American citizen, he was acutely conscious of the importance of the separation of church and state within the American constitutional system, and he consistently relied upon the nation's legal system to protect the rights of his people and ensure the freedom of his Church.

For two decades the bishop's wise counsel and prudent judgment went far toward determining that the eventual integration of immigrant Irish Catholics into the social and political life of the oldest Puritan community in America would take place in a gradual and nonviolent manner. This was John Bernard Fitzpatrick's legacy to his Church, to his people, and to his native city.

+≡ ADDITIONAL READING

The second volume of the three-volume *History of the Archdiocese of Boston* continues to be an indispensable source for any work on the history of the Catholic Church in New England during the early nineteenth century. Throughout his episcopacy, which extended from 1846 to 1866, Bishop John Bernard Fitzpatrick continued to keep the *Bishop's Journal,* which provides an insight into his personal thoughts and daily activities. Thomas H. O'Connor, *Fitzpatrick's Boston, 1844–1866* (Boston, 1984), provides a biographical study of Boston's third bishop and the times in which he lived; Richard Shaw, *Dagger John* (New York, 1977), presents a contrasting view of New York's archbishop, John Hughes. Alfred S. Foley, *Bishop Healy: Beloved Outcast* (New York, 1951), is a valuable introduction to James Healy and his family that needs further expansion and documentation. David Dunigan's *History of Boston College* (Milwaukee, 1947), has been significantly updated by Charles F. Donovan and Paul FitzGerald, *History of Boston College* (Chestnut Hill, 1990).

A good background to the rebuilding of nineteenth-century Boston is Harold Kirker, *Bulfinch's Boston, 1787–1817* (New York, 1964). A contemporary view of the renewal work accomplished by Boston's "Great Mayor," Josiah Quincy, may be found in Josiah Quincy, *Municipal History of the Town and City of Boston* (Boston, 1852), while Robert McGaughey, *Josiah Quincy* (Cambridge, 1974), provides a modern treatment of the city's second mayor. Samuel Eliot Morison, *Maritime History of Massachusetts* (Boston, 1921), is an important study of the commercial underpinnings of the Bay State's economy; Thomas H. O'Connor, *Lords of the Loom* (New York, 1967), traces the development of the new industrial enterprises of the region. Digby E. Baltzell, *Puritan Boston and Quaker Philadelphia* (New York, 1979), offers a stimulating contrast of the leadership in two major Protestant cities.

Cecil Woodham-Smith, *The Great Hunger: Ireland, 1848–1849* (New York, 1962), has furnished a vivid description of the terrible Irish famine from the vantage point of English sources. John Percival, *The Great Famine: Ireland's Potato Famine, 1845–51* (New York, 1995), accompanied a television production commemorating the 150th anniversary of the massive tragedy. Thomas Gallagher, *Paddy's Lament* (New York, 1982), offers an analysis of the Irish emigration during 1846–47; Kerby Miller, *Emigrants and Exiles* (New York, 1985), is perhaps the best one-volume history of the entire sweep of the exodus from the ruined lands of Ireland to the busy streets of America. Oscar Handlin, *Boston's Immigrants, 1790–1880* (New York, 1959), remains the classic and essential work on the immigrant experience in the city. Hasia Diner, *Erin's Daughters in America* (Baltimore, 1983), has opened a fresh approach to the study of Irish immigrant women in the nineteenth century. Peter C. Holloran, *Boston's Wayward Children: Social Services for Homeless Children, 1830–1930* (Rutherford, N.J., 1989), offers an insightful study of the social services available to homeless children in Boston; Robert Lane, *Policing the City: Boston, 1822–1885* (Cambridge, 1964), deals with the topics of crime and law enforcement in an urban setting.

Ray Allen Billington, *The Protestant Crusade, 1800–1860* (New York, 1938), continues to be the standard treatment of nineteenth-century nativism. Leonard Richard, *"Gentlemen of Property and Standing"* (New York, 1970), and Michael Feldberg, *The Turbulent Era* (New York, 1979), analyze the structure and motives of mob violence during the 1830s; Michael Feldberg, *The Philadelphia Riots of 1844* (New York, 1975), describes the bloody ethnic conflict in that city. Carleton Beals, *The Brass-Knuckle Crusade* (New York, 1960), is a popular account of the Know-Nothing conspiracy, but John R. Mulkern, *The Know-Nothing Movement in Massachusetts* (Boston, 1990), provides a more accurate and scholarly account of the faction in the Bay State. Dale T. Knobel, *Paddy and the Republic: Ethnicity and Nationality in Antebellum America* (Middletown, Conn., 1986), examines the complexities of Irish assimilation.

Intemperate drinking was of serious concern to church leaders during the early nineteenth century. Colm Kerrigan, *Father Mathew and the Irish Temperance Movement, 1835–1849* (Cork, Ireland, 1992), is a recent account of the Irish background; Ian R. Tyrrell, *Sobering Up: From Temperance to Prohibition in Antebellum America, 1800–1860* (Westport, Conn., 1979), and Robert Hempel, *Temperance and Prohibition in Massachusetts, 1813–1852* (Ann Arbor, Mich., 1982), view it from an American perspective. Maurice Dinneen, *The Catholic Total Abstinence Movement in the Archdiocese of Boston* (Boston, 1908), is an older work that is extremely valuable for the data it provides on local total abstinence societies.

The 1830s and 1840s were decades of powerful social change, much of it centering in Massachusetts. Alice Felt Tyler, *Freedom's Ferment* (Minneapolis, 1944), provides a comprehensive listing of the major reform movements of the era. Clifford S. Griffin, *Their Brothers' Keepers: Moral Stewardship in the United States, 1800–1865* (Rutherford, N.J., 1960), and William W. Sweet, *Religion in the Development of American Culture, 1765–1840* (New York, 1953), offer insights into major moral and ethical influences at work in American society. Louis Filler, *The Crusade against Slavery* (New York, 1960), is an introduction to the organized reaction against the institution of slavery in the United States. James Stewart, *Holy Warriors: The Abolitionists and American Slavery* (New York, 1976), and Ronald G. Waters, *The Antislavery Appeal: American Abolitionism after 1830* (Baltimore, 1976), are two works that have updated the story of the abolition movement. Russel Nye, *William Lloyd Garrison and the Humanitarian Reformers* (Boston, 1955), places the abolition movement and its leader in the larger context of antebellum reform; Laurence Lader, *The Bold Brahmins* (New York, 1961), concentrates on the impact of the antislavery crusade in the Boston community. Madeleine Hooke Rice, *American*

Catholic Opinion in the Slavery Controversy (Gloucester, Mass., 1964), treats the slavery issue from the point of view of Catholic public opinion; John Francis Maxwell, *Slavery and the Catholic Church* (London, 1975), examines the topic from an institutional point of view.

James McPherson, *Battle Cry of Freedom* (New York, 1988), is generally regarded as the best one-volume history of the Civil War. Allan Nevins's eight-volume series, *The Ordeal of the Union* (New York, 1947–71), is the most comprehensive treatment of the critical years from the close of the war with Mexico to the end of the Civil War. Benjamin J. Blied, *Catholics and the Civil War* (Milwaukee, 1945), is a pioneering study of how Catholics in the North and the South reacted to the crisis of the Union; Loretta Clare Freiertag, *American Public Opinion on the Diplomatic Relations between the United States and the Papal States, 1847–1867* (Washington, 1933), is concerned with international aspects of the war. Ella Lonn, *Foreigners in the Union Army and Navy* (1951), is a detailed study of enlistments by noncitizens in the Union cause; William L. Burton, *Melting Pot Soldiers* (Ames, Iowa, 1988), describes the new-immigrant regiments in the Union army; Eugene Murdock, *One Million Men* (New York, 1971), analyzes the controversial aspects of the Civil War conscription laws. Basil Lee, *Discontent in New York City, 1861–1865* (New York, 1943), Irving Weinstein, *July, 1863* (New York, 1952), and Adrian Cook, *Armies of the Streets* (Lexington, Ky., 1974), are studies of the New York draft riots, in which Irish Catholics played a prominent role. Thomas H. O'Connor, *Civil War Boston: Home Front and Battlefield* (Boston, 1997), provides an overview of the effects of the war upon Boston's civilian population, including the Irish Catholics.

4 Growth and Assimilation

THE CIVIL WAR HAD SIGNIFICANT AND BASICALLY positive effects upon the social and economic status of Irish Catholics in Boston. After years of nativist charges that Roman Catholics could never become dedicated American citizens or be fully assimilated into American culture, the newcomers took advantage of the great national crisis to demonstrate their loyalty to their adopted country, either by joining the Union army or by doing war work in one of the nearby armories, factories, or shipyards. The much-heralded courage of the Irish regiments on the battlefields, and the outstanding service of immigrant workers on the home front, caused even dyed-in-the-wool Yankees to relax their defensive posture and show a much greater degree of tolerance.

The awarding of an honorary degree by Harvard College to Bishop John Fitzpatrick in 1861 was a calculated public demonstration by city leaders of a new level of respect, and this initial gesture of friendship was soon followed by other concessions of a similar nature. The Massachusetts legislature, for example, passed a bill instructing the school committees of the various cities and towns of the commonwealth that they were to conduct daily readings of the Bible "without written or oral comment." The bill further stipulated that no students could be required to read from any particular version of the Bible that went against "the conscientious scruples" of their parents or guardians. This piece of legislation, the *Pilot* was happy to observe, was a "long stride" from the intolerant Know-Nothingism of 1854, and was a clear acknowledgment of the loyalty displayed by "the adopted citizens in this hour of national trial." The state legislature also repealed the 1859 law that had required a two-year waiting period before new citizens would be able to vote; a short time later, city authorities announced that patients in the Boston City Hospital could now be attended by a clergyman of their own choosing. Clearly there were tangible signs that Catholics could expect to enter a new and less hostile phase of their lives as residents of Massachusetts.

The four years of national conflict marked a significant period of transition not only in the social status of Irish Catholics but in the improvement of their depressed economic circumstances as well. By joining the Union army and getting a generous bonus, or by gaining employment in nearby armories, factories, ironworks, and shipyards, the newcomers had their first real opportunity to make a little money on a regular basis. They also gained a greater measure of acceptance by a community that usually regarded them as little more than shift-less wastrels and lazy loafers.

Although the names of many skilled Irish craftsmen are to be found on the rolls of various trade unions of the period, listed as long-shoremen, carpenters, tailors, stonecutters, and waiters, most immigrants before the war had still been generally categorized as "labour-ers"—untrained and unskilled workmen. By the time the war started, however, the invention of the sewing machine, as well as the introduc-tion of many other new mechanical devices, had made it possible even for "greenhorns" to perform fairly complicated tasks that had once been the exclusive province of highly skilled craftsmen. As a result, many more Irish workers were able to obtain employment in garment shops, textile mills, and shoe factories throughout the area. As the size of the Union army expanded and the demands of the battlefield increased, employment directly connected with the needs of the war opened up even greater opportunities for work. Irish men found many well-paying jobs across the channel in the lower end of the South Boston peninsula, where several large iron foundries turned out guns, cannon, and artillery shells for the Union army, and where shipyards were busily constructing new ironclad monitors for the navy. Many Irish women, too, took their places on assembly lines, some making ammunition at the Watertown arsenal, others working in business offices, newspaper rooms, clothing stores, and food markets closer to the city.

In addition to jobs in war-related industries, the extensive construction work that was going on throughout the city of Boston during the war years also provided the Irish with chances for work that otherwise would not have been available. The construction of the new city hall and several other buildings in the downtown area; the completion of the work involved in laying out the streets and parks of the South End; the erection of the Boston City Hospital, the Church of the Immaculate Conception, and Boston College; the enormous task of filling in the Back Bay that would continue well into the 1870s and 1880s, all furnished welcome jobs for engineers, steam-shovel operators, wagon drivers, and day laborers. Even though the work was hard, the hours long, and the wages low, the combination of war work and city construction provided the first real opportunity for most Irish workers to bring home a day's pay on a regular basis. They had taken a small but significant step on the first rung of the ladder to eventual financial success.

The marked improvement in the economic livelihood of Irish Catholics during the immediate postwar period was demonstrated by a demographic mobility that kept pace with their new-found material prosperity. In the years following the end of the war, more Irish than ever moved out of the old, crowded waterfront sections of downtown Boston—out of the North End, the West End, the South End—into the nearby neighborhoods of South Boston, Charlestown, Brighton, Dorchester, and Roxbury. The fact that Roxbury was annexed to the city in 1867, Dorchester in 1869, and Charlestown, Brighton, and West Roxbury in 1873 gives dramatic evidence of the speed with which immigrant families were creating whole new residential districts. Before long, these predominantly Irish communities would be sending representatives to serve on the city's board of aldermen and its common council. With new homes, schools, and businesses to be constructed, police and fire departments to be organized, roads and streets to be paved, and water mains and sewer lines to be installed, a whole range of municipal services had to be developed in these new neighborhoods. And such services not only accommodated the needs of incoming families but also provided full-time jobs for many able-bodied Irish-Catholic workers.

Considering the traditional absence of heavy industry and large factories in the Boston area, which absence had for so long denied unskilled immigrant laborers the opportunity to get work, the arrival during the postwar period of such new public utility companies as the New England Telephone and Telegraph Company, the Boston Edison Electric Company, the Massachusetts Electric Company, and the Boston Gas Company was particularly welcome to Irish workmen. These companies brought in new technologies and opened up badly needed sources of employment that had never before existed in Boston—work that Irish Americans did not have to take away from native Boston workers. With new and healthier areas of the city in which to live, and with brand new job opportunities available for first- and second-generation immigrant families, the prospects for Irish Catholics looked brighter than anyone might have suspected only a dozen years earlier when the Know-Nothing movement was at its peak and oppression at its worst.

And with all this expansion, leaders of the Catholic Church in Boston were hard-pressed to meet the enormous demands for new buildings, new pastors, and new priests. The task of confronting these challenges, and dealing with the complex problems of a rapidly growing

Church in the midst of a significant transition, fell to John Joseph Williams, who in 1866 had succeeded John Bernard Fitzpatrick as bishop of Boston. Williams was the son of Michael Williams, a blacksmith from Tipperary, and Ann Egan, immigrants from Ireland who had settled in Boston and who were married at the old cathedral on Franklin Street. Born on April 27, 1822, while Jean Cheverus was still bishop, young John was baptized at the cathedral and grew up on Broad Street, where his family ran a boarding house and grocery store. After the death of his father in 1830, his mother remarried and the family moved to the North End. John attended public school for a year near Fort Hill; for the next six years he was a student at Bishop Fenwick's "pay school," which was run by seminarians and young priests. Williams was a quiet, thoughtful, serious boy, and when he showed an interest in the priesthood Bishop Fenwick guided him to the minor seminary conducted by the Sulpicians at Montreal, where he remained for eight years. In 1841, at the age of nineteen, Williams followed the example of his older friend, John Fitzpatrick, traveled to Paris for his theological studies, and was ordained to the priesthood on May 17, 1845.

On October 10, the new priest returned to his home town to take up his duties at the Chapel of the Holy Cross, a basement church in the cathedral designed for children. Here he served for ten years, carrying out his various functions and taking on the added responsibilities of teaching Sunday School and catechism classes. During the early 1850s, Williams assumed two additional services connected with the cathedral—the Chapel of the Guardian Angels and the Chapel of the Holy Family. On January 20, 1856, the thirty-four-year-old curate was appointed rector of the cathedral, and in July of the following year he was named pastor of St. James Church on Harrison Avenue. It had recently been established to meet the needs of immigrant families who had moved into an area called the South Cove in the southeast corner of Boston where it adjoins the South End. Father Williams directed affairs at this new parish for nine years, reducing the considerable parish debt and reorganizing its affairs.

John Joseph Williams succeeded John Fitzpatrick in 1866 as the fourth bishop of Boston. In 1875, Boston became an archdiocese, and Williams became the first archbishop in Boston's history. Respected for his quiet wisdom and thoughtful confidence, Williams was often called upon to resolve difficulties and disputes. At one time he was rumored for the honors of cardinal and papal delegate in the United States. (Courtesy of the Archdiocese of Boston.)

Because of the deteriorating health of Bishop Fitzpatrick, Williams was raised to the rank of vicar-general of the diocese in late summer 1857. This left him as virtual administrator of the diocese between May 1862 and September 1864, while Bishop Fitzpatrick was in Europe. At the consistory of January 8, 1866, Pope Pius IX formally named Williams titular bishop of Tripoli and coadjutor of Boston with right of succession—something that Bishop Fitzpatrick had been strongly urging for several years. After Fitzpatrick's death in February 1866, Williams succeeded to the rule of the diocese, and was formally elevated to the episcopacy on March 11 at a solemn ceremony in St. James's Church.

When he assumed his responsibilities as the fourth bishop of Boston in 1866, Williams found he had 116 priests and a total of 109 churches to serve the religious needs of a Catholic population that he estimated to be at least 300,000—a number that was rapidly increasing now that the Civil War was over. Boston now ranked as the second largest diocese in the country, surpassed only by New York, but the quality of its services left much to be desired. Although eight parishes were able to support their own religious schools, and nuns conducted three private academies for girls, there was no formal parochial school system as such. Two insubstantial hospitals served the needs of the immigrant poor, and three homes had been established to care for orphaned and destitute children. Almost every other American diocese had a seminary of its own; Boston still had none. Indeed, it was a moment when the bishop of Boston did not even have his own cathedral. Back in September 1860, Bishop Fitzpatrick had disposed of the small Franklin Street cathedral with the intention of building a grand new cathedral in the South End, and for this purpose he had engaged the services of Patrick C. Keely, a well-known church architect from New York. Only a few months later, however, the election of Abraham Lincoln had triggered the secession of seven states from the Union, and in April of the following year the Confederate attack on Fort Sumter signaled the outbreak of the Civil War. The conflict caused plans for the new cathedral to be put aside indefinitely. For a while, Sunday

Masses were conducted in the Melodeon Theater on Washington Street; after 1862 they were held in a former Unitarian church that had been purchased to serve as a temporary cathedral.

There was obviously much the new prelate had to do, and in typical matter-of-fact style he set about doing it almost immediately. Within the first five years of his episcopacy, Bishop Williams had authorized the construction of no fewer than fifteen churches, and, according to the diocesan historian, it was "a rare year" in which he did not dedicate at least eight to ten new churches. During the same period, he brought into the diocese a number of new religious orders to supplement the work of the Jesuits and the Augustinians, as well as the Sisters of Charity, the Sisters of Mercy, and the Sisters of Notre Dame, in opening more schools, staffing hospitals, and operating new charitable institutions for the poor, the aged, and the homeless. In 1866, he brought down the Grey Nuns from Montreal; in 1868 the Oblates of Mary Immaculate and the Sisters of the Third Order of St. Francis; the following year the Redemptorists and the Sisters of the Good Shepherd; and in 1870 the Little Sisters of the Poor. In 1873 the Franciscans came to Boston; the next year the Brothers of Charity joined the ranks of the new religious orders that were providing a greater number of services for an expanding population.

One of those services was medical care, and Williams increased the involvement of the Church in that respect also. Andrew Carney, an Irish-born businessman and philanthropist, had purchased property in South Boston for the creation of a hospital building designed to serve the needs of the working-class population in that district. After his death, the task of maintaining what became known as the Carney Hospital fell to Sister Ann Alexis, Sister Ann Aloysia, and other members of the Daughters of Charity, St. Vincent de Paul, who staffed the institution. For nearly four years, these nuns begged daily in the streets of Boston for enough money and food to keep the hospital open and the indigent patients fed. When Archbishop Williams heard about the condition of the hospital and the plight of the nuns, he organized a massive charity bazaar that realized the enormous sum of $25,000. The sisters used these funds to construct a new four-story hospital capable of housing more than a hundred bed patients. From that point on the Carney Hospital became a major source of medical care for Catholics throughout the diocese.

In addition to his work within Boston, Bishop Williams also participated in the larger work of the Catholic Church as it reorganized its structures to meet the needs of a changing postwar society. The new prelate had hardly been installed in office before he was off to Baltimore in October 1866 to take part in the Second Plenary Council of Baltimore, presided over by Archbishop Martin J. Spalding, and designed to establish canon law in America on firmer foundations. Accompanied by his two theologians—Father Alexander Sherwood Healy, the younger brother of Father James Healy, and Father William Blenkinsop, pastor of SS. Peter and Paul's Church in South Boston—Williams attended the conferences, said very little, but gained invaluable insights into the ideas and attitudes of his fellow bishops as they discussed more efficient ways of organizing the Church in America, improving religious standards, and establishing religious schools wherever possible. Although several bishops raised the question of making the diocese of Boston a metropolitan see, Williams did not display any discernible interest in the subject, and the issue was set aside for the time being. Obviously inspired by the spirit of the Baltimore Council, when he returned home Williams proceeded to hold his own diocesan council, the Second Synod, at which 140 priests assembled in November 1868—a dramatic contrast to the 30 priests who had been present when Bishop Fenwick held the First Synod in 1842. Bishop Williams placed before the assembled clergy a series of carefully prepared "constitutions" that laid down the proper procedures to be followed in dealing with such subjects as preaching, the sacraments, divine worship, cemeteries and burials, ecclesiastical property, clerical behavior, and more than two hundred other topics related to the life of the Church.

In 1868, Bishop Williams went to Rome at the invitation of Pope Pius IX to attend special ceremonies commemorating the martyrdom of SS. Peter and Paul. Hardly had the new prelate come back to America when he had to return to Rome after the pope called for a General Council to meet at the Vatican on December 8, 1869. According to the Church historian Father James Hennesey, the First Vatican Council was essentially "a European event in a church with a predominantly European membership." To a great extent, the meeting was an effort to reestablish the authority of the papacy and to reinforce the structures of the Church in the face of violent political changes and radical social upheavals that were sweeping through western Europe in the late 1860s and early 1870s. Indeed, the meetings of the council were held even as Italian armies were taking over the papal States and threatening to occupy Rome itself. In addition to proclaiming the doctrine of papal infallibility, the First Vatican Council defended the temporal power of the pope, reaffirmed the position of Pope Pius IX against the most dangerous "errors" of the day, and established a more effective canonical structure for the Catholic Church. Williams attended the meetings of the council along with other American bishops, but as one of the newest and youngest members of the assemblage he took little part in the formal discussions. In the space of only a few short years, however, the forty-six-year-old prelate had acquired a wealth of experience attending major Church councils, both in Europe and America, participating in conferences, listening to discussions about serious concerns of the Church by the most prominent clerics of the period, and quietly assessing the issues and problems that lay ahead of him as bishop of Boston.

As a result of the rapid growth of the Catholic population in New England, as early as 1868 Bishop Williams asked permission from Rome to consider dividing up the diocese of Boston. At the meeting of the bishops of the New York Province (of which the diocese of Boston was a part) in June 1869 he presented his plan to separate the five counties of western and central Massachusetts and form them into a new diocese with Springfield as its see city. A year later, Pope Pius IX signed the bull that created the new diocese. At another provincial bishops' meeting in April 1871, Williams suggested cutting off three counties in southeastern Massachusetts so that another see could be created that would also encompass Rhode Island. Although Rome agreed to the new diocese of Providence, it grew so fast that the three Massachusetts counties had to be organized into their own diocese of Fall River. Despite these geographic divisions, the diocese of Boston continued to grow at such a remarkable rate that on February 12, 1875, Pope Pius IX confirmed the transformation of Boston from a diocese to an archdiocese, whose province would include all the dioceses of New England. The news was received by Boston Catholics with great rejoicing as an appropriate tribute to the remarkable progress of the Church in New England; it could now boast of over eight hundred thousand Catholics, four hundred priests, five bishops—and now an archbishop.

On Sunday, May 2, 1875, Bishop John Williams was elevated to the rank of archbishop, with Cardinal John McCloskey, archbishop of New York, the first American to be made cardinal, coming to Boston to perform the installation ceremonies in the still uncompleted cathedral. Some four thousand persons, representing all segments of the community, filled the half-finished structure. In addition to thirteen bishops, two hundred priests, a papal delegate, and members of several foreign consulates, Governor William Gaston and Mayor Samuel Cobb headed a list of distinguished members of the state and city governments who were in attendance.

It was not long after Williams's installation as archbishop of Boston that work on the new Cathedral of the Holy Cross in the South End of the city was finally completed. One of his first official acts when he succeeded Bishop Fitzpatrick in 1866 had been to meet with the architect, Patrick C. Keely, reaffirm the original plans, and lay the foundation of the structure on June 25, 1866. Supported by annual collections, private contributions, and a series of highly successful

"Cathedral Fairs," the building project was supervised by Father Patrick Lyndon, rector of the temporary cathedral. In 1875, after nine years of work, Boston Catholics were able to enjoy the sight of a magnificent new cathedral, built in an early English Gothic style, that was almost as large as Notre Dame in Paris or St. John Lateran in Rome. According to the original plans, the structure was to have had two lofty towers, but the shortage of funds made that impossible. In the basement of the new cathedral was a large chapel containing the high altar from the old Franklin Street cathedral, as well as the remains of Bishop Fitzpatrick, which Archbishop Williams moved from their resting place in the St. Augustine cemetery in South Boston to a crypt in the rear of the chapel.

Building a seminary had always been one of Williams's foremost concerns, but the cost of the new cathedral, as well as the demands of numerous other projects, caused him to postpone it. In the past, potential seminarians always had to go to Baltimore, Montreal, or Paris to study for the priesthood. Bishop Fenwick's dream of a seminary at his Benedicta Community in Maine had failed to materialize, and Bishop Fitzpatrick had chosen to help sponsor the provincial seminary of St. Joseph at Troy, New York, in an effort to bring trained priests to the Boston diocese. Now that Boston was no longer a part of the New York Province, but the archdiocesan see of its own New England Province, the necessity of having its own seminary became apparent. Once the new cathedral had been completed in 1875, therefore, Williams turned his attention to finding an appropriate site for a seminary. In March 1880, the archbishop purchased a twenty-six-acre estate previously owned by Jacob Stanwood, a wealthy Boston merchant, in the attractive rural suburb of Brighton. Work on Theology House began in April 1881; three years later an L-shaped building, constructed in a simple, Norman style, which would accommodate a hundred students studying for their theology program, was complete.

After obtaining a charter from the Massachusetts legislature in 1883 for a degree-granting institution officially designated as the Bos-

When the original church on Franklin Street proved too small for Boston's grow-ing Catholic population, Bishop Fitzpatrick in 1860 made plans for a much larger cathedral in the South End. Because of the Civil War, work was not begun on the new church until 1866, and the structure was not completed until 1875. A magnificent cathedral in early English Gothic style, the Cathedral of the Holy Cross is almost as large as Notre Dame Cathedral in Paris.

ton Ecclesiastical Seminary, Archbishop Williams was prepared to open what he called St. John's in honor of his own patron saint. For seminary teachers, he decided to rely upon those who had been his own instructors and those of Bishop Fitzpatrick—the priests of the Society of St. Sulpice in Paris. In the summer of 1884 a group of Sulpicians arrived from Paris and from Maryland ready to serve as instructors, bringing with them a large stock of books that would provide the foundation of the seminary library. Several months later, the new institution opened its doors to thirty-two aspirants for the priesthood; most of them were well along in their studies at other seminaries, so in December 1884 the first group of ten young men was ordained at Brighton.

But Archbishop Williams was not finished with his plans for the training of his priests. The program at St. John's Seminary, as with that of most American seminaries during the nineteenth century, was based on the Roman model. A prospective candidate who entered St. John's with two years of college behind him began his formal studies in Philosophy House, where his program centered on philosophy. Upon completion of the philosophy program, or after graduating from a Catholic college with a strong philosophy curriculum, the student entered Theology House. Here he pursued a four-year program that culminated in ordination. To house students in the initial phase of their studies, the archbishop purchased the eighteen-acre Plummer Estate adjoining the Stanwood property in order to construct Philosophy House, which was dedicated on October 23, 1890. Several years later, Williams arranged for the noted architects Maginnis and Walsh to design a beautiful chapel as an addition to Theology House. It was built in the Romanesque style so popular at the turn of the century, and the archdiocesan historian has described the chapel as "a jewel of ecclesiastical architecture." St. John's Seminary was Archbishop Williams's pride and joy. He visited it frequently, presided each year at its final ceremonies, and took special pleasure in personally awarding its graduates the degree of bachelor of philosophy.

A decade earlier, when he was first beginning to involve himself in the work of constructing his new seminary, Archbishop Williams had also become involved in further plans to adjust the functions of the Church to the needs of a changing society. As a newly appointed prelate, he had attended the Second Plenary Council of Baltimore in 1866, and two years later he had participated in the deliberations of the Vatican Council in Rome. The Catholic Church in the United States, like many other social and religious institutions, had grown to sudden maturity in the sprawling vastness of the American continent. Over the course of the next twenty years it had developed to the point where Church leaders felt that even more canonical direction was required for its ecclesiastical management and that a greater degree of supervision was needed for its doctrinal teachings. Despite some of the administrative improvements that had been made by the First Vatican Council in 1866, the continued growth of the Catholic Church in America during the years following the Civil War, and the casual nature of its rather loose organizational structure, occasionally resulted in some embarrassing disputes between priests, pastors, and bishops.

Even the subject of proper clerical attire came up for discussion. In many parts of the world at this time, it was not unusual for priests and bishops to dress in the kind of clothing customarily worn by the general population. Archbishop Williams, for example, was usually seen driving his own small buggy around Boston dressed in a conservative black suit and a somber necktie. The historian Dorothy Wayman tells of the experience of William O'Connell, a young seminarian from Lowell, who was studying at the North American College when Archbishop Williams arrived for a visit to Rome. He was accompanied by Father William J. Daly, pastor of St. Joseph's Church in the West End, who wore a wide-open vest over a white shirt with huge emerald studs. "This sort of array will end pretty soon," quipped one Italian prelate, dressed appropriately in the Roman collar and the long black cassock so familiar on the streets of the Eternal City.

In hopes of dealing with a wide variety of religious differences and cultural peculiarities, the Third Plenary Council met at Baltimore late in 1884 under the direction of the city's archbishop, James Gibbons, soon to become America's second cardinal. Among the seventy-two U.S. prelates assembled in council was Archbishop Williams, now a much older man, a more senior archbishop, and a highly respected participant. A wise and thoughtful man of very few words, he kept his own counsel, listened to all sides of a question, and rarely offered his own views. Often, however, he worked behind the scenes as a mediator, trying to bring conflicting views into some kind of reasonable consensus. At various council meetings and conferences, it became common for fellow bishops to take him aside and seek out his advice on difficult issues and complex problems, safe in the knowledge that he would never violate a confidence.

As a church administrator back in Boston, Williams might be considered a counterpart to many American corporate executives of the late nineteenth century who operated their businesses in accordance with the principles of laissez-faire management. In selecting his various pastors, for example, Williams took the time to make thoughtful decisions and judicious appointments, and then sat back and let his pastors run their parishes with little interference from their archbishop as long as things were going well. When difficulties appeared or disputes arose, he tended to wait things out, let nature take its course, and allow the difficulties to resolve themselves whenever possible. If all remedies had been exhausted, however, and the difficulties still remained, Williams could make decisions quickly and effectively.

A number of changes came from the Third Baltimore Council, most of them designed to eliminate confusing lines of authority and bring about in the United States a more effective system of church administration on a national level. A number of structural changes called for establishing diocesan chanceries and clarifying regulations concerning priestly duties and services. A national Catholic university, envisioned chiefly as a center of advanced studies in philosophy and theology, was projected, and all local parishes were called upon to open a primary school within two years. The council also urged the preparation of a standardized manual of prayer and a uniform catechism that would set down the basic principles of Catholicism. This latter decision would ultimately result in what became popularly known as the "Baltimore Catechism," prepared in the question-and-answer style ("Who Made You? God Made Me. Why Did God Make You?" . . .) that was to become so familiar to American Catholics in the twentieth century.

The importance of Catholic education was a serious issue discussed at great length by the council. Unfortunately, the subject of parochial schools was something to which Archbishop Williams had already been forced to turn his attention as a result of disturbing circumstances in the archdiocese. Although Bishop Fitzpatrick and Archbishop Williams had both agreed that a parochial school system was a desirable long-range objective, the impoverished condition of the Famine immigrants during the 1850s, followed by the dislocations of the Civil War years during the 1860s, persuaded both prelates that it would be better for the time being to allow immigrant children to be educated in the city's public schools while Church leaders focused their attention on the youngsters' religious training and catechetical instruction.

Despite concessions to local Catholics in the wake of the Civil War, and assurances that Catholic schoolchildren would no longer be required to take part in religious exercises that went against their consciences, conditions in the public schools of the period had not shown any substantial improvement. Most textbooks continued to present an essentially Protestant view of world history, distorting Catholic teachings, ridiculing the customs of Catholic countries, and denigrating the character of historical Catholic figures. Responding to longstanding complaints that Catholic schoolchildren throughout the archdiocese were still experiencing constant embarrassment and unwarranted humiliation at the hands of insensitive schoolteachers and unresponsive school committees, Williams began to think seriously of establishing a parochial school system for the archdiocese. Launching something as complex as a private and independent school system, however, created honest differences of opinion among various pastors throughout the archdiocese, who came up with serious and reasonable explanations for their points of disagreement.

Many pastors had serious doubts about whether their parishes would be able to afford the costs of such an ambitious undertaking. Some continued to believe that if Catholics worked patiently with the various school committees, and appealed to the courts to adjudicate problems, Catholic children could be educated in the public schools with a minimum of discrimination. Others feared that creating a separate school system would stigmatize Catholic schoolchildren and endanger peaceful relations with the Yankee community. Many immigrant families, eager to become "Americanized" as soon as possible, not only feared the financial obligations of parochial schools but were also apprehensive about removing their children from the American public school system and having them stigmatized as "foreigners."

There were, on the other hand, a number of pastors—often referred to as "the Schoolmen"—who were enthusiastic about the idea of Catholic education and eager to construct a comprehensive parochial school system as soon as possible. The leader of this group was Father Thomas Scully, a vigorous and dynamic priest who had made a name for himself as the chaplain of the Ninth Massachusetts Regiment (the Irish regiment) during the Civil War, and who in 1867 took over as pastor of St. Mary's Church in Cambridge. Assisted by his devoted curate, Father John Mundy, the energetic pastor constructed a beautiful church, and then proceeded to open a school for girls in 1870, a school for boys in 1875, and then a mini-college in 1881. In addition to this extraordinary school system, Father Scully also came up with a boys' uniformed drum corps, a baseball team, several rowing crews, and one gymnasium for boys and young men and another for girls. He also provided a library for his schools, a billiards room, an active debating society, and a large parish hall for dramatic and musical productions. To encourage attendance at his parish schools, as well as to promote the whole idea of Catholic education, Father Scully denounced from the altar those parishioners who continued to send their children to public schools, and on many occasions he denied such persons the sacraments. Clearly, Father Scully hoped that the success of his various enterprises would provide an inspirational model for other parishes.

Many outraged members of St. Mary's parish, however, went public with their complaints about Father Scully's "tyrannical" behavior and brought the local "school question" to national attention. Despite efforts by Archbishop Williams to keep the issue under control and to moderate the more violent excesses of persons on both sides, the controversy continued unabated—especially after it had come to involve Father John O'Brien, pastor of the neighboring Church of the Sacred Heart in East Cambridge. Father O'Brien also constructed an impressive complex of parish buildings across the Charles River, and he too organized activities for his parishioners, ranging from a debating society to a bowling league. In addition, in 1888 he began to edit and publish a weekly religious magazine, the *Sacred Heart Review*, which grew into a popular journal with a nationwide circulation. In contrast to Father Scully, however, Father O'Brien did not believe in Catholic parishes' developing their own parochial schools. He not only came out strongly in support of the public school system but actually served with distinction as a member of the Cambridge School Committee as part of his public efforts to promote better relations between Catholics and the Protestant community. But Father O'Brien, too, came under fire from both sides. During the fall of 1880 a number of Catholic critics denounced him as a "Protestant priest," whereas various Protestant critics attacked him for his Catholic beliefs and his "Papist" teachings.

As the school controversy raged, letters went back and forth to and from Rome, causing Church authorities to wonder what was going on in the Boston archdiocese and to call upon Archbishop Williams to remedy the situation as soon as possible. Although the documentation is scarce, it appears likely that Williams stepped quietly into the dispute and let it be known to his pastors that he was planning to institute a parochial school system throughout the archdiocese, thereby undercutting the efforts of the school opponents. The results of such a decision became evident almost immediately. Back in 1879, only sixteen parishes in the archdiocese had their own schools; by 1884, Archbishop Williams could report to the Third Baltimore Council that thirty-five of his parishes had parochial schools, with many more to come.

Williams's decision to create a parochial school system for the archdiocese caused shock waves among members of the non-Catholic community. In Boston, as in many other U.S. cities during the late 1880s and early 1890s, native-born Americans experienced a definite sense of fear and apprehension concerning the remarkable growth of the Catholic Church and the increasing influence of its members in the life of the nation. The demographics clearly indicated that in numbers alone the future was overwhelmingly in favor of the Irish Catholics for generations to come. "New England Protestants will do well to remember that the Catholic population gains on them every year, as well by natural increase as by emigration," observed the eminent Boston historian Francis Parkman. He went on to bemoan the fact that the size of his Protestant friends' families in the wealthy Beacon Hill area had "dwindled in numbers generation after generation through all this century." Perhaps even more disconcerting than their raw numbers was the realization that members of the Irish-Catholic community were taking on a much more independent attitude, as well as showing positive signs of a definite group consciousness. No longer the poor, meek, and humble immigrants who assumed a deferential attitude toward their "betters" and gave every indication of "knowing their place" in a country where they were looked upon as "guests," a new generation was emerging whose members insisted on their rightful place as equal citizens in the land of their own birth. The new Irish Catholics were no longer "adopted citizens." They were native sons.

A practical demonstration of this trend lay in how Irish Catholics were moving up from political activity at the various ward levels to begin taking their places in city, state, and even national politics. The city of Lawrence chose its first Catholic mayor, John Breen, in 1881; Lowell selected John J. Donovan as mayor in 1882; and in 1884 Boston chose Hugh O'Brien as the first Irish-born Roman Catholic mayor of the city. "Hugh O'Brien, Mayor of Boston!" exclaimed the *Pilot*. "Shades of Cotton Mather, what a change!" And that was only the beginning. By 1887, an Irish Catholic had become chairman of the city's board of aldermen, while other Catholics were serving as president of the common council, city clerk, and chairman of the Boston School Committee. And local Catholics were also moving up to important political positions at the national level. In 1894 John F. Fitzgerald, young ward boss of Boston's North End, was elected to the United States House of Representatives from the Ninth Congressional District, succeeding Joseph O'Neil, who had held the post for over a decade; and Joseph F. O'Connell of Dorchester went to Washington from the Tenth Congressional District, a seat that would be taken over in 1910 by James Michael Curley of Roxbury.

The rise of an educated, articulate, and increasingly influential laity in the archdiocese of Boston was a relatively new phenomenon that did not go unnoticed. Archbishop Williams recognized the emerging role of lay people and made responsive efforts to make them more actively involved in the life of the Church. He promoted, for example, the practice of having periodic "missions" for lay people in each parish, usually conducted by members of various religious orders, and he encouraged the formation of lay religious organizations. The Sodality of the Blessed Virgin Mary became very popular among female parishioners, and by 1881 membership was practically universal throughout the archdiocese. The League of the Sacred Heart, begun in 1887, was found in almost every parish by 1907, and by the end of the Williams era the Holy Name Society was already beginning to gain widespread appeal among men. In 1882, the Forty Hours' Devotion was made obligatory for all parishes, and the Society for the Nocturnal Adoration of the Blessed Sacrament, started in 1882 at the new cathedral in the South End, soon became a popular observance.

The early years of Williams's episcopacy also saw the appearance of various lay societies, clubs, and associations of a literary and cultural nature that were promoted by Church leaders. Many parishes sponsored reading clubs, debating societies, and literary groups, but toward the end of the century there seemed to be a greater interest in musical programs, dramatic productions, and sports activities. Father Robert Fulton, SJ, capitalized upon this new spirit in 1875 when he founded the Young Men's Catholic Association of Boston College, which had widespread appeal. In addition to societies of a religious and social nature, Catholic laymen during this period also found community and companionship in a number of fraternal organizations. The Massachusetts Catholic Order of Foresters, for example, was founded in 1879; the Knights of Columbus, which had started in New Haven, Connecticut, in 1882, established its first council in Massachusetts a decade later.

The virtue of charity was always close to Archbishop Williams's heart, and in 1861, when he was pastor of St. James's Church in downtown Boston, he established the first Conference of the St. Vincent de Paul Society, a volunteer organization of laymen designed to meet the needs of the poor, the homeless, and the disadvantaged within the parish. After Williams became bishop, the number of such Conferences increased dramatically, and they were brought under the direction of a central organization called the Boston Particular Council. As president of this council (and later of the Boston Central Council, which had jurisdiction over all New England), it was a layman, Mr. Thomas Ring, who exercised a vigorous and tireless leadership role. His successor, Dr. Thomas Dwight, Parkman Professor of Anatomy at the Harvard Medical School, continued the work and became one of the archbishop's closest personal friends. The St. Vincent de Paul Society grew into one of the most active and effective voluntary agencies of charity in the archdiocese, and in 1882 Pope Leo XIII spoke approvingly of its efforts. "Christian charity," he said, "unites the rich and the poor by the sweet bonds of holy affection."

In 1873, Pope Pius IX issued an appeal for lay people everywhere to unite in the face of the various world movements he felt were attacking the Catholic Church and undermining traditional Christian values. Responding to this appeal, Archbishop Williams encouraged a group of twenty-five prominent Catholic laymen in the city to form what he called the Catholic Union, both to demonstrate loyalty to the Holy See and to defend the principles of the Catholic faith. The first public demonstration of this new lay organization was the massive Catholic Festival held on November 13, 1873, at Boston's Music Hall to celebrate the golden jubilee of Pope Pius IX's ordination to the priesthood. The impressive occasion was highlighted by the appearance of New England's best-known Catholic figures, and it was attended by thousands of lay people from all parts of the archdiocese.

After that auspicious beginning, the Catholic Union gradually settled down to about four hundred active members, who purchased a building on Washington Street as a permanent location where members could meet, hold public lectures, plan programs, and undertake various charitable activities. Archbishop Williams had great hopes for the Catholic Union and attended the Wednesday evening meetings as often as possible. In keeping with his own reserved and deliberate nature, he made it quite clear that although he did not want "aggressive" Catholics, neither did he want "cowardly" Catholics. He wanted Catholics, he told the members, who would "stand on their rights as American citizens; no more." He looked forward to an organized group of Catholic laymen, he stated, who would be "strong, steadfast, firm, not afraid of any one, ready to defend their Faith, ready to speak the truth." "But," he added pointedly, "they should know how to speak it, and do it."

The expanding role of the laity in Boston also focused greater attention upon the need for more-effective communication throughout the archdiocese. The *Boston Pilot* had been started by Bishop Fenwick in 1829 in response to the many attacks then being made against Catholic beliefs and teachings. After several years, the bishop became discouraged by declining circulation, and in 1834 he turned the newspaper over to a twenty-five-year-old typesetter named Patrick Donahoe, who had arrived from Ireland only ten years earlier. Through careful management and shrewd financing, and by adding political news from Ireland and America to the basic religious orientation of the paper, Donahoe was able to turn the *Pilot* into one of the most successful Irish-Catholic newspapers in the country. Although his enterprise had no official ties with diocesan authorities, it was clearly to Donahoe's advantage to keep on good terms with the local bishop. This became evident during 1847–48, when Donahoe praised the "glorious progress" of various revolutionary movements in Europe that he said were shaking "thrones and despotism." Bishop Fitzpatrick was not pleased by such radical views. He set up a rival conservative newspaper, *The Observer*, which quickly sobered Donahoe and brought the *Pilot* into line. Thereafter, the *Pilot* generally reflected the views of diocesan authorities, although officially it continued to be an independent publication.

By the 1870s, Patrick Donahoe was not only the editor and publisher of a thriving newspaper but also the owner of a publishing house, a bookstore, a church-goods store, and a travel agency—all located in a six-story granite block called the "Donahoe Buildings" on Franklin and Hawley Streets. His enterprises were completely wiped out, however, in the Great Fire of November 1872 that devastated most of Boston's business district, and later attempts to rebuild were frustrated by a succession of smaller fires. The collapse of the insurance companies, followed by the financial depression of 1873, finally forced Donahoe into bankruptcy.

At this point Archbishop Williams stepped in and purchased the *Pilot*, with the intention of using the profits to pay off Donahoe's creditors. Cooperating with the archbishop in this undertaking, and serving as the paper's new editor, was a young Irish Catholic named John

Boyle O'Reilly. Born June 28, 1844, in County Meath, on the outskirts of Drogheda, O'Reilly grew up near the site of Oliver Cromwell's savage massacre of Royalist and Catholic men, women, and children. Coming from a family of educators, O'Reilly traveled to England to work as a printer's apprentice; he then enlisted in the British army, where he worked to convert Irish-born soldiers to the cause of Irish independence. When his illegal activities were uncovered, O'Reilly was arrested and sent off to a penal colony in Australia, but he made a daring escape and eventually found his way to Boston. There, in the spring of 1870, he was befriended by an Irish-American poet, Robert Dwyer Joyce, who helped him find an apartment in the West End and a job as a reporter for the *Pilot*. During his initial years with the newspaper, O'Reilly displayed an intense American patriotism, became critical of violence in the Irish nationalist movement, and called upon Catholics and Protestants in America to reconcile their differences.

O'Reilly's graceful style of writing, his staunch patriotism, and his conciliatory attitude toward native Bostonians quickly made him a favorite in Brahmin literary and social circles, and in 1872 he was invited to join the exclusive Papyrus Club. The following year, however, perhaps to indicate that he had not forgotten his Catholic roots and "gone over to the other side," O'Reilly helped Archbishop Williams form the organization of laymen called the Catholic Union. Williams admired the young writer, and when he took over the *Pilot* from Donahoe in 1876 he asked O'Reilly to join him in the acquisition and to assume the position of editor.

O'Reilly's direction of the *Pilot* during the 1880s charted a new and more lofty direction for the newspaper. He employed not only his own considerable literary skills but also those of outstanding staff writers like James Jeffrey Roche and Katherine E. Conway. A native of Rochester, New York, Conway was a devout Roman Catholic who earned her living as a writer, editor, and lecturer; until Leila Little held the position from 1990 to 1993, she was the only woman to have served

A political prisoner in British prisons in Ireland, England, and Australia, John Boyle O'Reilly escaped to America. He achieved a distinguished career as a public speaker, civil rights leader, poet, novelist, and editor of the Pilot. O'Reilly did much to bridge the late nineteenth-century divisions between the Yankee-Protestant and the Irish-Catholic communities of Boston. His unexpected death in 1890 was termed a "public calamity" by Cardinal Gibbons. (Courtesy of the Bostonian Society.).

as editor in chief of the *Pilot*. Conway was a founding member of the Boston Authors' Club and of Boston's League of Catholic Women, a trustee of the Boston Public Library, and a member of the Massachusetts Prison Commission. Active in the New England Women's Press Association, she held various executive positions over a period of forty years.

After accepting John Boyle O'Reilly's job offer, Katherine Conway served as editorial assistant from 1883 to 1890. For the next fifteen years she was the associate editor, becoming editor in chief in 1905. In 1912, Pope Pius X awarded Conway the papal decoration *Pro Ecclesia et Pontifice* for her various creative achievements on behalf of the Church. In 1908, when the archbishop took over the *Pilot*, Conway left the paper and for several years taught at St. Mary's College in Indiana. In 1916 she returned to Boston to become managing editor of John F. Fitzgerald's political weekly, *The Republic*, staying on until it folded in 1926. She contributed unsigned editorials to the *Pilot* until her death at seventy-four in January 1927.

In his role as editor of the *Pilot*, John Boyle O'Reilly also used the Catholic weekly as a vehicle for defending Boston Catholics' position on a number of disputed subjects, arguing the case for an independent Ireland and exploring such controversial issues as the rights of African Americans and the interests of Native American Indians. He often pointed out tragic similarities between the discrimination practiced for so long against Irish Catholics and the oppression visited upon other racial and ethnic minorities in America. O'Reilly's sudden and unexpected death in 1890 at the age of only forty-six was termed by Cardinal Gibbons "a public calamity." When he died, observes historian Mark Schneider, in his study *Boston Confronts Jim Crow*, the opportunity slipped away for some kind of progressive association between Irish Catholics and members of Boston's small African-American community. "The light of 'green' and black unity," he writes, "flickered and died."

There were many local Bostonians who were pleased to observe the

Katherine Eleanor Conway was the last editor of the Pilot *before it became the official newspaper of the archdiocese. A native of Rochester, N.Y., she was hired by John Boyle O'Reilly in 1883 on the strength of two novels she had published. A professional journalist, poet, novelist, and lecturer, Conway was a founding member of the Boston Authors' Club and was instrumental in founding the League of Catholic Women.*

growing influence of educated and articulate Irish Catholics in their native city. After he was elected mayor in 1884, for example, Hugh O'Brien came as a refreshing surprise; he was a chief executive of efficiency and integrity, displaying none of the disturbing characteristics Yankees usually associated with immigrants from Ireland. He was seen as the kind of Irish Catholic whom Yankees would seek out and encourage to become leaders of the Boston Irish. John Boyle O'Reilly, too, was seen as an invaluable asset in bringing immigrants into the mainstream of American society. He was hailed as a leading New England writer, welcomed to speak before prominent Boston organizations, and invited to give the main address at the dedication of the Plymouth Rock monument in 1889.

But others in the Yankee community resented the increasing power of the Papists in their midst and feared the inevitable consequences of their increasing numbers. Many Protestant leaders in Boston, for example, reacted in alarm at the announcement by Archbishop Williams that he was starting a parochial school system. For the first time, there was a real prospect that a whole new generation of immigrant children might grow to maturity without the painstaking guidance of Yankee headmasters and the careful instruction of traditional New England schoolteachers, who could be counted on to steer them in the "right" direction. Some native citizens were certain that Roman Catholics would be making their way to the state legislature, looking for the same kinds of public funding for their Church-supported schools that Protestants had long received for their own favorite institutions. Others feared that without trained teachers or a standardized curriculum, Catholic schools would lower educational standards, undermine old Puritan values, subvert republican principles, and provide an inferior style of religious indoctrination. In 1888 and again in 1889, bills were proposed in the Yankee-controlled state legislature requiring Massachusetts to establish local boards of education to inspect and supervise all private schools in the commonwealth.

Still other Bostonians, however, saw in Williams's plan for parochial schools even more serious implications for their hold over the city's future. Up to that point, the public school system had been one of the most effective methods by which the Brahmin community had been able to keep immigrant children under its surveillance and control. Serious and well-trained Boston teachers could use the public school system as what one modern writer has called a "culture factory" to instill in immigrant pupils a proper respect for the Puritan tradition and the Anglo-Saxon heritage. In this way, the sons and daughters of ill-bred and barely educated foreigners could be gradually transformed into disciplined, obedient, and respectful versions of second-generation Bostonians. If Catholics now built their own parochial schools, and took their children out of the public schools, Yankees feared that it would mean the end of their earlier popular and optimistic assumption that native-born Anglo-Saxon people could absorb and assimilate the inferior peoples who migrated to the United States.

The historian Doris Kearns Goodwin has observed that by this time many Brahmin families had already taken their sons out of the city's public schools and enrolled them in such private academies as Middlesex, Groton, St. Paul's, and St. Mark's, insisting at the same time that Irish children should remain in the public schools. The very fact that so many Roman Catholics were "still essentially foreigners," claimed the local publisher Edwin D. Mead, constituted a major reason that they, "above all others," should be kept for as long as possible in the public schools. Once a large segment of these immigrant children—presumably the more intelligent ones from better-off families—were able to move into a school system of their own design, operating in accordance with their own social values and their own religious beliefs, they would be beyond the reach and the influence of the Boston establishment. As a result of this decision, the division already existing between the Irish community and the Yankee community would only widen the breach that was being caused by contemporary political developments.

The formal establishment of a parochial school system by Archbishop Williams meant not only an increase in the number of schools and students but also a remarkable increase in the number of Catholic sisterhoods, whose members would staff these schools and teach these children. Pastors, anxious to find sisters to work in their new parochial schools, often traveled to many parts of the United States and Canada, visiting motherhouses in Maryland, Kentucky, Nova Scotia, New Jersey, and Indiana to find suitable teachers. In 1870, the number of sisters in the archdiocese of Boston had numbered slightly over two hundred; in 1940, there were over four thousand. Although by the 1890s most sisters were American born, coming predominantly from working-class families, studies by Sister Mary Oates, CSJ, indicate that most of them had foreign-born fathers, the overwhelming majority of whom had emigrated from Ireland. Working on the staffs of numerous parochial schools, hospitals, orphanages, and social agencies, sisters in the archdiocese outnumbered the total of priests, brothers, and seminarians *combined* by a margin of two to one. Nearly three-fourths of the sisters belonged to one of the ten largest communities, with the remaining numbers scattered among some twenty-eight other religious groups.

The two dominant teaching communities in the archdiocese of Boston were the Sisters of Notre Dame de Namur and the Sisters of St. Joseph; in 1920, these orders accounted for 44 percent of the city's sisters. Members of the Sisters of Notre Dame first arrived in Boston in 1849 to specialize in the care and education of young girls. Since their motherhouse was in Belgium, at first the nuns made efforts to reproduce in their convents and schools the European traditions and lifestyle of Namur; gradually, however, they were overwhelmed by the local Irish influences. Between 1850 and 1880, the Sisters of Notre Dame had the largest representation of teachers in the Massachusetts Catholic schools. The Sisters of St. Joseph, on the other hand, had been brought into the archdiocese in 1873 by Monsignor Thomas Magennis of St. Thomas's parish in Jamaica Plain at Archbishop Williams's suggestion. Under the direction of Mother Mary Regis, an immigrant girl named Ann Casserly who had arrived in the United States at the age of nine, a small community of four nuns who specialized in the education of boys and girls gradually became the largest teaching order in the archdiocese, with a community that expanded to fourteen hundred members.

By 1940, nearly two-thirds of all sisters in the archdiocese were employed in parochial schools. The individual parishes actually owned their schools and their convents, and the nuns received their housing and a small annual stipend from each parish. As employees of the parish, they could be dismissed by the pastor—and occasionally they were, especially when a pastor wanted the sisters to perform duties that a tough-minded mother superior determined were not appropriate to the training of the sisters or to the mission for which her particular order was qualified. "Sisters saw themselves as women in the vanguard of social and educational reform," writes Sister Mary Oates. "In a Protestant state, they valued their role in the development of Catholic schools, hospitals, and orphanages."

The combination among Irish Catholics of increasing numbers, a more self-assured attitude, a growing political ascendancy, and a separatist parochial school system, together with a frightening influx of new foreign immigrants from southern and eastern Europe, caused many Protestants to revert fearfully to the kind of defensive nativism that had characterized the pre–Civil War years. Even though the old Know-Nothing movement, as an organized political force, had been effectively crushed by the impact of the slavery controversy and the subsequent crisis of the Civil War, the spirit of anti-Catholicism continued to flare up in various forms and in different locations during the postwar years.

Local nativist groups with patriotic names, like the Order of the American Union, the Templars of Liberty, the Patriotic League of the Revolution, and the Order of American Freedom, made their appearance during the 1870s and 1880s. They warned of the international

Catholic conspiracy, opposed parochial schools, called for Bible-reading in the public schools, and opposed the election of Catholics to public office. Salacious books by runaway nuns and apostate priests sustained a lucrative publishing business during the same period by keeping alive old rumors of wrongdoing in convents and monasteries. The skillful cartoonist Thomas Nast drew a series of venomous lampoons against the Catholic Church in the popular magazine *Harper's Weekly*, while many Republican political leaders continued (at least indirectly) to warn the voting public of the dangers of "Rum, Romanism, and Rebellion" inherent in the Democratic party.* For the most part, however, the anti-Catholicism of the postwar years had not yet matched the force and violence of the pre–Civil War movement. But in the late 1880s, the "APA" appeared on the scene.

The American Protective Association operated mainly in the staunchly Protestant upper Mississippi Valley, but its influence was felt throughout the nation. Organized in 1887 at Clinton, Iowa, by Henry F. Bowers, a man addicted to bizarre fantasies of Catholic conspiracies, the APA spread rapidly through the Middle West as its followers warned of the dangers of Catholic political power and denounced parochial schools as an imminent danger to all American institutions. Calling for restrictions on further immigration, the APA made its members promise never to vote for a Catholic, never to hire one, and always to promote the teaching of the "American" language in the public schools. The organization achieved its greatest prominence in 1893, when it spread rumors that a papal decree had absolved Catholics of all oaths of allegiance to the United States and that a massacre of "heretics" was planned for September 5 (erroneously believed to be the feast day of St. Ignatius Loyola, the founder of the Jesuits).

As a national movement, the APA soon vanished almost as quickly

* The Republican presidential candidate, James G. Blaine, lost his chance for election in 1884 when he did not denounce this memorable anti-Catholic phrase in a public speech by one of his supporters.

THE AMERICAN RIVER GANGES.

The Priests and the Children.

The Nativist fears of the early nineteenth century, that the Catholic Church was involved in a vast conspiracy to take over the United States, came to life again in the latter part of the century as Catholic parochial schools grew more numerous. Thomas Nast, in the September 30, 1871, issue of Harper's Weekly, *provided an ingenious anti-Catholic cartoon using bishops' mitres as the jaws of ferocious crocodiles as they come ashore on American soil.*

as the Know-Nothings of the 1850s, swallowed up by the Populist movement and the free-silver agitation that rocked the prairie states during the mid-1890s. Nevertheless, its paranoia concerning Catholic conspiracies, its bitter resentment of immigrants, and its fears of the mongrelization of the Anglo-Saxon race by so-called inferior peoples met a welcoming response in many places throughout the Northeast. In parts of Massachusetts, the APA grew to some considerable strength after it was largely taken over by British-Americans and "Orangemen" from northern Ireland. The movement was especially active in cities and towns north of Boston, among them Chelsea, Somerville, Lynn, and Gloucester. Reportedly, the APA recruited as many as 75,000 members in some 175 to 200 councils in various parts of the commonwealth.

Until the fall of 1892 there was little APA activity reported in Massachusetts, but after that time various political parties (except the Democrats) began catering to the anti-Catholic mood in order to capture the votes of APA supporters. They included in their political platforms various phrases and slogans clearly pertaining to matters of church and state, the issue of parochial schools, and the importance of keeping the spirit of Americanism alive. Even prestigious journals like *Harper's Weekly* and the *Atlantic Monthly* began printing anti-Catholic articles and tasteless anti-immigrant cartoons as regular features.

Things became even more ugly in the summer of 1895, when the local chapter of the APA received permission from the governor to march in East Boston's Fourth of July parade. The event went off as scheduled, and the police were able to maintain order during the parade itself, a procession marked by floats carrying the symbol of the Little Red Schoolhouse, which everybody recognized as an attack against parochial schools. But when the parade broke up and the APA marchers were going home, they were taunted by a hostile crowd. In the midst of a scuffle, members of the APA drew guns, fired into the crowd, and killed a Catholic named John W. Willis. Charging that peaceful marchers had been set upon by a "murderous gang of thugs" and that they had fired in self-defense, members of the APA held an "indignation meeting" at Faneuil Hall to protest the attack on their parade and the violation of their civil rights. After an inquest in East Boston Court, two APA members were subsequently arrested on suspicion of murder, but both persons were later discharged. Even the *Pilot*, the Catholic weekly, chided the Irish residents for not recognizing that members of the APA had a constitutional right to hold their own parade.

By the late 1880s and early 1890s, there were clearly plenty of reasons for nativists in Boston to be apprehensive about the eventual impact of Irish Catholics on the traditional religious, social, and educational patterns of their beloved city. But certainly one additional cause for concern was directly related to the unexpected flood of immigrants coming into Boston from entirely new points of the compass. The influx of these "new" immigrants was a phenomenon that not only helped fuel the organized opposition of various antiforeign groups in the city but also presented Archbishop Williams and the members of the local hierarchy with a distinct challenge to the unity and stability of the Boston archdiocese.

✢ ADDITIONAL READING

The forty-year episcopacy of Archbishop John Williams, extending from the end of the Civil War to the beginning of the twentieth century, was the longest in the history of the archdiocese of Boston and cries out for serious historical study. Unfortunately, the laconic archbishop offers little help in his own cause. Not only was he a man of few words but he also discontinued the practice of keeping the *Bishop's Journal*, so that historians do not have a record of his personal reflections or an account of his day-to-day activities. Fortunately, however, Father Robert H. Lord, author of the section dealing with Williams in the third volume of the *History of the Archdiocese of Boston*, has provided a series of chapters that not only stand on their own to form a professional historical monograph but also provide valuable source materials for future scholars. Mother Augustine (Eulalia Tuckerman) prepared an extensive typewritten manuscript, "Life of Archbishop Williams," which is available to scholars in the Archives of the Archdiocese of Boston. The archbishop's close friend Dr. Thomas Dwight contributed a brief but sensitive essay about the life of Williams for *The Centenary of the See of Boston* (Boston, 1909).

The changing demographics of the Irish population in Boston is effectively presented by Sam Bass Warner, Jr., *Streetcar Suburbs: The Process of Growth in Boston, 1870–1900* (New York, 1974), not only documenting the changes in public transportation during the postwar decades but also describing the nature of immigrant housing as the Irish moved out from the waterfront into the neighborhoods. Thomas N. Brown, *Irish-American Nationalism, 1870–1890* (Philadelphia,

1966), is the leading scholarly work on the influence of Irish affairs on political developments in America; William D'Arcy, *The Fenian Movement in the United States, 1858–1886* (Washington, 1947), studies the efforts of Americans to fight for the freedom of Ireland; and Michael A. Gordon, *The Orange Riots: Irish Political Violence in New York City, 1870 and 1871* (Ithaca, N.Y., 1993), shows the extent of ethnic hatred that persisted in the aftermath of the Civil War. Ronald Formisano and Constance Burns, eds., *Boston, 1700–1980* (Westport, Conn., 1984), contains several chapters that are relevant to the second half of the nineteenth century. Dale Baum, *The Civil War Party System: The Case of Massachusetts, 1848–1876* (Chapel Hill, N.C., 1984), traces Bay State political history into the post–Civil War period; Thomas H. O'Connor, *The Boston Irish*, offers an overview of Irish political development at both the city and ward levels during the years following the Civil War. An early biography of Patrick Collins (Boston's first Irish-born Roman Catholic mayor), Michael Curran's *Life of Patrick Collins* (Norwood, Mass., 1906), was updated by Sister M. Jeanne d'Arc O'Hare, "The Public Career of Patrick Collins" (Ph.D. diss., Boston College, 1959). Lesley Ainley, *Boston Mahatma: Martin Lomasney* (Boston, 1949), is a fascinating but undocumented account of the life and career of the West End's colorful ward boss; John H. Cutler, *"Honey Fitz": Three Steps to the White House* (New York, 1962), is a valuable firsthand account of John F. Fitzgerald's rise to political prominence; Doris Kearns Goodwin, *The Fitzgeralds and the Kennedys* (New York, 1987), provides a panoramic view of three generations of an influential Boston family.

Arthur Mann, *Yankee Reformers in the Urban Age* (New York, 1954), and Geoffrey Blodgett, *The Gentle Reformers: Massachusetts Democrats in the Cleveland Era* (Cambridge, 1966), are insightful works dealing with major efforts to change politics and society during the late nineteenth century. James Jeffrey Roche, *Life of John Boyle O'Reilly* (New York, 1891), is an older study by a friendly contemporary. Jack Tager and John Ifkovic, *Massachusetts in the Gilded Age*

(Amherst, Mass., 1985), have edited a series of essays dealing with various aspects of the post-Reconstruction period. The chapter by Arthur Mann, "Irish Catholic Liberalism," in his *Yankee Reformers in the Urban Age*, and Francis R. Walsh's essay "John Boyle O'Reilly, the *Boston Pilot*, and Irish-American Assimilation, 1870–1890," in *Massachusetts in the Gilded Age*, shed a great deal of light on O'Reilly's role as a progressive reformer. Mark Schneider's chapter "Irish-Americans and the Legacy of John Boyle O'Reilly," in his book *Boston Confronts Jim Crow, 1890–1920* (Boston, 1997), analyzes the potential role O'Reilly and Boston Catholics might have played in establishing relations with members of the city's African-American community. Francis G. McManamin, *The American Years of John Boyle O'Reilly, 1870–1890* (Washington, 1959), provides a sound basis for further study of this brilliant, complex figure. A. G. Evans, *Fanatic Heart: A Life of John Boyle O'Reilly, 1884–1890* (Nedlands, W. Australia, 1997), is the most recent biography that sheds light on the penal years in Australia. Mary Jo Weaver, *New Catholic Women: A Contemporary Challenge to Traditional Religious Authority* (San Francisco, 1985), Karen Kennelly, *American Catholic Women: A Historical Exploration* (New York, 1989), and James J. Kenneally, *History of American Catholic Women* (New York, 1990), provide the basis for further study into the role and contributions of women in the Catholic Church.

The decision of Archbishop Williams to establish a parochial school system had a significant impact on the Boston community. Louis S. Walsh, *Archdiocese of Boston: Growth of Parochial Schools in Chronological Order, 1820–1900* (Newton Highlands, Mass., 1901), provides valuable historical source materials for researchers. Daniel F. Reilly, *The School Controversy, 1891–1893* (Washington, 1943), studies the subject on a national level; James W. Sanders, "Boston Catholics and the School Question, 1825–1907," in *From Common School to Magnet School: Selected Essays on the History of Boston Schools* (ed. J. W. Fraser et al., Boston, 1979), provides an informative treatment of the issue as it affected the archdiocese. Dennis Ryan, *Beyond the*

Ballot Box (Amherst, Mass., 1989), offers a fascinating study of the social history and cultural contributions of the Boston Irish from 1845 to 1917.

At the end of the century there were violent explosions of anti-Catholic sentiment. Josiah Strong, *Our Country, Its Possible Future and Present Crisis* (New York, 1885), is typical of a number of contemporary works that pointed out the many dangers that Catholicism posed to the American Protestant way of life. Humphrey J. Desmond, *The A.P.A. Movement: A Sketch* (Washington, 1912), and Gustavus Myers, *History of Bigotry in the United States* (New York, 1943), are two older works that are helpful in describing the methods and goals of the American Protective Association; John Higham, "The Mind of a Nativist: Henry Bowers and the A.P.A.," *American Quarterly* 4 (1952), offers a view of the association against a broad background of nativist sentiments. Donald Kinzer, *An Episode in Anti-Catholicism: The American Protective Association* (Seattle, 1964), and John Higham, *Strangers in the Land: Patterns of American Nativism, 1860–1925* (New York, 1965), are more recent treatments of this unfortunate episode of religious and ethnic bigotry.

5 A Changing Church

U NTIL WELL INTO THE LATER YEARS OF THE nineteenth century, while John Williams was still serving as archbishop of Boston, Catholics of Irish background, because of the large numbers in which they had emigrated to America, clearly played a prominent role in shaping the religious beliefs and social practices of the Catholic Church. A French priest, l'Abbé Félix Klein, a graduate of Saint Sulpice and a professor at the Institut Catholique in Paris, visited the United States in the late 1800s and observed that the Catholic Church he found there was essentially an Irish church. "Many of the priests were born in Ireland; almost all are the sons of Irishmen," he wrote. "Most of its communicants come from Ireland; and if other countries, Germany, Italy, Austria, today add more immigrants, it must be remembered that these are received and must settle in communities that are . . . based on Irish zeal and American patriotism."

Until about 1890, the archdiocese of Boston certainly reflected the major patterns that characterized early emigration from Europe to America. During the early part of the nineteenth century, most immigrants to the United States had come from northern and western

Europe—from various parts of the British Isles, from the northern parts of France and Germany, and from the Scandinavian countries. By the 1880s, however, the national character of immigration had begun to change dramatically, and by the 1890s the bulk of those entering the country were coming from southern and eastern Europe— from Italy, Austria-Hungary, Greece and the Balkans, present-day Poland and Lithuania, and Russia. Fleeing from high taxes, low wages, drought, famine, political oppression, and religious persecution, the members of this so-called new immigration no longer came from easily assimilable groups whose cultural traditions and political institutions were at least vaguely similar to those of the United States.

The new immigrants had been drawn by America's celebrated image as a nation of freedom and a land of opportunity, and they were determined to build for themselves a new and more hopeful future. Together with other northern states like New York, New Jersey, and Pennsylvania, the commonwealth of Massachusetts also received its share of the new European immigrants in the decade between 1900 and 1910; over 150,000 Italians entered the Bay State, along with some 80,000 Poles and nearly 25,000 Lithuanians. Most of these newcomers headed for such major urban centers as Boston, Brockton, Lowell, and Lawrence in search of jobs and homes. These were the men, women, and children who would greatly change the nature and character of the Catholic Church in the archdiocese of Boston.

Note, however, that long before these "new immigrants" arrived, members of other nationalities had already contributed significantly to the vitality and diversity of the Faith. People of French origin, for example, were critical to the establishment of the Catholic Church in Boston—first, because of the alliances Americans made with the French government during the Revolution, which bound the two nations more closely together; and, second, because of the presence of so many French Catholics in the town in the years that followed independence. A series of French priests helped start the first Catholic parishes in the Puritan town, in the days before the arrival of Father

François Matignon and then Father Jean Cheverus created a stability and dedication that transformed a small immigrant parish into a permanent Catholic diocese. As Boston's first Roman Catholic bishop, Cheverus succeeded with Gallic charm in blending the religious and cultural traditions of the Old World with the emerging democratic spirit of the New.

Catholics from various German states also began arriving as early as the 1820s. Among the first were the three Kraemer brothers, Melchior, Sebastian, and Mathias, clockmakers from Baden, who came to Boston from Philadelphia in 1827 and operated a very profitable import business. By 1830, more German immigrants had arrived in the city, most of them from the western and northwestern parts of the German states.

Because the "American" church was an "Irish" church, however, it was not long before the Germans made it clear that they wanted a priest of their own, one who could preach to them and hear confessions in their own language and who could help them observe their own religious feast days. For example, they celebrated Christmas as a special holy day, and Germans actually introduced Bostonians to the custom of Christmas trees and greeting cards. Bishop Benedict Fenwick tried to respond to the needs of the newcomers, and between 1836 and 1848 he brought in several priests from the German lands to serve the small congregation. None of them remained in Boston very long, however, usually choosing to move westward, where much larger German communities were being established in America's vast farmlands.

Without a permanent priest of their own, the Germans were increasingly irritated at having to submit to the jurisdiction of an Irish bishop and the direction of Irish pastors. Until some permanent solution could be found, Boston's immigrant German community was visited several times a year by Father John Raffeiner of New York, who heard confessions and dispensed the other sacraments. Seeing the need for a permanent German parish, in 1840 Father Raffeiner raised some money and purchased a plot of land. In June 1842 he laid the cornerstone of a new church at the intersection of Lucas and Suffolk Streets (later Shawmut Avenue) in Boston's South End, with Bishop Fenwick in attendance. In June 1844, Father James Rolof of Maryland celebrated the first Mass in the basement of what was named Holy Trinity Church—although most Bostonians referred to it simply as "the German Church."

When the elderly Father Rolof left Boston, relations between the members of the German parish and several succeeding pastors became so bitter that the new bishop, John Fitzpatrick, finally ordered the church temporarily closed. Fortunately, further trouble was avoided with the installation in August 1848 of a Jesuit priest, Rev. Gustavus Eck. A kind and affable man who won the affection of his parishioners, Eck was able to reconcile many of the conflicting interests by establishing a variety of sodalities and societies that brought people together. This was particularly important because, during the late 1840s, the number of German immigrants coming into America increased substantially. A combination of natural disasters (Germany, too, had a ruinous potato famine in the mid-1840s), an upsurge in military conscription, and the violent political revolutions of 1848 brought so many new German refugees to Boston that Father Eck felt it necessary to build a larger church. Although Bishop Fitzpatrick had serious misgivings because the original church still had a debt outstanding, in 1853 Father Eck went ahead with his plans—only to leave the project unfinished when he returned to Germany.

Over the course of the next few years, several Jesuit pastors came and went until, in 1859, Rev. Ernest Reiter, SJ, arrived at Holy Trinity Church, where he would remain for the next eleven years. Father Reiter tried to return the parish to the custody of the diocese, but Bishop Fitzpatrick was unwilling to assume the financial burdens. Bowing to the inevitable, Father Reitter made such extraordinary efforts at fundraising that in a short time he not only was able to pay off the original debt but found himself with enough money to resume building a new church on the corner of Cobb Street and Shawmut Avenue. On November 10, 1872, the day after the Great Fire that destroyed nearly the entire downtown business district, Bishop John Williams laid the cornerstone of the new Holy Trinity Church. Five years later, two years after he had become Boston's first archbishop, Williams dedicated the new church, which could accommodate twelve hundred parishioners in its upper level and seven hundred more in its basement.

But German-speaking parishioners were not the only newcomers for whom Archbishop Williams provided special arrangements. More French-speaking immigrants had come into the archdiocese over the years, and they required being treated with care and sensitivity. As the textile mills in the Merrimack Valley had expanded their operations in the decades after the Civil War, and had begun replacing the former Yankee "mill girls" with immigrants from various European countries, many French-speaking persons came down from Canada to take such jobs as well. Settling into the American communities, but clinging tenaciously to their heritage *(La Foi, La Langue, La Culture)* they sought French-speaking priests who could deliver sermons and hear confessions in their native language.

As time went on, relations between the French newcomers and the older Irish residents of Lowell became increasingly tense, especially after one newspaper announcement stated that "no one but an Irish Catholic" would be allowed to be buried in the local cemetery. In 1867 a French-speaking layman from Lowell, John Dozois, planning a business trip to Canada, was asked by his friends to present their spiritual needs to Bishop Ignace Bourget of Montreal. This prelate gave Dozois a personal letter of introduction to Archbishop Williams, and suggested that because Williams had studied at the Sulpician seminary at Montreal he might well be receptive to their desires. Williams was, indeed, receptive, and within a year, in 1868, he managed to recruit French-speaking Oblates of Mary Immaculate to staff the first French parish of St. Joseph (later changed to St. Jean-Baptiste) in Lowell. A few of the older priests of Irish birth or descent had been trained in Canadian seminaries and had some acquaintance with the French language. For example, Father Cornelius Reardon and Father John Mullen, who served at St. Michael's parish in Hudson during the 1910s, were able to read the Gospel, make announcements, hear confessions, and give simple sermons in French.

But this proved to be the exception rather than the rule. For the most part, younger diocesan priests of Irish background had neither the language proficiency nor the cultural orientation to adapt easily to French-speaking congregations. Fortunately, because of New England's proximity to Canada, and an abundance of vocations in that region, Archbishop Williams was able to recruit as many as twenty-seven French-speaking clerics from Canada, and even some from France. To further accommodate the desires of Canadian immigrants, the Boston prelate brought the Marist Fathers into Haverhill in the 1870s. By 1938, when the last French parish (St. Theresa) was founded in Methuen, French Canadians could claim as many as twenty-five parishes at various locations throughout the archdiocese.

French-speaking persons from Canada had been much slower in congregating in Boston than in the various manufacturing towns in the outlying areas, where opportunities for unskilled workers were more plentiful. Not until 1880 did Church authorities feel that there was a sufficient number of French-speaking residents in Boston itself to support a church of their own. Father A. Léon Boulard, an eloquent and flamboyant French-born priest who had been serving in Rhode Island parishes, was given permission to undertake the building of such a church. Settling his first parishioners in a temporary chapel in the downtown area, the new pastor solicited funds, first in Boston and then in France and Rome, for what he proposed to call the Church of Notre Dame des Victoires. After the erratic cleric returned from a trip to Europe, the money disappeared—and so did he. Fortunately, however, the Marist Fathers took over the abandoned project, and as a result of their hard work and dedication they were permanently entrusted with the project in Boston, as well as with the responsibility for St. Anne's parish in Lawrence. In 1885, the Marists purchased a site on Isabella Street in Boston's Back Bay district, and in 1892 the building was finally completed—a red-brick Gothic structure that most Bostonians familiarly referred to simply as "the French Church."

The next of the newer Catholic immigrant groups to form part of the commonwealth's diversified population were the Portuguese. Sailing across the Atlantic during the 1830s to engage in the whaling industry that was flourishing in various New England seaports, the earliest arrivals came principally from the islands of the Azores to settle in New Bedford; they then spread out to Fall River and the Cape Cod regions, north to Boston and Gloucester, and then to Lowell and Lawrence. These first newcomers were later joined by fellow countrymen from the Cape Verde Islands, and then by natives of Portugal itself. Until 1890, no more than two thousand Portuguese entered the United States each year. Between 1899 and 1910, however, Massachusetts alone took in 45,466 Portuguese immigrants—an average of four thousand a year.

To respond to the presence of these new arrivals, Archbishop Williams wrote to a bishop in the Azores, who sent Father João Encarnacao to work among the Portuguese, first in New Bedford and then, in 1873, in Boston. At the outset, his congregation shared St. John the Baptist Church in the North End with Italian immigrants, until the Italians acquired a church of their own. Partly as a result of ensuing financial difficulties, combined with some political intrigues involving the Portuguese consul, the Portuguese congregation became divided by controversies, causing an unhappy Father João to return to his homeland.

Again Archbishop Williams recruited a priest—this time an old Dominican friend, Welsh-born Father Henry Hughes, who had been educated at Lisbon, who knew twelve different languages, and who had served as a translator at the Vatican Council. Though feeble in health and virtually blind, Hughes nevertheless served for eight years at his Boston post. He succeeded in restoring peace among the parishioners, and even organized a small school staffed by sisters of the Third Order of St. Dominic. Gradually, however, the small Portuguese community in the North End dwindled away, and the original structure on North Bennett Street eventually became the North End Branch of the Boston Public Library. At the turn of the century, in 1901, Father Antonio J. Pimentel established a parish of St. Anthony in Lowell for Portuguese immigrants; he set up another parish with the same name the following year in Cambridge, where he served for the next half century.*

In addition to newcomers from Portugal, immigrants from Italy made up a significant part of Boston's new Catholic population. In 1880 an estimated 109,000 Italians, devastated by floods, droughts, and disease, left their homes and their farmlands to come to America. By 1881, the average number of immigrants from Italy was up to 154,000; by 1886, it had reached 222,000, with many of the newcomers arriving in Boston. This was not the first time that the city had seen a community of Italian Catholics. Some twenty years earlier, a number of Italian families had moved into South Boston. This was probably because in 1868 Archbishop Williams had appointed an Italian Franciscan priest, Father Emiliano Gerbi, as pastor of the newly constructed Gate of Heaven Church in the center of the peninsula district. Until his death five years later, Father Gerbi served the parish, regularly assisted by one or two other Italian Franciscans; their presence undoubtedly persuaded a number of Italian families to become permanent residents of the predominantly Irish neighborhood.

But it was in the late 1880s and early 1890s that the vast majority of Italian immigrants arrived in Boston. At first, they congregated along the waterfront of the city's North End, where the Italian population grew from a thousand in 1880 to seven thousand in 1895. Gradually they moved across the harbor to East Boston, as well as into the

---

* Cardinal Humberto Medeiros later established Our Lady of Fatima Church in the city of Peabody for the benefit of Portuguese parishioners.

various surrounding neighborhoods, which still had large Irish populations.

As the number of the city's Italian arrivals rapidly increased, it became obvious that steps would have to be taken to meet their spiritual needs. Although the Italians were mostly Roman Catholics, as were the Irish, like most other newcomers from Europe they preferred to establish their own separate churches, where they could hear their own priests speaking to them in their own language. But there were some deep-seated cultural reasons for the slowness with which the predominantly Irish Church responded to repeated Italian requests for their own churches and their own priests. For one thing, many Irish parishioners were never quite sure whether the Italians, with their preference for a certain number of saints, their colorful religious festivals, and what one Irish priest described as their "superstitious emotionalism" were "real" Catholics. Then, too, the frequent expressions of anticlericalism among Italian men, who sent their wives to church on Sundays while they waited outside and smoked, also raised questions about the depth of their faith. The Irish, whose priests and bishops had come from the ranks of the working classes and had stayed close to their parishioners through the oppressions of the British and the disasters of the Famine, failed to appreciate that in Italy, as in most European countries, Church leaders had generally come from the ranks of the aristocracy and often took the side of the ruling classes in conflicts with farmers and laborers. It would take time for the customs of the old country to adjust to the realities of the adopted land.

For a time the new Italian immigrants joined with early Portuguese arrivals to share services at the small Baptist church on North Bennett Street that had been transformed by Father Joachim Guerrini, a Franciscan from New York, into the Church of St. John the Baptist. Early in 1875, however, Father Guerrini responded to requests from his Italian parishioners for a separate church of their own, purchased some property on Prince Street, and in 1876 completed the construc-

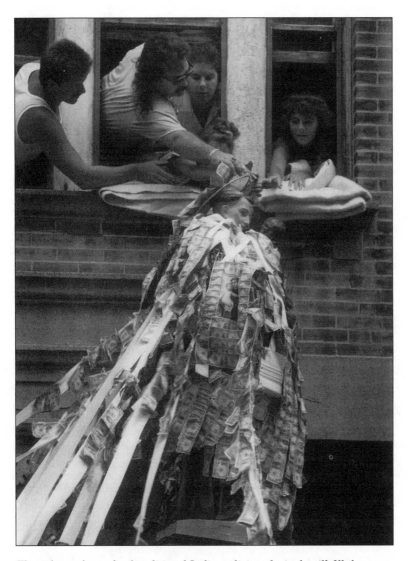

The sights and sounds of traditional Italian religious festivals still fill the streets of Boston's North End; here residents join in the custom of pinning money to a statue of St. Anthony. Arriving in great numbers during the late nineteenth and early twentieth centuries as part of the "new immigration" from southern and eastern Europe, Italian Catholics quickly became an important part of Boston's religious and political communities. (Photo by Susie Stevens.)

tion of St. Leonard's Church. Unfortunately, divisions within the congregation led one faction, headed by members of the San Marco Society, to break away and form their own meeting house in North Square. They hoped that Church authorities would sanction this site for religious use, functioning under their own jurisdiction. Archbishop Williams, however, absolutely refused to authorize the North Square edifice as a church, unless the title was transferred to him unconditionally as evidence of archdiocesan jurisdiction. The San Marco Society refused, and the resulting standoff divided members of the North End for some five years. Finally, members of an Italian religious order called the Missionaries of St. Charles Borromeo (popularly known as the "Scalabriniani") negotiated a settlement. The San Marco Society agreed to cede the title to the North Square property to the archbishop; the archbishop, in turn, agreed to permit St. Leonard's Church to continue functioning under the Franciscans, while authorizing a new Church of the Sacred Heart to serve the Italian community under the Missionaries of St. Charles.

Beyond providing for the spiritual needs of the Italian immigrants in Boston, the Catholic churches also provided the basis for a number of community benevolent associations, social organizations, and religious schools. In 1903, for example, St. John's School was opened under the auspices of the Missionary Sisters of the Sacred Heart. It operated thus until 1912, when the school was added to the parish of the Sacred Heart Church and the teaching duties were taken over by the Sisters of St. Joseph. During the 1920s, St. Leonard's Church sponsored St. Anthony's School, a parochial grammar school that provided further religious instruction in the closely knit neighborhood. The religious life of the North End was also reflected in a number of social clubs, whose responsibilities included honoring their patron saints at yearly festivals. Former villagers from San Sossio Baronia, for example, celebrated the feast of La Madonna delle Grazie, whereas Sicilian fishermen honored La Madonna de Soccorso each year for her help in protecting them while they were at sea. A procession, during which a statue of the Madonna or some special saint like St. Anthony, St. Joseph, or St. Rocco was carried through the narrow streets of the North End, was always a colorful part of the Italian religious festivals, keeping alive the traditions of *la via vecchia*—the "old way of life."

As the Italians were moving into one part of the city, immigrants from Poland—many of them Roman Catholics—were moving into another. By the turn of the century, nearly ten thousand Poles had settled in the Boston area, most of them near the boundary between South Boston and Dorchester, just off Andrew Square. Their apostolate began with Father John Chmielinski, a Russian-born Polish priest who had studied for the priesthood in Italy as a Scalabrini father, and who had originally come to Boston in 1893 to work among Italians. As soon as local Polish people heard about him, they invited him to start a Polish parish; up to this time, most of them had been attending religious services either at the German Church on Shawmut Avenue or at St. Margaret's Church (the "Irish Church") in nearby Dorchester. With the approval of his religious order, Father Chmielinski became affiliated with the archdiocese of Boston. Now a diocesan priest, he purchased a tract of land extending from Dorchester Avenue to Boston Street, and in November 1894 he dedicated a wooden structure in honor of Our Lady of Czestochowa. The Polish population of the area continued to grow, and it quickly became a small but active part of the peninsula district. As a pioneer clergyman, Father Chmielinski traveled to various locations in the archdiocese like Lowell and Salem to minister to other groups of Polish immigrants. From 1893 to 1918, Archbishop Williams and his successor, William Cardinal O'Connell, sanctioned as many as fifteen Polish parishes, with which the diocese experienced many successes, along with a few failures.

Misunderstandings, lack of sensitivity on the part of Irish pastors who often failed to understand why the foreigners couldn't learn to speak English like everybody else, and disputes over such issues as the ownership of church property, the appointment of pastors, and the character of parochial schools caused a variety of problems and sometimes led to schisms—especially when exacerbated by national and political rivalries. Lithuanians in Chicago, for example, formed a separate national church, with allegiance to their own bishop. A year later, Polish groups in Buffalo set up the Polish Catholic Independent Church in America, which later affiliated with a group based in Scranton, Pennsylvania, known as the Polish National Catholic Church. By 1901 the Polish separatist movement had reached Boston, when St. Casimir's Church in Cambridge became the first of an eventual four Polish schismatic parishes to break away from archdiocesan control. In 1925, separatist groups organized Immaculate Conception Church in Lawrence; in 1938 two more were established, one in Cambridge and one in Lynn, both called Holy Cross.

There were many reasons for these breaks, with faults on both sides, including a dearth of Polish-speaking personnel and a lack of pastoral sensitivity. One of Archbishop Williams's last acts in 1905 was his invitation to the Polish Conventual Franciscans to head St. Stanislaus parish in Chelsea. This arrangement was followed in 1931 by Cardinal O'Connell, who put the Conventuals in charge of St. Joseph's parish in Peabody and also used this order of Franciscans to replace diocesan clergy at Holy Trinity parish in Lawrence, at St. Michael's in Haverhill, and at Our Lady of Czestochowa in South Boston. Happily, since 1984 there has been an ongoing dialogue between some Roman Catholic spokespersons and Polish National Catholic leaders.

Also around the turn of the century, about one thousand Lithuanian immigrants arrived in Boston, most of whom made their homes on the northern side of the South Boston peninsula. Reflecting the strong nationalist impulse of the 1880s that called upon the Lithuanian people to retain their native language and preserve their traditional customs, local leaders wrote back to their homeland and urged seminarians to come to America and serve their people. Archbishop Williams adopted one of these young Lithuanian theological students, Joseph Gricius, and enrolled him in St. John's Seminary to complete his training. After his ordination in 1895, Father Gricius was assigned to work among the city's Lithuanian immigrants in South Boston, where he established St. Joseph's Church.

Unfortunately, difficulties between the inexperienced young pastor and members of his congregation became so extreme that, when the church burned down in February 1899, the parishioners refused to help rebuild it. Instead, they erected another church of their own (St. Peter's) and persuaded Archbishop Williams to appoint a new pastor. Once he took over and Father Gricius moved away to another part of the country, parish life gradually settled down. Meanwhile, five other Lithuanian parishes were established in various parts of the archdiocese—in Brockton, Lawrence, Lowell, Cambridge, and Norwood—where groups of Lithuanian immigrants had gone in search of work. In most cases, Archbishop Williams had very few diocesan priests who could speak Lithuanian, and therefore he had to rely upon other clerics of varying degrees of effectiveness. In 1916, internal disputes and personal difficulties caused a split in the Lithuanian church in Lawrence, resulting in the establishment of the Sacred Heart Church as a separatist parish.

Many old-time Yankees of Boston, as Barbara Solomon has perceptively demonstrated in her study *Ancestors and Immigrants*, were at a complete loss to comprehend the magnitude of this sudden and completely unexpected inundation of their ancient and honorable city by European foreigners at the end of the nineteenth century. The Irish Catholics who had arrived fifty-some years earlier had been bad enough; but at least they had been able to speak English, and usually had some acquaintance with basic Anglo-Saxon customs and traditions. But these *new* people—swarthy Italians, black-bearded Jews, and a motley collection of Poles, Lithuanians, and Portuguese—spoke a babel of tongues, followed entirely different social customs, and lacked any firsthand experience with the democratic process. Things had reached the point, according to Dr. Oliver Wendell Holmes, where a New Englander would feel more at home among "his own people" in London, England, than "in one of our seaboard cities."

Lithuanian Catholics were among the new wave of immigrants from eastern Europe who came to Boston at the turn of the century. Here, members of today's active Lithuanian community, representing St. Joseph's Schools in Holbrook and in Lowell, and St. Peter's School in South Boston, celebrate the six hundredth anniversary of Lithuanian Christianity on October 4, 1987, at a liturgy presided over by Bernard Cardinal Law at the Cathedral of the Holy Cross. (Photo by Sister Rita Murray.)

Some Bostonians simply threw up their hands in despair and moved out to the rural suburbs of Dover, Marblehead, Hamilton, and Pride's Crossing, far from the sights, the sounds, and the smells of this latest wave of unwanted immigrants. Other native Bostonians, literally terrified of the disastrous effects these barbarians would have upon the Athens of America, formed the Immigration Restriction League of Boston. This organization, founded in 1894, was designed to promote national legislation restricting any further immigration of "inferior races" to America and confining those already in the United States to the status of a permanent underclass of manual laborers and humble domestics. Still other Bostonians, however, bowed to the inevitable and worked to fashion a wide array of civic organizations, educational programs, and neighborhood associations to introduce the children of the new immigrants into the folkways of America, to teach them about the democratic political process, and to transform them into useful and responsible citizens.

Leaders of the Catholic Church in the archdiocese of Boston, many of them Boston-born and most of them of Irish parentage, were also taken aback by the number and variety of European immigrants flooding into the city during the late 1880s and early 1890s. Since a significant number of these newcomers were Roman Catholics, Church leaders faced the challenge of how to bring them into an organizational structure that was predominantly Irish and universally English speaking.

From an administrative point of view, it was important to make sure that these newcomers from various parts of Europe realized that in religious matters they were subject to the authority of the archbishop of Boston, and that whatever churches they established would fall within the organizational structure of that archdiocese. This understanding was viewed as essential to maintaining centralized episcopal power and the unity of the ecclesiastical system. From a human-relations point of view, however, Archbishop Williams was astute enough to recognize that if the new European immigrants found themselves alienated by a system that did not allow them to have their own priests, use their native languages, enjoy their traditional feast days, or follow their national religious practices, they might well decide to form their own national churches outside the jurisdiction of the archdiocese. The task of the archbishop, then, was a delicate one—working closely and sensitively with the newcomers, and permitting them as much national expression as possible in their religious observances, while using his considerable persuasive skills to keep the new churches and their congregations under his episcopal authority.

After the Civil War, the continued increase in the number of immigrants coming from Ireland, as well as a growing influx of newcomers arriving from the various countries of southern and eastern Europe, placed even greater demands upon the financial resources of the archdiocese of Boston. New immigrants found themselves in the midst of America's "Age of Big Business"—a time of vast technological and mechanical changes, with which most of the new arrivals were totally unfamiliar. Although it is true that rapid industrialization opened up numerous job opportunities for the mass of unskilled laborers, it is also true that most workers were badly exploited in the sweatshops and factories of the period and were confined with their families in unheated apartments and overcrowded tenements. Workdays of from twelve to sixteen hours in shops with inadequate ventilation and little or no safety equipment were the norm. Workers who were injured on the job, or who became ill from unhealthy conditions, were provided with no medical care, workmen's compensation, or funeral expenses. Widows left alone, wives abandoned by their husbands, or women who could not withstand the rigors of the sweatshops often took to the streets as prostitutes in desperation. And when little boys could not find jobs selling newspapers or shining shoes in order to supplement the family's meager income, they could often be found hanging out in pool halls and saloons, shooting dice in back alleys, or sleeping in the gutters.

Social problems associated with the poor, the unemployed, and the homeless in the major cities of industrial America became the object of numerous social agencies and charitable institutions during the years after the Civil War. Two church-sponsored institutions that had their origins in Great Britain were adapted to meet the social needs of persons in the United States. The Young Men's Christian Association (YMCA) and the Young Women's Christian Association (YWCA) expanded their branches during the 1870s and 1880s, working among urban derelicts to save their bodies and win their souls. It was also during this period that the Salvation Army began its work in the United States, providing food, shelter, and clothing for the poor while caring for their spiritual welfare. The American Baptist Home Missionary Society, too, worked among urban immigrants, and social activists in many cities established settlement houses and neighborhood centers, such as Jane Addams's Hull House in Chicago, where they could provide advice, comfort, and assistance to the poor and the dislocated. In 1874, delegates from seventeen states met in Cleveland to form the Women's Christian Temperance Union (WCTU); it agitated for the total prohibition of alcoholic beverages, which many of the group's leaders regarded as the particular curse of the immigrant population.

That same year, the Greenback party was organized in Indianapolis to support the elimination of the gold standard, a change that would help poor farmers and laborers pay their debts. Although cities like Boston continued to use the screening processes of the office of the overseer of the poor to assign helpless and impoverished people to municipal hospitals, sanitariums, asylums, almshouses, and reform schools, a number of states were beginning to discuss the advisability of using legislation to control, or even eliminate, the worst abuses connected with the labor of women and children.

Most Catholics, however, tended to avoid the institutionalized social agencies of the period, especially those that functioned under the auspices of some religious group. They generally preferred to deal with the problems of "their own people" in their own way. For one thing, Catholics continued to suspect that one of the intentions of non-Catholic charitable organizations was to conduct a subtle process of proselytism, taking Catholic children out of their immigrant environment, bringing them into comfortable Protestant surroundings, and gradually weaning them away from their traditional Catholic beliefs. There was also a feeling of apprehension among nineteenth-century Catholics that any type of government involvement in the private life of the family or the personal decisions of individuals would inevitably strengthen the power of centralized government and thereby diminish the primacy of parental authority, as well as reduce the role of the Catholic Church in the everyday lives of its parishioners.

Then, too, it was the general belief of both priests and their congre-

Young basketball players from the South End, members of the Cathedral Young Men's Catholic Association of Boston, pose with their spiritual director, Father Thomas Robert McCoy, who attended St. John's Seminary, was ordained in 1899, and became pastor of St. Ann's, Somerville. Athletic programs such as these were intended to keep young men close to the Church and away from the many temptations of the modern city. (Photo by Paul Winik Photography.)

gations that such social problems as poverty, crime, homelessness, illegitimacy, and alcoholism were not the results of any particular defect of society. They were, instead, the inevitable consequences of either individual weakness or personal immorality, usually resulting from a lack of religious faith. The solution to such problems, therefore, lay in promoting a spirit of moral self-control and personal self-discipline on the part of the less fortunate, not in passing a series of laws or in creating a complex system of secular institutions.

Along these same lines, it was a traditional Catholic view that for the public sector to take over the dispensing of charity would be to deprive the ordinary Catholic of an important, if not essential, source of spiritual grace. The ability to gain salvation, according to Church doctrine, lay not only in faith but also in good works. For government agencies or public institutions to take over the care of the poor, the abandoned, the elderly, and the homeless would be to deprive individual Catholics of the opportunity to practice the virtue of charity and thereby gain grace. Furthermore, acts of charity carried out by family, friends, and neighbors were generally regarded by members of the Irish community as much more personal and humane than the cold and anonymous process of institutional assistance. Martin Lomasney, the ward boss of the West End, once referred to the latter as "the inquisitorial terrors of organized charity"; John Boyle O'Reilly cleverly ridiculed it as "the organized charity, scrimped and iced, / In the name of a cautious, statistical Christ."

It was during the episcopacy of Archbishop John Williams, then, that the archdiocese greatly expanded the number of charitable institutions designed to meet the needs of its Catholic population. St. Vincent's Orphan Asylum for girls, begun by Bishop Fenwick in the South End, continued to function throughout the Williams years. Over the course of eight decades it was reported by the *Pilot* to have provided a healthy and happy home for as many as ten thousand little girls. For those who were not so fortunate, in 1867 Archbishop Williams invited the Sisters of the Good Shepherd to come down from New York and staff the House of the Good Shepherd, a home for wayward girls on Allen Street in Boston's congested West End. This program expanded so rapidly that in 1870 the archbishop purchased new property on Huntington Avenue, Roxbury, where he constructed a larger home that could shelter as many as 350 to 450 clients at a time.

The House of the Angel Guardian, originally founded by Bishop Fitzpatrick to provide a sanctuary for homeless boys, not only continued during the Williams era but actually expanded when, in 1874, it was placed under the direction of the Brothers of Charity of Montreal, an order recognized for its work with the disabled and the disadvantaged. Under a series of excellent superiors, the program prospered during the late nineteenth century, initiated an effective vocational

training program for the older boys, and over the course of its existence provided a home and an education for some fifteen thousand
youngsters.

The welfare of neglected young children continued to be of concern
to the archdiocese. In 1867 Archbishop Williams, with the assistance
of Patrick Donahoe of the *Pilot,* bought a piece of property on Harrison Avenue in Boston's South End and invited the Sisters of Charity
of Emmitsburg to take charge of what he called a Home for Destitute
Children. Supported by the charitable contributions and fundraising
activities of concerned Bostonians, the home was able to sustain itself
over the years and provide a safe haven for neglected, abandoned, and
abused children. The number of abandoned babies and neglected
infants had become such a problem in itself, however, that in 1868
the responsibility of caring for foundlings was assigned to the Carney
Hospital in South Boston. In 1870 the Sisters of Charity purchased a
location in Dorchester, where they incorporated their specialized activities under the name of St. Mary's Infant Asylum and Lying-in
Hospital. After a number of years, during which pressing financial
problems required a series of physical moves and managerial changes,
Archbishop Williams persuaded the Sisters of Charity of Emmitsburg
to assume fiscal control of this much needed institution, which was
taking in an average of six hundred babies a year.

There were also disturbing reports of a growing number of homeless juveniles who were roaming the streets of Boston at night, sleeping in stables, alleyways, and vacant lots. In 1881, Father David
Roche received permission from the archbishop to establish the
Working Boys' Home in Boston as a refuge for newsboys, bootblacks,
messengers, and other young workers who had no homes of their own
and did not make enough money to rent a decent room. In 1886, a
four-story structure was erected on Bennett Street to house the Working Boys' Home, and Franciscan sisters were brought in to manage
the operation. Open to all homeless boys aged twelve to seventeen,
the home was quickly filled to overflowing. Those residents with jobs

paid a modest sum for board and room; those without jobs paid nothing, while efforts were made to find them work.

With a heavy mortgage and mounting expenses—especially as an increasing number of boys arrived with no jobs and no income—the home was plagued for many years by internal problems of finance and management. In 1890, the trustees decided to put up another building in the suburban town of Newton, called St. John's Industrial School. There, the younger boys could receive a basic Catholic education taught by the Franciscan Sisters; the older boys could receive industrial training, taught by lay instructors, in such occupations as baking, laundering, tailoring, carpentry, and farming. Even though the work was of vital importance, oppressive financial problems resulting from the operation of two homes—one in Boston, the other in Newton—created a heavy burden for the succession of priests who labored to keep the operation going into the twentieth century.

Archbishop Williams also established a similar working home for older girls, aged twelve to seventeen, with the construction of the Daly Industrial School in Dorchester. It was named after Father Patrick Daly, pastor of St. Francis de Sales Church in Roxbury, who made a generous contribution to get the project off the ground. The Sisters of St. Joseph staffed the home, where they provided instruction in typing, bookkeeping, accounting, dressmaking, and the domestic sciences as a means of helping the girls get decent and well-paying jobs when they entered the labor market. But with so many young Catholic women leaving their homes and their families to come into the big cities to work in a variety of occupations, the archbishop was especially conscious of the dangers and temptations they faced in the modern world. Anxious to provide these young women with a safe, decent, and pleasant place to live, in 1888 he invited the Grey Nuns of Montreal to come down and staff the Working Girls' Home on Dover Street, close to the downtown working district. In 1891 he purchased property in the South End, at the corner of Harrison Avenue and Union Park, directly behind the cathedral, where he constructed a four-story brick building called St. Helena House. It would serve for many years as a home away from home for Boston's Catholic working women. In the city of Lowell, at about the same time, Father Michael O'Brien opened St. Patrick's Home for Working Girls, conducted by the Franciscan Sisters, which served much the same purpose as its Boston counterpart.

With low-income urban families restricted to the confines of small tenements and cramped apartments, the future of the poor, elderly, and disabled persons among them was fast becoming a serious social problem. In an effort to provide tender and humane care for the aged poor, Archbishop Williams invited the Little Sisters of the Poor to establish a home in the Boston area. In 1870, six members of the Little Sisters of the Poor arrived in Boston from France with just the clothes on their backs and only ten cents in their pockets. A mere two years later, with what the archdiocesan historian describes as "a very lively confidence in the assistance of St. Joseph," the sisters purchased a piece of property at Dudley Street in Roxbury and opened their doors to elderly people who were destitute, homeless, and friendless. And throughout the archdiocese of Boston during this same period, in cities such as Lowell, Lawrence, Salem, and Newburyport, pastors and parishioners were creating their own orphanages, homes for destitute children, dispensaries, schools for the deaf, and centers for the aged in an effort to provide for the needs of their own Catholic people.

While the archdiocese was supporting this expanding range of social agencies and charitable institutions it was also funding at least three major Catholic hospitals designed to provide the kind of professional medical care that the indigent might not be able to receive elsewhere. The first of these was the Carney Hospital in South Boston, which had been founded in 1863 when John Fitzpatrick was bishop, and which was capably supervised by the Daughters of Charity of St. Vincent de Paul. During the late 1860s, a substantial bequest in the will of Andrew Carney—a Catholic immigrant from County Cavan who had started out as a tailor, invested his money wisely, and become a wealthy philanthropist—made it possible for the sisters to add a brick-and-stone wing to the original building, as well as a new chapel. In 1891, the original structure was greatly enlarged, doubling the size of the hospital and allowing it to expand its medical services. Ten years later, when its outpatient department was constructed, the Carney Hospital was the third largest hospital in Boston, still servicing a substantial number of poor and working-class patients who had little or no income.*

The archdiocese's second Catholic hospital was St. John's in Lowell, which was started in 1863 by members of the Sodality of St. Patrick's Church as a modest infirmary designed to serve the needs of parish members. When the Sisters of Charity came to Lowell, Father John O'Brien welcomed their idea of turning the dispensary into a full-fledged hospital. With the approval of Archbishop Williams, they acquired a site on Bartlett Street, and shortly thereafter St. John's Hospital was duly chartered by the state legislature. In 1864, a four-story brick structure was erected; an annex containing a chapel was added in 1882; an outpatient department went up in 1888; and another large addition in 1893 contributed to its growing size and reputation.

The third-oldest hospital of the Williams period was St. Elizabeth's, in Boston, which was started in 1868 by five laywomen. They had taken the vows of Sisters of the Third Order of St. Francis, and they hoped to create a hospital that would specialize in ailments and diseases peculiar to women. The new institution steadily expanded its medical services as well as its surgical staff, and in 1882 began admitting male patients as well as women. In 1884, the Franciscan Sisters took over its administration, and by the end of the century St. Elizabeth's had become one of the most important hospitals in the city.

Considering the relative youth of the archdiocese and the limited

---

* Of the 70,069 patients admitted during the Carney Hospital's first fifty years, 25,755 paid in full; 15,231 patients paid in part; and 29,083 paid nothing at all, being treated free of charge.

Daughters of Charity of St. Vincent de Paul leaving the Cathedral of the Holy Cross in Boston's South End, October 24, 1932, after attending a Mass said by Cardinal O'Connell in honor of the hundredth anniversary of the Daughters of Charity. The distinctive white "wings" of the Daughters of Charity became a familiar sight as the sisters walked through the city on their errands of mercy. (Courtesy of the Archdiocese of Boston.)

nature of financial resources, it was a remarkable performance. Determined to care for "their own" instead of sending needy Catholics off to secular institutions, the leaders of the archdiocese had erected an impressive network of Catholic charitable organizations that included schools, orphanages, old-age homes, hospitals, nurseries, and homes for disadvantaged boys and girls. "The Church was seen as the mother to all her children," writes the historian Susan Walton, "and, like any mother, could not abandon her children." And Walton sees these various institutions serving the additional function of helping to strengthen Irish-Catholic group identity in what most of them still viewed as a hostile Yankee city. The Catholics who furnished the charity not only benefited their own souls by performing "good works" but also deepened their commitment to the task of the Church itself. The broader network of charitable institutions throughout the archdiocese also provided a focus of identity for all those in the larger Catholic community who contributed money, engaged in fundraising, served as volunteers, or in some other way participated in the beneficent purposes of the various charities. And finally, beyond the purely charitable aspects of their enterprises, Catholics could also feel that they were an integral part of the battle for souls—doing their part to prevent the poor and the disadvantaged from being swallowed up in the machinery of non-Catholic philanthropic organizations where they might lose their faith.

Of course, the changes, the strains, and the tensions in the archdiocese of Boston during the 1880s and 1890s were only minor reflections of events taking place throughout the United States at this time. The remarkable expansion of numbers and the impressive upward mobility of the older American Catholic community by the late nineteenth century, combined with the staggering influx of a new wave of immigrant Catholics from southern and eastern Europe, brought size, strength, and diversity to the American Church. At this point, many of its leaders paused to reflect seriously upon the distinctive character of the Catholic Church in the United States and the direction in which it should be headed as the world entered the twentieth century. What began to emerge out of these considerations was something that the historian Father James Hennesey has called an "internal identity crisis."

There were, on the one hand, prelates who argued that the Catholic Church in the United States had become so large and so powerful that it should be capable of governing itself in accordance with the unique social, economic, and political environment of the New World. They generally saw no necessary antagonism between the Catholic Church and American democracy, and they felt that the experience of a truly pluralist society was something that could be put to good use in other parts of the world as the Church moved away from its conservative European traditions. Although continuing to insist upon loyalty to the Holy Father, the pope, as the spiritual head of the universal Church, they also suggested a decentralization of authority in keeping with the social and cultural differences in various parts of the world, as well as a greater degree of collegiality among the bishops in each country.

There were, on the other hand, prelates who felt that the blatantly materialistic and secular values of American society were incompatible with the spiritual values of the Roman Catholic Church, and who felt that there were serious dangers in trying to reconcile the ideals of Catholicism with those of democracy. They believed that it would be better for the Church in the United States to continue to follow the traditional European models of church governance. Sometimes referred to as the "Ultramontanes" because they looked for leadership "beyond the mountains" in Rome, they insisted there was no such thing as an "American Church" or an "American" form of Catholicism. The Church was one and indivisible, the same everywhere, perfectly defined by the infallible pope whose jurisdictional power was "immediate"—everywhere in the world.

With reasonable arguments on both sides, the "Americanists" and the "Romanists" (who at a later time would probably be labeled "liberals" and "conservatives") engaged in a period of serious debate concerning the future character of the Church in America. Archbishop John Ireland of St. Paul, Bishop John Keane, rector of the Catholic University of America, and Father Denis O'Connell, rector of the American College in Rome, were strong supporters of the idea that Catholicism was perfectly compatible with the ideals of American democracy, and they urged a greater degree of episcopal individuality under the guidance of the Holy Spirit. Cardinal James Gibbons of Baltimore was generally favorable to the views of the Americanists, as was Bishop John Lancaster Spalding of Peoria. The Paulist magazine, the *Catholic World*, and Notre Dame's popular journal, *Ave Maria*, also reflected the views of this group.

The Romanist opposition was led by Archbishop Michael Corrigan of New York, Bishop Bernard McQuaid of Rochester, and several German bishops in the Middle West. They had a substantial number of Vatican officials on their side, many of whom still viewed the United States as mission territory. Their ideas were supported by the influential *American Ecclesiastical Review,* as well as by the *Messenger of the Sacred Heart,* published by the Jesuits, who had close ties to Rome. These conservative churchmen feared that the Americanist influence would water down doctrine and compromise teaching. Moreover, they were concerned that it would draw the Catholic Church into controversial economic and social issues that would only breed division.

Since he spoke so seldom and wrote so little, it is difficult to tell exactly where Archbishop Williams stood during this controversy, especially since he was on very good terms with most of the leading personalities involved. Given his rather moderate, down-to-earth approach to complex issues, as well as his tendency to let things work out by themselves without too much interference, it is probable that Williams could see good points on both sides of the argument. It is clear, however, that in the final analysis he supported the conservative position and earned the warm friendship of Pope Leo XIII. Indeed, rumors were rife during 1885–86 that because of his loyalty, and especially because of his conciliatory work at the Third Council of Baltimore, Williams was to be made the next American cardinal. According to the archdiocesan historian, however, Williams did not want this honor for himself, and actually wrote to the pope requesting that it be given to Archbishop Gibbons of Baltimore.

The philosophical debates between the Americanists and the Romanists took place amidst the more practical political and economic events of the day. This was a time in European history when a large number of radical, often violent, and usually anticlerical secret societies were at work seeking to undermine monarchies, dislocate governments, overturn churches, and generally revolutionize traditional society. In light of these developments, most European churchmen tended to see all secret societies and fraternal organizations everywhere throughout the world as essentially anticlerical and anti-Catholic—and therefore off-limits to all Catholics.

In the United States, however, all kinds of clubs, orders, organizations, and societies were flourishing. As almost every European visitor observed, Americans were inveterate "joiners." "Americans of all ages, all conditions, and all dispositions form associations," wrote Alexis de Tocqueville during his famous visit to the United States in 1834. "The Americans make associations to give entertainments, to found seminaries, to build inns, to construct churches, to diffuse books, to send missionaries to the antipodes. . . . If it is proposed to inculcate some truth or to foster some feeling," he commented with obvious amusement, "they form a society." And Americans were still joining all kinds of organizations, many of which had elaborate uniforms, funny hats, hidden handshakes, and secret passwords. Some were private clubs and fraternal organizations; others were devoted to social benefits and charitable purposes. During the 1870s and 1880s, many working-class American Catholics were also active in a variety of labor organizations, such as the National Labor Union, the Knights of Labor, and (after 1886) the American Federation of Labor.

Fearful that American Catholics were being drawn into dangerous secret organizations with secular philosophies, anti-Catholic prejudices, and socialist agendas, a number of conservative Church leaders in the United States and Europe struck out hard. They forbade Catholics to join any secret societies—including labor unions—sometimes under pain of excommunication. American bishops like Gibbons, Ireland, and Keane communicated with Rome and pointed out the essential differences between the American and the European experiences, emphasizing that the American labor movement had none of the socialist or communist ideologies of its European counterparts. Indeed, when Gibbons went to Rome in 1887 to receive his cardinal's hat, he used the occasion to persuade the pope that the rumors about the Knights of Labor being a socialist and anarchistic organization were not true. Pope Leo XIII's subsequent encyclical, *Rerum Novarum*—with its emphasis on the right of workers to bargain collectively and the necessity for a living wage, along with its defense of private property and the importance of family life—helped reconcile some of the more extreme differences between liberals and conservatives. But it was clear that the question of the role of the Catholic Church in the modern industrial world still remained the focus of serious dispute between the Americanists and the Romanists.

The publication of a book in 1891 created a storm center around which swirled some of the most violent charges and countercharges connected with the Americanist controversy, which by this time had taken on many of the characteristics of a major heresy. Father Walter Elliott, a Paulist priest, had written a flattering biography of Father Isaac Hecker. Born in New York, Hecker had been ordained in 1849 as a Redemptorist, but he was later encouraged by Pope Pius IX to form the Congregation of the Missionary Priests of St. Paul the Apostle (popularly known as the Paulists) to serve native-born Americans and to win converts to Catholicism. Hecker subsequently founded the *Catholic World* in 1865, published the *Young Catholic*, and established the Paulist Press to explain the Catholic faith to the non-Catholic population of the United States. In his biography, Elliott depicted Isaac Hecker as an intelligent and courageous man of action who worked to make the Catholic Church in America responsive to contemporary issues. Although this portrait was appealing to the Americanists, the Romanists saw it as symptomatic of the new trends of the Church in the United States, which they viewed as incompatible with conservative European traditions.

Conservative Church leaders, with strong backing from Rome, used the occasion of this most recent controversy to suppress the leadership of the Americanist movement. In 1895, for example, Father Denis O'Connell was removed as rector of the American College in Rome and replaced by the much more conservative Father William Henry O'Connell of Boston; the following year, Bishop John J. Keane was ousted from his position as rector of the Catholic University of America. In 1899, Pope Leo XIII came out strongly in a papal encyclical, *Testem Benevolentiae*, against the kinds of ideas said to be abroad in the United States, such as relaxing doctrine to gain converts, putting increased reliance on direct inspiration, and placing emphasis on active rather than passive virtues. Although there were occasional outbursts of disappointment over the conservative resolution of the contest, it was obvious that since *Roma locuta est* then *causa finita est*. The so-called Americanist movement quickly died out, and the Catholic Church in the United States entered the twentieth century in closer step with the universal pattern of the traditional Church.

Meanwhile, the passage of time had begun to take its toll on Archbishop Williams. He had succeeded Bishop Fitzpatrick in 1866, just after the end of the Civil War, and by the turn of the century the seventy-eight-year-old prelate had already served for thirty-four years. Although he recovered from cataract surgery in 1904, his waning physical powers convinced him that it was time to bring in a "younger and more vigorous hand" as his coadjutor to attend "properly" to the affairs of the diocese. In April 1905, therefore, the consultors and rectors of the diocese compiled a list of candidates; it was reviewed by the bishops of the province, and then forwarded to Rome for a final decision. Heading the list were the names of Bishop Matthew Harkins of Providence, Rhode Island, and Bishop William O'Connell of Portland, Maine. Word finally arrived in Boston early in 1906 that Rome had decided upon Bishop O'Connell as Williams's successor.

The archbishop continued to follow his usual rounds of episcopal duties, and then in July 1907 he went off to upstate New York for a summer vacation. Williams returned to Boston on August 21 feeling fatigued and unwell, and on August 30 quietly passed away at the age of eighty-five, after forty-one years of devoted service. All the bells of Boston announced the news of Williams's death, and thousands of mourners filed past the casket as the prelate lay in state at the cathedral he had built. Cardinal James Gibbons was the celebrant of the funeral

Mass, and the new archbishop of Boston, William Henry O'Connell, delivered the eulogy. When the last absolution had been given, the body of Archbishop John Williams was laid to rest in the basement of the cathedral, alongside his two close friends, Bishop John Fitzpatrick and Father Patrick Lyndon. With the passing of Williams, a distinctive era of Boston Church history had come to an end.

+⇒ ADDITIONAL READING

The arrival of the "new immigrants" from the nations of southern and eastern Europe at the turn of the century, many of them members of the Roman Catholic Church, ushered in a new chapter in the history of the archdiocese of Boston. Once again, the painstaking work of Father Robert H. Lord in the third volume of the *History of the Archdiocese of Boston*, describing the character of the new arrivals, analyzing the reaction of Church leaders to their spiritual needs, and documenting the establishment of their national churches, provides the basis for all future research. James M. O'Toole, "'The Newer Catholic Races': Ethnic Catholicism in Boston, 1900–1940," *New England Quarterly* 65 (March 1992), studies in more detail the responses of many Boston religious leaders to the "new immigrants."

Oscar Handlin, *The Uprooted* (New York, 1951), is a popular and inspiring treatment of the great migration that shaped modern America; Nathan Glazer and Daniel P. Moynihan, *Beyond the Melting Pot* (Cambridge, 1963), speculate on the long-range consequences of an immigration policy that was unlike any other in the annals of history. Barbara Solomon, *Ancestors and Immigrants: A Changing New England Tradition* (Cambridge, 1956), examines the reactions of Boston Brahmins to the influx of new European immigrants, and analyzes their reflections on the meaning of the newcomers to the future of the historic city. Dolores Liptak, ed., *Immigrants and Their Church* (New York, 1988), contains essays on Irish, Germans, Italians, French Canadians, Poles, Slovaks, Lithuanians, African Americans, and Hispanics as they became part of the Church in America.

Emmet H. Rothan, *The German Catholic Immigrant in the United*

States, 1830–1860 (Washington, 1946), and Colman Barry, *The Catholic Church and German Americans* (Milwaukee, 1953), are good background studies; Thomas J. Archdeacon, *Becoming American: An Ethnic History* (New York, 1983), analyzes the effects of economics and demographics on German emigration. An early work dealing with the formation of a German community in Boston, Francis X. Weiser's, *Holy Trinity Parish, Boston, Massachusetts* (Boston, 1844), has been considerably updated by the work of Robert Sauer, *Holy Trinity German Parish* (Boston, 1990). Gerard J. Breault, *The French-Canadian Heritage in New England* (Hanover, N.H., 1986), describes the influences of French Canadians. Luciano Iorizzo and Salvatore Mondello, *The Italian Americans* (Boston, 1980), supply a good background study of Italian immigration, while Paul Todisco, *Boston's First Neighborhood: The North End* (Boston, 1975), and William De Marco, *Ethnics and Enclaves: The Italian Settlement of the North End of Boston* (Ann Arbor, Mich., 1980), focus on the formation of the city's Italian community. Thomas H. O'Connor, *South Boston: My Home Town* (Boston, 1994), provides a study of a major Irish-Catholic neighborhood; William Marcione, *The Bull in the Garden* (Boston, 1986), offers a history of the Allston-Brighton community. Reed Ueda, *The West End House, 1906–1981* (Boston, 1981), recounts the history of a major settlement house in one of Boston's most densely populated multiethnic neighborhoods. The preeminent historian of immigrants from Poland and Lithuania is a priest of the archdiocese of Boston, Father William Wolkovich-Valkavicius. He has written many scholarly articles and essays dealing with immigration from eastern Europe, and his *Immigrants and Yankees in Nashoba Valley, Massachusetts: Interethnic and Interreligious Conflict and Accommodation of Irish, French-Canadians, Poles, Lithuanians, and Italians* (West Groton, Mass., 1981) is a fascinating study of the interaction between members of the "old" and "new" immigration. Theodore Andrews, *The Polish National Catholic Church in America and Poland* (London, 1953), and Father William Wolkovich-Valkavicius, "Religious Separatism among

Lithuanian Immigrants in the United States and Their Polish Affilia-
tion," *Polish American Studies* (Autumn 1983), provide a background
for this subject. Silvano Tomasi, *A Scalabrinian Mission among Polish
Immigrants in Boston, 1893–1909* (New York, 1986), deals with changing ethnic communities in Boston.

The story of increasing urban hardships among poor and working-
class people in an industrial era is an integral part of Catholic Church
history, and a subject that needs further exploration. Joseph Hussein,
The Christian Social Manifesto (Milwaukee, 1931), Charles C. Mor-
rison, *The Social Gospel and the Christian Culture* (New York, 1933),
and Robert T. Handy, ed., *The Social Gospel in America, 1870–1920*
(New York, 1966), offer reflections on the role of churches in industrial America during the late nineteenth century. Peter C. Holloran,
*Boston's Wayward Children: Social Services for Homeless Children,
1830–1930* (Rutherford, N.J., 1989), and Eric C. Schneider, *In the
Web of Class: Delinquents and Reformers in Boston, 1810s–1930s* (New
York, 1992), supply valuable information regarding the search for personal and social security in the Boston area; the work of Regis College
professor of economics Sister Mary J. Oates, *The Catholic Philanthropic Tradition in America* (Bloomington, Ind., 1995), breaks new
ground in the social history of the Catholic Church.

The vibrant and often controversial history of the Church in the
United States during the late nineteenth century has attracted many
writers. James Hennesey, *The First Council of the Vatican: The American Experience* (New York, 1963), is very helpful in explaining the
complexities of European developments to American readers. Jay P.
Dolan, *Catholic Revivalism* (Notre Dame, Ind., 1978), describes how
Catholicism developed in the United States during the nineteenth
century; Donna Merwick, *Boston Priests, 1848–1910: A Study of Social
and Intellectual Change* (Cambridge, 1973), provides an interesting
analysis of the ways in which the formation of Boston's priests corres-
ponded to the changing character of American society.

The story of the Americanist controversy at the turn of the century is related in Félix Klein, *Americanism: A Phantom Heresy* (Cranford, N.J., 1951), and in Thomas T. McAvoy, *The Great Crisis in American Catholic History, 1895–1900* (Chicago, 1957). Gerald P. Fogarty, *The Vatican and the Americanist Crisis, 1885–1903* (Rome, 1974), concentrates on the activities of Father Denis O'Connell, rector of the American College; Patrick H. Ahern, *The Life of John J. Keane, Educator and Archbishop* (Milwaukee, 1955), explores the life of the first rector of the Catholic University of America. John Tracy Ellis, *The Formative Years of the Catholic University of America* (Washington, 1965), and Neil McCluskey, *The Catholic University: A Modern Appraisal* (Notre Dame, Ind., 1970), provide valuable accounts of the early stages of Catholic higher education. Walter Elliott, *The Life of Father Hecker* (New York, 1891), is the laudatory biography of the founder of the Paulists; it acted as a lightning rod for much of the Americanist controversy at the end of the nineteenth century. Fergus Macdonald, *The Catholic Church and Secret Societies* (New York, 1946), and Henry J. Browne, *The Catholic Church and the Knights of Labor* (Washington, 1949), are also helpful in understanding some of the concerns that often caused differences between American prelates and their European counterparts.

6

A
Sense
of
Solidarity

WHEN WILLIAM HENRY O'CONNELL SUCCEEDED John Williams as archbishop of Boston in 1907, the new prelate was forty-seven years old, had studied in Rome, had traveled extensively, and brought with him a reputation as a conservative churchman, a tough-minded administrator, and a person of cultivated tastes and scholarly pursuits.

Born December 8, 1859, in Lowell, Massachusetts, O'Connell was the eleventh child of John and Brigid O'Connell, a devout Irish Catholic couple who had emigrated from County Cavan in 1850 in the aftermath of the famine years. The family settled at first in upstate New York, and then moved down to Lowell, where construction offered steady employment for John, an experienced brick mason. The O'Connells were able to purchase a single house for themselves and also build additional property for rental income. Although William was only six years old when his father died of throat cancer, the family managed to stay together thanks to their mother, Brigid, who managed the rental property and provided a comfortable home.

Young Willy was a bright child, determined and independent, with a definite gift for music. After graduating from grammar school, he decided to work in the mills, but after one morning spent amid the roaring machines and suffocating air of a textile plant he decided that school was not so bad. By the time he graduated from Lowell High School in 1876, he had begun discussing a vocation for the priesthood with several local clerics; at the age of seventeen he entered St. Charles College in Maryland, a seminary run by the French Sulpicians.

For a young man fresh from a household of ten noisy brothers and sisters, the imposed silence of seminary life was depressing, despite the opportunity to direct the student choir. After one more year, O'Connell transferred to Boston College, then located in the city's South End, to complete his education under the Jesuits. He found life in Boston much more agreeable—closer to home, a stimulating curriculum, and a chance to play the organ at a parish in Wakefield. In June 1881, O'Connell graduated from Boston College with a gold medal in philosophy, a silver medal in physics, and another medal in chemistry.

Although he had completed his academic studies on a high note, the question of his vocation remained unresolved until one morning in 1882, when he heard Archbishop John Williams give a sermon at the Cathedral of the Holy Cross. It was highly unusual for the tight-lipped old prelate to give a public sermon, but the recent death of a young seminarian he had sent to the North American College in Rome had prompted him to deliver the eulogy at the young man's funeral. According to O'Connell, the prelate's moving description of the young seminarian's life, and his eloquent appeal for others to take his place, was overwhelming. The next day he visited Archbishop Williams at his small rectory on Union Park Street and told him of his desire to become a priest. After listening to him sympathetically, the archbishop asked simply: "Would you like to study in Rome?"

Rome it was. With the financial assistance of his mother's personal savings, young O'Connell sailed from East Boston on his way to Rome to begin his seminary studies at the North American College. Founded in 1859 at the request of Pope Pius IX as a seminary that would enable Americans to study for the priesthood within close proximity to the Holy See, the North American College quickly became a place where U.S. bishops sent the brightest of their seminarians. The expectation was that a few years spent in the Eternal City, becoming acquainted with members of the hierarchy, making influential friends, and becoming accustomed to "Roman" ways of thinking and doing things would be immensely helpful after the young men returned to the United States and began to move up the ecclesiastical ladder.

After a short stay in Ireland (where he toured Dublin and then visited the family homestead at Fartagh), followed by brief stopovers in London and Paris, O'Connell traveled by train to Rome, and on October 27, 1881, arrived at the North American College on the Via dell'Umilità. In addition to undertaking the religious and scholastic routines of seminary life, O'Connell also found an outlet for his love of music. He became director of the seminary choir, and composed a hymn, "*Iuravit Dominus*," that was later sung at all ordinations. During his years at the seminary, he had an opportunity to see at first hand notable prelates of the Church in all their elaborate regalia, as well as to make the acquaintance of a number of prominent American officials and tourists visiting the Holy City for business or pleasure. On June 7, 1884, William O'Connell was ordained a priest in ceremonies at St. John Lateran; he then returned to America, where he reported to Archbishop Williams at the small rectory in the South End.

After spending the Christmas holidays with his family in Lowell, Father O'Connell was assigned as a curate at St. Joseph's Church in Medford. There, he learned the varied routines of a parish priest— saying Masses, baptizing infants, hearing confessions, going out on sick calls, conducting funerals, training altar boys, and working with the choir. With the death of the pastor and the arrival of a replacement, in October 1886 O'Connell was transferred to St. Joseph's Church in Boston's West End, where the earlier population of Irish immigrants was giving way to Italians, Jews, Greeks, and other new

William Henry O'Connell left his post as bishop of Portland, Maine, to officially succeed the aged John Williams in 1907 as archbishop of Boston. Young
and vigorous at the age of forty-seven, O'Connell exerted a strong personal influence not only on the management of church affairs but also on the character
of Catholicism throughout the archdiocese. He was elevated to the Sacred College in 1911, becoming Boston's first cardinal. (Courtesy of the Archdiocese of
Boston.)

arrivals from southern and eastern Europe. The change from life in a small rural parish to serving in one of the most congested city parishes in the heart of downtown Boston was a definite culture shock for the young priest. With five thousand families crowded into unheated tenements, with toilets located in the back yards, and with alleyways littered with garbage, the presence of numerous saloons and brothels only added to the squalor of a city slum. In addition to dispensing the sacraments, the routine duties of a priest in this kind of urban parish now included sessions with drunkards, pregnant girls, and runaway boys, as well as visits to nearby jails, prisons, and hospitals. It was also a time when ward politics dominated the local scene, with Martin Lomasney, the "boss" of Ward Eight, dispensing favors and ruling the ballot box with a heavy hand. Although they were approximately the same age (twenty-seven) at this time, O'Connell and Lomasney differed significantly in their social attitudes and political philosophies. With their strong egos and dominant personalities, the priest and the politician carefully avoided one another as they went about their daily chores.

In 1895, a sudden turn of events plucked young O'Connell out of the slums of Allen Street and into the grandeur of Rome. Ten years earlier, a bright young priest named Denis O'Connell, a protégé of Cardinal James Gibbons of Baltimore and Archbishop John Ireland of St. Paul, had been appointed rector of the North American College. Because of his close association with "Americanists," who supported the idea of a more decentralized Church organized along national lines, Denis O'Connell fell into disfavor with some powerful Italian "Romanists," and in 1895 he was asked for his resignation. To replace him, Rome decided not to accept any of the names put forward by the American archbishops but selected, instead, William Henry O'Connell of Boston. As a graduate of the North American College, an outstanding student who spoke Italian fluently, and a decided Romanist who pledged absolute allegiance to the pope, O'Connell had exactly the qualifications the conservatives were looking for—both at this moment and well into the future.

Rome was not at all disappointed with its choice. As rector of the North American College, Father O'Connell worked hard for the next four years to reinvigorate the seminary, create new spiritual programs, and increase its enrollments. At a time when the Americanist controversy was still raging, O'Connell assured Archbishop Williams back in Boston that as rector of the college he remained "absolutely neutral," although in his instructions to the seminarians he emphasized that "nationality" was something that belonged "in the bosom of the universal Church." The sons of America, he counseled, should return home "cosmopolitan" in mind and in heart, with "a firm attachment to the Vicar of Christ."

During these same years, O'Connell also mingled with Roman society, establishing new contacts among the hierarchy and reviving many old ones. He renewed his acquaintance with his former seminary professor, Archbishop Francesco Satolli, who became the first apostolic delegate to the United States, and he established a particularly close friendship with Bishop Rafael Merry del Val, son of an English mother and a Spanish-ambassador father, who would soon become secretary of state for the Vatican.

In 1897, during a visit by Archbishop Williams to Rome, and in an obvious acknowledgment of O'Connell's accomplishments at the college, Pope Leo XIII made the priest from Boston a monsignor—one more indication in Church circles that O'Connell was a young man on the way up. Even as he was looking forward to his fifth year as rector of the North American College, the announcement was made on April 11, 1901, that the Holy See had named William Henry O'Connell as bishop of Portland, Maine, to succeed Bishop James A. Healy of Boston, who had died the previous August. Rome had decided to disregard the three names proposed by members of the Maine clergy and select a man it obviously regarded as a known quantity and a trusted spokesman.

On June 28, 1901, O'Connell landed in Boston, and after a series of gala receptions traveled to Portland, where he raised quite a few Yankee eyebrows when he arrived in true Roman fashion—with a small retinue of Italian servants. The stalwart figure of the new bishop in all his resplendent finery, together with the ostentatious manner of his arrival, only further alienated many of the local clergy, who would have preferred one of their own people as bishop.

If O'Connell was aware that some New Englanders resented his appointment, he gave little evidence of it as he moved around his far-flung diocese. He visited among the older Catholic families in the Portland area; he ministered to the devoted Catholic Indians at Old Town and at Eastport; and he became familiar with the many French-speaking inhabitants who occupied the northern farming regions. During his time in Portland, the new bishop also traveled frequently—to Boston, to Lowell, to Washington, and in 1904 to Rome for his first *ad limina* visit, the formal report each bishop is expected to render in person every five years. It was while he was in Rome that the other New England bishops agreed upon three names for Rome to consider in appointing a coadjutor for the ailing Archbishop Williams of Boston—Bishop Matthew Harkins of Providence, Auxiliary Bishop John J. Brady of Boston, and Vicar-General William Byrne of Boston.

While the question of Williams's successor was still under consideration, in August 1905 Pope Pius X sent Bishop O'Connell on a diplomatic mission to persuade the government of Japan to allow the Jesuits to reestablish a Catholic university in that country. After four weeks, as a result of the cooperative spirit of the Japanese leaders, O'Connell could report that his mission had been accomplished. The pope agreed that his efforts had produced "a success far greater than our highest expectations." Six months later, on February 21, 1906, came the announcement that William Henry O'Connell had been named coadjutor, with right of succession, to the Metropolitan See of Boston, Massachusetts. Replacing him as bishop of Portland would be another Bostonian, Father Louis S. Walsh. For a third time, the Holy See had preferred to pass over a list of other qualified candidates in favor of a young bishop whose recent success in Japan had further demonstrated his abilities and his loyalty.

Boston was greatly excited by the announcement of O'Connell's appointment, although a number of those who had supported other candidates complained that the new coadjutor owed his appointment to his political activities in Rome and to his close friendship with several high-ranking Church officials. O'Connell was confident, however, that his appointment was the result of his hard work and notable accomplishments, and he lost no time in coming to Boston to assume officially his office before a gathering at the Cathedral of the Holy Cross. Those attending included Archbishop Williams; about five hundred diocesan clergy, many of whom did not want O'Connell; and some three thousand lay people, most of whom did not know him. Instead of ascending the pulpit, the new coadjutor strode to the center of the sanctuary and established his presence in no uncertain terms: "Rome has made her irrevocable decision," he began, leaving no doubt concerning the source of his power or the nature of his authority. "He who from this day breaks the sacredness of order and harmony in this Diocese," he warned, "will have small claim to respect from any of us who rule or labor in it." But then he adopted a more conciliatory tone as he asked the members of the assemblage not only for their hearts but also for their minds in full cooperation. "I claim now the right to be judged only by my own acts, not for what others do or say." "The past is dead," he concluded. "The future is at the door. *Procedamus in pace*—Let us go forward in peace."

A little over a year later, while O'Connell was still winding up his affairs in Portland, Archbishop John Williams died on August 30, 1907. Cardinal Gibbons came to Boston to pontificate at the funeral Mass, and Archbishop O'Connell delivered the eulogy. Less than six months later, on January 29, 1908, at a service at the Cathedral of the Holy Cross attended by a throng of notable ecclesiastical figures and prominent civic dignitaries, the pallium was conferred upon O'Connell by Cardinal Gibbons as a symbol of his assuming the office of archbishop.

At the time of his accession, Archbishop O'Connell assumed responsibility for an archdiocese that covered about twenty-five hundred square miles and served some 850,000 Roman Catholics. The archdiocese contained almost two hundred parish churches, and had nearly six hundred priests and almost sixteen hundred sisters of various religious orders. Fifty thousand students attended Church-related schools, from the elementary grades to the college level, and some seventy thousand cases a year were handled by the various hospitals and charitable agencies operated by the archdiocese.

Despite what had already been accomplished under his predecessor, however, there was considerable work for O'Connell to do in building even more churches and creating more parishes. It was necessary for the Church to keep pace with the continuing growth of the Catholic population and its rapid expansion into new suburban communities. In older neighborhoods, this usually meant breaking up parishes that had grown too large and creating smaller ones. In South Boston, for example, St. Monica's and St. Eulalia's were new parishes positioned at either end of the peninsula; in nearby Dorchester, St. Paul's and St. William's parishes were created out of the district originally served by St. Peter's. In more recently developed suburban communities, where more well-to-do congregations made up new parishes, the impressive structure of the Holy Name Church reflected the prosperity of West Roxbury, whereas the Blessed Sacrament Church in Cambridge was only the first of four new Catholic churches that would make their appearance on the other side of the Charles River. From Winthrop and Revere to Lynnfield, Danvers, and Newburyport, the spires of new churches were like banners signaling the steady advancement of the Catholic population into the cities and towns of the North Shore.

North of Boston, the bustling textile centers of Lowell and Lawrence, as well as the neighboring communities of North Andover, Tewksbury, and Dracut, continued to attract new immigrant families, and well into the twentieth century the archdiocese was kept busy supplying priests and dedicating new churches to meet their spiritual needs. South of Boston, the spectacular growth of the town of Quincy was clear indication of the movement of Catholics into Norfolk County. St. John's Church served as the basis for a network of several other new churches and mission stations in the Quincy area during the O'Connell years, and new parishes were created in the nearby towns of Braintree, Weymouth, Milton, and Randolph during this same period. Along the seashore areas of Hull, Cohasset, and Scituate, as well as in Plymouth, Kingston, and Duxbury, a number of new churches were constructed, whereas several temporary missions were converted into full-scale parishes. The numerous industries in the Brockton area, offering employment opportunities for unskilled laborers, attracted large numbers of working-class Catholic immigrants from southern and eastern Europe. Starting with St. Patrick's, several large churches were erected in Brockton itself, and the Catholic populations of such nearby towns as Whitman, Bridgewater, and Middleboro also began to grow in both size and distribution.

During this same period, the number of churches authorized to serve Catholics who did not speak English also showed a significant increase. When Archbishop Williams died in 1907, for example, there were seventeen French-speaking churches in the archdiocese; when Cardinal O'Connell died in 1944, there were twenty-nine such churches—most of them conducted either by the Oblates in Lowell or by the Marists in such places as Lawrence, Haverhill, Everett, Waltham, Salem, Beverly, and other Massachusetts towns with substantial French-Canadian communities. The number of Italian and Polish churches also saw significant increases during the O'Connell years. The seven Italian churches functioning in 1907 grew to fifteen by 1945, heavily concentrated in the North End of Boston and in East Boston, but also spreading out to Revere, Somerville, and Everett, as well as Lawrence, Waltham, and Salem. The six Polish churches operating in 1907 also expanded to fifteen by 1945, serving Polish-speaking congregations not only in South Boston but in such North Shore communities as Haverhill, Peabody, Salem, and Ipswich, as well as in South Shore communities like Brockton, Middleton, and Norwood. During the first eighteen months of his episcopacy, according to his biographer Dorothy G. Wayman, Archbishop O'Connell could point to thirty-one new parishes, twenty-nine additional priests, nine more parochial schools, two more orphan asylums, and three new religious orders of nuns added to those already serving the archdiocese.

The new archbishop made his presence felt not only by the confidence with which he took over the direction of the archdiocese, and the speed with which he went about building new churches, but also by the self-assured manner in which he established a clear and direct chain of command that formed the basis of his personal management style. Archbishop Williams reflected the image of the "laissez-faire" executive of the nineteenth century, who appointed his subordinates and then let them run their departments with little or no interference from the top. Archbishop O'Connell, however, was more the corporate executive officer of the twentieth century, who centralized management in his own hands and kept a close eye on every facet of corporate operations.

From the very beginning of his tenure, observed the historian James M. O'Toole, the new archbishop engaged in "frenetic activity" to portray himself as such a modern executive. He was determined to establish a highly centralized system of management control over the remarkably diverse network of Catholic churches, schools, hospitals, homes, asylums, and orphanages that had grown up at an incredible rate during the last twenty years of the Williams administration. The new chancery office on Granby Street in the Back Bay became a bustling place where the archbishop was personally in charge, meeting with his aides and assistants and then sending them off to type out the necessary correspondence and file the appropriate responses.

Somewhat critical of his predecessor's good-natured tendency to let the affairs of the church go "bumbling along" without any sort of effective supervision or personal accountability, O'Connell set out to impose order and direction on what he perceived to be chaos and drift. There is no question that many times the new archbishop could be sharp, abrupt, and abrasive. In many instances, though, he obviously felt that this was the only way to make persons in authority recognize that the old ways were over and a new way of doing things was in place.

In addition to his administrative labors, Archbishop O'Connell also maintained an active and demanding schedule of consecrating new bishops, ordaining new priests, administering the sacrament of Confirmation, laying cornerstones for new churches, speaking at schools and colleges, and lecturing before religious organizations and civic associations. So much activity created a high degree of visibility, which immediately attracted the attention of all the local newspapers. The extent of the coverage was so great that the archbishop soon decided that it would be beneficial for the archdiocese to have its own source of news—the *Pilot* being the obvious choice. Founded in 1829 by Bishop Fenwick, the *Pilot* had been an independent publication for many years under the direction of Patrick Donahoe, but by the turn of the century it had fallen on hard times. After arranging to buy up the paper's stock, in September 1908 O'Connell announced that henceforth the *Pilot* would be the official diocesan newspaper. With copies distributed to every church in the archdiocese, and with Catholic families as dutiful subscribers, circulation picked up almost immediately; with increased advertising, the paper was reivitalized and began to show a substantial profit. The new archbishop had found one more way in which he could expand his influence throughout the archdiocese and more effectively communicate the views of the Catholic Church to the clergy and the laity everywhere.

In the fall of 1911, word began to circulate in the United States that Boston's young archbishop would be among three new American cardinals who would be named by Pope Pius X. Since the 1870s, there had been only one cardinal at a time in the United States—first John McCloskey of New York, and later James Gibbons of Baltimore. By 1910, however, the number of Catholics in the country had grown so large and their influence so extensive that the addition of more American cardinals was almost inevitable. On October 28, 1911, the public announcement came that the pope had named three Americans to be cardinals—Archbishop Diomede Falconio, the apostolic delegate to the United States, and a naturalized American citizen; Archbishop John Farley of New York; and Archbishop William O'Connell of Boston. The news caused a sensation in Boston, which greeted the prestigious appointment as being as much an appropriate tribute to the historic city as a rare distinction for the recipient. On November 11, O'Connell set sail for Rome, arriving two weeks later to participate in the impressive ceremonies in St. Peter's Basilica and to receive his red hat from the hands of Pope Pius X. Returning to Boston in mid-January, the new cardinal was swept up in a series of parades, celebrations, and receptions attended by the mayor of the city and the governor of the commonwealth. The small boy from the textile town of Lowell was now a prince of the Church.

To many of O'Connell's implacable enemies, the red hat was the last straw. The young archbishop's aggressive administrative style and effective publicity campaign over the previous three years had not at all endeared him to a number of older pastors and well-established curates throughout the archdiocese. Under Archbishop Williams's easygoing regime, they had usually been left alone to operate their parishes, conduct their business, and organize their financial affairs pretty much at their own pace and in their own manner. O'Connell, however, insisted that all business be conducted by mail; refused to allow pastors of churches, superiors of religious orders, or administrators of schools and hospitals to expend any sum of money or engage in any sort of construction without specific written authorization; and insisted upon prompt written responses to his communications. Some adjusted gradually to the new man and his new ways, whereas others never became reconciled to O'Connell. They criticized his policies, objected to his personal mannerisms, charged him with arrogance and ambition, and complained about the ways in which he played up to the press. Several of his critics used whatever opportunities they could to undermine his authority and to weaken his influence in the Church. Toward this end, they made a special point of informing authorities in Rome about the scandalous double life being led by O'Connell's young nephew James.

The son of the cardinal's older brother Matthew, James O'Connell entered the seminary and was eventually ordained by his uncle in 1906 while he was still bishop of Portland. When he moved to Boston, the coadjutor brought his nephew along to help him with administrative work. James showed such a decided flair for budget matters and financial investments that in 1914 the cardinal appointed him chancellor of the archdiocese. While carrying out his ecclesiastical duties in Boston, however, the young priest had married a divorced woman and was living a comfortable life in New York City as a real estate speculator, traveling back and forth to Boston each week by train. By 1918, however, rumors began to circulate about the chancellor's scandalous behavior, and before long Vatican authorities were in possession of most of the facts in the case. In June 1920, Rome ordered James O'Connell formally excommunicated and saw that he was dismissed from office. While the embarrassed cardinal defended himself in Rome, his enemies used the ugly affair to buttress their earlier arguments that O'Connell should be removed as archbishop of Boston, insisting that the prelate had known all along about his nephew's secret life. The charges and countercharges flew back and forth during the early 1920s, but finally the controversy had dragged on for so long that arguments faltered and the episode became yesterday's news. By 1924, Rome appeared to accept as fact that a doting and somewhat naive uncle had been duped by his slick nephew, who had engaged in his deceitful lifestyle without the cardinal's knowledge.

The historian James M. O'Toole has suggested that as a result of the political attacks of his enemies Cardinal O'Connell's influence in Vatican circles showed a marked decline. Whether or not that was the case, the prelate's standing in the greater Boston community certainly appeared to be as powerful as ever. Many of the older Irish parishioners may have enjoyed referring to the prelate irreverently (but good-naturedly) as "Gangplank Bill" because of the regular newspaper reports of his numerous cruises, but most of them retained a deep-seated and almost awesome respect for their imposing cardinal archbishop.* If this exalted churchman dressed in elaborate robes, spoke in lordly phrases, and conducted himself with grave solemnity, that was what parishioners expected of a prince of the Church at that time. The same generation of emerging Irish families who took such delight in beholding James Michael Curley resplendent in a pearl-gray cravat, tailored morning coat, and elegant striped trousers would have tolerated nothing less in the appearance of their cardinal archbishop. For most Bostonians of the first half of the twentieth century, "the Cardinal" meant only one person. There was no question to whom they were referring when members of the state legislature spoke of "Number One." City councillors hesitated to act on any issue before they heard of "Lake Street's" position. And newspaper reporters often referred to the prelate as "Number Eighty" from the license plates of his automobile. In 1931 O'Connell received an honorary degree from Boston College; in 1934 he was similarly honored by Catholic University; and in 1932 he was appointed by James Michael Curley to a seat on the Boston Public Library's board of trustees. In 1937 he received an honorary degree from Harvard University, and, three days later, he

---

* Transatlantic travel did not always work in the cardinal's favor. In 1914, travel delays prevented him from arriving in Rome in time to participate in the election of Pope Benedict XV. In 1922, similar delays caused O'Connell to miss the conclave at which Achille Ratti was elected as Pope Pius XI. Only in 1939 did improvements in travel make it possible for the cardinal from Boston to arrive in time to join the other cardinals in the Sistine Chapel to elect Eugenio Pacelli as Pope Pius XII.

presided at the first Mass ever celebrated in Harvard Stadium. If the cardinal had lost any of his personal or ecclesiastical influence, there was little evidence of it on this side of the Atlantic.

It was under O'Connell's influence, too, that the Catholic Church in the archdiocese of Boston assumed a conceptual solidarity and impressive visibility that it had never seen before and would never see again. "It wasn't just the buildings that made the Catholic presence so impressive," observes the historian James O'Toole. "It was the culture. That culture pervaded every aspect of Catholic life, attracting an amazing diversity of people and ideas." By the twentieth century, most Catholics in the archdiocese of Boston not only lived in neighborhoods that were overwhelmingly Catholic but developed an intimate relationship with the particular Catholic parish in which they worshiped, and where their families quickly became homeowners in order to establish their socioreligious connections on a permanent and generational basis. "For all Euro-American Catholic groups," writes John T. McGreevy in his study of the American parish phenomenon, "neighborhood, parish, and religion were constantly intertwined." Sales of homes and apartments were advertised by parish ("a few minutes' walk from St. Peter's"), and individuals identified themselves by their local church ("I'm from St. Ann's, are you from Sacred Heart?"). As a result, Catholic spirituality and Catholic social structure combined to produce a powerful unifying force that made religion a vital and all-embracing influence throughout the archdiocese for at least half a century.

Whether they worshiped at English-speaking churches or at churches where they heard sermons and announcements given in a variety of other languages, Boston Catholics participated in a perpetual calendar of familiar religious devotions that not only drew them into the universality of the Roman Catholic faith but also bound them more firmly together as members of their own distinctive parishes. Taking part in the seasonal rounds of religious activities in most neighborhoods was as much a total community effort as a matter of private devotion. During the period of Advent in late November and early December, for example, persons of all ages prepared for the coming of the Christmas season by attending daily Mass. They then enjoyed the celebration of midnight Mass on Christmas Eve, often followed by festive early morning breakfasts with friends and relatives. In the penitential season of Lent, during the cold, gray winter months of February and March, parishioners tramped through the snow and ice to attend daily Mass, and conscientiously gave up such things as candy, gum, cigarettes, and liquor as personal acts of abstinence. Families would join together to participate in a Lenten schedule that usually included a Wednesday-night service of the rosary, a sermon, and benediction, as well as a Friday-night service that featured the stations of the cross and solemn benediction. One of the high spots at the close of the Lenten season came on Holy Thursday evening, when the streets of Boston's neighborhoods would be crowded with groups of friends, neighbors, and classmates "making the seven churches," a pious custom based on an old Roman tradition of Saint Philip Neri. This called for Catholics to walk (driving a car was forbidden except in case of illness) to seven different churches to visit the Blessed Sacrament, which was left exposed to public view during the Holy Thursday services. After the completion of Lent and the subsequent Eastertime festivities, parishioners usually considered their liturgical year to end with the extremely popular "May Procession." This was a Sunday afternoon promenade that started out from the church and wound through the streets of the parish. It featured the young children of the parish, all dressed in white, escorting a litter that carried a large statue of the Blessed Virgin Mary. The procession would end up back at the church (at an outdoor shrine if weather permitted), where a young girl would "crown" the statue with a small chaplet of flowers while the parishioners stood around and sang favorite hymns to the Blessed Mother.

Within this broad spectrum of devotional activity, there were many other practices going on within the archdiocesan parish network that

Against a background of the three-decker houses characteristic of Boston's ethnic neighborhoods, priests of the archdiocese hold a solemn procession through the streets of Roxbury during the Clergy Marian Days. Frequent public displays of religious devotion by both clergy and lay people demonstrated the strong religious atmosphere that prevailed during the 1940s and 1950s.

created what Thomas Wangler has called "a second devotional calendar." This series of rituals further intensified the strong religious bonds that held the various communities together, competing (but not conflicting) with the regular Church calendar and its traditional Easter-to-Christmas cycle. Parishioners accepted the custom that each month was assigned to some specific aspect of faith and belief—March, for example, was set aside for St. Joseph, May for the Blessed Mother, June for the Sacred Heart, July for the Precious Blood, and October for the Holy Rosary. Confessions were held regularly on Saturday afternoons and evenings, as well as on the Thursday evening before the First Friday of every month. First-Friday devotions to the Sacred Heart were very popular during the 1920s and 1930s, as were

"Holy Hour" devotions, where parishioners would spend an hour in church kneeling in adoration before the Blessed Sacrament on the altar. Novenas—nine consecutive days or weeks of prayer—were also expressions of religious piety, with parishioners either attending their own parish or perhaps another that specialized in some particular devotion. Novenas to Our Lady of Perpetual Help were conducted at Roxbury's Mission Church; the Miraculous Medal Novena was held at St. Cecilia's Church in the Back Bay; and the Novena of Grace in honor of St. Francis Xavier drew thousands to the Immaculate Conception Church in the South End. Every parish had its own cluster of devotional groups and associations, but Cardinal O'Connell assigned the Holy Name Society a special role as the leading male religious organization in the Boston archdiocese. In addition to this association, most parishes also had the Legion of Mary for women, different Third Order groups for lay persons (of St. Francis, St. Dominic, Our Lady of Mount Carmel, and others), and various sodalities for both married and single women. It was standard practice for every parish in the archdiocese to have a mission or a retreat at least once a year. These were periods of intensive meditation, repentance, and spiritual renewal, usually directed by a vigorous orator belonging to such religious orders as the Oblates, the Passionists, the Redemptorists, or the Jesuits. Generally speaking, a mission was customarily a two-week affair, with men involved one week and women the next. A retreat, by contrast, was usually a single week, with men and women mixed.

In every Catholic neighborhood during the 1920s and 1930s, the Church was an integral part of almost every aspect of family life, from the cradle to the grave. A large crucifix, along with pictures of the Sacred Heart of Jesus, the Blessed Mother, and St. Joseph, was prominently displayed in almost every Catholic home, dramatizing the Holy Family as the universal model for all working-class families. Religious pamphlets, inspirational literature, and copies of the *Pilot* were found in most houses, and entire families knelt together every night before going to bed to recite the decades of the rosary.

Mass, of course, was the central event in the life of the parish, and

Sunday was the big day of the week. Parents usually went to early Mass so that the mother could prepare the breakfast, whereas the youngsters went to the "children's Mass" at 9:30 A.M. There was always a lengthy sermon at Sunday Mass, usually centering on one of three major topics: the importance of the Blessed Sacrament and the benefits to be derived from regular attendance at the Holy Sacrifice of the Mass; the loyalty and obedience Catholics owed to the Holy Father in Rome as the successor of St. Peter; and the special devotion all Catholics should have to the Blessed Virgin Mary, Mother of God. Cardinal O'Connell encouraged these themes, and they were repeated from the pulpit over and over during the course of the year until they became, in the words of one elderly parishioner, "part of the mental and religious furniture of our minds." After returning from Mass to a large breakfast, the children went back to the church in the early afternoon for Sunday School—boys upstairs and girls downstairs. For about an hour the children recited their catechism and received instruction in the basic beliefs of Catholicism—most of it in the familiar question-and-answer form of the Baltimore Catechism (Q. "Who made you?" A. "God made me." Q. "Why did God make you?" A. "To know Him, to love Him, and to serve Him in this world, and to be happy with Him forever in the next."). After the children returned from Sunday School, the whole family usually sat down for the main meal of the day, which almost always featured a roast beef, a roast chicken, or a baked ham. In most Irish homes, the Sunday meal was an absolute necessity. It started precisely on time, nothing was allowed to change the menu, and every member of the family was expected to attend.

But the influence of Catholicism was not limited to the sermons at Mass or the routines of Sunday. Throughout the entire week, men and women engaged in various voluntary activities that usually had some religious connection. Almost every parish had a rosary society and a scapular society, as well as a St. Vincent de Paul Conference, which had originally been developed by Archbishop Williams to bring comfort and assistance to parishioners who were poor or homeless. Parish priests, too, were involved in a number of activities that went far beyond saying daily Mass and hearing weekly confessions. They often operated small clubhouses close to the church where they offered a variety of religious and social activities for parishioners during the week. Pastors organized choirs for the church, and arranged plays, minstrel shows, and operettas where members of the parish could display their musical and dramatic talents once or twice a year. They ran colorful outdoor bazaars during the spring months to help pay off the parish debt and provide an opportunity for parishioners to get together after the long Lenten season. The priests also took a strong personal interest in encouraging parish sports programs, not only for their importance to the health and well-being of the parishioners but also because they acted as a physical and moral deterrent in keeping young men away from the temptations of the pool hall, the barroom, and the brothel. These same priests were plainly visible at all hours of the day and night in most neighborhoods, walking the streets in their black cassocks with their birettas on their heads, talking to parishioners, buying penny candy for the little children at the corner store, and making sure that teenagers were not loitering in the alleyways after dark.

It was not always sweetness and light, of course. There were always those crusty old Irish pastors (the "iron hats") who ruled their fiefdoms like feudal barons. They terrorized the entire parish, roared at altar boys for not saying the Latin properly, sent weeping nuns back to their motherhouses for not agreeing to take on more classes, and reduced fresh young curates to various states of fright and frustration. And what the old priest couldn't accomplish on his own his sturdy Irish housekeeper did, guarding the lace-curtained portals of the rectory like a modern-day Cerberus and endangering the digestive systems of visiting curates with her cooking. But the occasional upsets and tensions were generally taken in stride by most loyal and long-suffering parishioners as typical of the daily trials and tribulations they were led to expect in this "vale of tears." This was a period, after all, when battered wives were admonished by many confessors to return home, cook a tasty supper, and avoid upsetting their hard-working husbands any further. Most parishioners shrugged stoically, agreed to "offer it up," and continued to follow their Church and their priests with few questions. Under the supervision of the pastor, the parish was the world in which Catholics lived, a world where a strong and abiding religious faith infused almost every aspect of their daily lives. "Your parish is the most important society to which you as laymen can belong," one Cleveland pastor told the members of his congregation, according to the historian John T. McGreevy in his *Parish Boundaries*. "Your parish speaks not only with the voice of your pastor and your Bishop, but with the voice of the Holy Father, who speaks to you the words of God."

The visible presence of so many priests and nuns in every parish throughout the archdiocese was a clear reflection of the remarkable growth of religious vocations during the O'Connell years. This was a time when neighborhoods vied with each other over how many of their young people had gone into the priesthood or had left for the convent, a time when it was the dream of every father and mother to have at least one son become a priest and one daughter become a nun. This spirit can be seen in the statistics for the period: between 1907 and 1942, the number of priests in the archdiocese went up from 598 to 1,582, while the number of students enrolled in St. John's Seminary rose from 86 to 241. The number of young women going into the convent during the same thirty-five years was even more remarkable—the number of female religious orders grew from 29 to 44, sending the number of nuns from 1,567 in 1907 to 5,469 in 1942. Given this strong spiritual impulse, fostered by parents and nurtured by nuns, priests, and pastors, Catholic neighborhoods were characterized by a distinctive set of moral principles. The ideals of the sacredness of life, the sanctity of the home, and the permanence of the matrimonial bond were constant themes in the church and in the home, and they became deeply ingrained in the whole culture of the community. The importance of unqualified sexual abstinence outside the formal state of marriage was both a social and religious tenet of the neighborhood, and the virtues of purity, modesty, and virginity were accepted as articles of faith without question or condition.

The strikingly devout spirit of Catholicism that characterized the religious life of the parishes of the archdiocese during the early part of the twentieth century was even further intensified by the expansion of the parochial school system. This took place under the personal direction of Cardinal O'Connell, who was determined to liberate the Catholic Church in Boston from what he regarded as the stifling oppression of Anglo-Saxon Protestantism and to fashion the character of American Catholics in a completely new mold. Throughout the nineteenth century, the general tendency of Boston's Catholic hierarchy had been one of diplomacy and accommodation. The town's first bishop, Jean Cheverus, established cordial relations with the Yankee community, and later bishops such as John Fitzpatrick and John Williams continued to work with their Protestant neighbors in a cooperative and nonaggressive fashion. These early Church leaders encouraged peaceful coexistence between the insecure members of their immigrant flock and a hostile native-born establishment through a policy of what the historian Paula Kane has called "withdrawn entrenchment."

By the time William Henry O'Connell took over as archbishop of Boston in 1907, however, the balance of power had clearly shifted, and a policy of religious accommodation seemed outmoded, impractical, and unnecessary. Irish Catholics were no longer the meek and oppressed minority they had been half a century earlier. With the election in 1905 of John F. Fitzgerald as the first Boston-born Irish-Catholic mayor of Boston; with David Ignatius Walsh becoming the commonwealth's first Irish-Catholic governor in 1914, and then going on to serve nearly thirty years in the United States Senate; with Joseph O'Connell, an 1893 graduate of Boston College, being elected to the

Further evidence of the growing political power of Irish Catholics in the twenti-
eth century came with the election of John F. Fitzgerald in 1905 as the city's first
Boston-born Catholic mayor. A former political boss of the North End, and
elected to the U.S. congress in 1895, Fitzgerald ("Honey Fitz") was the father
of Rose Fitzgerald Kennedy, and would become the maternal grandfather of
President John F. Kennedy. (Courtesy of the Print Department, Boston Public
Library.)

United States House of Representatives in 1906; and with William
Henry O'Connell himself raised to the exalted rank of cardinal in
1911, it was clear that the Irish had already begun moving into positions of considerable power and influence. O'Connell urged the faithful to adopt an independent attitude and to focus on their own distinctive culture instead of striving to adapt themselves to the traditions of
their host society. The religious splendors of the rich medieval past,

together with the colorful traditions of their glorious Gaelic culture, he insisted, provided the Irish with far more inspirational models than those of the cold-roast-beef Anglo-Saxon forms. From the outset, O'Connell insisted that the old tide of Protestantism was receding and that a new wave of Irish Catholicism was sweeping over the region. "The Puritan has passed; the Catholic remains," he announced bluntly in his sermon on the occasion of the diocesan centennial in 1908.

Although the cardinal himself maintained close and even affectionate relations with many prominent members of the city's Protestant establishment, he warned the faithful of the archdiocese to avoid Protestant churches and non-Catholic rituals and ceremonies—even on such semisocial occasions as marriages and funerals. Youngsters were cautioned not to join Boy Scout troops, not to participate in YMCA or YWCA activities, and not to attend social gatherings at local neighborhood clubs, which O'Connell felt were imbued with anti-Catholic attitudes. Instead, he encouraged Church leaders to organize a series of parallel, exclusively Catholic social activities for the young people of the archdiocese—a sort of "shadow" network of clubs and associations fashioned after non-Catholic models. Catholic Boy Scout and Girl Scout troops, for example, provided young people with the opportunities of healthy outdoor recreation within a Catholic atmosphere. And the Catholic Youth Organization (CYO) was established to give boys and girls a chance to join sports teams, debating clubs, and marching bands without going outside the boundaries of their own parishes.

Using the impressive dignity of his position and the intimidating force of his personality, Cardinal O'Connell established a pattern of separatism throughout the archdiocese of Boston that was carefully designed to disentangle Catholics as much as possible from local Protestants and to free the Irish from all forms of Yankee influence. Through this deliberate strategy of "separatist integration," O'Connell shaped a "triumphalist, separatist Catholic subculture," according to Paula Kane, which was "sacred but equal, separate but integrated." He exerted pressure on pastors and curates, mothers and fathers, to make sure that children attended parochial schools and Catholic colleges. He was deeply suspicious of Harvard and other Ivy League institutions because they had moved away from their original religious affiliations and therefore had few, if any, sound moral or ethical principles. They did not possess "the whole truth, the real truth, the fundamental truth," he said. When it became known that young Rose Fitzgerald, the daughter of Mayor John F. Fitzgerald (and future wife of Joseph P. Kennedy), intended to go to Wellesley College, Cardinal O'Connell spoke to him, indicated his displeasure, and pointed out the impact of such a decision on other Catholic girls because of the mayor's position in the community. The following day, "Honey Fitz" informed his daughter that she was "too young" for Wellesley and subsequently enrolled Rose in the Academy of the Sacred Heart. This was consistent with the prelate's view that Catholic education was indispensable to a proper moral and religious life. "There is, as you know, just one point of view," he declared in 1930, "and that is, Catholic children should attend Catholic schools."

It was no coincidence, however, that by the early twentieth century so many of the new schools and colleges were being located in the western suburbs rather than in the center of Boston itself. During the Civil War period, at the time that the Catholic Church had decided to build a new and larger cathedral, the South End of Boston had been regarded as the area that would become the new and fashionable section of the city. In anticipation of this prospect, the Jesuits had constructed their handsome Immaculate Conception Church on Harrison Avenue and had started the first classes at Boston College. The early prospects for the South End quickly soured, however, with the filling in of the north side of Boston Neck and the elegant extension of Commonwealth Avenue. The area that became known as the Back Bay quickly eclipsed the south side of the Neck as Boston's most desirable residential address. By the end of the century, while the Back Bay was flourishing the South End had become a run-down and neglected neighborhood. Its once handsome bowfront brick mansions had been converted into inexpensive boarding houses, dingy saloons, and hole-in-the-wall shops. The stately Cathedral of the Holy Cross was all but obscured by the dark, ugly skeleton of the elevated railway, which ran along Washington Street with a deafening clatter that drowned out sermons and interrupted devotions.

O'Connell began moving many of the operations of the Catholic Church out of the congested streets of the South End and into the more expansive areas of the western suburbs of Brighton and Newton, where Archbishop Williams had earlier established St. John's Seminary. Thanks to an unusually generous bequest from the family of Benjamin F. Keith, a vaudeville magnate, O'Connell was able to realize many of his ambitions for creating a "little Rome" in the suburban hills west of Boston, where the work of the Church could take place in a more inspirational setting.* He used a portion of this bequest to make substantial changes to St. John's Seminary in Brighton, adding new wings to Theology House, rebuilding Philosophy House after a serious fire in 1936, and naming the new structure Saint William's Hall. In 1937 he provided a new library building, and three years later he established a new junior seminary, St. Clement's Hall. It was on the site of St. John's Seminary that the cardinal constructed a new chancery building in the Italian Renaissance style, and then a new archbishop's residence, an impressive palazzo done in the same style.

Renovations at St. John's Seminary were not restricted to bricks and mortar, however. Perhaps as a reaction to his earlier experience as rector of the North American College, Cardinal O'Connell always showed an active and personal interest in all aspects of life in the Brighton seminary. He was convinced that an increase in vocations and a more effective priesthood depended on a professional and in-

* Benjamin F. Keith's wife was a devout Catholic. When their son, Paul, died without heirs in 1918, he left to the cardinal, in his mother's memory, an outright gift of cash, investments, and real estate amounting to nearly three million dollars.

spiring educational program. When Archbishop Williams had first organized St. John's Seminary in 1884, in the absence of local academic talent he entrusted its direction and management to priests of the French order of the Society of St. Sulpice. The Sulpicians had acquired a reputation as seminary directors, and both Archbishop Williams and his predecessor Bishop Fitzpatrick had studied at their seminaries at Montreal and at Paris.

By the time he had become archbishop of Boston, however, O'Connell believed that it was time for him to take over the management of his own seminary and staff it with qualified diocesan priests of his own choosing. He was convinced that young men studying for service in an essentially American ministry should be thoroughly acquainted with the social and cultural circumstances of their assignments. After the responsibilities of the Sulpicians had been terminated, St. John's reopened in the fall of 1911 under the overall jurisdiction of the archbishop. Father John B. Peterson, a professor at the institution since 1901, was the new rector; he supervised a faculty composed of eleven priests of the archdiocese, five of whom had been teaching there for several years. In addition to these administrative changes, the program of courses at St. John's Seminary was also greatly amplified and improved. Under the direction of diocesan priests who felt challenged by the cardinal to provide schooling that at least matched the standards of the Sulpicians, many future seminary graduates professed to feel a new shared vision of a priestly calling that shaped their lives and their work in the parishes.

The cardinal encouraged other large Catholic institutions to establish themselves in more spacious locales outside the central city. For example, he vigorously supported the efforts of Father Thomas I. Gasson, SJ, to move Boston College (O'Connell's alma mater) out of the congested streets of the South End. In June 1909, ground was broken and work begun on the first of a complex of buildings in the English Gothic style, designed by the firm of Maginnis and Walsh. They were set on a magnificent site formerly owned by the family of the Episcopalian bishop William Lawrence in the fashionable Chestnut Hill section. The cardinal also gave his support to the founding of Emmanuel College in Boston's Fenway area; operated by the Sisters of Notre Dame, it was the first local Catholic college for women. During the same period, the Religious of the Sacred Heart moved its academy (which had originally been located in the South End, and later in the Back Bay) to Centre Street in Newton, where it became the College of the Sacred Heart for female students. In like fashion, when the Sisters of St. Joseph opened Regis College for women, they located their new institution on a beautiful campus in the suburban town of Weston. Cardinal O'Connell also used part of his funds from the Keith family to build a new chapel for St. Elizabeth's Hospital, which had moved from its crowded South End site to a more spacious location in Brighton, fairly close to the seminary.

Not content with transforming Boston's traditional Anglo-Saxon culture into a modern Celtic one, or with organizing a comprehensive Roman Catholic community devoted to a system of unchanging moral values, the cardinal was determined to put it all on public display. He wanted the city and the commonwealth to see the extent to which the new "Catholic Americans" were now a powerful force to be reckoned with. Emphasizing the theme of the "Church militant," O'Connell went out of his way to demonstrate dramatically, in the words of one local journalist, that "the once brow-beaten Irish-Catholics have come into possession of Boston." From his own point of view, the archbishop was making a conscientious effort to preserve the faith and morals of those souls who had been entrusted to his episcopal care, to help Catholics realize their "full duty to themselves," as well as to promote in the community at large "a fair attitude toward the Church." He insisted that Roman Catholics, especially young people, should no longer be pale imitations of Yankee role models. By becoming conscious of their own heritage and their own history, he believed Catholics would gain a greater awareness of their own values and their own principles.

O'Connell's version of American Catholicism was no puny thing; indeed, it took on many of the characteristics of a more aggressive age. In 1899, just back from his military exploits in Cuba, Theodore Roosevelt ushered in the twentieth century by exhorting his fellow countrymen to live vigorously and to engage in "the strenuous life." He urged Americans to extinguish "the soft spirit of the cloistered life" and boldly face "the life of strife." There was much of this same muscular and militant spirit in Cardinal O'Connell's approach to American Catholicism, and several of the popular hymns he composed for his parishioners contained lyrics that almost paraphrased the competitive fervor of the Rough Rider. "Fierce is the fight / For God and the right," went the words of the hymn that was sung with great enthusiasm by members of the Holy Name Society. In the cosmic "battle" between the forces of morality and religion, and the advocates of secularism and materialism, the cardinal called upon his people to be prepared for "storm and trial" and to assert themselves with "manly firmness" in defending their faith.

Throughout his years in Boston, O'Connell used a succession of religious events and public occasions to put on displays of the power and prestige of "triumphant Catholicism." In late October 1908, little more than nine months after he assumed his responsibilities as archbishop, O'Connell hosted a series of celebrations commemorating the centenary of the Catholic Church in New England. A pontifical high Mass was held on October 28 at the Cathedral of the Holy Cross; the papal legate, Archbishop Diomede Falconio, presided, and Archbishop O'Connell delivered the centenary sermon. With archbishops and bishops from all parts of the country, Governor Curtis Guild, Jr., and Mayor George A. Hibbard, and several hundred priests from throughout the archdiocese of Boston in attendance, the cathedral was packed to the doors, and thousands more were lined up on the streets and sidewalks outside. That same evening, the governor and the mayor joined bishops, priests, and people at Symphony Hall at an event in which a number of prominent Catholic laymen commemorated the lives and accomplishments of the bishops—Cheverus, Fenwick, Fitzpatrick, and Williams—who presided over the diocese during its first hundred years. On Sunday, November 1, nearly forty thousand members of the Holy Name Society from every parish in the archdiocese, organized in military ranks, paraded through the streets of Boston to the music of eighty military bands. Archbishop O'Connell, joined by Cardinal James Gibbons, who had come up from Baltimore to participate in the grand event, observed from a flag-draped reviewing stand as the Catholic men marched along to the applause of almost half a million spectators who lined the streets and sidewalks along the route. It was the start of an era that most Bostonians would not soon forget.

And the celebrations continued. In May 1926, in observance of the cardinal's silver jubilee as a bishop, a series of Masses, religious celebrations, and civic receptions provided another colorful opportunity for local and national press coverage. Five years later, in 1931, the fiftieth anniversary of the cardinal's graduation from Boston College set the stage for an elaborate commencement, an honorary degree, and further press coverage of the prelate's scholarly and cultural achievements. In 1934, however, the golden jubilee of O'Connell's ordination to the priesthood saw perhaps the most extensive series of events publicizing the scope of diocesan influence. A solemn high Mass on Friday, June 8, with special greetings from His Holiness, Pope Pius XI, drew thousands of the region's most prestigious religious and political figures. The following day, Saturday, was set aside as "Children's Day," with some twenty-five thousand pupils from the parochial schools of the archdiocese gathered on the campus at Boston College to celebrate the occasion with songs and prayers. And on Sunday, June 10, thousands of the faithful packed Boston's Fenway Park at a "civic ceremony" that brought the period of solemn festivities to a resounding conclusion. The city and the commonwealth could not help but be impressed by the size, the dedication, and the enthusiasm of the Catholic population.

In shaping the moral values of second- and third-generation Catholics in the archdiocese of Boston, the cardinal was trying to shape their political attitudes as well. Although much has been written about O'Connell's opposition to "Americanist" views in the earlier philosophical debates with "Romanists," this should in no way cast doubt on his deep patriotism and his sincere devotion to his native land. He spoke out strongly and movingly on the issue at the Cathedral of the Holy Cross after returning to Boston to celebrate his appointment as cardinal: "My American citizenship I prize as one of God's choicest gifts to me—mine to honor with the best that is in me and to defend with my last breath." He brushed aside the claim of some critics that Roman Catholics could not be good Americans because they owed allegiance to Rome. O'Connell rejected the idea of any kind of "divided loyalty," arguing that such a notion would be like saying that a son could not love his father and his mother at the same time. The motto For God and for Country that appeared over the main entrance of many parochial schools in the archdiocese was a public declaration that devotion to God and loyalty to the country were indivisible in the hearts and souls of American Catholics.

O'Connell's particular brand of Americanism took the conservative form usually associated with members of the Republican party and most representatives of the American business community. During the 1920s and 1930s, the prelate's natural conservative tendencies were further strengthened by two developments on the international scene in the years following the end of World War I.

The first was the rise of atheistic Communism, which had been given a foothold by the victory of the Bolsheviks in Russia and which had then developed into a worldwide revolutionary movement directed by the leaders of the Soviet Union. O'Connell was formidable in his opposition to everything Communism stood for in pursuing socialistic goals and persecuting organized religion. And he was vigilant in his determination that Communist ideas and principles should never gain a foothold in the United States.

The other development was the rise of totalitarian governments in many parts of the world. Fascism in Italy and Nazism in Germany, along with Communism in the Soviet Union, established evil dictatorships that destroyed the rights of individuals, curtailed the functions of organized religion, and replaced the role of the family with external authoritarian rule. O'Connell's fear of centralized government power and its consequent effects upon parental authority and upon the traditional values of American family life became almost obsessive during the 1920s and 1930s. This helps to explain his strong opposition to various proposals for federal legislation that would establish regulations controlling such things as wages, hours, and conditions of employment. It also accounts to some extent for his opposition to liberal social and political movements within the Catholic Church itself directly following World War I.

When the United States declared war against Germany in 1917, young American Catholics, anxious to display their loyalty and patriotism, flocked to the colors and provided at least 1 million among the 4,791,172 men who served in the armed forces. The number of Catholic chaplains soared from a mere 28 to a total of 1,525; volunteers representing the Knights of Columbus provided food, recreational facilities, and religious counseling for American troops in army camps throughout the United States, as well as for members of the American Expeditionary Force in Europe. During the virulent epidemic of influenza that afflicted the country in the fall of 1918, priests made their tragic rounds visiting the sick and giving the Last Rites, while nearly a thousand Catholic nuns of the archdiocese, representing twenty different sisterhoods and ninety convents, went from house to house caring for families, preparing meals, washing clothes, and dispensing medicines. The Daughters of Charity, who staffed the Carney Hospital in South Boston, became a particularly familiar sight during the height of the epidemic, their distinctive headdresses flowing like great white wings as they traveled about the city bringing medicines to the sick and comfort to the dying. At the end of the terrible year, Boston's mayor, Andrew J. Peters, wrote a letter expressing his gratitude "for the valuable services rendered to the City of Boston by the Carney Hospital during the influenza epidemic."

Cardinal O'Connell, too, supplied valuable resources to the community during these dangerous times. In order to relieve the congestion in regular hospitals, he offered the facilities of St. John's Seminary to the Massachusetts Emergency Public Health Committee as a home for convalescents, as well as a central location for the large number of army trucks and other vehicles that were pressed into service to transport the dead. Richard Cardinal Cushing later recalled that as a young seminarian he saw stacks of coffins piled up outside Cassidy's Funeral Home in South Boston. When the worst of the epidemic had passed, on the evening of November 11, 1918, hundreds of people flocked to the Cathedral of the Holy Cross to attend a special Mass of Thanksgiving and hear Cardinal O'Connell sing a joyous *Te Deum* heralding both the end of the epidemic and the announcement of the armistice that brought the war to a close.

The unusual demands of World War I, and the obvious lack of coordination among those working to help the war effort, suddenly revealed that, except for the annual gathering of the nation's archbishops, the Catholic Church in the United States had no effective national organization. With the approval of Cardinals Gibbons, O'Connell, and Farley, a meeting of prominent Catholic priests and laymen took place in Washington, D.C., in August 1917; it resulted in the National Catholic War Council. The NCWC would represent the Knights of Columbus and numerous other Church groups in the United States in working with the War Department and with parallel Protestant and Jewish agencies. This cooperation among religious organizations serving the troops in World War I was a first in American history, according to the historian James Hennesey.

With the war coming to an end, and with servicemen beginning to return to civilian life, several NCWC leaders felt that the time had come for the Catholic Church to become more actively involved in social questions and political issues. Father John A. Ryan, a priest from Minnesota who had completed his doctoral work in economics at Johns Hopkins University in 1906, was especially interested in developing a Catholic system of political economy in which a spirit of Christian ethics would provide a humane response to free-enterprise capitalism. Transforming the NCWC into the National Catholic Welfare Conference, Ryan and other Catholic social liberals had their new organization approved by Pope Benedict XV in 1919. Basing many of his ideas on his book *A Living Wage*, Ryan argued for the necessity of a minimum wage, old-age insurance, low-cost housing programs, government control of monopolies, and restrictions on the labor of women and children. As director of the newly renamed NCWC's Social Action Department, Ryan wanted to develop a progressive social reform movement for the Catholic Church in the United States.

The change of the NCWC's mission from wartime cooperation in serving American troops to postwar advocacy of social reforms met with strong and vocal resistance from many of the nation's religious leaders, who accused Father Ryan and his supporters of being socialist agitators engaged in a plot to promote labor unions. During 1921–22, Cardinal O'Connell and Cardinal Dennis Dougherty of Philadelphia spearheaded an unsuccessful movement to have the National Catholic Welfare Conference suppressed. Seeing the new version of the NCWC as a resurrection of the old "Americanist" philosophy that would weaken the central authority of the Church, they denounced the program as contrary to the American spirit of individual freedom and insisted that it should not be associated with the name of the Catholic Church. Most prelates had little complaint with the Church encouraging its members to tend the sick, help the poor, care for the widow and orphan; but they had little sympathy with the Church, as an institution, involving itself in larger questions of social policy or political action, especially if it suggested expanding the powers of the federal government. The place of the clergyman was on the altar or in the pulpit on Sunday, they insisted. They went on to argue that the function of the Church was saving souls, not running factories, engaging in labor disputes, or lobbying for social legislation in the halls of Congress. And few members of the Catholic population at large, at a time when they were striving to conform to "100 percent American" ideals and practices, appeared to show much desire to get involved in any liberal social movements that might label them as alien, foreign, or socialist. American Catholics clearly did not want to be regarded as "different."

Cardinal O'Connell refused to reveal his personal political beliefs or party affiliations, and he carefully refrained from expressing opinions for or against specific political candidates. For example, although he had personal misgivings about the appropriateness of women moving into politics, the cardinal held back on any public opposition to a proposed constitutional amendment in 1913 to give American women the suffrage. This was especially the case after the first Catholic governor of Massachusetts, David I. Walsh, went out of his way to back the amendment strongly. Walsh failed to get reelected, and the suffrage proposal went down to defeat, but in 1920 the Nineteenth Amendment was finally ratified. O'Connell received the decision with good grace and urged all Catholic women to take the opportunity to use their vote wisely and well.

He did, however, become a powerful voice during the 1920s and 1930s on certain broad policy issues that he saw as involving the doctrines of the Catholic Church or the traditions of the Catholic family. In 1924, O'Connell, typically suspicious of any reform movement he felt smacked of Bolshevism when it substituted the authority of the state for the authority of the parent, came out in strong opposition to a proposed amendment (supported by Father Ryan and the NCWC) that would ban child labor. A month before the election, he ordered all pastors in the archdiocese to speak against the amendment from their pulpits, and at the last minute even James Michael Curley backed off from his longtime support of the proposal in the face of such episcopal displeasure. It came as no surprise that Bay State voters

A word of admonition from William Cardinal O'Connell often made the head-lines in the daily press, as happened in this instance in the 1930s when His Emi-nence told his listeners, "Don't go near the movies." During the same period, the cardinal also lashed out at the "bleating and whining" of such popular crooners as Bing Crosby and Rudy Vallee; he was fearful of the effects this "immoral slush" would have on young people. (Courtesy of the Pilot *Archives.)*

soundly defeated the Child Labor Amendment. Another case involved contraception. Cardinal O'Connell was always opposed to birth control, both as a matter of religious doctrine and as a matter of moral principle. Although he was now in his eighties, and in increasingly feeble health, he leaped to the attack when efforts were made in Massachusetts in 1941 and 1942 to liberalize the birth control laws through a ballot initiative. Marshalling the efforts of friendly legislators, loyal priests and pastors, and the editors of the *Pilot*, the archdiocese launched an effective campaign that saw the birth control measure go down to defeat.

O'Connell was consistent in his political views, however, even when they did not coincide with current public opinion. During the mid-1930s, Father Charles E. Coughlin, known as the Radio Priest, spoke to nationwide audiences concerning such subjects as Franklin Delano Roosevelt, New Deal programs, and the influence of international bankers. Every Sunday morning after Mass, thousands of parishioners snatched up copies of the popular priest's newspaper, *Social Justice*, piled up alongside the regular Sunday newspapers outside Catholic churches. Every Sunday afternoon following dinner, they gathered around their radios to hear Coughlin's tirades against New Dealers and Jews. Cardinal O'Connell had always been opposed to members of the clergy assuming political roles and involving themselves in partisan issues. Although he did not mention Coughlin by name, he lashed out against "hysterical addresses" by priests who were "talking nonsense" and indulging in "emotionalism." This may not have been a popular position to take in Boston, which Mayor James Michael Curley once boasted was "the strongest Coughlin city in the world," but the cardinal was always one to let the chips fall where they might.

And besides, O'Connell, now that he was a cardinal, did not display any greater regard for Curley's populist brand of big-city politics than he had for that of the old ward boss Martin Lomasney when he was a young curate in the West End thirty years earlier. At a time when the prelate was trying to elevate the social standards and intellectual levels of his Irish-Catholic parishioners, he could not help but be embarrassed by the graft and corruption so often associated with Irish political leaders who thrived on demagoguery and patronage. Although the cardinal continued to maintain a studied silence on matters of partisan politics, it is clear that he gave whatever encouragement he could to Irish candidates whom he regarded as men of honesty and integrity. In 1930, for example, when James Michael Curley put himself forward as a candidate for a third term as mayor of Boston, he was opposed by a number of rivals, including Frederick W. Mansfield. Despite his Yankee-sounding name, Mansfield was an Irish Catholic, a Democrat, president of the Massachusetts Bar Association, and had earlier been a Democratic candidate for governor. Not only did Mansfield receive the backing of the Good Government Association, but he was also rumored to have the unofficial blessing of the cardinal, who would certainly see such a distinguished lawyer as a vast improvement over a rogue like Curley. Ponderous and methodical—"as spectacular as a four-day-old codfish," quipped Curley—Mansfield was no match for his fast-talking opponent, and he lost his first mayoral race. Four years later, however, Mansfield succeeded in getting elected. He served as mayor of Boston from 1934 to 1938, after which he became legal counsel for the archdiocese.

Evidence that O'Connell still wielded considerable political influence could be seen in 1937, when Curley tried for a fourth term as mayor of Boston. This time he was opposed by tall, handsome Maurice J. Tobin of Roxbury's Mission Hill district, who was viewed by many voters as a younger, more capable, and more honest alternative to the Rascal King. Election day, November 2, 1937, fell on All Soul's Day, and as thousands of the faithful came out of morning Mass they saw below the masthead of the *Boston Post* a statement by Cardinal O'Connell complaining: "The walls are raised against honest men in civic life." These words—actually delivered at an event six years earlier—were followed by a ringing endorsement of Maurice Tobin as "an honest, clean, competent young man." Most readers failed to notice that the endorsement was not part of O'Connell's original statement, but had been cleverly appended by the *Post's* editors. Citizens went to the polls and dutifully voted the way they assumed His Eminence wanted—and Curley's bid for a fourth term failed.*

By the time that Mayor Curley's political influence began to wane, and events in many parts of Europe and Asia began to suggest the terrifying prospects of another world conflict, Cardinal O'Connell showed signs of slowing down as old age began to take its inevitable toll. Now in his early eighties, the prelate had enjoyed relatively good health throughout his long life and career, despite a mild diabetic condition and a cataract operation in 1937. But his eyesight was now failing fast, and his mobility was increasingly limited, so that by the spring of 1944 he was pretty much confined to his Brighton residence, where he could reflect upon his thirty-five years as archbishop of Boston.

There was no doubt that under O'Connell's personal and energetic direction the archdiocese had expanded both in membership and in institutions. Despite restrictive immigration laws during the 1920s that reduced the flow of newcomers from southern and eastern Europe, followed by a disastrous depression during the 1930s that discouraged the immigration of unskilled workers, the Catholic population passed the one million mark by 1940, making Boston the third largest diocese in the United States, surpassed only by Chicago and New York.

To provide for the spiritual welfare of these additional Roman Catholics, the number of parishes was increased from 194 in 1907 to 322 in 1942, with the number of churches going from 248 to 375 during this same thirty-five-year period. The number of diocesan priests rose from 488 to 947, while the number of priests in various religious

* According to Jack Beatty, Curley sent an emissary to the cardinal's residence to beg him to disavow the "endorsement." O'Connell sent word that he was too busy to see him.

orders went up from 110 to 625—a total increase of 263 percent in only a single generation. Clearly the archdiocese still had no problems recruiting an adequate number of candidates for ordination. In 1907, there had been only 86 seminarians enrolled in St. John's; in June 1943, however, 214 candidates were listed on the seminary's rolls. Indeed, at several points during the middle and late 1930s, no doubt reflecting the impact of the lean depression years, the number of seminarians so far exceeded the facilities of the seminary and the positions that would be subsequently available in the parishes that steps were taken to limit the number of candidates who could be accepted each year.

Even more remarkable was the number of young women entering the various female religious orders during the O'Connell years, obviously reflecting the increase in the number of schools, hospitals, and charitable institutions that required their invaluable services. As the number of female religious orders expanded from 29 to 44, the number of women involved more than tripled, rising from 1,567 to 5,469. By this time there were over 90,000 pupils enrolled in parochial schools throughout the archdiocese. In 1907 there were 76 parishes that maintained grammar schools, while only 22 supported high schools; by 1942 there were 158 parishes operating grammar schools, while as many as 67 were supporting high schools.

By the end of O'Connell's episcopacy, the archdiocese was responsible for three major hospitals in Boston—St. Elizabeth's, St. Margaret's, and the Carney Hospital—as well as St. John's and St. Joseph's Hospitals in Lowell and the Holy Ghost Hospital in Cambridge. In addition to such facilities for young people as the House of the Angel Guardian, St. Vincent's and St. Peter's Orphan Asylums, and St. Mary's Infant Asylum, the archdiocese also supported numerous homes for the poor, the elderly, and the homeless. The St. Vincent de Paul Society continued its charitable work, expanding the number of its councils and increasing its membership, but during the years of the Great Depression there was a pressing need for more-organized efforts. Accordingly, the archdiocese created the Diocesan Charitable Bureau, which set up a network of offices, agencies, and bureaus, to bring specialized forms of relief and assistance to those in need. And diocesan leaders did not neglect a unique Boston tradition in helping to meet the needs of Catholic priests and nuns working as missionaries in various parts of the United States and in places throughout the world. The Society for the Propagation of the Faith was established as a diocesan bureau to encourage parishes, church organizations, business associations, and groups of working men and women to provide financial contributions for the work of Catholic missionaries.

Even more impressive than the external corporate and institutional structure of the Boston archdiocese was the strength and vitality of the parish life that pulsated within it. In every parish, where church boundaries were as rigid and clearly defined as the ethnic neighborhoods in which those churches existed, parishioners followed a set pattern of religious devotions and traditional rituals that everyone knew by heart and that had few, if any, variations. Catholic churches were filled to overflowing at Masses on Sundays and Holy Days of Obligation, many parishioners attended early morning Mass regularly, and entire families would kneel down together to recite the rosary every night before going to bed. First-Friday devotions continued in every parish; retreats and novenas attracted thousands of the faithful; first Holy Communions, Confirmations, and May Processions were an accepted part of community life in Catholic Boston. Despite the great number of parishes, churches, schools, hospitals, and other institutions that had grown up throughout the archdiocesan community, Cardinal O'Connell had been able to weld all the separate and highly individual elements into a remarkably coherent and comprehensive force that impressed friend and foe alike. He had succeeded in taking members of what had still been an immigrant Church out of the fears and insecurities of the nineteenth century, making them conscious of their own distinctive religious and cultural heritage, and setting them on the road to a more confident and self-assured future as Catholic Americans in the world of the twentieth century.

Despite its impressive physical growth and its remarkable numerical expansion, however, the Catholic Church during the 1930s and 1940s tended to become more parochial, more separate, more insular. Consciously and deliberately, Boston Catholics set themselves apart from their non-Catholic neighbors, drew themselves together within their own parish boundaries, developed their own social and cultural networks, and showed little or no interest in, or awareness of, the attitudes and interests of other groups. This emphasis on provincial solidarity created an attitude among many Catholics that they had all the answers and needed no one else to enhance their lives or to inform their minds.

Cardinal O'Connell had consciously encouraged the Catholics of Boston to separate themselves from the Protestant, Anglo-Saxon traditions of the Puritan city and to find a new and proud consciousness in their Celtic origins and their Catholic past. In the process, however, the cardinal unwittingly and certainly unintentionally supplied a socioreligious dimension to the political and fiscal policies of Irish bosses like James Michael Curley that divided Boston into two separate, distinctive, and highly antagonistic camps. "The new assertive mood in the church," observed Jack Beatty, Curley's biographer, "closely paralleled the new ethnic policies." As Curley divided the city between the Irish and the Yankees, between those who lived in the neighborhoods and those who lived downtown, O'Connell was adding to the urban dichotomy by separating Catholics from Protestants in religious practices and in social intercourse. This had beneficial results in establishing a new level of personal self-consciousness, a renewed feeling of ethnic pride, and a vigorous sense of self-assurance among members of the emerging Catholic laity. Even so, it could not help contributing to a more intensive sense of division and antagonism among citizens of a city whose political system, social relationships, and physical infrastructure were already showing the unfortunate results of petty feuds and violent confrontations.

Whether the Roman Catholic population of Boston, which was becoming larger, better educated, more affluent, and more politically influential every year, could continue to remain such a separate and disassociated part of the general community was something only time would tell. But certainly, the impact of World War II would go far toward changing the dynamics of American society in ways that most observers could never have thought possible.

ADDITIONAL READING

William Henry Cardinal O'Connell, in contrast to his predecessor, was an eloquent public speaker, a prodigious record keeper, and a prelate with a keen sense of his place in history. A collection of letters covering the early years of his life was published in 1915, *Letters of His Eminence William Cardinal O'Connell, Archbishop of Boston* (Cambridge, 1915); eleven years later he published *Reminiscences of Twenty-Five Years* (Boston, 1926). The celebration of the cardinal's golden jubilee as a priest was the occasion for an expanded work, *Recollections of Seventy Years* (Boston, 1934), and in that same year Monsignor Hugh F. Blunt edited a collection of the cardinal's writings and sermons called *Readings from Cardinal O'Connell* (New York, 1934). Father Robert H. Lord, in the third volume of the *History of the Archdiocese of Boston*, provides a detailed summary of the growth of the archdiocese under O'Connell's direction. Robert E. Sullivan and James M. O'Toole, eds., *Catholic Boston: Studies in Religion and Community, 1870–1970* (Boston, 1985), is a collection of essays by several Boston historians who employ a newer historical methodology to explore the forces that helped shape the Catholic community during the O'Connell years.

Dorothy G. Wayman, *Cardinal O'Connell of Boston: A Biography of William Henry O'Connell, 1859–1944* (New York, 1955), is a respectful work that is especially informative in describing O'Connell's youthful life and his early training and experiences in Rome. James M. O'Toole, *Militant and Triumphant: William Henry O'Connell and the Catholic Church in Boston, 1859–1944* (Notre Dame, Ind., 1992), is a more scholarly study that draws upon Vatican archival sources and concentrates on O'Connell's years as archbishop. Henry A. Brann, *A History of the American College of the Roman Catholic Church of the United States, Rome, Italy* (New York, 1910), has been updated by the work of Robert F. McNamara, *The American College in Rome* (Rochester, N.Y., 1956), in describing the institution where O'Connell studied and where he later became rector.

Thomas H. O'Connor, *Bibles, Brahmins, and Bosses: A Short History of Boston* (3rd ed., Boston, 1991), is helpful in establishing the broad outlines of the city's changing political scene at the turn of the century. Richard M. Abrams, *Conservatism in a Progressive Era: Massachusetts Politics, 1900–1912* (Cambridge, 1964), provides an understanding of the prevailing political ideology in the Bay State. Doris Kearns Goodwin, *The Fitzgeralds and the Kennedys* (New York, 1987), is extremely helpful in describing conditions in the North End, as well as the early life of John F. Fitzgerald, who would become the city's first Boston-born Irish-Catholic mayor in 1905. Dorothy Wayman, *David I. Walsh: Citizen Patriot* (Milwaukee, 1952), has supplied a much-needed biography of the Bay State's first Roman Catholic governor. James Michael Curley, *I'd Do It Again: A Record of All My Uproarious Years* (Englewood Cliffs, N.J., 1957), is Curley's autobiography, written at the end of his political career. Joseph F. Dinneen, *The Purple Shamrock: The Honorable James M. Curley of Boston* (Boston, 1949), is a popular and readable biography of the colorful Boston politician, but Jack Beatty's *Rascal King: The Life and Times of James Michael Curley, 1874–1958* (Reading, Mass., 1992) will remain for some time the most comprehensive study of this controversial figure who was the political champion of the city's people while O'Connell was their religious leader.

William M. Halsey, *The Survival of American Innocence: Catholicism in an Era of Disillusionment, 1920–1940* (Notre Dame, Ind., 1980), and Robert K. Murray, *Red Scare: A Study of National Hysteria, 1919–1920* (Minneapolis, 1955), concentrate on the aftereffects of World War I on American life and society. Timothy J. Meagher, ed.,

From Paddy to Studs: Irish-American Communities in the Turn of the Century Era, 1880–1920 (New York, 1986), is a valuable collection of essays describing the changes in Irish-Catholic attitudes and behavior in the course of the twentieth century. Patrick W. Gearty, *The Economic Thought of Monsignor John A. Ryan* (Washington, 1953), and Francis L. Broderick, *Right Reverend New Dealer: John A. Ryan* (New York, 1963), are studies of the controversial priest who led the movement toward Catholic action during the 1920s and 1930s; John A. Ryan, *Social Doctrine in Action* (New York, 1941), presents the priest's own views. Robert D. Cross, *The Emergence of Liberal Catholicism in America* (Cambridge, 1958), Aaron Abell, *American Catholicism and Social Action: A Search for Social Justice, 1865–1950* (Garden City, N.Y., 1960), and David O'Brien, *American Catholics and Social Reform* (New York, 1968), deal with the larger, philosophical issues of Catholic social action. James J. Kenneally, "Catholicism and Woman Suffrage in Massachusetts," *Catholic Historical Review* 5 (1967), has provided an insightful article about an issue that concerned Cardinal O'Connell. Alan Brinkley, *Voices of Protest: Huey Long, Father Coughlin, and the Great Depression* (New York, 1982), and Charles H. Trout, *Boston, the Great Depression, and the New Deal* (New York, 1977), focus on changing Irish political and social attitudes during the depression years. William V. Shannon, *The American Irish: A Political and Social Portrait* (2d ed., Amherst, Mass., 1989), has some very insightful comments about the reasons for Catholic reaction to the Great Depression and Irish Americans' support for Father Coughlin. John T. McGreevy, *Parish Boundaries: The Catholic Encounter with Race in the Twentieth Century Urban North* (Chicago, 1996), is especially good on relating the religious, ethnic, and political lines of Catholic parishes.

7 Winds of Change

THE YEAR 1945 WAS A SIGNIFICANT ONE IN THE history of the United States. On May 8, after Allied forces had accepted the unconditional surrender of Germany, Americans everywhere celebrated "V-E Day"—victory in Europe over the Nazis. On September 2, the signing of another unconditional surrender led Americans to celebrate "V-J Day"—victory over Japanese forces in the Pacific. Rejoicing at the conclusion of World War II was dampened only by the awesome implications of the weapon that, although it had hastened the end of the conflict, had also ushered in the terrifying Atomic Era.

The year 1945 also proved to be a significant one in the religious history of Boston. On Saturday, April 22, 1944, William Henry Cardinal O'Connell had died quietly in his bed at the age of eighty-four. After remaining at the Brighton residence over the weekend for private viewing, his body lay in state at the Cathedral of the Holy Cross in the South End, where a quarter of a million persons solemnly filed past to see the prelate laid out in his ceremonial robes. An impressive funeral Mass was held on Friday morning, presided over by the apostolic delegate, Archbishop Amleto Cicognani, and attended by state and local dignitaries. Twenty-five hundred persons were seated inside the cathedral, and ten thousand others stood outside listening to the services through an amplifying system. The casket was returned to Lake Street, and then escorted to a small chapel behind St. John's Seminary, where Cardinal O'Connell was buried. It was the end of a remarkable era.

The question now was, who would succeed O'Connell? Five years earlier, his auxiliary bishop, Francis J. Spellman, had left Boston to replace the late Cardinal Patrick Hayes as archbishop of New York. This meant that Richard J. Cushing, then aged forty-four, who had moved up to become auxiliary bishop of Boston, appeared to have become the logical successor to O'Connell. But in the past Rome had made some unexpected decisions where the see of Boston was concerned, and there were other names and more-senior candidates under consideration. Then, too, young Cushing had some potential drawbacks. Although he had a reputation as an effective administrator, and was well known for his support of the missions, he had not attended the North American College, he had never been to Europe, he spoke no foreign languages, and he had no personal friends in Vatican circles. And so everyone waited to learn what the final decision would be. The wait was not long. On September 28, 1944, official word came from Pope Pius XII that Richard J. Cushing, at the age of forty-nine, was the new archbishop of Boston.

He was the son of Patrick Cushing of Glanworth, Ireland, who left his job as a nail maker and sailed out of Cobh in 1879 to join his brother Richard in Rye, New York. After a two-year apprenticeship as a blacksmith, Pat moved to South Boston, where he worked in the repair pits for the Boston Elevated Railway. In 1890 he married Mary Cahill in the Gate of Heaven Church; the couple lived in a three-decker on East Third Street, a short distance from the car barn where Pat worked. After the birth of two daughters, in 1895 Richard James was born to the Cushings. The boy grew up in the uniquely Irish, staunchly Roman Catholic, and solidly working-class neighborhood of South Boston. After the family moved to O Street in St. Eulalia's Parish, Dick attended the local public schools, where he was regarded as a bright youngster with a quick memory and a good speaking voice. During these early years, Dick also became involved in the parish, doing odd jobs, mowing lawns, and shoveling snow; he also came under the influence of the church's first pastor, Father Mortimer F. Twomey. Indeed, many years later, Cushing said that it was Father Twomey who first planted the seed in his mind of becoming a priest.

After graduating from the Perry School in 1908, young Cushing entered South Boston High School, but he decided to drop out and go to work. An uncle in New York, however, made it possible for him to go to the Jesuit-run Boston College High School, then located in Boston's South End. At first, Cushing kept up with his studies quite well, but by his junior year his various outside jobs began to take a toll on his health as well as on his grades. The prefect of studies sent for Cushing's father and suggested that Dick might be happier elsewhere; recognizing the importance of schooling, however, Patrick Cushing quietly advised his son to give up the outside work, concentrate on his studies, and remain at B.C. High. "Do the best you can," he said. "'Tis all God asks. He'll do the rest." Dick took his father's advice, attended to his schoolwork, and began to improve his academic standing. In his senior year, he was designated the best speaker in the Bapst Debating Society, and was chosen as one of the three orators for the graduation exercises. He won the Edward J. Campbell Medal for scholastic excellence, and took second prize for academic achievement in Latin and Greek. Although in later years Cushing usually downplayed his academic accomplishments, contemporaries remember him as a bright, serious, hard-working student, with a puckish sense of humor, a penchant for raising money, and a talent for organization.

Cushing had thought about joining the Jesuits after high school graduation, but in September 1913 he enrolled at Boston College, which had just moved out of its original South End location and was now situated at Chestnut Hill. A tall, husky young man, with a square lantern jaw and the build of a football player, Richard Cushing traveled back and forth to school on the streetcar and entered into the excitement of college life. Even so, he was still doing a few odd jobs at St. Eulalia's and keeping in contact with Father Twomey. In his sophomore year, Cushing was elected vice president of his class, and he won several medals, including one in debating. The idea of becoming a priest was still in the back of his mind, however, and at the conclusion of his second year he decided to move in that direction. In September 1915, however, after the sinking of the *Lusitania* by a German submarine, Cushing enlisted in the U.S. Army, only to be quickly discharged because of a serious asthmatic condition. After that, he took the plunge. With a strong letter of recommendation from Father Twomey, the young man enrolled at St. John's Seminary.

There were few indications that Cushing was an exceptional intellect, but he was obviously a "plugger" who worked hard at his studies. By the end of his second year at the seminary, he made the honors list and was one of three top seminarians chosen by Cardinal O'Connell to go to the prestigious North American College in Rome. But with hostile German submarines patrolling the Atlantic, the rector of St. John's prudently canceled the trip rather than risk the lives of the three seminarians. Cushing, therefore, never acquired the Old World panache and the same spirit of *Romanità* that so often flavored the ideas and pronouncements of his cardinal.

At St. John's Seminary in 1919 he was elected secretary of the Mission Academia, a student organization designed to promote the missions, and in his senior year he was elected its president. In that same year he was named second prefect, meaning that he was the second best scholar in his class. After six years of study, he was ordained by Cardinal O'Connell on May 20, 1921, in the Cathedral of the Holy Cross. On the following Sunday, he said his first Mass at his home parish of St. Eulalia's in South Boston with his mother and other members of his family in attendance. After serving several short stints at three different parishes, he finally decided that he was not cut out for parish work. Going directly to Cardinal O'Connell, young Father Cushing asked to be sent off to the missions—to China, or Africa, or the Solomon Islands—"Anywhere, I'm big and strong," he told the bemused prelate. A few weeks later, Cushing was assigned to go around speaking on behalf of the Society for the Propagation of the Faith. After a year and a half, he was assigned to work under Monsignor Joseph McGlinchey as assistant director of the society in the Boston office on Granby Street. His major tasks were to encourage religious vocations, collect money, and make Boston Catholics much more aware of the importance of foreign missions.

Although Cushing attended to meeting all these goals, it was as a fundraiser that he achieved perhaps his greatest success and recognition at the time. No matter that he had not studied in Rome or traveled through Europe—by priestly instinct, by the encouragement of Cardinal O'Connell (who was a generous benefactor of the foreign missions), and by his years with the Society for the Propagation of the Faith, he developed a comprehensive understanding of the universality of the Catholic Church. "I have always pictured myself on the deck of the bark of St. Peter," he once said, "looking out on the Universal Church." Working around the clock at the Granby Street office, Cushing devised all kinds of methods to meet the appeals from nuns and priests in China, Africa, the Pacific Islands, and throughout Latin America.

It was in recognition of his work with the missions that in 1939 Pope Pius XII raised Cushing to the rank of monsignor, and only two months later that the pontiff named the young priest from South Boston the city's auxiliary bishop. After Bishop Spellman left for New York, Cushing continued his work with the Society for the Propagation of the Faith. But he also served as what one writer called Cardinal O'Connell's "action man" until he himself was finally apointed archbishop of Boston in 1944. Even in his new post, Cushing continued his efforts on behalf of the foreign missions. To support such efforts in China, he formed the Sen Fu Club for women and a comparable organization for men called the Father Jim Hennessy Club, named after a priest friend who had been killed in the South Pacific during World War II.

In 1958, after he had become archbishop, Cushing created the Society of St. James the Apostle. This was an organization of diocesan priests who would volunteer to serve in Latin American countries where Cushing feared that grinding poverty and a scarcity of priests would open the way for Communism. By 1962, the Society of St. James had over seventy priests (working with priests from Ireland, and later from other countries) serving more than four hundred thousand Latin Americans in Ecuador, Bolivia, and Peru. In the summer of 1960, during a eucharistic congress, Cushing himself visited Peru and later Bolivia, seeing at first hand the desperate circumstances of the people. Upon his return to Boston, he stepped up his fundraising efforts in order to supply more priests and more money for his missionary work.

The journalist Joseph Dever described Cushing's efforts as a pleader for financial aid to the foreign missions as positively "shameless and irrepressible." Well-to-do industrialists, prominent businessmen, supportive politicians, successful sports figures, and assorted sympathetic millionaires turned over substantial checks after a tearful story and a hearty handshake. With a creative sense of public relations that was the envy of most professionals, he drew on the idea of the old medieval guilds to form associations that not only supported Catholic action but also served as effective sources of money for his charities.* From devoted groups of men and women at the Boston Gas Company, the Boston Edison Company, the Boston Fire and Police Departments, the Boston City Employees, the Gillette Razor Company, and many other downtown organizations the archbishop received regular and generous contributions. Cushing's interest in working people, on

* St. Luke's Guild, for example, was for doctors; St. Appollonia's for dentists; St. Agatha's for nurses; St. Michael's for communication workers; St. Ives's for lawyers; St. Francis de Sales's for journalists; and St. Joseph's for all workers.

the other hand, was demonstrated by the numerous workers' chapels he set up in such locations as Logan Airport, the South Station railroad terminal, the Fish Pier, and on Arch Street (St. Anthony's Shrine) in the midst of Boston's downtown shopping district. And he also encouraged the men, women, and children of every parish in the archdiocese to support him in his worthy causes. At parish reunions and church bazaars, at testimonial banquets and regional conferences, with weekly envelopes at church and special mailings at home, he took up collections for his building programs and other efforts.

In 1945, as Richard J. Cushing was starting to take over leadership of the Archdiocese of Boston, the Catholic Church, both in the United States and in New England, seemed particularly strong and healthy. Despite dire predictions that spiritual impulses would gradually disappear after World War II, organized religion in the country during the late 1940s and 1950s actually showed a great deal of vitality. Catholics in the 1950s manifested "a real buoyancy and hopefulness," recalled Rev. William J. Leonard, SJ, of Boston College, shortly after he returned from military service as a chaplain in the Philippines during World War II. "The threat of atomic devastation did not deter us from putting up buildings as if they would stand forever." Indeed, there was a rapid rise in total church membership in all major denominations throughout the United States, growing from 64 million persons in 1940 (49 percent of the total population) to almost 87 million in 1950 (57 percent), and then exceeding 100 million (61 percent) in 1955. Clearly, organized religion was continuing to grow at a vigorous rate.

The American public displayed a lively interest in spiritual themes relating to the turmoil of persons' inner lives in an unstable world. Dr. Norman Vincent Peale's *Power of Positive Thinking*, Rabbi Joshua Liebman's *Peace of Mind*, and Thomas Merton's *Seven Storey Mountain* were some of the most widely read books of the period; millions more Americans listened to the sermons of the Reverend Billy Graham, or tuned in to the television programs of Bishop Fulton

J. Sheen. Books dealing with inspirational themes crowded the best-seller lists, newspapers gave increased attention to religious topics, and magazines expanded their sections devoted to religion. Motion pictures such as *The Song of Bernadette, Going My Way, The Bells of St. Mary's,* and *The Keys of the Kingdom* were box-office successes, and leading actors like James Cagney, Bing Crosby, Pat O'Brien, and Spencer Tracy were cast in positive and compassionate roles as Catholic priests.

Another factor that no doubt helped to solidify the influence of religion in America during the 1940s and 1950s was the beginning of the "Cold War" between the United States and the Soviet Union. The intense struggle against the expansion of World Communism after World War II led many to concentrate upon all those features of the Communist system of the East that differed from those of the capitalist system of the West. One of the main differences was, of course, religion. Since Communism was dogmatically atheistic, it logically followed that Americans should hold a strong and equally dogmatic belief in God. In this manner, the culture of the 1950s saw organized religion in general, and the Catholic Church in particular, not only as a source of personal reassurance in an age of great anxiety but also as a highly visible means of identifying which nation had the protection of Almighty God in the struggle against World Communism.

Archbishop Cushing took up the crusade against Communism with ferocity and determination. He greatly admired J. Edgar Hoover, chief of the FBI, as an outstanding champion in the war against World Communism, and he later extended the same type of praise and support to the anti-Communist activities of Senator Joseph McCarthy. In his inimitable fashion, Cushing tended to label people whom he identified as holding left-wing, liberal, or radical views as either full-fledged Communists or as dangerous "fellow travelers." It was very simple: anyone who was an enemy of Communism was a friend of Cushing's—and vice versa.

As the new archbishop of Boston, therefore, Richard Cushing inherited both a strong religious organization and a supportive attitude of social acceptance. After the war, Catholic life in most parishes moved along old familiar paths, continuing to offer its adherents an active and fulfilling spiritual life. And the congregations responded with eagerness and enthusiasm. During the late 1940s and early 1950s, Catholic churches were still filled to overflowing at each Mass on Sundays and Holy Days of Obligation; parishioners went to confession every Saturday night; the altar rails were crowded with communicants every Sunday morning. These were years when parishioners could kneel in reverential awe at a Solemn High Mass with three celebrants on the altar, moving in unison with slow, measured pace in their gold-encrusted robes, intoning the Latin liturgy as the sounds of a mighty organ echoed through the soaring vaults of a great Gothic church. Old people and young people trudged through the snow on cold February mornings during Lent to attend early morning Mass; families joined together on Christmas Eve for the colorful tradition of midnight Mass, where well-trained choirs sang out the Yuletide message; mothers and fathers still lined the streets of the neighborhoods to watch their children take part in the annual May Procession. Novenas, retreats, stations of the cross, noctural adoration services, and other devotional activities flourished throughout the archdiocese. Devout Catholics regularly attended holy-hour devotions in large numbers, especially on the first Friday of the month, where solemn benediction would take place to the ringing of bells and the sweet odor of incense, while every member of the congregation joined the choir in chanting *Pange Lingua* and *Tantum Ergo* (everyone knew the Latin words) and then, after the final prayers, sang the favorite closing hymn, "Good Night, Sweet Jesus."

The active participation of parishioners in the numerous liturgical activities throughout the archdiocese showed no signs of slowing down. Overflow crowds still attended novena services every Wednesday night at the Mission Church, where the well-known Redemptorist preacher Father Joseph E. Manton held his listeners spellbound with his eloquent oratory. Retreats for men and women, with special services for young people, continued to be a regular part of each parish's religious calendar, providing at least one major opportunity each year for a period of intensive personal reflection and spiritual renewal. The archbishop himself led numerous pilgrimages overseas, many of them with groups of disabled and retarded children, to such sacred shrines as those at Lourdes and at Fatima so that the inspiration of the universal Church could be brought back to Boston. Devout Catholics continued the practices of wearing the scapular medal underneath their clothing, pinning their miraculous medals on their outer clothing during the entire month of May, and sprinkling their houses with holy water to safeguard their loved ones and protect their homes. The recitation of the rosary continued to be a favorite source of personal devotion to Catholics of all ages, bringing solace to patients in hospitals, comfort to the elderly in nursing homes, and sustenance for entire families who knelt down together in the evening to pray.

Archbishop Cushing was well aware of the value of keeping in touch with his flock in prayer, especially with the sick and the infirm. "His residence became a sort of radio studio," recalled Bishop Lawrence Riley. He would say Mass every Sunday morning over the radio, and recite the rosary every morning and every evening. After the rosary on one night every week he would give a fifteen-minute meditation; on another evening he would give a forty-five-minute prayer service, ending with benediction. Each evening, the distinctive sound of him bellowing out "Hai-i-i-l Mary!" in his nasal twang brought smiles of pleasure to untold thousands of bedridden souls, who found comfort in the voice of a friend who understood their pain and loneliness. To continue this kind of modern apostolate, in 1955 Cushing established WIHS-TV, the first specifically Catholic television station in America—the only such facility in the United States owned and operated by a Catholic see.

During the 1940s and 1950s, societies and associations that had first started under Archbishop Williams and then expanded remarkably under Cardinal O'Connell took on new size and vigor under Cushing. Women's sodalities had substantial enrollments, and members worked to help parishes care for their churches, maintain schools, and raise funds for parish improvements. The League of Catholic Women, which had been founded in 1910, had attained an enrollment of at least 7,500 members during the 1940s; it provided volunteers who sponsored lectures, prepared educational programs, worked in hospitals and nursing homes, and raised money for archdiocesan charities. The Proparvulis Club of Boston (meaning "for the little ones"), founded by Cardinal O'Connell in 1922 as a means by which young women could work to benefit needy children, was thriving. For the men of the archdiocese, the Knights of Columbus offered an opportunity for both fraternal association and organized Catholic action. The Holy Name Society, however, was perhaps the most active and comprehensive outlet for vigorous displays of Catholicism throughout the archdiocese during the postwar years. In June 1945, for example, a month after V-E Day, some 30,000 members of the Holy Name Society gathered at Fenway Park to commemorate the nearly 4,000 Catholic servicemen from the archdiocese who had died for their country; three months later, 45,000 young people filled Boston College Alumni Field to observe a holy hour; and the following June, 40,000 men crowded into Braves Field for another holy hour at which Archbishop Cushing awarded citations to Catholic chaplains. Here were impressive public displays of loyalty and devotion that demonstrated the continued vitality of the archdiocese of Boston.

And there were signs that this growth and vitality would continue well into the future. Returning veterans had already started their families, had their children baptized in the Catholic Church, and were beginning to send these children into the local parochial schools, which were expanding at a phenomenal rate under the archbishop's energetic building program. The Catholic Youth Organization (CYO) had developed into a major group for young Catholic boys and girls, providing opportunities for religious formation through catechetical

A dramatic indication of the extraordinary size and enthusiasm of Catholic action can be seen in this diocesan congress of the League of Catholic Women at Boston's Statler Hilton Hotel. Founded in 1910 as a means by which Catholic women could provide volunteer programs and charitable assistance for the archdiocese, the league achieved an all-time high membership of about 7,500 women during the 1940s. (Courtesy of the Archdiocese of Boston.)

programs, weekend retreats, and similar spiritual activities, while also offering opportunities for cultural development with public-speaking programs and musical activities. There was hardly a civic celebration, a patriotic event, or a St. Patrick's Day parade that did not feature several CYO bands from parishes throughout the archdiocese. The Catholic Church in Boston was still looking confidently to the future and preparing its young people to take their place as leaders of tomorrow. "Nuns still prepared boys in bow ties and girls in white dresses for first communion, parishes sponsored dances and dinners, altar boys struggled to learn Latin responses," the historian John McGreevy remarks of the postwar decades. "The Catholic world," he concludes, "remained encompassing."

In this comfortable and familiar setting, the new archbishop continued many of the policies of his predecessor—although with an approach that was all his own. Moving into the palatial residence in Brighton, he replaced the old cardinal's retinue of servants with a group of nuns, who thereafter staffed the residence. A number of rare paintings and expensive pieces of furniture disappeared in favor of a collection of filing cabinets, typewriters, mimeograph machines, and other equipment that turned the palazzo into a working office. From here, Cushing administered a multimillion-dollar operation whose property was listed under the name of "The Roman Catholic Archbishop of Boston" as a corporation sole.

In many ways, Cushing's plans for the archdiocese were fairly traditional, and he carried on a number of the programs and projects begun during the O'Connell years. Immediately upon assuming office in 1944, he commenced the prodigious building program that soon made him a legend in the field of fundraising. He was convinced that Catholic education was not only a means of raising the intellectual and cultural standards of young Catholics but also a means by which they could convey the spirit of Christ (as "lay apostles") in their homes and offices, in their professions, and in government service, "making moral principles known and respected."

From 1944 to 1960, the Catholic population of the archdiocese was going up at a rate of about 250,000 to 300,000 every five years—an aggregate of well over half a million new parishioners in the first fifteen years of Cushing's episcopacy. Although the number of parishes also increased during this period, growing from 325 in 1944 to 396 in 1960, the rate of increase was much smaller than the overall increase in population. Similarly, the number of diocesan priests serving in the Boston parishes did not change much beyond the 1,292 recorded in 1944. Indeed, following a dramatic jump after the end of World War II that brought the number of priests to 1,939, the total gradually declined to 1,152 in 1960. A few observers were already expressing concern that the number of Catholics in the archdiocese was rising much faster than the number of priests available to serve them.

What concern there was about the future, however, was quieted by statistics showing an encouraging number of young people going into religious life. In 1944, there were 4,054 young women serving in 44 female religious orders throughout the archdiocese; by 1960 that figure had risen to 5,543, representing 63 different orders, and reports indicated that the ranks of nuns and sisters would continue to grow. Likewise, the number of young men enrolling at St. John's Seminary gave every indication that Boston would have a plentiful supply of priests to serve the growing Catholic population. When Cushing became archbishop in 1944, there were 253 seminarians; six years later there were 277, and in 1960 the figure jumped to an all-time high of 418. Indeed, the archdiocese had so many priests that Cushing developed a unique "lend-lease" policy, named after the military-assistance program of World War II, by which he could send priests from Boston to dioceses in many other parts of the country where there were serious shortages. In 1946, five Boston priests were sent to the diocese of Sioux Falls, South Dakota; in following years, others received assignments to Utah, Louisiana, Florida, Texas, Colorado, Wyoming, and other places where they were needed.*

Confident of a loyal base of support and a steady supply of money, Archbishop Cushing launched an ambitious building program to construct more churches for his parishioners and more schools for a new generation of Catholic children. Starting with 66 diocesan high schools in 1944, he supervised the construction of 6 more, bringing the total to 72 by 1960. Similarly, the 158 diocesan elementary schools in 1944 grew to 169 by 1955, and then to 211 by 1960, marking the addition of 53 new elementary schools in a little over fifteen years. From all accounts the prospects looked bright, and there seemed to be no reason why Cushing should not go on building, well into the future, what John H. Fenton of the *New York Times* described as "one

* Cushing's program still continues. In August 1997, for example, Boston priests received assignments to Charlotte, North Carolina; Santa Fe, New Mexico; and Phoenix, Arizona.

of the most extensive and best-equipped Catholic parochial school systems in the country."

Despite what appeared to be the established and unchanging nature of the American religious scene, however, two developments were to have significant effects upon traditional attitudes and beliefs. One was the gradual disappearance of the excessive denominalization that had characterized American religions and the emergence of greater cooperation among the various churches. Stimulated by the numerous interdenominational activities that had taken place during World War II, a number of leading Protestant denominations began to explore new methods of reducing rivalries and encouraging greater cooperation. In November 1950, twenty-five Protestant denominations and five Eastern Orthodox bodies joined together in the National Council of Churches of Christ. In 1957, the Congregational Christian churches and the Evangelical Reformed churches merged into the United Church of Christ. In 1958, Presbyterian groups formed the United Presbyterian Church; in 1960 various Lutheran groups merged into the American Lutheran Church; and the following year Unitarians and Universalists combined to create the Unitarian-Universalist Association. For the first time in history, too, Protestants and Catholics—the two largest religious groupings in the United States—entered into what was called an ecumenical movement, which promised great advances in mutual understanding and cooperation.

The other major reason for changing religious attitudes during the 1950s and 1960s was related to the maturing of a new generation of young American Catholics, shaped by the experiences of World War II and transformed by the social and economic forces of the postwar years. Most of these young people were second- and third-generation Americans of Irish, Italian, and German descent, born, raised, and educated in the United States. Most of them came from middle-class backgrounds, and a number of them were the first members of their families to attend college. As a result of their travels and experiences during World War II, they tended to be less defensive about their ethnic origins and less parochial in their religious convictions. During their years in the armed forces, most of them had attended Mass in the same multipurpose post chapel where Jewish services had been held the previous evening, and where a variety of Protestant services took place at other hours on Sunday. They had seen a Jewish rabbi consoling a wounded Irish-Catholic soldier from Brooklyn, or they had watched a Catholic priest giving the last rites to a dying Baptist sailor from Georgia. Suddenly the old ways of doing things just didn't seem the same any more; the old restrictions and formalities seemed ridiculously out of date. The new generational reactions were more open and tolerant—remarkably consistent with the new so-called ecumenical movement that was making headway throughout the nation.

Archbishop Cushing read the signs. He saw that new times called for new approaches—that the rising generation of younger, more mature, and more self-assured Irish Catholics was looking for something different. And Cushing, certainly, was something "different." A crusty, unpredictable, outgoing cleric from South Boston, who had made a name for himself by successfully directing the local office of the Society for the Propagation of the Faith, the archbishop set a new course for himself and for his people that was dramatically different from that of his predecessor. Cushing concerned himself with updating the Church and making it relevant to the everyday lives of ordinary people. Breezy and extroverted, he welcomed publicity, courted photographers, mingled with all sorts of people from the very rich to the very poor, and generally showed a remarkable grasp of the potential of the modern media to dramatize his policies and his goals.

But Cushing was more than just a new man in town with a charismatic personality and an effective public-relations campaign. He was genuinely interested in defining a new level of human and spiritual relations in an archdiocese that heretofore had not been particularly noted for being warm, welcoming, or tolerant toward those who were new and those who were "different." Geared to the interests of the rising generation of Catholics, he worked in the current spirit of ecumenism, and pledged to refrain from "all arguments with our non-

Catholic neighbors and from all purely defensive talk about Catholics." The archbishop unceremoniously began to brush aside many of the barriers that for so long had separated his Catholic parishioners from their non-Catholic neighbors.

Ecumenism did not come easily to Boston, a city that never took kindly to change in any form. The divisions between Yankee and Celt, Protestant and Catholic were unusually deep and went back hundreds of years. There were still many Catholics who could remember the signs that hung on factory gates announcing No Irish Need Apply; there were just as many Protestants who could not let go of their suspicions of a Papist conspiracy orchestrated by the Vatican.

Despite his determination to put old rivalries behind him, and his promise to refrain from sectarian disputes, Cushing nevertheless was drawn into religious controversies during the late 1940s and early 1950s. One reason was Paul Blanshard's best-selling book, *American Freedom and Catholic Power.* It resurrected the old nineteenth-century fear of a Catholic conspiracy, and it charged that the principles of the Church still could not be reconciled with the American ideals of freedom and democracy. Indeed, just when the United States was becoming involved in the Cold War with the Soviet Union, Blanshard went so far as to suggest that Rome and Moscow were remarkably similar in the techniques they used to control the minds of their adherents. He used the occasion of a series of large public gatherings of Catholics in Boston during 1945 and 1946 as evidence of intimidation on the part of the Church. Blanshard professed to see in these, and in similar gatherings, deliberate attempts by the Catholic Church to put its power on display in order to encourage its friends and frighten its foes. His views received outright support and approval from local Protestant leaders like the Reverend Harold J. Ockenga, pastor of the Park Street Church, who agreed that growing Catholic power was a threat to the future of America, and they got a sympathetic hearing from many other non-Catholics in whose hearts and minds Blanshard's attacks had struck a responsive chord.

Despite these and other occasional disputes with various Protestant leaders,* the archbishop continued to push for more cordial relations with the non-Catholic community. Anticipating many of the changes that would come with the Second Vatican Council, he preached to Protestant groups, spoke before Jewish audiences, and generally worked to promote feelings of fellowship and goodwill among large numbers of ethnic and religious groups in the greater Boston area. This was something that would have been unthinkable during the 1930s and 1940s, when Catholics were forbidden to set foot in the churches or temples of other religious groups or to participate in the functions of non-Catholic faiths. But the sincerity of Cushing's style, the friendliness of his manner, and the obvious warmth of his compassion caused people to accept the new episcopal approach as the most natural thing in the world.

In reaching out to establish better relations with the non-Catholic community, the archbishop was especially concerned with relations between the Catholics of Boston and their Jewish neighbors. For a long time there had existed in many of Boston's Catholic neighborhoods an ugly undercurrent of anti-Semitism, fueled in part by the popular misconception that since the Jews were responsible for the crucifixion of Jesus Christ they were "Christ killers." This attitude was undoubtedly promoted by the anti-Semitic tirades of Father Coughlin in his weekly radio programs during the late 1930s and early 1940s, and it resulted in an outbreak of Jew-baiting in Dorchester, Brookline, and Chelsea. Young hoodlums, claiming to be patriots and Christians, invaded Jewish neighborhoods, broke windows, stoned houses, and beat up Jewish boys and girls on their way to school. In the 1944 St. Patrick's Day parade in South Boston, a gang of young Irish Americans attacked several Jewish members of a marching band from Malden, and a short time later John W. McCormack, the district's popular congressman, was vilified for having appointed a Jew

* Cushing also clashed openly and angrily with several local Protestant ministers who visited Tito's Yugoslavia in 1947 and reported that Catholics enjoyed freedom of worship.

In October 1964, Richard Cardinal Cushing met for the first time with Dr. Billy Graham, who was conducting one of his "crusades" in Boston. Cushing urged young people to go to the Boston Garden and hear the evangelist. "His message is one of Christ crucified, and no Catholic can do anything but become a better Catholic after listening to him." The evangelist said he considered Cardinal Cushing "the leading ecumenist in America today." (Courtesy of NC Photos.)

to the United States Naval Academy. Although there was never any indication that members of the Catholic hierarchy were involved in these episodes, many people criticized the clergy for not having taken a stronger public stand against anti-Semitism.

It was against this historical background that Archbishop Cushing came out publicly against anti-Semitism in any form. In November 1948, he addressed the fifteen hundred delegates of the American Hebrew Congregations, who were meeting in Boston. "No man could have my faith concerning Christ," he told them, "without desiring to be more like Him and, therefore, seek, like Him, to help and befriend all men without exception—white, black, Gentile, Jew." He asked the members of his audience not to believe the malicious charges many Christians were making about Jews. "These are lies," he exclaimed, "and they are uttered in order to delude us." And he followed through on this position. When further troubles threatened in some neighborhoods, Cushing had his priests speak out against anti-Semitism at Masses on Sunday, and in several instances he sent priests into private homes to speak to the parents of young people causing the trouble. Moreover, he himself made every effort to meet with members of the Jewish community, speaking at their breakfasts, attending their meetings, developing close personal friendships, and supporting Jewish charities. And he boasted that his own brother-in-law, a man he praised as a "devoted husband" and a "great example to me," was Jewish.

In light of his efforts to establish more cordial relations between the Catholic Church and the non-Catholic communities, the "Feeney Affair" in the early 1950s caused Cushing much personal pain and embarrassment. Father Leonard Feeney was a Jesuit priest who taught at Boston College during the 1930s and later gained a popular following with his witty books and charming essays. Not long after becoming a chaplain at St. Benedict's Center in Cambridge, where Catholic students from Harvard and Radcliffe gathered, he began to proclaim that "outside the Church there is no salvation." He became inflexible in his pronouncements, refused to countenance dissenting views, and gathered a small but fanatically devoted following. On Sunday afternoons, Father Feeney could be found preaching on Boston Common, directing his wrath against Protestants, Jews, and anyone else who would not come into the Church.

Although Feeney was removed from St. Benedict's Center, and later expelled from the Jesuit order, he continued his public diatribes against "outsiders." Archbishop Cushing was clearly annoyed by the problems Feeney was causing for his ecumenical attempts to promote friendlier relations with non-Catholics, but he held off as long as possible before taking official action. He knew Father Feeney personally, and hoped to persuade him to cease his scandalous activities, but Rome stepped in and took matters out of his hands. Father Feeney was formally excommunicated. Shortly thereafter, he and his most devoted followers moved away to a small town on the outskirts of Worcester, where, as "Slaves of the Immaculate Heart of Mary," they formed their own religious communities. In his later years, Father Feeney was reconciled with the Church, and on November 22, 1972, the excommunication was lifted quietly and without publicity in Cambridge.

In addition to promoting a spirit of ecumenism among various religious groups in the non-Catholic community, the new archbishop also promoted the idea of greater involvement with members of his own community. Preaching a gospel of inclusion, he reached out to those he felt had been restricted to the margins of human compassion. He said Mass for inmates at Walpole State Prison, accompanied groups of nuns to baseball games at Fenway Park, and personally sliced turkey and sang songs at annual Thanksgiving dinners for elderly people at Blinstrub's Village in South Boston. He dedicated himself to improving the lives of mentally retarded and physically disabled children (whom he called "special children"), and in 1947 he brought the Sisters of St. Francis of Assisi of Milwaukee to Boston. They established a school for the children on a 175-acre site at Hanover; originally

In addition to his love for the foreign missions and the establishment of the Society of St. James the Apostle for work in Latin America, Cardinal Cushing always had a special concern for children with mental and physical disabilities, referring to them as his "special children." He is buried, at his own request, in the Portiuncula Chapel, Hanover, on the campus of a school for retarded children. (Courtesy of the Archdiocese of Boston.)

called St. Coletta-by-the-Sea, it was later renamed the Cardinal Cushing School.*

It was easy to underestimate the new archbishop from South Boston and to underrate his accomplishments. With his high-pitched raspy voice (the voice of a fish peddler, laughed one priest friend), his open, friendly, genuinely glad-handed manner, and his constant assurances that he really did not understand complicated theological

---

* Cardinal Cushing chose the Portiuncula Chapel at Hanover, a replica of the chapel in Assisi, Italy, where St. Francis lived and died, as the site of his own final resting place.

issues ("I'm no theologian," he often croaked), Cushing created a non-threatening image that allowed him to accomplish things that otherwise might not have been possible. But this surface congeniality and easygoing manner also kept many people unaware of a deep and abiding spirituality, a devotion to the hidden purposes of Almighty God, that gave purpose and meaning to his own designs and purposes for the faithful of the archdiocese. Coincidentally but significantly, the new archbishop's ecumenical approach was also clearly in tune with the political exhortations of Mayor John B. Hynes, who had defeated James Michael Curley in November 1949 and who was urging the citizens of Boston to put aside their differences and work together for the renewal and reconstruction of the city. To have the prestigious religious leader of the community voicing the same humanitarian ideals and moral sentiments as the city's political leader could not help but create a new and healthier climate in which fundamental improvements could finally take place.

Halfway through his years as archbishop, Cushing was afflicted by a series of illnesses that endangered his life and threatened to end his episcopacy. Already burdened by chronic asthma and the early stages of emphysema, in December 1953 he was operated on for a gall bladder condition and also had his prostate gland removed. A short time later, a cancerous tumor was taken from his kidney. Despite the loss of over forty pounds, which left him looking haggard, Cushing refused to retire. He plunged back into his active routine with no discernible letup, "running here and there, dictating correspondence to three secretaries," said Monsignor Thomas Finnegan, a close friend and the cardinal's last chancellor. "He was dynamic," recalled Finnegan, "building parishes, convents, schools, and hospitals—and, of course, on the phone begging for financial assistance."

In August 1958 Cushing traveled to Europe, stopping at Rome to visit with the ailing Pope Pius XII. After going to Lourdes, he crossed over to Ireland, where he was greeted by the people of Cork with wild rejoicing. He had hardly returned to Boston in mid-September when he learned that the pope had died; subsequently, Angelo Giuseppe Roncalli, archbishop of Venice, was elected head of the Roman Catholic Church as Pope John XXIII. Many observers viewed the new pontiff as (at age seventy-eight) a humble and pious old man, a "caretaker pope" who would keep the papal seat warm until a younger and more sophisticated replacement could be found. Once in office, however, Pope John became a veritable dynamo of energy who set in motion a series of events that would change history and transform the Roman Catholic Church.

At eleven o'clock at night, on November 16, 1958, Archbishop Cushing received a telephone call from the apostolic delegate, Archbishop Amleto Cicognani of Washington, informing him that in recognition of his "glowing charity" and his "burning zeal for souls" he would be elevated to cardinal. All Boston, young and old, Catholic and non-Catholic, rejoiced in the announcement. Cushing reveled in the cheers and applause from priests, nuns, seminarians, schoolchildren, and parishioners—but warned everyone that his new exalted position would make no difference in how he carried out his duties as archbishop. He would continue to visit prisons, orphanages, old people, the disabled, and the retarded. Knowing little about Cardinal Roncalli before he became Pope John XXIII, Cushing was delighted to learn that the new pope was a kind and humble man, that he came from a working-class family, and that he too visited prisoners and comforted the sick and the dying. On December 10 Cushing arrived at Logan Airport, and moved through cheering throngs at the Alitalia terminal as the Boston Police Band played "Southie Is My Home Town." In company with Archbishop Cicognani and Archbishop John O'Hara of Philadelphia, who had also been designated as cardinals, Cushing took the first of several planes headed for the Eternal City.

Arriving in Rome, Cushing first expressed his pleasure at receiving Santa Susanna as his titular church, and then went off to be measured for his new scarlet robes. On December 16, he was at the North

American College, where he received his *biglietto*, the document delivered by a papal messenger officially notifying him of his elevation. After that, Cushing, Cicognani, and O'Hara left to attend a private consistory at the Vatican Palace, where they received ecclesiastic symbols of their new office. Two days later, December 18, more than thirty thousand persons witnessed the public consistory at St. Peter's Basilica as Pope John was carried to the papal throne. Cushing was tenth in the scarlet line of candidates slowly approaching the pontiff, who embraced each one, exchanged a few words, and bestowed the *galero*, a wide-brimmed tasseled hat, the special badge of their rank.* For a second time in the history of the archdiocese, an archbishop of Boston had become a prince of the Church. The following day, the new cardinal, along with a group of pilgrims, had a private audience with Pope John under more informal circumstances. It pointed up the extraordinary warmth and affection that had almost immediately developed between these two simple and saintly men.

Four years later, in 1962, Pope John called for the assembling of an ecumenical council—the first since the Vatican Council of 1869, and the second since the Council of Trent began in 1545—in order to examine the internal structure of the Church and assess its relationship with the modern world. It was hoped that in restructuring the Church's organization and clarifying many of its basic doctrines, a major step might be taken toward reunion with those other Christian denominations that had become separated from the Catholic Church during the Reformation. Although Pope John died in June 1963, at the end of the first sessions of Vatican II, the second session of the council reconvened in September 1963 under the direction of John's successor, Pope Paul VI. Cardinal Cushing traveled to Rome to attend the meetings of the council, but he was obviously ill at ease listening to long-winded speeches concerning complex theological issues, and

---

* The *galero* was worn only at this consistory. It would not be seen again until the cardinal died, when it was suspended from the roof of the cathedral.

he was clearly frustrated by the use of Latin he could not easily understand. As a result, he spent only short periods in Rome during the
first two sessions of the council, returning to Boston to supervise his
numerous charitable activities and to increase the number of his ecumenical associations in the greater Boston area.

With the third session coming up, Cushing again departed for
Rome, this time determined to speak out on issues that affected him
greatly. During the first two sessions of the council, the bishops from
the United States had been working hard to obtain definitive statements supporting the separation of church and state, ensuring religious liberty, removing traditional denunciations of Jews, and denouncing racial discrimination. On September 23, 1964, speaking on
behalf of "almost all the bishops of the United States," Cardinal Cushing made his first "intervention" at the council by speaking out boldly
in support of the proposed declaration of religious liberty. The time
had come, he declared, for the Church to show herself clearly as "the
champion of liberty, of human liberty, and of civil liberty, especially
in the matter of religion." The same freedom in civil society that the
Church had always insisted upon for herself, he said, she must now
also champion "for other churches and their members, indeed for every human person." Urging that no more amendments be added that
would undermine the proposed declaration, he demanded action:
"I praise and approve this declaration," he said simply. The eventual
declaration, incorporating Cushing's suggestions, was subsequently
passed on December 7, 1965 (*Dignitatis Humanae*), and became the
Church's official teaching on religious freedom.

The force and intensity of the cardinal from Boston were even more
in evidence the following week when, on September 28, Cushing
threw the full weight of his support behind the proposed statement
on the Jews. Speaking in Latin (or at least his version of it) before
the assembled members of the council, Cushing urged the Church to
"manifest to the whole world and to all men a concern which is genuine, an esteem all embracing, a sincere charity." He called for a clear

and positive statement (not a "timid" one) of love for the Jews as "the blood brothers of Christ"; he proposed an explicit statement denying that the Jews had any culpability in the death of Christ; and he urged a public admission that Christians had not always been faithful to the teachings of Jesus Christ in their relations with their Jewish brothers. Looking up from his notes, his eyes swept over the assemblage as he barked out sharply in his raspy voice: *"Dixi"*—"I have spoken." The assembled bishops broke the rules and burst into applause. The Council Fathers may not have understood every word of Cushing's faulty Latin, but they clearly understood the implications of what he had called for. Although there was further discussion and debate, Cushing's suggestions were to be found in the final document of the Second Vatican Council, leaving no doubt of the high regard with which the cardinal from Boston was held among the leaders of the Church and his importance at a critical point in the council's deliberations.

The extent of the changes that Vatican II brought about in the Catholic Church was truly extraordinary. "At no time in Church history, perhaps, had so vast a cultural change come about in so short a time," writes Father William Leonard. Almost no aspect of Catholic life, customs, devotion, piety, or ritual remained untouched. Despite efforts by conservative prelates (the Italians called them *immobilisti*) to halt the changes, or at least slow them down, many traditional forms of worship underwent substantial revisions. The celebrant of the Mass now faced the members of the congregation; they surrounded the altar and participated more actively in liturgies, which were modernized to include new forms of worship. Catholics were allowed to use the vernacular (the local language) in place of Latin in most parts of the Mass and in their sacraments, so that the meaning of their religion would be clearer to Catholics and non-Catholics alike. A number of fasts, rituals, and ceremonies that had once been obligatory now became voluntary—the ban on eating meat on Friday, for example, disappeared in 1966 after the first Sunday of Advent. Many fond and familiar sacramentals—like prayer books, missals, breviaries, scapulars, hymnals, novena booklets, medals, holy cards, sacred pictures—gradually receded into the mists of history. Most religious orders modified their traditional European habits and cassocks in favor of more modern styles of dress, and many left contemplative environments to work with the poor and the underprivileged in urban neighborhoods. And recognizing that American Catholics had become generally more educated and informed, bishops began to encourage lay people to work with pastors on parish councils and financial boards. "A whole subculture vanished at a speed unprecedented, perhaps, in the history of the Church," commented Father Leonard. "Young people now have simply no idea of what it was like to be a Catholic in 1940—or even in 1960."

Even before Vatican II, however, there had been American Catholics, many of them in the Boston area, who could see that World War II was ushering in a completely new phase of world history, when things would no longer be the same. "We may not like it, we may not even admit it," Father William Leonard told Boston College students at the annual Mass of the Holy Spirit in 1947, "but it is a fact that the culture and the civilization our fathers knew are fading forever." Groups of teachers, scholars, nuns, priests, theologians, biblical experts, and concerned lay people felt that they had an obligation to become the "architects" and the "builders" of a new Christian Commonwealth that would be infused by the spirit and principles of Christ, where all would be equal, and where the people would come "not to be served but to serve." Feeling that the spiritual experience of the faithful—the ways in which they worship—would be central to their active participation in such a Christian society, the "builders" began working to make the traditional Latin liturgy more understandable and accessible to the people of God. The language to be used in saying Mass, the location of the altar, the arrangement of the pews, the degree of active participation by the laity at services, the opportunity for evening Masses, the rules of the eucharistic fast, the nature of sacred music, the possibility of dance, the function of sacramentals—liturgists felt that these and many more topics should be studied against the teachings of the Scriptures and the traditions of the Church.

In 1948, Archbishop Cushing invited the national Liturgical Conference to hold its annual "Liturgical Week" in Boston. At first he was unsure about the objectives of the liturgists, and uneasy about any "excessive enthusiasm" that might be displayed by some of the three thousand delegates. At the closing session, however, the prelate extended to the liturgists the facilities of the archdiocese and offered them the cathedral for their educational programs. After two years of preparation, the Boston group traveled to different parishes throughout the archdiocese to put on a variety of lectures and programs; they found, however, a general lack of interest both among lay people and among priests and pastors. Many members of the laity found some of the proposed liturgical innovations unusual, even bizarre. The liturgists discontinued their efforts for a while, turned to further research, and tried to come up with ways of communicating their ideas in a more acceptable manner.

During the 1950s, Pope Pius XII himself showed a personal interest in liturgical reform, writing a long encyclical on the subject of sacred music. In 1956, at the close of the first International Congress on Pastoral Liturgy, held at Assisi, the Holy Father further demonstrated his encouragement by delivering the concluding address in Rome. Stimulated by such reassuring signs of support, during the late 1950s the American liturgists gave lectures and sermons at seminaries, novitiates, retreat houses, high schools, and parishes throughout the country. Each year they gathered for Liturgical Week at various Catholic colleges and universities. Concentrating on Christian life and worship, the participants discussed education, ecumenics, the role of the laity, social worship, biblical studies, interracial justice, art, music, and church architecture. Leaders urged a change from passive and contemplative individual worship to a more active and participatory role in a liturgical celebration they felt should involve the whole community. With the cooperation of the National Council of Catholic Men, the liturgists made film and television productions and designed programs for training lectors and commentators.

In a field of growing interest, researchers and theologians in the greater Boston area made significant contributions to exploring the relationship between early Church teachings and public worship. At St. John's Seminary, Father Philip J. King achieved a national reputation as a leading American archaeologist and biblical scholar. Monsignor J. Joseph Ryan divided his time between the seminary and the Medieval Institute at Toronto, researching the medieval traditions of the Church and their relevance to modern theology. Father Thomas Carroll, director of the archdiocesan Guild of the Blind, was an active proponent of liturgical change, and Mr. Theodore Marier of Cambridge introduced original ideas concerning how new forms of church music could be adapted to community worship. Father William Leonard and his friend Father Joseph Collins inaugurated a series of monthly lectures dealing with new liturgical ideas at Fontbonne Academy in Milton for the sisters of the archdiocese. Held on Sunday afternoon, these programs attracted appreciative audiences of never less than five hundred, predominantly members of the Sisters of St. Joseph. The Fontbonne series proved so popular that the liturgists started one for the sisters in the northern area of the archdiocese and another in the west. Father Leonard found the sisters who attended these sessions active and enthusiastic, "avid for anything that would help them in their apostolic labors."

Clearly, not all Catholics were happy about the kinds of unfamiliar, if not strange, innovations being proposed by the various liturgists; moreover, they were not convinced that many of the innovations were in keeping with the admonitions of the Second Vatican Council in its "Constitution on the Sacred Liturgy," or the subsequent teachings of Pope Paul VI. Sharp, bitter, and sometimes violent reactions took place in many parishes and among many parishioners over the speed with which and extent to which changes should be made in the traditional rituals and practices of their religion. Some Catholics argued that the changes had already gone much too far and were working to the detriment of the Church. Others argued that they had not gone far enough, and were necessary to bring the Church into the modern world. People everywhere took sides: pastors disagreed with their curates; parishioners fought with their pastors; pastors took issue with their bishops; parishioners broke up into "liberal" and "conservative" factions over such questions as using English instead of Latin, singing modern folk music instead of Gregorian chant, and removing statues of favorite saints from the churches. Pastors accused lay people of trying to go too far too fast; parish groups accused pastors of dragging their feet in implementing the mandates of Vatican II. Pastors insisted that lay boards were to serve only in an advisory capacity; lay boards insisted they should be allowed to make policy decisions. It was the beginning of an unsettling and confusing time in the religious life of Catholics who had always viewed their Church as unchanging and unchangeable.

Complicating these tensions and divisions were the numerous strikes, marches, and demonstrations that were sweeping across the nation during the late 1960s, challenging traditional authority and rejecting established institutions. Generally headed by young people, these movements demanded freedom of speech, equality for women, civil rights for African Americans, liberalized sex codes, and an end to the Vietnam War. Student protests and rallies, from Berkeley to Cambridge, paralyzed the nation's colleges and brought the work of many of them to a complete halt. As one of the country's leading academic centers, with a large and diverse student population, Boston became the focal point of strikes and protests, sit-ins and pray-ins, occupations and demonstrations—all designed to overturn the existing order.

The Catholic Church was certainly not immune to these waves of unrest and controversy; in one instance, its own seminary was caught

up in the excitement. Feeling that the restrictive rules of the institution did not allow them to read modern journals and magazines,
engage in dialogues with theologians of other faiths, or leave the
seminary grounds to participate in civil rights activities, a group of
students at St. John's Seminary appealed directly to Cardinal Cushing
for a meeting to air their grievances. When he did not respond, late
in March 1966 more than a hundred seminarians carried signs and
marched outside St. John's auditorium, where the cardinal was addressing an assembly of Boston pastors on the meaning of Vatican II.
Cushing, furious at what he considered a display of ingratitude and
disobedience, refused to allow the *Pilot* to report on the incident and
expelled eight of the ringleaders. Early in April, sympathetic lay
Catholics picketed the cardinal's residence, and later organized a four-
day Easter prayer vigil on behalf of the students. Cushing had made
up his mind, however, and he would not change it. Some clerics and
members of the laity supported the cardinal for punishing the "strik-
ers," insisting that stern discipline was an integral and essential part
of seminary life. Other priests and more-liberal parishioners, on the
other hand, criticized the cardinal for publicly championing freedom
of conscience and the right of dissent while punishing seminary students for demanding precisely those rights.

Over the course of the next two years, it seems that Cushing reviewed the situation and introduced reforms similar to those that were
being undertaken in most other Catholic seminaries in the United
States. In 1968, he merged the seventeen-year-old Cardinal O'Connell minor seminary in Jamaica Plain with the eighty-four-year old St.
John's major seminary in Brighton, thereby inaugurating a complete,
four-year, liberal-arts college program for his seminarians. Instead of
taking a two-year college course, followed by six years of seminary
training, students would now divide the eight years into two equal
parts. After receiving a bachelor's degree at the end of the first four
years, they would then take seminary courses (with emphasis on philosophy and theology) during the second four years. The cardinal also

arranged for seminarians to have more freedom on evenings and weekends, and encouraged them to read newspapers, listen to the radio, and watch television.

In the long view, the seminary "strike" was probably a brief and relatively insignificant event in archdiocesan history. At the time, however, it was a startling symbol of change, a microcosmic picture of the forces dividing the parishes, and a powerful indication, for persons who chose to see it, that the traditional world of Richard J. Cushing was changing. During the 1960s, the decline in the number of diocesan priests began to signal a serious problem throughout the archdiocese. In the past, it was very unusual for a man to leave the priesthood to get married or to go into another vocation; after 1960 it became a common and troublesome phenomenon. Even more unsettling was the precipitous drop in seminary enrollments during the same period. In June 1964, Cardinal Cushing ordained twenty-seven young men to the priesthood, the same number ordained in his own seminary class some forty years earlier—and Cushing was heartbroken about it. "We are losing vocations that should be going to the seminary, and are not," he told Joseph Dever in an interview. "Frankly, it's a serious problem to keep seminarians in the seminary itself." In an effort to alleviate the shortage, in 1963 Cushing established in Weston, Massachusetts, the Pope John XXIII National Seminary for Delayed Vocations; twenty-three men, ranging in age from twenty-seven to fifty-four, made up the first class. A geologist, a chemist, a school administrator, a psychiatrist, an attorney, and several businessmen were among those who were ordained into the priesthood in May 1968. Because they had "rubbed shoulders with the world," the cardinal hoped this group would be better able to "understand it than we are."

Cushing was right to be concerned about the ways in which "the world" operated, because by this time the financial foundation of the archdiocese of Boston was showing dangerous cracks. In order to pay for the new churches, schools, convents, rectories, hospitals, colleges, orphanages, and other institutions he was fostering, the cardinal once told newspaper reporters candidly that he had to raise about $30,000 per day—about $11 million a year. By the 1960s, however, the archdiocese was paying out much more than it was bringing in. A significant problem was that the costs of the cardinal's building programs were rising higher and faster than the initial costs of construction. It was one thing to build schools, colleges, and hospitals, but it was another thing to keep up with the salaries, maintenance costs, development grants, and research expenses these institutions inevitably generated.

Furthermore, although the cardinal's one-man style and freewheeling ways were wonderful for public relations, they were disastrous for accurate record keeping. Cushing tended to be his own manager, his own secretary, his own press agent, and to a great extent his own treasurer. It was not uncommon for him to take in six-figure checks at some charitable event and either stuff them into his cassock or hand them over to some missionary priest who needed a new roof or to some poor nun who had no food in her convent. Money meant literally nothing to him personally, except as something to be given out to those who were in need. Unfortunately, this open-handed generosity had practical consequences.

Compounding these problems, the nation was beginning to experience a period of inflation at the same time that the federal government was reducing the amount of money it appropriated for domestic spending. Because of the escalating costs of the Vietnam War, Congress was forced to cut back severely on monies not only for renewal projects and housing programs but also for financial aid to scholarship programs and research projects in colleges, universities, and hospitals. With its enormous expenditures, large mortgages, and long-term financial commitments, the archdiocese faced the prospect of bankruptcy. Although the cardinal and his staff succeeded in paying off some $45 million of the debt, the archdiocese was still carrying a remaining debt of at least $40 million.

In addition to divisions within parishes, controversy in the seminary, a decreasing number of priests, and a growing indebtedness of serious proportions, the Catholic Church was also caught up in the complex problems of race relations. Although there had been a number of African Americans listed on the rolls as communicants at the first Cathedral of the Holy Cross on Franklin Street, by the early 1800s most of Boston's black population preferred to attend their own Protestant churches situated where they lived on the north side of Beacon Hill. There were exceptions, of course. Father James Healy, the son of an African mother and an Irish father, was named the first chancellor of the diocese of Boston and was appointed bishop of Portland, Maine, in 1875. Robert Morris, a distinguished black lawyer who served as counsel in the famous Sarah Roberts case (a suit on behalf of an African-American girl denied admittance to a Boston school because of her race) and later fought for the rights of black soldiers in the Fifty-Fourth Massachusetts Regiment, was also a devout Catholic. For the most part, however, the members of Boston's small, self-contained African-American community remained overwhelmingly Protestant—Baptist, Methodist, Pentecostal—even as they moved across town at the turn of the century to settle in the South End.

Immigration from various parts of the Caribbean and the West Indies during the late nineteenth century gradually increased the number of Roman Catholics as the city's black population grew from 2,280 in 1860 to nearly 14,000 in 1910. Nevertheless, until the 1940s the overall size of the black community was remarkably small for a city of Boston's size and importance. The mechanization of cotton farming, the dream of greater racial justice, and jobs made available by the outbreak of World War II brought millions of African-American workers out of the rural South to seek employment in the urban North. Boston's black population nearly doubled in only a decade, rising from some 23,000 in 1940 to over 40,000 in 1950, with the number of black Catholics going up proportionately—an estimated 2,635 in 1940, reflected as 849 families.

Seeing that African Americans were already a significant part of the archdiocese, Cardinal Cushing took steps to meet their spiritual needs. In 1945, assisted by a gift of $50,000 from Father Maurice O'Connor, pastor of St. James, Arlington, the cardinal announced that he was establishing St. Richard's parish in Roxbury and dedicating it to the "colored people of the area and of the Archdiocese." Staffed by white Josephite priests, the church was to have the same status of "national parish" as those built for the French, the Italians, the Poles, and other immigrant groups. In the face of some criticism that he was isolating black Catholics, Cushing insisted that the new parish was not to be seen as a "segregated" one. African Americans would not be forced to attend St. Richard's; they were free to be members of any of the other local parishes. "There is not now, and there never has been, any place in the religious life of the Archdiocese of Boston for segregation of any ministry," he wrote. "All our churches have equal place for all who share our Faith."

Although many members of Boston's black Catholic community welcomed the idea of having their own church as a place of worship, Cushing himself appeared to have reservations as issues involving race and racism became more complex during the late 1950s and early 1960s. Inspired by the ideals of the Reverend Martin Luther King, Jr., by civil rights successes in the South, and by the centennial of the Emancipation Proclamation in 1963, the black community in Boston, as in other American cities, began to demand equal rights in housing, education, and employment. Pressured by the lack of adequate housing, by the late 1950s and early 1960s African Americans were moving beyond their traditional Roxbury boundaries and settling along the fringes of such formerly all-white and predominantly Catholic neighborhoods as Dorchester, Jamaica Plain, Roslindale, and Hyde Park. Residents of these white neighborhoods reacted in panic and alarm when they realized that black people were not staying "where they belonged" and were moving into districts that had always been reserved for white immigrant populations and for equally white Catholic parishes. Politics and race, turf and class were all coming together to form a highly explosive mixture.

Cardinal Cushing displayed sympathy for the cause of civil rights on many occasions, and on Pentecost Sunday, 1964, he spoke out strongly against racism in Boston, calling upon all Catholics to "love all men, and especially love Negroes, because they have suffered so much for lack of love." At the same time, however, he was uneasy with the confrontational methods being employed by civil rights leaders to dramatize their objectives, regarding their approach as provocative and disruptive. When African-American residents, for example, called for a boycott of the city's schools in order to protest segregation, the cardinal complained that such an act was "a very, very dangerous thing." And yet he felt that some action was necessary to show that the Church was interested and involved. Working through Monsignor Francis J. Lally, editor of the *Pilot* and a highly respected member of the Boston community, Cushing encouraged the formation of a Boston unit of the Catholic Interracial Council under the direction of Father Paul Rynne, and in 1966 he established a human rights commission to handle civil rights matters for the archdiocese.* In December of that year, the cardinal issued a pastoral letter entitled "The Servant Church," which broadly condemned the "scandal of racism," among other social evils.

But events in Boston were moving faster than Cushing could imagine, and many of his own clerics were already taking the initiative in matters involving race. In 1963, a number of seminary students had gone into Roxbury to work with community activists in the vicinity of St. Richard's Church; the following year, two priests from St. Brigid's Church in Lexington were arrested in North Carolina for trying to integrate a restaurant. In the spring of 1965, more priests, nuns, and seminarians went to Selma, Alabama, to march with Martin Luther

* Cardinal Cushing reconsidered the status of a separate black church, and in November 1961 changed St. Richard's from a "national parish" to a mission of St. Joseph's Church. He also appointed the Josephite Fathers as assistants in St. Joseph's parish.

King. In 1967, a group of twenty inner-city priests, impatient with the quiescence of Church leaders, formed the progressive Association of Boston Urban Priests and later endorsed the candidacy of black NAACP leader Tom Atkins for a seat on the Boston City Council. After condemning the Vietnam War and supporting the position of Catholic protestors like the Berrigan brothers, in June 1969 the association issued a "public criticism" of the failure of the Boston Church to "preach and live the gospel" where racial segregation was concerned.

The old cardinal, overwhelmed by age and illness, beset by the problems of an archdiocese under siege, seemed unable to make the right moves. Whatever he did, he found himself caught in the middle. He was denounced by black civil rights leaders for not using his remarkable influence to promote the cause of racial equality, and he was denounced by Irish-Catholic parishioners for turning his back on his own people. Cushing was making the painful discovery that this was an issue where, as J. Anthony Lukas would later observe in his Pulitzer Prize–winning book, there was no "common ground." For the first time in Boston's long political history, the issue of race became a factor in the city's mayoral election. Kevin Hagan White, former secretary of state of Massachusetts, was locked in a bitter struggle with Louise Day Hicks, former school committee member and champion of the white neighborhoods, who refused to concede that the Boston public schools were segregated. Although White defeated Hicks in November 1967 by 12,429 votes, it was clear that Boston faced a bitter showdown on the race question in the very near future.

If Cushing had been strong, healthy, and resilient, perhaps he could have better faced the numerous problems with which he was confronted. But by the late 1960s this was not the case. After his series of medical problems back in 1953, it is true that he had regained his health and resumed his incredibly busy schedule of travel, fundraising, public speaking, administrative duties, and construction projects. But the hard work took an increasingly heavy toll on his already frail and weakened constitution, and his exhausting visit to Latin America during the summer of 1960 was the last straw. From then on, Cushing's health went downhill rapidly as he suffered from recurring asthma attacks, splitting headaches, a painful case of shingles, and occasional fainting spells. In almost continuous pain, the sixty-five-year-old cardinal became increasingly petulant and quarrelsome, given to fits of self-pity and depression. His disposition was not at all improved by the results of the mayoral election of November 1959, in which his good friend Senator John E. Powers of South Boston was defeated by John F. Collins in a startling upset. Although Cushing eventually developed a warm personal friendship with Collins, the unexpected defeat of John Powers was still a cruel blow.

And only three years later came perhaps the cruelest blow of all—the assassination of President John F. Kennedy. Over the years, Cardinal Cushing had become closely associated with the Kennedy family, going back to the days when as an auxiliary bishop he first met Joe Junior and his younger brother Jack when they were students at Harvard. He soon developed a friendship with the boys' father, Joseph P. Kennedy, and as time went on the relationship with the Kennedy family became closer. The senior Kennedy gave the cardinal a large sum of money to establish the Kennedy Memorial Hospital for retarded children;* Cushing later raised a million dollars to help ransom the Bay of Pigs prisoners and get them home for Christmas in 1962.

Cushing formed a particularly warm attachment with Jack Kennedy. He officiated at his marriage with Jacqueline Bouvier, and he watched proudly as the young man moved up the political ladder. With his own shrewd sense of politics, however, Cushing carefully avoided making any kind of public statements during the 1960 presidential race that might inject the church-state issue into the campaign and harm Kennedy's chances. January 20, 1961, was a very happy

* The hospital was named in honor of young Joseph Kennedy, who was killed in a plane crash in World War II. The announcement was that "Big Joe" gave the cardinal a million and a half dollars for this project; Cushing later complained that he received only $600,000.

President John F. Kennedy joins with Richard Cardinal Cushing in commemo-
rating the hundredth anniversary of the founding of Boston College. Behind
Cardinal Cushing is Nathan Pusey, president of Harvard University; behind
Dr. Pusey is Congressman Thomas P. ("Tip") O'Neill. In the center is Rev. Mi-
chael P. Walsh, SJ, president of the Catholic university that was the inspiration
of Bishop John Fitzpatrick. (Courtesy of the Archdiocese of Boston.)

occasion, as Richard Cardinal Cushing delivered the invocation at the inauguration of John F. Kennedy as the first Roman Catholic to be elected president of the United States. But that happiness was not to last very long. On November 22, 1963, President Kennedy was assassinated in Dallas. Cushing had the heartbreaking task of saying the funeral Mass for his young friend and consoling his widow and two children. It was a devastating experience for the sixty-eight-year-old prelate, who professed: "My heart is broken with grief over his martyrdom for the cause of the free world." And things did not get any better. Only five years later he had to preside at the funeral of

Jack's younger brother, Senator Robert F. Kennedy, after he had been assassinated in Los Angeles.

Even while he was again comforting the members of the grief-stricken Kennedy family, it was clear that the old man could not comprehend the mindless violence of the times. He was so shocked, he told reporters, that he could scarcely think: "What is this country coming to?" he asked. "Are we going to run a political campaign with bullets or debates?" It was terribly wearing on the prelate's already precarious health and disposition. Now going on seventy-four, gaunt and emaciated, he complained about recurring fainting spells, bleeding ulcers, and other physical ailments. "I can't eat," he told one radio reporter in 1969. "My emphysema is terrible. I'm like a dead man, like a statue. Unless I have oxygen, I can't breathe." So serious had his physical condition become that it was agreed that he would retire the following August, on the occasion of his seventy-fifth birthday. And already there was speculation about his successor. Archbishop John Dearden of Detroit and Archbishop Paul Hallinan of Atlanta were two possibilities; Bishop Ernest Primeau of Manchester, New Hampshire, Bishop John Mussio of Steubenville, Ohio, and Bishop Bernard Flanagan of Worcester were mentioned; and the Boston auxiliary bishops Daniel Cronin, Jeremiah Minihan, and Thomas Riley were also named as possible candidates. Everyone knew that nobody could really replace someone as lovable, irascible, and unpredictable as "the Cush," but they wondered who would be the one to try.

⇌ ADDITIONAL READING

Seldom has such a well-known and highly publicized world figure as Richard Cardinal Cushing turned out to be such an intensely private person. This paradox is reflected in the various books and articles that have been written about his life. Even though they draw heavily upon newspaper reports, magazine pieces, personal interviews, and extensive television coverage, they usually lack references to personal papers or original documents. To a great extent this is the result of

Cushing's stubborn insistence that he did not want outsiders digging into his own private life or that of the members of his family. As he grew older, Cushing came to distrust reporters, journalists, and writers, feeling that because they did not understand him (he often said he could not understand himself) they would twist his words and distort his intentions. Most of the time he simply refused to cooperate: "I don't care what they write about me or what they don't write about me," he once told the writer Joe Dever, boasting that he kept no personal memoirs, letters, or records that could be later used to prepare an official biography.

Cushing proved an irresistible subject, however, and even before his death there were three major biographies under way. Joseph Dever, *Cushing of Boston: A Candid Portrait* (Boston, 1965), is perhaps the most forthright and personal study, since Cushing seems to have felt comfortable with a young journalist who was a native of Boston and a graduate of Boston College. John H. Fenton, *Salt of the Earth: An Informal Portrait of Richard Cardinal Cushing* (New York, 1965), is the work of a journalist for the *New York Times* who is capable of seeing the far-reaching influence of the Boston prelate as an international figure. John Henry Cutler, *Cardinal Cushing of Boston* (New York, 1970), is valuable for the extensive background he provides on the role Boston's political and social history played in Cushing's life and career. A firsthand and utterly charming account of the life of a priest during the Cushing years is John P. Carroll, *Golden Memories* (Boston, 1997). Monsignor Carroll served as director of the Catholic Youth Organization (CYO) from 1948 to 1968.

H. Paul Douglass, *Christian Unity Movements in the United States* (New York, 1934), Stephen C. Neill, *Towards Church Union, 1937–1952* (London, 1952), and Matthew Spinka, *The Quest for Christian Unity* (New York, 1969), provide a general background for the postwar ecumenical movement. George H. Tavard, *The Catholic Approach to Protestantism* (New York, 1955), and John M. Todd, *Catholics and the Ecumenical Movement* (London, 1956), supply a Catholic perspective. Francis J. Lally, *The Catholic Church in a Changing America* (Boston, 1968), offers insightful views by an influential Boston priest and journalist. David Caute, *The Great Fear: The Anti-Communist Purge under Truman and Eisenhower* (New York, 1978), supplies a national background for the issue of Communism; Donald J. Crosby, *God, Church, and Flag: Senator Joseph McCarthy and the Catholic Church, 1950–1957* (Chapel Hill, N.C., 1978), views the subject from a Catholic perspective.

Paul B. Marx, *Virgil Michel and the Liturgical Movement* (Collegeville, Minn., 1957), gives a national view of the liturgical movement, while William J. Leonard, *The Letter Carrier* (Kansas City, Mo., 1993), is both a fascinating autobiography of a Jesuit from Boston College and an analysis of the early liturgical movement at the local level. Xavier Rynne (the pseudonym of Francis X. Murphy) wrote the perceptive and readable *Vatican Council II* (New York, 1968); also see Ralph M. Wiltgen, *The Rhine Flows into the Tiber: The Unknown Council* (New York, 1967). Giuseppe Alberigo et al., eds., *The Reception of Vatican II* (Washington, 1987), and Adrian Hastings, ed., *Modern Catholicism: Vatican II and After* (New York, 1991), provide a series of essays dealing with Vatican II and its aftereffects. Peter Hebblethwaite has written two biographies of the conciliar pontiffs with *Pope John: Shepherd of the Modern World* (New York, 1985) and *Paul VI: The First Modern Pope* (New York, 1993).

Mary Jo Weaver and R. Scott Appleby, eds., *Being Right: Conservative Catholicism in America* (Bloomington, Ind., 1995), contains essays focusing on the conservative reaction to Vatican II. Hans Küng, *The Council, Reform, and Reunion* (New York, 1961), offers the views of a noted liberal theologian of the 1960s. Robert T. Hall, *The Morality of Civil Disobedience* (New York, 1971), and Francine du Plessix Gray, *Divine Disobedience: Profiles in Catholic Radicalism* (New York, 1970), comment on the involvement of Catholics in civil disobedience activities. John D. Donovan, *The Academic Man in the Catholic College* (New York, 1964), and Joseph H. Fichter, *The Parochial School: A Sociological Study* (Notre Dame, Ind., 1959), are sociological studies of Catholic education. Mary Daly, *The Church and the Second Sex* (New

York, 1968), is a controversial examination of the role of women in the Church from a feminist point of view. Daniel Callahan, *The New Church* (New York, 1966), Andrew Greeley, *The Church and the Suburbs* (New York, 1959), and Gibson Winter, *The Suburban Captivity of the Churches* (Garden City, N.Y., 1962), offer some analytical views on the Church in the postconciliar era.

Nat Hentoff, *Boston Boy* (New York, 1986), provides some personal insights into the difficulties faced by a Jewish boy growing up in an Irish-Catholic neighborhood. John T. McGreevy, *Parish Boundaries* (Chicago, 1996), offers a brilliant analysis of the changing nature of Catholic parishes in response to the modern civil rights movement. E. Franklin Frazier, *The Negro Church in America* (New York, 1963), James H. Cone, *Black Theology and Black Power* (New York, 1969), and J. R. Washington, *Black Religion: The Negro and Christianity in the United States* (Boston, 1964), present the background of African-American religious views. John LaFarge, *The Catholic Viewpoint on Race Relations* (Garden City, N.Y., 1956), William Osborne, *The Segregated Covenant: Race Relations and American Catholics* (New York, 1967), and Cyprian Davis, *The History of Black Catholics in the United States* (New York, 1991), provide a national view of race relations; William C. Leonard has provided a local view in "The History of Black Catholics in Boston, 1790–1840" (M.A. thesis, Northeastern University, 1993). Leonard has also written "A Parish for the Black Catholics of Boston," *Catholic Historical Review* (January 1997), a valuable study of the decision of Cardinal Cushing to establish a black parish in the city. J. Anthony Lukas, *Common Ground* (New York, 1984), is a kaleidoscopic account of the busing crisis as seen through the eyes of three Boston families; Ronald P. Formisano, *Boston against Busing: Race, Class, and Ethnicity in the 1960s and 1970s* (Chapel Hill, N.C., 1991), is a scholarly analysis of the same controversy, whose effects are still felt in the city. Michael B. Friedland, *Lift Up Your Voice Like a Trumpet* (Chapel Hill, N.C., 1998), provides a perceptive study of the white clergy and the civil rights movements from 1945 to 1973.

8 Meeting the Future

ONCE AGAIN ROME DID THE UNEXPECTED WHERE the see of Boston was concerned. Contrary to expectations, the Holy See announced that Humberto Sousa Medeiros, Bishop of Brownsville, Texas, would succeed Cardinal Cushing as archbishop of Boston. The new man was someone few people knew, and most Bostonians had never heard of. The appointment certainly came as a great surprise.

Humberto Medeiros was born in 1915 in the Portuguese Azores, the oldest of the four children of Maria and Antonio de Sousa Medeiros. Antonio raised vegetables and ran a small variety store until 1931, when he moved his family to America and settled in the town of Fall River, some fifty miles south of Boston. Humberto attended St. Michael's, the local Portuguese church, and spoke little English until he was enrolled in a "special" school for children who had mental or physical disabilities. Humberto's natural intelligence brought him to the attention of his teachers, who wanted to further develop both his academic and his artistic talents. Anything like advanced schooling was out of the question during the lean depression years, and so the seventeen-year-old lad took a job as a sweeper and "bob-watcher" at the Sagamore Mills for sixty-two cents a day. Every evening and weekend, however, he worked on his English, French, Latin, and mathematics; eventually, his two brothers became old enough to replace him in the mills and let him go back to school. Admitted to Durfee High School as a sophomore, Humberto completed the four-year program in only two and a half years, graduating first in his class of 1937.

Pursuing his boyhood desire to become a priest, young Medeiros studied at the Catholic University of America, where he earned a master of arts degree in 1942 and a licentiate in sacred theology in 1946, before being ordained on June 15, 1946. Father Medeiros returned to his hometown of Fall River, was assigned to St. John of God Church, and for the next five years served the spiritual needs of the local Portuguese community. In 1949 he was asked to pursue doctoral studies in Washington and then in Rome, where he earned a doctorate in sacred theology in 1951 from the Gregorian University.

After returning to Fall River, Medeiros was assigned by Bishop James Cassidy to Holy Name Church in a well-to-do Irish parish and was also named assistant to the chancellor of the diocese. Cassidy could see that the population of Fall River was fast becoming more diversified, and he felt that Medeiros had the qualities for future leadership. Cassidy's successor, Bishop James Connolly, continued to move Medeiros up the ecclesiastical ladder—vicar for religious, vice-chancellor, and finally chancellor—obviously grooming him for higher positions. In 1958 Medeiros was made a monsignor, and in 1960 he became pastor of St. Michael's Church.

On April 14, 1966, Pope Paul VI named Monsignor Medeiros the second bishop of Brownsville, Texas, located in the lower Rio Grande Valley where the great river empties into the Gulf of Mexico. Brownsville was one of the nation's newest and smallest dioceses, most of whose communicants were desperately poor Mexican Americans earning eighty-five cents an hour in the fields, struggling to feed large families on twenty to thirty dollars a week. Medeiros arrived in

Brownsville in June, just as Cesar Chavez and the United Farm Workers were calling the fruit pickers out on strike, demanding a $1.25-an-hour minimum wage and union recognition. The growers, wealthy landowners, responded by bringing up Mexican "green-carders" from the other side of the border to harvest the melons while the strike was on. Trying to act as peacemaker, Medeiros urged both workers and growers to settle their differences "in a Christian manner." Although he refused to become directly associated with either side, he was conspicuously sympathetic to the workers' demands for a living wage; he also strove vigorously to integrate the valley's segregated churches. During his years at Brownsville, Medeiros earned a reputation as a Church leader who spoke out boldly in favor of human rights without completely alienating the powerful growers, who provided the fields that were necessary for the workers' survival. Medeiros was named by *Critic* magazine as one of twelve leading American bishops who held "the most promise for the future of the Church in the United States."

So it was that when Cardinal Cushing of Boston reached his final days it was Humberto Medeiros who was chosen to replace him. Whether it was his success in reconciling ethnic tensions in Brownsville that made him an attractive candidate for a city whose racial tensions were reaching the boiling point; whether it was an effort by the Holy See to provide new bishops who would better reflect the growing ethnic and racial diversity in American cities; whether it was to provide one of the nation's renowned academic centers with an archbishop known for his intellectual attainments—or for all of these reasons—many religious observers felt that it was a wise appointment, made at an appropriate moment in Church history. In view of the increasing number of Portuguese, Hispanic, and African Americans who had become an integral part of Boston's population in recent years, the arrival of Medeiros was greeted with a great deal of enthusiasm by most city leaders.

In August 1970, on his seventy-fifth birthday, Cardinal Cushing's

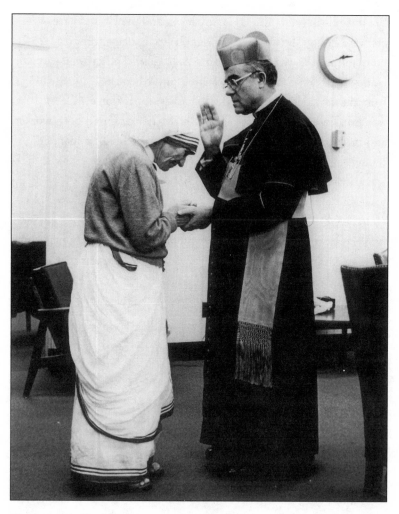

Humberto Cardinal Medeiros greets Mother Teresa of Calcutta on her visit to Boston in June 1982. In their compassion for poor and suffering people and their concern for social justice in accordance with the teachings of the Gospel, these were two preeminent Catholics. By reducing the debt, organizing parishes into regions, and expanding the role of the laity, Cardinal Medeiros did much to move the archdiocese into the post–Vatican II era. (Courtesy of the Archdiocese of Boston.)

resignation was accepted officially by the Holy See. His successor, the Most Reverend Humberto S. Medeiros, was installed as archbishop of Boston on October 7, 1970. Despite his weakened condition, Cardinal Cushing insisted on attending the ceremony at the Cathedral of the Holy Cross to offer his successor his prayers and his blessing. When it was suggested that he might take a shorter route to avoid the exertion of the long procession, he rasped sharply: "I'll march!" Anyone who was in the cathedral that day, later recalled Bishop Joseph Maguire, would never forget Cushing's brief but touching farewell, which ended: "Pray for me as I pray for you—and God bless you all." The vast throng surged to its feet in one spontaneous burst of emotion, and gave the aged cardinal a five-minute ovation.

Then, straightening himself up, pulling his thin shoulders back, and calling upon one last reserve of strength, Cushing made his final walk down the cathedral's long center aisle. Waving his biretta to the emotion-filled congregation, a showman to the end, wrote Bishop Maguire, it was almost as though he was saying, "Take a good look at me, now. For when I'm gone, you'll not see the likes of me again." Only a few weeks later, on All Souls Day, Richard Cardinal Cushing closed his eyes and slipped into the history of an archdiocese that had taken him into its heart. His passing produced a massive outpouring of sorrow and affection. In the four days that followed, more than half a million persons filed past his catafalque in the cathedral, and as the funeral procession moved along Washington Street the mourners stood ten deep, silently watching the cortege of eleven cardinals and fifty bishops lead the body of the beloved prelate to its final resting place.

As with every new person who is promoted to high position ahead of others who, their supporters feel, deserved better, Medeiros had his share of critics at the outset. A small number of detractors were troubled by his dark skin and foreign origins, but many more simply resented the fact that he was an "outsider." For the last century and a half, every archbishop of Boston had been born in the United States and had been of Irish parentage, and some people did not know why that tradition had to change. Then, too, there were the inevitable comparisons with his popular predecessor. Everyone agreed that the colorful and legendary Cushing was a hard act to follow. And Medeiros knew it. Occasionally, he made a valiant attempt to re-create the old illusions—singing Irish songs, taking nuns to Nantasket, riding with children in roller coasters, posing in silly hats—but it fell flat. "They want me to be Cardinal Cushing, but I'm not. I am Humberto Medeiros," he once exclaimed to his secretary, Father William Helmick. "I can succeed him, but I can't replace him." It was clear from the outset that he would have to be his own man, his own person, regardless of the consequences. He was too honest and too intelligent to do anything else.

Any executive taking over a leadership role in any major American institution in the year 1970 faced serious difficulties, and Archbishop Medeiros was no exception. The war in Southeast Asia dragged on, and the bitterness it generated permeated American society. Any hopes that a new administration in Washington would bring the conflict to an end were dashed when President Richard Nixon, in April 1970, ordered an incursion into Cambodia. Massive demonstrations rocked colleges and universities throughout the nation; four students were killed during a demonstration at Kent State University in Ohio, and two more were killed at Jackson State College in Mississippi. At the same time, African-American citizens everywhere were accelerating their demands for equal rights and equal opportunities, and in the Boston area black leaders continued to pressure the school committee to admit that de facto segregation existed in the Boston public school system. To make matters worse, by 1970 the American economy was in serious trouble as the Vietnam War caused already inflated prices to rise each year. President Nixon called for a tight-money policy and higher interest rates, but the reduction in consumer purchasing, cutbacks in business operations, and rising unemployment only produced "stagflation"—a stalled economy in a period of inflation. All of these circumstances produced a climate of anger, bitterness, and uncertainty that made the Medeiros years very difficult ones.

By 1970, changes and developments within the Catholic Church itself added to the atmosphere of anxiety and uncertainty. By now, most of the fasts, rituals, and ceremonies that had formerly been required were generally voluntary. Latin was a thing of the past; the clergy were no longer wearing clerical dress; lay boards and advisory councils were functioning in many parishes. A number of priests were demanding permission to marry, and many were leaving the Church to do so. Theologians were discussing the modification of traditional stands on such issues as birth control and divorce, and liberals were calling upon the Catholic Church to speak out more boldly on matters of social concern. In some cases, when the Church did not react quickly enough or boldly enough, some individuals took action on their own. In 1968 two priests, Philip Berrigan and his brother Daniel, were jailed for antiwar activities; in Milwaukee, Father James Groppi became nationally famous as a fiery civil rights fighter; in March 1969, nine Catholics—priests, nuns, and laymen—vandalized the Washington offices of the Dow Chemical Company. In 1970, Rev. Robert F. Drinan, SJ, dean of the Boston College Law School, ran for a seat in the United States House of Representatives on a declared antiwar platform; he and Father Robert J. Cornell of Wisconsin were the first Catholic priests in modern times to serve in Congress.*

Disturbing changes were evident throughout the archdiocese of Boston itself in many other areas. Between 1960 and 1978, attendance at Mass by Catholics in greater Boston was reported to have declined from 75 percent to 55 percent. Even though the number of parish priests showed a slow but steady rise, going from 1,152 in 1960 to 1,263 in 1973 (for a total increase of 111 priests in 13 years) the number of incoming seminarians at St. John's continued its discouraging

---

* Father Gabriel Richard, a Sulpician, was the first Catholic priest to serve in the U.S. Congress. Before Michigan became a state in 1837, Father Richard was its territorial delegate to the House of Representatives from 1822 to 1825.

descent from an all-time high of 418 in 1960. By 1970, their numbers had fallen to only 220; by 1973 there were 172; by 1975 they were down to 126. Archbishop Medeiros was acutely conscious of what was happening, and he described the decline in priestly vocations as "a grave danger for us and a source of sadness for the Church." In a homily on priestly vocations, he pointed out that twenty-five years earlier the archdiocese had ordained over fifty seminarians, as compared with the seven young men who were being ordained in 1981. And the loss of older priests made the situation even worse. "At present we lose through death, retirement, illness, incapacity, and other causes between twenty-five and thirty of our priests every year," he said. "In four years we could lose over one hundred priests!" And the archdiocese's parochial school system was also showing signs of decline and retrenchment during this same period. The 72 parochial high schools that were in operation in 1960 had dropped to 60 in 1970, and then to 44 in 1973; the 211 elementary schools still operating in 1970 were reduced to 182 in 1973, and then to 157 in 1975. Between 1965 and 1973, the total enrollment of students in archdiocesan schools fell from 151,582 to 86,469. The condition of parochial schools became even more precarious during the late 1960s and early 1970s, when the decline in the number of teaching nuns forced schools to hire lay teachers at competitive salaries, thus leading some schools to close and others to raise tuitions.

Many parishes throughout the archdiocese continued to show evidence of conflict over post–Vatican II changes in traditional rituals and practices. By the early 1970s, parishioners generally were becoming more comfortable with the new-style Masses, the use of the vernacular, unaccustomed liturgies, and unfamiliar music. There were, however, still enough unresolved difficulties over the extent of lay participation in parish affairs, service on budget committees, and membership on planning councils to produce the kinds of controversies between pastors and parishioners that were reminiscent of the old battles over lay trusteeship during the early nineteenth century. Con-

Priests, Nuns, and Seminarians in the Archdiocese of Boston,
1944–1994

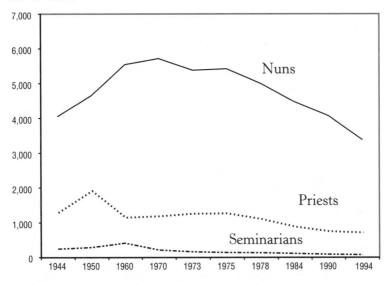

tinued factionalism and occasional disruptions in various parishes
provided one more complex and disturbing problem with which the
new archbishop would have to deal.

Archbishop Medeiros's most immediate and pressing problem,
however, was the size of the archdiocesan debt. Although Cardinal
Cushing had paid off about $45 million of that debt before his retire-
ment, the remaining $40 million loomed as a terrible spectre over the
heads of Church authorities, especially given changing times and
changing circumstances. Part of the difficulty was the nature of the
debt itself: it was for the most part for maintaining projects long after
their completion. There was nothing particularly exciting or stimulating about the kind of fundraising Archbishop Medeiros would have
to undertake.

Another part of the difficulty was the character of the fundraising
process. Under Cushing, asking for money was highly personal, often
colorful, and usually newsworthy. It was a one-man show, with Cush-

Parishes, Parochial Elementary Schools, and High Schools in the Archdiocese of Boston, 1944–1994

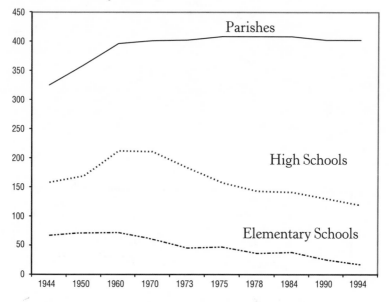

ing glad-handing wealthy donors who enjoyed giving their checks personally to the cardinal archbishop of Boston while television cameras recorded the event. Under Medeiros's direction, the process was much more efficient, but it was also much more routine and bureaucratic. He set about to solve the problem of a $40 million debt in a thoughtful, methodical, and professional manner, employing capable financial advisors and using modern management techniques. He established the Archbishop's Stewardship Appeal to assess each parish a portion of the goal he set out to achieve each year in order to reduce the debt. It was a long, slow, and painful process, but in the end Medeiros accomplished what many cynical observers regarded as impossible. Between 1970 and 1977, he cut the budget by 40 percent, closed a number of facilities, curtailed the activities of forty-three archdiocesan agencies, and brought the debt down to a manageable $15 million. But although he received the plaudits and admiration of those who worked closely with him in the process, he got little appreciation from some pastors and parishioners who were not always aware of the magnitude of the debt and the implications of its importance. They tended to see the tedious fundraising process as an unwarranted demand on their hard-pressed parishioners and an unnecessary burden on their overworked clergy.

While working on the burden of the archdiocesan debt, Cardinal Medeiros was also planning ways to modernize the organization of the Church itself. He had studied the ways in which a system of regional bishops had worked in other dioceses, and he decided to implement such a program in the archdiocese of Boston, which now had a population of nearly two million Catholics. He originally set up three episcopal regions: the North Region, under Bishop Jeremiah Minihan; the South Region, under Bishop Joseph Maguire; and the Central, or Greater Boston, Region, under Bishop Lawrence Riley. (The number of regions was later increased to four with the addition of a new West Region.) Each regional bishop was expected to have a more intimate knowledge of his particular area, keep the archbishop informed about regional developments, and make recommendations regarding personnel changes and appointments. Each of the regions was subdivided into four smaller vicarates so as to provide an even more effective and highly personalized network of information and control. The institution of the regional system, according to Bishop John M. D'Arcy of the Fort Wayne–South Bend Diocese, formerly one of the early regional bishops appointed by Cardinal Medeiros, "was one of the best steps ever taken in the Boston Archdiocese."

In order to promote vocations and to stimulate increased lay participation in the life of the Church, Cardinal Medeiros moved to restore and revitalize the office of the permanent diaconate. Before taking action, however, he ordered a serious study of the nature of the diaconate itself, the unique function of the office, and the distinctive qualities of those individuals called to serve in this capacity. This analysis, supervised by Father Arthur Driscoll, eventually produced a structure that provided a deeper theological understanding of the diaconate, as well as a more effective screening process that involved not only the candidate but also his wife.* A booklet incorporating the new reforms for the diaconate helped pave the way for further reforms in other dioceses throughout the United States and in other parts of the world. In May 1976, the first class of permanent deacons was ordained in the Cathedral of the Holy Cross. It was also Medeiros who brought the Catholic Church even closer to the laity by authorizing eucharistic ministers in all parishes in the archdiocese.

A scholar himself, with a deep respect for higher learning, Cardinal Medeiros recognized that the Boston-Cambridge region was one of the nation's most widely recognized centers of advanced studies, with well over a quarter of a million students in the area. Proceeding in his usual methodical manner, he appointed a commission—headed by Bishop John D'Arcy and consisting of priests, nuns, and religious—that visited the various colleges and universities, spoke with their officials, and assessed the prevailing condition of campus ministries. On the basis of these reports, the cardinal drew up new guidelines to reform and reinvigorate the campus ministry. Under the direction of Father John Boles and a staff of trained priests and nuns, the ministry at Harvard became so effective that on one occasion President Derek Bok informed the cardinal that the Catholics had "the best ministry" at the University. Similar progress was made at Wellesley College, Northeastern University, Simmons College, and various state colleges. In 1978, the cardinal also launched a project to professionalize the management of the archdiocesan archives. Supervised by Bishop Thomas V. Daily, a professional archivist was employed to guide the effort to collect, preserve, and make available to scholars and to the entire community the valuable documents and records of the archdiocese.

* The analysis included studies by Father John Farrell, a noted patristic scholar, and by Sister Jane Carew, a recognized theological expert.

Although he was conscientious about vigorously implementing the liturgical changes called for by Vatican II, Cardinal Medeiros was equally vigorous in establishing clear boundaries beyond which experiments in doctrine and innovations in teaching would not be tolerated. He refused to engage in discussions about modifications in divorce, the question of clerical celibacy, or the ordination of women, and he came out very strongly against the "new barbarism" of abortion, which he defined as the "destruction of human life at its source" and "objectively evil." To reinforce the spiritual faith of his flock in a positive manner, he became the only bishop in the United States to establish an office of spiritual development. This was a pastoral office geared entirely to the spiritual renewal of individuals and parishes, and designed especially to bring people back to the sacraments after many years of absence. The program culminated in a series of parishwide missions throughout the archdiocese. Medeiros's own spiritual concerns were deep and far ranging, evidence of an extraordinarily profound faith that was apparent to all who knew him well. In his periodic pastoral letters, he addressed such serious contemporary issues as abortion, aid to the poor, the pernicious influence of drugs, the necessity for penal reform, pastoral care for homosexuals, and the threat of nuclear disaster.*

In obvious recognition of the dedication and loyalty of the archbishop of Boston, on February 2, 1973, Pope Paul VI named Humberto Medeiros to the college of cardinals. He participated in the election of Pope John Paul I (the "September pope") in August 1978, and then, in October of the same year, in the election of John Paul II, the first non-Italian pontiff in centuries. The following year, Pope John Paul II made his first pastoral visit to the Church in the United States. He stayed in Boston for two days, spending the night of October 1, 1979, in the cardinal's Brighton residence after having said a spectacu-

---

* In 1984, the Daughters of St. Paul compiled and indexed a collection of pastorals and addresses by Humberto Cardinal Medeiros under the title *"Whatever God Wants,"* covering the period from 1970 to 1983.

lar outdoor Mass on Boston Common. It seems clear that in ecclesiastical matters and doctrinal issues Humberto Medeiros had earned the respect and admiration of the Holy See.

The sure grip and decisive approach Cardinal Medeiros displayed in spiritual affairs and ecclesiastical matters, however, eluded him once he became involved in the deadly labyrinth of Boston politics. The cardinal tended to distrust politicians, who tried to use him for their own purposes, and he generally avoided news reporters, who he feared would trap him and catch him off-guard in order to misinterpret his words and manipulate their meaning. A person of clear words and precise thoughts, accustomed to careful planning and rational thinking, Medeiros could never come up with the kind of wisecracks and one-liners the media wanted for their television reports or morning headlines. Unfortunately, however, the issue of race had become so involved with local politics that it was almost impossible for the cardinal archbishop of Boston to avoid being drawn into the public arena over questions involving both race *and* politics.

The usually strong and generally warm political relations that had always existed between the Catholic Church and Boston's Irish-Catholic neighborhoods had begun to break down during the 1960s, when Cardinal Cushing and a number of his pastors were taken to be supporting politically driven urban-renewal programs that threatened to alter the city's traditional ethnic housing patterns. Cushing maintained personal friendships with two progressive mayors, John B. Hynes and John F. Collins; he apparently endorsed the destruction of the city's West End; and he gave his permission for Monsignor Francis J. Lally, editor of the *Pilot,* to serve as chairman of the Boston Redevelopment Authority (BRA). A number of local neighborhood leaders saw these decisions as indications that Catholic Church leaders were moving away from their working-class ethnic roots and taking up with upper-class liberal do-gooders and financial bureaucrats. For the first time, the certainty of many Irish Catholics regarding the loyalty and support of their own Church leaders began to show dangerous signs of weakening.

Accompanied by Humberto Cardinal Medeiros, Pope John Paul II arrives at Boston's Logan International Airport on September 30, 1979, and exits the Aer Lingus airplane that brought him to Boston. Later, at an outdoor Mass on historic Boston Common, the pope addressed a vast throng of people who braved torrential rains to participate in the first visit of a reigning pontiff to the capital of the Commonwealth. (Photo by Sister Rita Murray.)

That sense of uncertainty became even more evident during the late 1960s and early 1970s as the growing militancy of the city's African-American community was gaining greater political force. Humberto Medeiros had arrived to begin his episcopal duties in Boston in 1970, just as the city's race relations had reached a dangerous and more volatile level. Three years earlier, in November 1967, Kevin White had defeated Louise Day Hicks to become mayor of Boston; the campaign was bitter, and race played a prominent role for the first time in Boston's political history. The accelerating spread of the black population into traditionally white neighborhoods, the demands of African Americans for a more equitable share of city jobs and low-cost housing, and the continuing dispute between parents of black children and the all-white school committee over segregation in the city's public schools all contributed to a hostile environment that the nature of the campaign and the outcome of the election did nothing to improve.

After Mayor White's victory in 1967, African Americans' anger focused increasingly on the issue of segregation in the city's public schools. This came after the city's white establishment failed to demonstrate any real interest in enforcing the 1954 Supreme Court decision in the case of *Brown v. Board of Education of Topeka,* which outlawed racial segregation in public schools. Speaking for the black community, the NAACP charged that de facto segregation existed in the Boston public school system; the Boston School Commitee flatly denied the charge, and refused to consider any plans for a system of gradual integration. Frustrated by this lack of response, a number of black parents brought a class action suit—*Morgan v. Hennigan*—against the school committee.* Early in 1972, the case was assigned by lot to Judge W. Arthur Garrity, Jr., a graduate of Holy Cross College and the Harvard University Law School, and a former campaign

---

* The name of one parent was Tallulah Morgan; the name of the chairman of the Boston School Committee was James Hennigan.

worker for John F. Kennedy. After studying the case for two years, on June 21, 1974, Judge Garrity handed down his decision. He declared that the school committee had "knowingly carried out a systematic program of segregation" and that the entire Boston public school system was "unconstitutionally segregated." On the basis of this decision, he ordered a program to go into effect the following September that would bus some eighteen thousand schoolchildren in order to achieve a balanced mix of white and black students. At this point, with opponents of busing in the white neighborhoods vowing never to allow their children to be bused into all-black neighborhoods, and pledging never to permit black students to be bused into their neighborhoods, Boston was on the verge of racial war.

As they had done in most other critical moments in their lives, members of the city's predominantly white, Irish-Catholic population looked to the leaders of their Church for moral support and personal direction. There was no question that Humberto Medeiros was unalterably opposed to racism in any form and that he supported the idea of equality of all human beings. In August 1971, less than a year after his arrival in Boston, encouraged by the members of the archdiocesan Human Rights Commission and assisted by Father Thomas McDonnell, he issued a strong pastoral letter on racism that gained international attention. In "Man's Cities and God's Poor," Medeiros announced his opposition to the sin of racism and made an unequivocal commitment to education, housing, and racial and ethnic equality. He stated that one of his highest priorities as archbishop of Boston would be to alleviate the suffering of the poor. Medeiros also joined with leaders of all faiths to draft a statement they hoped would promote peace in the divided city. The resulting Covenant for Justice, Equity, and Harmony, complete with an olive-branch logo, was signed by over 250,000 people. Although he spoke out publicly on behalf of human rights and racial equality, Medeiros made it equally clear that he would neither bless nor oppose any specific elements of the school desegregation conflict in Boston. These were political and economic issues in which he insisted he had no special competence and which he felt should be resolved by the appropriate legal and professional authorities. In April 1974, the cardinal went to legislative hearings at the Massachusetts State House to testify in support of the state's Racial Imbalance Law, an unpopular but courageous act; after Judge Garrity handed down his decision two months later, Medeiros responded in his usual reasoned and measured fashion. "Busing may not be the most desirable way to integrate," he said, "but it's all we have right now. As long as people keep calm and quiet, all will be fine."

But opponents of busing had no intention of keeping calm and quiet. The cardinal's position of moral strength and quiet objectivity may have worked in Brownsville, Texas, but it did not work in Boston, Massachusetts. The Boston Irish did not want to listen to abstract theories or pious platitudes—they wanted action. They wanted their cardinal to join them in their prayers, lead them in their rosaries, march at the head of their parades. In the controversy over court-ordered busing, you were either "with us" or "against us," you were either a friend or an enemy—there was nothing more to be said. The Boston Irish would not accept the kind of "common ground" for which their cardinal was obviously searching.

The sincere and outspoken position that Medeiros took against racism, as well as his statements apparently supporting the order of the court, caused many members of his flock to react with dismay, protest, and even vilification. Catholics had been raised in the belief that parental control over their children's education took precedence over the power of the state. Now Church leaders seemed to be going against that tradition. It was at this time that a great deal of repressed anger and resentment boiled to the surface, as angry protestors found fault with the prelate's racial views and criticized his personal idiosyncrasies. The television camera was not always kind to Medeiros, often catching those inconsequential personal characteristics that were a natural and unconscious part of the prelate's ethnic persona—the sad brown eyes, the tilted head, the pious invocations, the hands meekly folded, the protestations of unworthiness—but that many Irish viewers now found lugubrious and sanctimonious. The cardinal often became the butt of cruel ridicule and caricature at the hands of those who felt betrayed by their Church leaders.

Still, most Catholic parishioners retained their basic faith in the Church and their confidence in their cardinal; on several occasions, he was requested to come to their neighborhoods and join with them in their activities. Medeiros, however, feared that, given the temper of the time and the high level of emotion, any public appearance would be misconstrued and any comments, however informal, would be misinterpreted in a way that would make it seem he was supporting one side or the other. On several occasions during 1975 and 1976, when residents of Charlestown felt that Medeiros might pay a visit to their neighborhood (on Bunker Hill Day, for example), the prelate failed to show up. The "townies" of Charlestown saw the cardinal's failure to accept their invitation as a public rejection of their cause. It was obvious that the harried prelate was becoming increasingly frustrated by criticisms from the black community and the white community that he was not speaking out strongly enough or decisively enough to make his position clear. When, in May 1976, one local newspaper suggested that he might go into such Irish neighborhoods as South Boston and Charlestown to clarify his stand on the racial crisis, the usually calm and controlled cardinal could no longer hold back his irritation: "Why should I go? To get stoned? Is that what they'd like to see?" he retorted angrily. "I've been turned off in South Boston, anyhow," he continued. "No one there is listening to me. Eighty percent of the Catholics in South Boston do not attend Mass or go to church. They wanted me to go to Charlestown, too. To get stoned." And the poor man continued on, obviously giving vent to the fears and frustrations that had been rising to the boiling point over the preceding several months. Irish Catholic residents of South Boston and Charlestown were shocked at the cardinal's questioning of their religious faith and his implication that they would throw stones at a prince of the Church. Medeiros

The bitter controversy over court-ordered busing in Boston during the mid-1970s, designed to promote racial integration in the city's public school system, deeply divided the religious as well as the political community. Many Catholic pastors were torn between upholding the civil rights of African Americans and supporting the parental rights of their own parishioners. (AP/Wide World Photos.)

subsequently made a public apology for his "unfortunate" remarks, explaining that he was only human and had reacted out of "fatigue and anger." Unfortunately, however, the damage had been done.

Feeling rejected and betrayed, many local Catholics could not understand why so many of "their own kind" had apparently turned against them, sided with "outsiders," and supported racial integration. Popular political figures such as Senator Ted Kennedy, Congressman Tip O'Neill, and Mayor Kevin White seemed to have gone over to the enemy; successful Irish businessmen, lawyers, and other professionals who had moved out into the wealthy suburbs criticized them as bigots and racists; and now their own Church leaders appeared to have deserted them and taken up with the liberals. Many neighborhood critics felt that they could no longer yield to the authority of the Church or accept the direction of the clergy.

Throughout the archdiocese itself, but especially in parishes in old

Irish neighborhoods like Charlestown and South Boston, the clergy themselves showed signs of confusion and division. Some priests came out in favor of civil rights, supported busing, and actually rode the yellow buses to protect the children. Other priests came out in open defiance of the court order, withheld their collections, and aligned themselves with their defiant parishioners. Most parish priests, however, found themselves in much the same position as the Irish police officers who patrolled the troubled streets or rode alongside the yellow buses on their motorcycles. As professionals, they were sworn to uphold the letter of the law and obey the orders of their superiors; as residents of these same neighborhoods, they were sympathetic to the fears and anxieties of their families, their neighbors, and their friends. Boston was a badly divided city throughout the 1970s, and the agonizing issues that disrupted homes, alienated families, and ended friendships were also reflected in the membership of the Catholic Church itself.

The years of hard work reorganizing the archdiocese, reinvigorating the Church, paying off the monstrous debt, and going through the agonizing ordeal of the city's racial problems took a heavy toll on the health of Cardinal Medeiros. Despite his normal appearance and apparently sturdy physique, Medeiros suffered from diabetes, severe hypertension, and a congestive heart condition that had increasingly worsened under the frustrating pressures of the city's racial problems and the violence generated by the busing crisis. By the summer of 1983, it was becoming obvious that the cardinal's health was declining. He underwent open-heart surgery with apparent success, only to die the following morning, September 17, 1983. Only in death was the pastoral leadership of Humberto Medeiros, and the deep spirituality he brought to his dealings with persons over the years, truly recognized and appreciated by the community at large, which shared in the outpouring of love and emotion at his funeral ceremonies.*

* William Helmick, *Cardinal Medeiros Remembered* (Boston, 1984). Monsignor Helmick served as secretary to Cardinal Medeiros, and compiled the sermons delivered by the auxiliary bishops of Boston at the noon and evening memorial Masses. Medeiros was buried in St. Patrick's Cemetery, Fall River, where his parents are also buried.

As it became increasingly evident that the cardinal was seriously ill, there was the usual speculation about his successor. Over the years he had built up a staff of extremely competent auxiliary bishops— Thomas Daily, John D'Arcy, Daniel Hart, Alfred Hughes, Joseph Maguire, Lawrence Riley, Thomas Riley, and several others, any of whom would make an acceptable replacement. But once again Rome did the unexpected. On January 24, 1984, the Holy See announced that the Most Reverend Bernard F. Law, bishop of Springfield–Cape Girardeau, would succeed Umberto Medeiros as the eighth bishop and the fourth archbishop of Boston.

Born in Torreón, Mexico, on November 4, 1931, Bernard F. Law was the son of a colonel in the United States Air Force. After attending various schools in North America, South America, and the Virgin Islands, he graduated from Harvard College in 1953, enrolled at St. Joseph Seminary in St. Benedict, Louisiana, and then attended Pontifical College Josephinum at Worthington, Ohio. After being ordained to the priesthood in May 1961, Father Law traveled to Jackson, Mississippi, where he served as the editor of the diocesan newspaper, after which he went to Washington, D.C., for three years as executive director of the Bishop's Committee for Ecumenical and Interreligious Affairs. This was a post that brought him into contact with numerous bishops and diocesan authorities in many parts of the United States. In 1973 he was appointed bishop of the diocese of Springfield–Cape Girardeau, Missouri.

Just why Bishop Law, aged fifty-two, was then named archbishop of Boston in 1984 is still not clear. Whether it was because he was an outsider who could assess the Boston situation objectively, a bishop known for his religious orthodoxy and loyalty to the pope, a graduate of Harvard College familiar with the environs of Boston, a well-traveled individual knowledgeable about Latin America and fluent in Spanish, or because of a combination of all these factors, clearly Bernard Law was Pope John Paul II's choice to head up the archdiocese of Boston. And Law's appointment was roundly greeted with enthusiasm by local residents as a welcome return to a more familiar Boston ecclesiastical tradition. Bright, affable, and compassionate, the new prelate made friends easily, moved about the archdiocese actively, displayed an early and serious concern for poor and homeless persons, and almost immediately set out to establish relations with the increasing number of "new" immigrants, mainly Hispanic and Asian, who were fast becoming part of the city's Roman Catholic population.

In a number of ways, conditions in Boston were far less menacing and confrontational for Archbishop Law in 1984 than they had been for his predecessor, Archbishop Medeiros, a decade earlier. For one thing, the most bitter displays of violence over court-ordered busing had largely subsided. Many white families had abandoned the neighborhoods in favor of the quieter surroundings of the suburbs. Furthermore, a number of families were avoiding sending their children to the public schools by enrolling them in nearby parochial schools. Despite stern directives by Cardinal Medeiros that no new students should be admitted if their acceptance would impede school integration, several Catholic high schools in the greater Boston area took on new life with increased enrollments, either from the children of new families that had just moved into the area or from nieces and nephews who registered from the addresses of aunts and uncles in the suburbs.* And finally, a form of mental and physical exhaustion had set in that gradually precluded any further agitation or demonstrations. Some community leaders became ill; others grew old; most simply got tired and decided to do something more enjoyable with the rest of their lives. The lessening of tensions could be seen in small but meaningful ways. The number of policemen on duty around the schools grew smaller; the noise of police motorcycles became fainter; the media reported fewer racial incidents; and the defiant slogans Never and Resist began to fade and peel on brick walls and wooden fences.

Then, too, the new archbishop arrived only a few months after the

* The statistics of what became known as "white flight" demonstrate the changing character of Boston's public schools. In 1973, one year before busing started, the percentage of white students was 60 percent; by 1980 the figure had dropped to 35 percent; by 1987 it was down to 26 percent.

1983 election of Raymond L. Flynn as mayor. There were many Bostonians who hoped that the new mayor would usher in a more tolerant racial climate, and certainly, in his inaugural address, he gave every reason for optimism in this regard. Although he assured the white neighborhoods of his sympathy and support, he also promised African Americans that he would protect their political rights and civil liberties. "The full weight of city government will be brought down," he declared, "on all those who seek, because of race or color, to deny anyone from any street, any school, any park, any home, any job, in any neighborhood in the city." The undercurrent of racism still continued in Boston, of course; as late as 1988, Cardinal Law came out in support of Mayor Flynn's stand against excluding anyone from public housing in South Boston by having members of the clergy read a pastoral letter at all Masses condemning racial bigotry and urging the peaceful integration of public housing. But the greater problems facing the new archbishop now had more to do with the internal problems and challenges facing the Catholic Church itself than with healing the conflicts of the civic community—although in a city like Boston these two areas could never be completely separated.

One of Archbishop Law's immediate concerns was the efficient and cost-effective management of his archdiocese. He retained the system of four regional bishoprics established by his predecessor, but he also looked for ways to further modernize diocesan operations and reduce financial expenditures.* Almost immediately, he appointed a special committee of religious leaders, prominent educators, and business executives to examine the existing organization of the archdiocese. In accordance with the recommendations of this committee, chaired by Bishop Robert Banks, the archbishop created a cabinet system with a series of cabinet secretaries who would provide greater direction and accountability for the eighty-seven agencies and offices that had for-

---

* Cardinal Law also added a fifth episcopal region, Merrimack, which incorporated parishes from the West, South, and Central regions.

merly operated as independent units. Not only did this system save an enormous amount of time for the archbishop, who previously had had to meet with each agency separately, but it also provided an opportunity for the agencies themselves to learn what their counterparts were doing, and how those activities fitted in with their own plans and programs. The secretary for social services, for example, would now supervise agencies working with the deaf, the aged, the handicapped, and persons with AIDS, as well as those working with charitable agencies, family counseling programs, and prison ministries. The Office for Health Care oversees not only such individual Catholic hospitals as St. Elizabeth's and St. Margaret's in Boston, and St. John's and St. Joseph's in Lowell, but also the newly formed associated Catholic hospitals under the Caritas Christi system. The secretary for pastoral services manages such traditional agencies as the Holy Name Society, the Legion of Mary, and the Society for the Propagation of the Faith, but it also heads up a series of apostolates dealing with such "old" national groups as the Italians, the Poles, and the Lithuanians, as well as with such "new" immigrant groups as the Cambodians, the Chinese, the Haitians, the Laotians, and the Vietnamese.

Archbishop Law takes his managerial responsibilities very seriously, meeting with his cabinet secretaries once a week, whenever possible, as well as at extended afternoon sessions at which written reports are presented and discussed. In his early years in Boston, he must have found such meetings extremely helpful in gaining firsthand information about what was going on in a large diocese about which he knew relatively little. In more recent years, the process has also become a way of keeping his finger on the pulse of the archdiocese, as well as helping him formulate his long-range goals as archbishop of Boston.

The archbishop also sought ways to pay off the last external indebtedness of the archdiocese. In place of the Stewardship Appeal, which comprised ten collections throughout the year and set a specific goal for each parish, he established the Cardinal's Appeal, which conducts

Bernard Francis Law came to Boston in 1984 to succeed Humberto Cardinal Medeiros as archbishop of Boston. Elevated to the Sacred College in 1985, Cardinal Law had been an outspoken defender of human life and a strong supporter of Church doctrine in accordance with the teachings of Pope Paul II. Presiding over a rapidly changing archdiocese, he has begun a program of pastoral planning designed to lead the Church into the twenty-first century. (Photo by Bachrach.)

a single major fundraising event each year, thereby providing the basis for a predictable annual budget upon which the archdiocese can plan its income and expenditures.

In addition to dealing with financial and managerial issues, however, Archbishop Law also had to confront fundamental demographic changes that were altering the ethnic structures of many old neighborhoods and transforming the traditional parish boundaries. Old gothic churches in depopulated urban areas where old congregations had either died off or moved away were often practically deserted, and devotional services that had once drawn thousands of faithful communicants now went largely unattended. In the lower end of South Boston, for example, the absence of a substantial congregation made it necessary for the archdiocese to close SS. Peter and Paul's Church, one of the oldest parishes in the Boston diocese. For similar reasons, in 1987 the archdiocese was forced to close St. Mary's-by-the-Bay, originally dedicated in 1928, one of three Catholic churches in the south shore town of Hull. The movement of tourists and vacationers to Cape Cod and other summer locations left St. Mary's without enough year-round parishioners to support the church. At the same time, the movement of new and younger populations into such recently developed suburban areas as Billerica, Chelmsford, Franklin, and Tewksbury made it necessary for the archdiocese to create new parishes and build new churches. This created a problem of double spending— money to take the old churches down, and money to put new churches up.

Issues of nationality and language, too, presented challenges involving both financial management and public relations. With second and third generations of young, English-speaking families growing up and moving to the suburbs, and with a diminishing number of priests competent in languages other than English available, a large number of the "old" German, French, Italian, Portuguese, Polish, and Lithuanian churches fell into serious disrepair, were virtually abandoned, and had to be closed down and sold off. These were always sad and painful experiences for original parishioners from the "old countries," who had been baptized, confirmed, and married in these churches and who expected the structures to remain standing forever. At the same time, however, a number of comparatively new ethnic and racial populations were rapidly developing within the Boston archdiocese. During the 1970s, the city's Latin-American population showed a remarkable increase, as refugees from Haiti, Cuba, El Salvador, Honduras, Colombia, and Nicaragua sought to escape the effects of organized crime and political oppression.

Then, during the 1980s, Boston neighborhoods received additional numbers of homeless immigrants from the war zones and refugee camps of Vietnam, Cambodia, Laos, and other parts of Southeast Asia. Although in 1980 the total population of Boston was still nearly 60 percent white, already the share of school-aged children who were white had dropped to 52 percent. By 1990 that number had fallen to 40 percent, making the number of white school-aged children much lower than the combined number of African-American, Haitian, Hispanic, and Asian youngsters. In a remarkably short time, these new immigrant peoples began moving into parts of Boston that had once been overwhelmingly Irish. In the Field's Corner section of Dorchester, for example, where solid three-deckers still stood as a reminder of the Irish-Catholic families who had once dominated the neighborhood, new and different ethnic groups changed the character of the community. St. Matthew's Church, built with the savings of Irish immigrants, began holding its liturgies in French for the benefit of its mostly Haitian immigrant congregation. And nearby, St. Peter's Church, also originally Irish, had three Vietnamese priests to minister to its Vietnamese parishioners. "When we have a parish celebration that involves *all* the community," said Father John Doyle, pastor of St. Peter's, "we use five languages—English, Vietnamese, Spanish, Portuguese, and French." By 1998, the archdiocese offered Mass in fifteen different languages, counted twenty-seven national groups among its members, and estimated that Boston-area worshippers spoke more

Bernard Cardinal Law has taken a strong personal interest in extending a warm welcome to Boston's new immigrants who have joined many of the parishes throughout the archdiocese. Here, the Missionaries of Charity have taken children from St. Peter's parish in Dorchester to attend morning Mass at the Cardinal's residence. After Mass, the Cardinal speaks with his young guests and gives each child a small present. (Photo by Lisa Kessler Photography.)

than thirty languages. "These immigrants are filling parishes that had been becoming almost empty," said Father Joseph Cogo, director of ethnic apostolates. "They are providing many churches with a brighter future."

The problems of population shifts and church closings, however, were merely symptoms of a much larger difficulty—the declining number of clergy in Boston and throughout the nation. The once dominant role and unquestioned authority of the Catholic Church had greatly diminished during the 1970s and 1980s, and the pervasive influence of pastors, priests, and nuns in the daily lives of parishioners had all but disappeared. And disturbing statistics indicated that this problem would become even more complex as time went on.

Throughout the United States, new vocations of priests and nuns were a mere fraction of what they had once been—nine thousand seminarians in 1966 down to three thousand in 1990—while the number of young people choosing to go into religious life appeared to be radically decreasing. By the 1990s, the average age of Catholic priests reached fifty-five, according to Charles H. Morris in his book *American Catholic,* and he reports that only 11 percent of American nuns are younger than forty-five. Because they once outnumbered priests by as much as five to one, and served as the indispensable workforce for parochial schools and Catholic hospitals, Morris feels that nuns have now become "particularly conspicuous by their absence."

Responding to these developments and showing a keen awareness of the meaning of the statistics, in March 1998 Cardinal Law assembled a convocation of some three thousand clergy and lay leaders at Boston's huge World Trade Center to outline a program of pastoral planning that he informed them might eventually result in the closing of forty to sixty parishes by 2008, the year of the archdiocese's bicentennial. Citing an estimated annual decline of 2 percent in regular Sunday Mass attendance over the preceding five years, and a projected 22 percent decline in the number of diocesan priests by the year 2005, the cardinal pointed out the need for proper planning in order to maximize resources to meet the needs of a multicultural Church with an ever-expanding mission.

Within the individual parishes themselves, statistics also pointed to similar problems as the population continued to rise while the number of priests and nuns continued to fall. As one means of ensuring that the work of the Church was carried out, a major effort was made to have members of the laity serve in a number of capacities. In some areas of the country where the shortage of priests was particularly critical, lay people were already serving as chancellors of dioceses and in various other administrative offices. About three hundred parishes in various parts of the United States are run by pastoral administrators, most of whom are women, usually nuns, who carry out all the responsibilities of a pastor, except for saying Mass and administering the sacraments. In Boston, a layman now serves as chancellor of the archdiocese, a nun serves as one of the judges on the diocesan marriage tribunal, and a number of nuns and lay people—lawyers, businessmen, educators, physicians—serve as cabinet secretaries under Cardinal Law. Both married and single men have become ordained deacons while continuing their professional occupations, and members of the laity carry out many functions that were traditionally the responsibilities of priests and nuns. At the parish level, men and women serve as council members, business administrators, eucharistic ministers, lectors, prefects of sodalities, religious education teachers, music directors, leaders of prayer groups, and organizers of youth ministries. These extraordinary developments would have been inconceivable and incomprehensible to most of the faithful as late as the 1960s.

Some Catholics feel that, in the absence of priests and the prospect of declining vocations, the work of the Church would be even more effectively served by either ordaining married men or allowing women to be ordained as priests—or both. These are proposals, however, that Pope John Paul II has definitively taught are contrary to the teaching of the Catholic Church, and that Cardinal Law fully agrees cannot be considered in light of Church tradition. The mere mention of such issues, however, points up some of the most serious and complex challenges that faced Boston's new archbishop. External issues involving administrative management, financial constraints, and personnel problems are certainly important considerations for any Church leader; but even more critical are internal issues involving doctrinal teachings, standards of moral behavior, and the future character of the Catholic Church itself.

The numerous cultural revolutions and social upheavals that permeated all of world society during the 1960s and 1970s generated demands for a whole series of moral, social, and religious changes. Defiance of established authority, along with rebellion against generally accepted norms of civilized behavior, produced a general rejection of such traditional institutions as the family, the law, and the church. "The world is new. The situation of 1960 is revolutionary. It is quite unlike the world of 1900," warned the Jesuit theologian Gustave Weigel in a public address. "World society and our own institutions are changing." Influenced by these powerful forces of change, and undoubtedly stimulated by the exhilarating spirit of Vatican II, many Catholics began calling for serious modifications in Catholic Church teaching in order to adapt to the new order of things. Proposals for a more tolerant attitude toward birth control, abortion, divorce, and premarital sex, as well as demands for admitting married men to the priesthood and ordaining women, raised serious questions about the traditions of the past and prospects for the future.

Contributing additional pressure for change in the Catholic Church during the 1990s was the extensive impact of the electronic media—radio, television, the Internet—which made all information instantaneously accessible and which no longer accepted any defining line between what is private, personal, or confidential and what is unconditionally available to satisfy the public's "right to know." The issue of divorce and annulment involving Catholics, for example, became a subject of public discussion and general speculation. Once privately adjudicated in church tribunals by specialists in canon law, the annulment process had for some time been discussed quietly by leaders in ecclesiastical circles. Whereas American bishops had tried in recent years to make the annulment process as painless and compassionate as possible, Rome had increasingly complained about the growing number of annulments granted in the United States. Now, however, the topic of annulment became an issue of open controversy, especially involving those who felt it was dishonest to say that a marriage had never taken place. Sweeping charges were made, often stimulated by gossip columnists and television reporters, that the Catholic Church had engaged in dishonest or deceptive practices in awarding

annulments, especially when celebrities or well-known political figures were involved.*

In much the same manner, electronic and print journalists brought
into the open the news of sexual scandals involving a number of pedophiliac priests in various parts of the country and in several parts of
the archdiocese of Boston, a shameful situation that had once been
kept discreetly out of sight. Before the 1960s, it was customary for
Church authorities to hush up such scandalous conduct to protect
the Church from the terrible curse of "scandal." In many cases, the
offending priest would be provided with medical care and professional
therapy, but then sent quietly off to some other unsuspecting parish
in the hope that he would either change his ways or be lost to view
altogether. All too often, however, the priest would continue his abuse
of the young boys and girls entrusted to his care until his victims, now
adults, finally refused to be silent any longer and went public with the
traumatic results of their childhood ordeals.

In the full light of the mass media, with major criminal indictments
bringing perpetrators such as Father James Porter to public trials and
convictions, and with multi-million-dollar lawsuits being brought
against various Catholic archdioceses, Church leaders began taking
steps to develop more sophisticated screening procedures for prospective priests and resolved to formulate more precise pastoral guidelines
for handling such matters. Acknowledging that any allegation of
sexual misconduct by clerics is "a serious matter," the archdiocese
requires a prompt investigation and thorough examination of the
charges by diocesan authorities, spiritual and psychological assistance
for the victim and his or her family, protection of the rights of the
accused, and appropriate notification to the parish and community

---

* The marital status of Massachusetts Congressman Joseph Kennedy, for example,
became the subject of nationwide interest and public discussion after his former wife
wrote a best-selling book in which she openly criticized the Catholic Church for its
policies and procedures regarding the annulment process.

involved. The sexual scandals were a tragic embarrassment to the Church, and although the perpetrators actually represented only a small proportion of the total number of priests, their misconduct certainly cast a pall over the lives of all those churchmen who devoted themselves to the Christian formation of children. Only by reviewing many of the policies and procedures of the past in light of modern social needs and technological developments is it possible to make whatever changes are necessary to reassure the public at large that the Church is truly a force for Christian love and a model for human compassion.

Officials of the Catholic Church in Rome were only too well aware of the mounting pressures for change in the wake of Vatican II, but they were also conscious that many of these demands posed serious and dangerous challenges to some fundamental Church teachings. One of the first significant reactions came in July 1968 when Pope Paul VI issued the encyclical letter *Humanae Vitae,* which reaffirmed the traditional ban on artificial contraception. This came as a shock to many American Catholics who had been expecting some kind of change in the official position. Further signs that Church policy would remain unaltered became evident in 1978 when Archbishop Karol Wojtyla of Kraków, Poland, was elected as Pope John Paul II, and even more so in 1982 after Cardinal Joseph Ratzinger took over direction of the Congregation for the Doctrine of Faith. Although Pope John Paul accepted both the reformist spirit and the ecumenical principles of Vatican II, he drew a sharp line defining the point beyond which any further changes or modifications in established Church doctrine would not be permitted. He eloquently proclaimed the equality of women and the importance of their role in the Catholic Church, for example; at the same time, however, he ruled that the impossibility of women's ordination was a fundamental truth of faith that allowed for no further discussion. In a similar manner, he emphasized the primacy of individual conscience as defined by the Second Vatican Council, but he also insisted that there are certain acts (abortion, for example) that are "intrinsically evil" and "always wrong." He promoted the ideals of pluralism and encouraged the concept of "inculturation" (by which the Catholic Church adapts to local conditions and different cultures), but at the same time he has limited the influence of national conferences of bishops and has steadily appointed bishops who are devoted to his more centralized vision of the Church.

Some critics of Pope John Paul II complained that his views were contradictory and paradoxical, creating confusion within the Church, bewildering pastors and priests, and causing individuals to make up their own minds about issues of personal morality. Supporters of the pontiff, on the other hand, argued that his authority is paramount, his leadership unquestioned, his definitions precise, and his positions on official Church teaching perfectly clear. They labeled as "cafeteria-Catholics" those who picked and chose which teachings of the Church they would follow and which they would not.

It was in the midst of these discussions and debates in the mid-1980s that Bernard F. Law assumed his new position as archbishop. As a city of renowned colleges and universities, Boston was acutely aware of the new theological and philosophical movements that were being discussed. As a city of famous medical centers and scientific laboratories, Boston was also responsive to the day's complicated moral and ethical questions. Many of these arose from a series of remarkable discoveries in medicine and biology involving contraception, abortion, in vitro fertilization, and artificial insemination, as well as from considerations of physician-assisted suicide, living wills, and even the possibility of cloning human life itself. A number of Bostonians assumed that since he was young, bright, well-traveled, and a graduate of Harvard College, the new prelate would hold more progressive theological views and would probably move the archdiocese away from traditional church teachings on many of these issues. ("Oh, God!" one diocesan priest recalls himself thinking when he first heard of Law's appointment, "we're getting a Midwestern liberal!")

Contrary to such expectations, however, Bernard Law has adamantly refused to make any of the modifications or concessions anticipated by those who had expected a different approach. From the outset, Archbishop Law demonstrated his loyalty to the pope and his obedience to the pontiff's statements regarding the acceptable body of Church teaching. He has allowed no deviation in dealing with such controversial topics as the sanctity of life in any of its stages from conception to death, refusing to accept anything that would violate the traditional natural-law teaching of the Catholic Church.

Law used the force of his office as archbishop of Boston as a public, forceful, and articulate supporter of the pro-life movement against abortion, and in 1997 he also came out publicly against an organized movement to restore the death penalty in Massachusetts. Although this was an unpopular position at a time when a series of particularly gruesome murders had generated much public support for capital punishment, the archbishop pointed out that consistency in his moral beliefs demanded recognizing that the sanctity of life applied as much to the murderer in prison as it did to the fetus in the womb.* In a similar manner, the new archbishop also refused to consider as a matter for fruitful discussion the ordination either of married men or of women. He is convinced that, under the effective supervision of his regional bishops and vicars and with the efficient direction of his cabinet system, an enlarged use of an informed, educated, and highly motivated laity can make up for the declining numbers of priests and nuns. Indeed, he has insisted that even if there was not a shortage of priests, he would continue to encourage the greater use of lay people in Church affairs, in keeping with the spirit of Vatican II that called for greater participation of the people of God in the life of the Church.

The writing of history requires not only an accumulation of source

* In April 1998, Cardinal Law was presented with the Ehrmann Award by the Massachusetts Citizens Against the Death Penalty for his efforts in opposing capital punishment.

materials and factual data but also a certain amount of distance and a sense of perspective in order to obtain the necessary objectivity. Attempts to analyze the personal qualities of the present archbishop and to assess the relative success of his current programs and policies must, therefore, be seen as the efforts of a writer witnessing a work that is still very much in progress. (I have every expectation that before long other historians, armed with more information and a greater sense of perspective, will arrive at more accurate assessments and decidedly different interpretations.) For the moment, however, there are certain trends and characteristics that seem worth observing.

As archbishop of Boston, Bernard Law presents a fascinating contrast with the preceding archbishops, most of whom came to be easily (and sometimes irreverently) categorized by the general public. Williams was said to be "taciturn" and "laconic"; O'Connell has been labeled "proud" and "authoritarian"; Cushing was variously described as "crusty" and "unpredictable"; Medeiros came across as "humble" and "pious." Even after some fifteen years in Boston, however, it is still difficult to come up with an adjective or a short phrase that captures the elusive personal qualities of Cardinal Law. In many ways he defies casual labeling or easy stereotyping, despite attempts by writers and commentators to use the prosaic terms of "conservative" or "liberal" to define his religious convictions or categorize his social views. Beneath a calm facade and stolid bearing, there is a slight hint of the mystic whose spiritual beliefs go very deep as he carries out his episcopal duties and performs his priestly rites. In his public persona he is careful, dignified, and controlled, purposeful in his movements and deliberate in his speech; in social settings and small gatherings he is a charming conversationalist who captivates his listeners with an easy smile and a delightful sense of humor. He is a man who can listen patiently and sympathetically; but he can also make decisions decisively and sometimes instantaneously.

Almost every priest comments on the deep personal interest the archbishop takes in their welfare. "Of all the four archbishops I have served under," recalled retired Monsignor John P. Carroll, former director of the Catholic Youth Organization, Law "is the most attentive and thoughtful of his priests. He visits with them when they are sick, he consoles them when death strikes their families, he tries to give them the Sacrament of the Sick when he can." One young curate described the archbishop simply as "a pastor for his priests." In a further effort to increase a sense of brotherhood among the clergy, the cardinal initiated the Emmaus Program, which brought priests of the archdiocese together for overnight convocations celebrating the priesthood, and then encouraged them to form smaller groups for monthly meetings. This attitude on the part of the cardinal has created a considerable measure of harmony and collegiality among the clergy, as well as increased loyalty and support for the prelate.

Although Cardinal Law moves around the city constantly, visits his parishes without advance notice, and has involved himself in municipal affairs of all kinds, he has still not become an integral part of "old Boston" as longtime residents think of it. This is so perhaps because he spent much of his youth traveling from one part of the country to another, from one school to another, without really putting down roots in any one place. But it is also perhaps because in so many ways the "old Boston" no longer exists the way it does in the memories of the oldtimers. Archbishop Law came to Boston when the city was changing dramatically—in the organizational structure of the Church, in the racial character of the city's population, in the structure of its economy, and in the ethnic composition of its neighborhoods.

Times had changed, and they have changed even more; it may well be that the new prelate saw this more quickly than many others. One clerical observer remarked that because of his extensive background, Law is perhaps the most "American" archbishop Boston has ever had. But in many ways Law seems to have transcended even this national identity, and has developed into something of a citizen of the world, without the parochial restraints or myopic limitations of those who have always been rooted in one particular region, one particular culture, one particular way of doing things. Many ordinary Bostonians seem to sense this when they speak admiringly of the cardinal and remark that he is intended "for something better" or that he is bound to go on to "something in Rome." What many of these people speak of in the familiar terms of a job or position may well be an unconscious recognition that Law has a vision of the Catholic Church that goes far beyond Boston, or even America—a more "catholic" vision that sees the archdiocese as part of a much broader realm of the universal Church.

It must be obvious to anyone who has met him that Cardinal Law has a clear understanding of power and a shrewd sense of what politics is all about. He has chosen, however, neither to flaunt his power nor to exercise his influence in the traditional mode of Boston politics. He is a strong believer in establishing quiet networks of personal friendships and engaging in extended dialogues in an atmosphere of mutual respect. In situations where he had decided that using the Church's influence is appropriate—especially where issues of equity and justice involving the less fortunate are concerned—he has tended to use the moral weight of his office not to provide solutions of his own but to bring the various parties together around a "table of trust" to work out their own decisions. He has used this influence as a sort of "moral broker," for example, in helping hard-pressed lobstermen acquire new docking facilities in Boston; assisting fishermen to get better health care in Gloucester; encouraging unemployed workers after a devastating fire in Lawrence; and supporting Hispanic residents seeking affordable housing in Lowell. His meetings with prominent businessmen have provided a valuable source of support for parochial schools in Boston; his close associations with groups of African-American ministers in the Greater Boston area have helped improve relationships among church leaders in the city.

The high degree of respect that Cardinal Law had established for himself as a moral spokesman of unquestioned integrity was very much in evidence in a time of unexpected crisis. In December 1994, a deranged young man named John Salvi burst into two women's health clinics in the town of Brookline and shot to death two young women and wounded several other people before he was apprehended, tried, and convicted. This violent and tragic episode became a catalyst in focusing public attention on the manner in which angry confrontations between pro-choice and pro-life groups had gradually escalated from peaceful demonstrations for and against abortion rights to loud and frequently menacing clashes involving vicious name calling and insulting epithets. Many community leaders feared that intense television and newspaper coverage of the Salvi shootings might raise the level of controversy over abortion to even more violent levels, and they called on both sides to limit their demonstrations and moderate their language. The fact that Cardinal Law could meet with Governor William F. Weld to review the situation and discuss ways in which peaceful demonstrations could be assured without endangering the peace of the community was a confirmation of the prelate's primary reputation as a moral and religious spokesman. No one suggested any hidden political motives or asked what his "angle" might be—everyone understood that as the leader of the Church in Boston he was standing up for the constitutional right of American Catholics to proclaim their religious beliefs in a peaceful, responsible, and public manner.

The work and accomplishments of Archbishop Law had proven to be more than acceptable to Pope John Paul II, for in 1985, after only a little over one year as archbishop, Bernard Law was elevated to the Sacred College of Cardinals.* Not long after his elevation, in a pastoral letter dated August 6, 1986, the new cardinal issued a call for the convening of the Eighth Synod of the archdiocese. In response to this call twenty-six subcommittees, composed not only of members of the clergy but also, for the first time in Boston Church history, of a sig-

---

* William Henry O'Connell had been archbishop of Boston for four years before becoming cardinal; Richard J. Cushing was in office for fourteen years before receiving the red hat; and Humberto S. Medeiros was named a cardinal after three years as archbishop.

nificant number of lay people, gathered to examine various aspects of the life of the Church in Boston. Questionnaires were sent out to the parishes of the archdiocese, where local committees of priests and lay people reflected on them, formulated responses, and returned their completed questionnaires to the synod. The subcommittee then selected two or three of the most important topics from each parish report and sent them back to the parish committees for further consideration and refinement. Long, serious, and painstaking, the Eighth Synod was a collaborative process involving literally thousands of pastors, curates, and parishioners; it gave members of the archdiocese an opportunity to develop a priority ranking of issues and concerns that would be formulated into the *Pastoral Plan for Mission.* The process also gave Cardinal Law an opportunity to learn what was going on throughout his archdiocese as well as the basis on which to develop his future agenda for Boston. The synod turned out to be a remarkable starting point for a new phase in the history of the archdiocese, providing a valuable document to which church leaders can refer in developing new programs as well as a basic yardstick against which future accomplishments can be measured.

One program that was put into effect to continue the momentum started by the synod was a system of regular parish visitations. Following the pattern of the regular five-year *ad limina* visit of each bishop to Rome to give an account of his stewardship, the archbishop, or one of the regional bishops acting on his behalf, would pay a formal visit once every five years to each parish in the archdiocese. In preparation for such a visit, each parish would review its activities, prepare a mission statement, and offer a projection of its activities for the next five years. The bishop would meet with the pastor and the curates, consult with members of the parish council and other groups, engage in a period of spiritual activities, respond to the parish report, and make suggestions as to which changes and innovations would be most appropriate over the next five years. The visitation program challenges the people of every parish to engage in serious planning not only in such areas as finances, construction, education, buildings and grounds—taking over responsibility for functions once seen exclusively as "the pastor's job"—but also in regard to various aspects of the spiritual life of the parish. At this point, even the selection of a new pastor involves serious consultation between the bishop and members of the parish in question.

As part of promoting more vigorous forms of parish life, Cardinal Law was also deeply concerned with making the fundamental teachings of the Church better known and more available to the modern generation of Catholics. At the synod of bishops that assembled in Rome in 1985 to commemorate the twentieth anniversary of the conclusion of the Second Vatican Council, it was Cardinal Law who made a formal presentation (known as an "intervention") calling for publication of a new Catholic catechism that would codify and clarify in modern language the basic doctrinal teachings of the Catholic Church. Not since the Council of Trent in the sixteenth century had a universal catechism been prepared (this provided the basis for the so-called Baltimore Catechism of the nineteenth century, from which most American Catholics received their earliest religious instruction in the familiar question-and-answer format). Cardinal Law took a personal interest in all aspects of the preparation of what ultimately appeared in 1994 as the *Catechism of the Catholic Church;* he at one point strongly supported the use of inclusive (non-sexist) language in the English translation wherever it would not compromise theological accuracy. A compendium of Catholic doctrine more than a thousand pages long, the *Catechism* was originally intended as a reference work from which local bishops could develop smaller doctrinal manuals for their parishioners. In its first year of publication, however, the American edition sold 2.5 million copies, and by the following year (1995) its total sales had reached the 4 million range, demonstrating a remarkably broad interest on the part of the general American Catholic community in the fundamentals of its religion.

In supporting the directives of the Second Vatican Council and the teachings of Pope John Paul II, and reemphasizing the point beyond which changes in Catholic doctrine will not be allowed to go, Cardinal Law has also indicated a number of areas in which he would encourage the Catholic Church to function in a positive and supportive manner. To emphasize Church teachings in confronting new developments in medical science and biological research, for example, he has favored a Catholic health-care network called Caritas Christi. This program has been bringing together various hospitals throughout the archdiocese in a merger calculated to offer patients professional medical treatment in a Catholic environment. In hospitals that are part of the Caritas Christi system, doctors are not permitted to perform tubal ligations, vasectomies, sterilizations, or abortions. The merger has been approved by the Public Charities Division and the Antitrust Division in the office of the Massachusetts attorney general, as well as by the U.S. Justice Department. At this point, the Catholic network, including St. Elizabeth's Hospital in Brighton and the Carney Hospital in Dorchester, serves some 250,000 residents in Massachusetts, New Hampshire, and Rhode Island. What the long-range prospects of this program will be in the light of objections from insurance companies, physicians' groups, and competing health-care companies is not quite clear, but the network does provide an example of a positive and workable alternative to what Catholic leaders regard as the "objective evil" of abortion.

The archdiocese has also provided means of preventing abortion before it reaches the medical stage. In 1973, in response to the *Roe v. Wade* decision by which the U.S. Supreme Court legalized abortion, a Boston organization called Pregnancy Help was founded to provide a positive, moral alternative to abortion. Now funded by the archdiocese, Pregnancy Help provides such services as pregnancy testing, counseling, referrals, and direct financial assistance to women contemplating abortions. Over the course of twenty-five years, the program has served more than twenty thousand women. Another program, called Project Rachel, also functions under the Pro-Life Office of the archdiocese, and provides spiritual consolation, medical advice, and therapeutic assistance to women who have had abortions and who wish to be reconciled to the Church.

The Catholic Youth Ministry, too, is an area of special interest to Cardinal Law. He hopes to attract teenagers back to the Church by convincing them that the Church takes them seriously and that it wishes them to feel not just wanted but actually needed. The former Catholic Youth Organization (CYO), which most Catholics recall from the 1950s and 1960s because of its impressive marching bands and successful baseball teams, has been gradually transformed into Catholic Youth Groups, which place greater emphasis on educational programs and social activities. Special "Life Teen" Masses and weekend retreats have been organized, and many parishes have encouraged young people to become involved not only in religious programs and liturgical services, but also in such charitable works as serving dinners to the homeless, buying food for the poor, and going shopping for the elderly. In the city of Quincy, nine parishes have combined their personnel and their assets to create a citywide youth ministry. In a further effort to stimulate the interest of young men and women in religious vocations, special Vocation Awareness teams have gone around to churches and schools, published pamphlets and leaflets, and produced television advertisements explaining the nature of the religious life and pointing up the spiritual benefits of doing God's work. In these and other diocesan programs, it appears that the cardinal has moved beyond the damage-control stage of restoring confidence and goodwill between the bishops and the laity. The new, more positive programs are intended to reach out to young people, newly arrived immigrants, and those who have been alienated from the Church and draw them into the Catholic community.

In November 1997, Cardinal Bernard Law joined hundreds of other bishops from North and South America in attending a special monthlong Vatican synod called by Pope John Paul II to explore ways of revitalizing the Roman Catholic Church in the Western hemisphere. The bishops expressed particular concern that the increasingly secular, materialistic, and highly individualistic character of United States society had greatly eroded "the concept of the common good and its ability to call people to something beyond themselves." Such "unspeakable crimes" as abortion and physician-assisted suicide, said Monsignor Dennis Schurr, general secretary of the National Conference of Catholic Bishops, "come to be embraced in the name of individual rights and democracy." Another concern voiced at the Vatican meeting was the need to minister to Latin American immigrants to North America so that they would not be drawn into a more selfish and secular lifestyle. The plight of the immigrant, however, was actually part of a broader concern on the part of the pope. He sought greater Church unity and solidarity throughout the Americas, and he hoped that Church leaders could somehow span the cultural and economic divide betweeen the North and the South of the world. There was every expectation that the speeches, workshops, papers, and reports prepared by the bishops and their staffs in the course of the synod would form the basis for future decisions regarding the Americas.

The Vatican Synod of America, however, took on an even greater significance in view of the decision by Pope John Paul II to visit Cuba early in 1998. While his primary concerns in visiting this Communist country (which has been under the dictatorial rule of Fidel Castro since 1959) were essentially religious—ministering to Catholics, winning more rights for Catholicism, strengthening a church that has suffered nearly forty years of Marxist harassment—the social and political significance of the pontiff's visit could not be ignored. After the collapse of world Communism in 1989, Cuba suffered not only ideological isolation as one of the few surviving Communist countries, but also severe economic depression as a result of Soviet withdrawals and the United States embargo. Although Pope John Paul II is known for his strong anti-Communist views, he has also been highly critical of the "savage capitalism" he feels has been displayed by the Western

Democracies—including the United States—and he has opposed American embargoes on humanitarian grounds. More than one national observer speculated that the pope's visit might well cause Europe and Latin America to unite behind a papal message of reconciliation that would persuade the United States to change a policy that imposes suffering on the Cuban people.

Given his birth in Mexico, his extensive travels in Latin America, and his personal friendship with Cuba's Cardinal Jaime Ortega, Boston's Cardinal Law has taken a keen interest in Latin American affairs. For fourteen years he was in continuous contact with the Church in Cuba, and he traveled to that country several times to meet with Catholic leaders. In January 1998 he led a group of 150 pilgrims from Boston, including 4 congressmen, 46 priests, and 5 nuns to Cuba to support the pope on his historic visit and to join in the prayers for religious freedom. Speaking two months later, before the American Academy of Arts and Sciences, Cardinal Law suggested that the time was right for a change in U.S. policy toward Cuba. He proposed the establishment of a bipartisan national commission on U.S.–Cuban relations, perhaps chaired by a former American president, to develop policy initiatives that could build on changes already perceived in Cuba since the visit of Pope Paul II.

It is impossible at this point to predict the long-range effects of Pope John Paul II's visit, or the impact it might have on Cuban–U.S. relations, but almost all observers agree that any changes will occur slowly. It is interesting to wonder, however, whether the increasing interest of North Americans in the social, economic, and religious affairs of Central and South America will provide the archdiocese of Boston with even greater opportunities to expand a missionary involvement that has become one of the hallmarks of Boston Catholics over their long and remarkable history.

+≕ ADDITIONAL READING

New studies are beginning to explore the far-reaching aftereffects of Vatican II throughout the Catholic Church in the United States and to analyze the challenges facing Church leaders as they enter the twenty-first century. The compilation of pastorals and addresses by Humberto Cardinal Medeiros of Boston, *"Whatever God Wants"* (Boston, 1984), is impressive simply because of the significant topics he chose to discuss. Subjects such as the evil of abortion, assistance to the poor, the need for priestly vocations, the importance of ethics in law, the threat of nuclear war, the curse of racism, pastoral care for the homosexual, and the danger of drugs demonstrate quite dramatically how acutely conscious the cardinal was of the problems facing the Church, and how clearly he perceived the need for addressing them in Christian terms. Monsignor Peter V. Conley has written an excellent biographical essay, "Humberto Cardinal Medeiros," in *The New Catholic Encyclopedia*, XVIII, pp. 287–88; Father Vincent A. Lapomarda, SJ, has furnished another essay, "Humberto Cardinal Medeiros," in *The Encyclopedia of American Catholic History*, pp. 899–901.

Other writers have also focused on the issues challenging the post-conciliar Church. Adrian Hastings has edited a series of provocative essays, *Modern Catholicism: Vatican II and After* (New York, 1991), and Ralph Martin, in *The Catholic Church at the End of an Age: What Is the Spirit Saying?* (San Francisco, 1994), covers many of the same topics. Jim Castelli and Joseph Gremillion, *The Emerging Parish: The Notre Dame Study of Catholic Life since Vatican II* (San Francisco, 1987), George Gallup, Jr., and Jim Castelli, *The People's Religion: American Faith in the 90's* (New York, 1989), and William V. D'Antonio et al., *Laity: American and Catholic: Transforming the Church* (Kansas City, Mo., 1996), are works that discuss the changing character of the traditional Catholic parish structure and the emerging role of the Catholic laity.

Richard A. Schoenherr and Lawrence A. Young, *Full Pews and Empty Altars: Demographics of the Priest Shortage in United States Catholic Dioceses* (Madison, Wis., 1993), analyzes the character of the priest shortage throughout the United States; Dean R. Hoge, *The Future of Catholic Leadership: Responses to the Priest Shortage* (Kansas City, Mo., 1987), outlines various suggestions to meet the current crisis. Eugene F. Hemrick and Dean R. Hoge, *Seminarians in Theology: A National Profile* (Washington, 1986), a study sponsored by the United States Catholic Conference, addresses the subject of new vocations. Andrew Greeley, *Religious Change in America* (Cambridge, 1989), provides valuable statistical information and discussion of sociological trends relating to changes in the modern Church. Jason Berry, *Lead Us Not into Temptation: Catholic Priests and the Sexual Abuse of Children* (New York, 1992), and Philip Jenkins, *Pedophiles and Priests: Anatomy of a Contemporary Crisis* (New York, 1995), are two of the works that address a serious problem.

The *Catechism of the Catholic Church* (San Francisco, 1994) is the most recent compendium of Catholic teaching; Boston's Cardinal Law played a significant role in its formulation. George A. Kelly, *The Battle for the American Church Revisited* (San Francisco, 1995), offers a conservative critique of what he regards as recent liberal excesses; Michael J. Wrenn, *Catechisms and Controversies: Religious Education in the Postconciliar Years* (San Francisco, 1991), presents an even stronger conservative view on a whole range of catechetical changes. William McSweeney, *Roman Catholicism: The Search for Relevance* (New York, 1980), also inquires into the direction the Church has taken since Vatican II.

Robert J. McClory, *Turning Point* (New York, 1995), provides historical background for the promulgation of Pope Paul VI's 1968 birth control encyclical, *Humanae Vitae*. Anthony Kosnik, ed., *Human Sexuality: New Dimensions in American Catholic Thought* (New York, 1977), and Donald E. McCarthy, ed., *Moral Theology Today: Certitudes and Doubts* (St. Louis, 1984), are two collections of essays by writers who focus on the morality of sexual issues. John T. Noonan, Jr., *Contraception: A History of Its Treatment by the Catholic Theologians and Canonists* (Cambridge, 1965), provides a serious analysis of Church teachings on the subject, while Peter Fryer, *The Birth Controllers* (New York, 1966), offers a historical treatment of the birth control movement in the United States.

Conclusion

⸸

THE CATHOLIC CHURCH, IN MANY WAYS LIKE THE city of Boston itself, seems never to change. It goes along over the years, the decades, and the centuries without any apparent twists or turns in its slow and inexorable passage through time, confident of its past and assured of its future. In fact, however, the Catholic Church has been almost continually changing in response to new ideas, new members, new movements, and new goals during its long history, and it has acquired the facility of incorporating many of these changes without appearing to do so. That, certainly, has been the case with the evolvement of the Catholic Church in the archdiocese of Boston.

In looking back over the history of the archdiocese during the more than two centuries of its existence, it is fascinating to observe the remarkable ability of Catholics to respond to a constant series of changes that often challenged their existence and usually called their future into question. As members of an outlaw church during the colonial period, American Catholics found themselves constantly threatened by social ostracism and physical harassment. Only political independence from Great Britain and the constitutional guarantees of a new government finally provided them a reluctant measure of personal freedom. During the early days of the Republic, however, the old bigotry of nativism was augmented by the newer paranoid hysteria of outright anti-Catholicism as waves of immigration brought increasing numbers of Catholics into the country. Thanks to the level-headed guidance of Bishop Benedict Fenwick and Bishop John Fitzpatrick, Boston Catholics were able to sustain themselves through the trials of a resurgence of nativism, the Know-Nothing era, and the Civil War without yielding their principles or resorting to senseless violence. Steadily, they continued to build their churches, develop their neighborhoods, and, under the guidance of Archbishop John Williams, expand their influence remarkably by the end of the nineteenth century.

By the beginning of the twentieth century, Boston Catholics were starting to emerge from their immigrant status and assume a more active and responsible role in the life of the community. On Christmas Day, 1997, the *Boston Globe* published an article reporting the retirement of Father Robert Boyle, seventy-one, former pastor of St. Mary's Church in Charlestown. In many respects, the career of this priest personified the spiritual lifetime not only of many of his own priestly colleagues but also of the many men and women of the laity who had lived their lives as Roman Catholics during the greater part of the twentieth century under four of Boston's eight bishops.

Born in 1926, Father Boyle had grown up as a young Catholic during the stern and spartan years of Cardinal William O'Connell, when the people of the archdiocese began to assume a new and more self-assured confidence in the primacy of their religious faith and the supremacy of their ethnic heritage. These were the times when the aesthetic culture of the Catholic Church was in full splendor, with the smell of incense and the full-throated sounds of the mighty organ forming the background for the three priests who moved in unison and chanted the Latin liturgy at a solemn high Mass.

Having attended St. John's Seminary, Bob Boyle was one of thirty-six young men ordained in 1951 by Cardinal Cushing. He first carried out his duties as a parish priest in suburbs such as Belmont and Acton, and later served the interests of inner-city youngsters as principal of Cathedral High School in Boston's South End. These were exuberant years, when John F. Kennedy was elected the first Catholic president of the United States, when the ecumenical movement broke down old barriers between Catholics and their non-Catholic neighbors, and when the physical growth of the Church, paralleling the growth of the "New Boston" itself, seemed destined to go on forever.

By the time Cushing was fading into retirement in the late 1960s, however, the good times were no more. It was almost as though the bullet that had taken the life out of the handsome young president had also taken the life out of those who had looked forward to some kind of new golden age. But it was much more than that, of course. Changes of great magnitude were taking place during the late 1960s and early 1970s, changes that took their toll as much upon Father Boyle as upon the parishioners with whom he had worked so long and so intimately. Some of these changes resulted from the numerous social and political upheavals sweeping through the nation in the wake of the Vietnam War and in response to calls for a new and more equitable society. As pastor at St. Mary's, Father Boyle, always a favorite among young and old, now often found himself the object of criticism and ridicule. First it came during the bitter clashes over urban renewal programs, when "townies" accused Church leaders of backing the political forces that destroyed the distinctive character of their old neighborhoods. A short time later it came during the violent racial tumult surrounding school integration and court-ordered busing, when Boston priests who were moved by the moral imperative to ensure full equality for all persons were roundly denounced by community leaders who believed they were defending the sanctity of their homes and the security of their children. Dedicated priests and many of their own loyal parishioners found themselves on opposite sides of the barricades. It was a heart-breaking time in Boston.

At almost the same moment, the city's Catholic Church was also being badly shaken by many of the unexpected aftereffects resulting from the changes set in motion by the Second Vatican Council. These often confused priests, divided parishes, and sent many Catholics stomping out of the Church in bewilderment, anger, or sheer disgust. Some criticized the Church for having gone too far in rejecting old practices and traditional liturgies; others complained that the Church had not gone far enough in liberalizing its doctrines to meet the demands of the modern age. A number of hitherto faithful, church-going Catholics felt abandoned by the Church they had loved all their lives and betrayed by the priests and bishops to whom they had pledged their loyalty and support. Although most of them insisted they still believed in God and belonged to His Church, they now took the position that they no longer needed their priests and bishops to tell them what to do. They would make up their own minds about what to believe and what not to believe. Religion was important, they said, but the Church had become largely irrelevant.

Starting with Cardinal Humberto Medeiros in 1970, and continuing under Cardinal Bernard Law in 1984, the archdiocese of Boston recognized the significance of this breakdown in what had always been an unusually warm and cooperative relationship between Boston Catholics and their religious leaders and took steps to deal with it. The first efforts seem to have been in the nature of damage control—immediate attempts to halt the worst effects of what was happening and to restore some semblance of normalcy and stability. If that could be accomplished, then it might be possible to reestablish more-effective lines of communication, generate new forms of cooperative partnerships, and perhaps offer new visions for the future. In preparing to deal with the problems of the moment, however, both Medeiros and Law made it clear that neither of them would offer or sanction any changes or modifications in the basic doctrinal teachings of the Catholic Church as promulgated by Pope John Paul II. Neither prelate would deviate from this position.

Beyond this point, however, both cardinals made efforts to demonstrate that the Catholic Church was indeed taking new shape and form in accordance with the principles laid down by the Second Vatican Council. By establishing a modern management system to eliminate duplication and ensure accountability, Cardinal Medeiros was able to send his bishops out into the various episcopal regions. There, they came into direct and frequent contact with the people of the Church, and on a regular basis they provided him with an up-to-date and accurate picture of what was going on at the parish level. Ironically, a strong, centralized episcopal base provided the opportunity to develop a more decentralized system of episcopal contacts and associations. Building on the new management model, and making use of a new system of parish visitations, Cardinal Law was able to modernize administrative procedures even more, as well as to reinvigorate the spiritual life of the parishes throughout the diocese. Sometimes this was done by reestablishing familiar forms of liturgical practices in the various parishes, such as Novenas, missions, and retreats. At other times it was accomplished by new forms of Confraternity of Christian Doctrine (CCD) programs, Bible study classes, reading groups, and special programs for young people and teenagers. Much of this was made possible by the increasing participation of lay people in almost all aspects of the life of the Church, in ways that would have seemed absolutely inconceivable a generation earlier. Gradually, old enmities died out and old wounds began to heal, as more fulfilling styles of liturgical worship and more respectful forms of spiritual dialogue created a greater spirit of cooperation between the leaders of the Church and the people in the parishes.

In looking to the immediate future, it appears that in view of a relatively stable Catholic population, serious budget constraints, and a continuing decline in the number of priests the archdiocese will not be launching any large-scale programs to build more churches, schools, or hospitals. Given the significant increase of new-immigrant groups from various parts of Asia and Latin America, combined with a national policy of reform that has dropped unemployed persons from the welfare rolls, the Catholic Church will undoubtedly be required to devote more of its funds to social and charitable purposes. Funds acquired through the Cardinal's Stewardship Appeal are already used to support a remarkable number of archdiocesan agencies. These range from services for the elderly, family counseling, marriage preparation, pregnancy assistance, and AIDS ministries to a variety of apostolates for black Catholics and for recent Asian, Haitian, Hispanic, and Irish immigrants to the greater Boston area. In all probability, the resources of the archdiocese will be directed even more toward meeting the pressing needs of the poor, the homeless, and the disadvantaged, not allocated to extensive construction programs.

It also appears likely that it will be necessary to curtail and even reduce the number of parishes in the archdiocese as the number of Catholics increases and the number of priests continues to decrease as a result of the aging of the clergy combined with declining vocations. Members of the laity, therefore, will go on taking over more and more functions previously considered to be the prerogative of priests. In many cases, baptisms and marriages will be handled by deacons, and spiritual direction, pastoral counseling, and financial management will be done by lay people.

In this process of lay involvement, it seems that the feminization of the Church is not just inevitable—it has already happened. At the parish level, laywomen now play prominent roles as eucharistic ministers, lectors, and religious educators; at the diocesan level, women serve as pastoral administrators, curial judges, and cabinet secretaries. In 1995, Mary Ann Glendon of the Harvard University Law School was appointed the pope's representative at the Beijing Conference on Women, where she was a persuasive advocate for the Catholic tradition. And in 1997, former congresswoman Lindy Boggs was named to succeed former Boston mayor Raymond Flynn as ambassador to the Holy See. There is no evidence that such a trend will not continue well into the future. Catholic women are a significant part of the extraordinary level of activity being generated by the laity in the spiritual life of the Church.

As Charles Morris has suggested in his book *American Catholic,* however, this new breed of active and committed lay Catholics can be a mixed blessing. They tend to be an unusually "prickly and contentious lot," he says, who now demand a "seat at the table" in decisions ranging from parish administration and the selection of a new pastor to questions of sexual ethics and policies regarding ministries for women. It is well recognized that the world has changed, the times have changed, and in many ways even the Catholic Church itself has changed. But what is sometimes overlooked is that over the course of several generations the people of the Church have changed as well. Today's Catholics are, for the most part, well educated, socially conscious, economically successful, and self-confident Americans. In their political lives and professional careers, they are accustomed to making informed decisions based on an intelligent review of factual information. As a result, they are much more apt to respond to reasonable explanations and logical conclusions than to officious directives or authoritative commands. At the local level, for example, Catholics are already more inclined to choose their own parishes than to passively accept the one assigned to them according to some geographical boundary. Older people seek out quiet, meditative liturgies; young families prefer churches with day-care facilities; teenagers attend parishes with Teen Masses; traditionalists look for the occasional church where the Mass is said in Latin. Inspiring music, stimulating homilies, and unconventional liturgies often prove more appealing than the convenience of proximity. Annoying as it might be, this tendency of American Catholics to be increasingly selective in their personal choices and moral decisions is not something that will go away. At a moment when Rome is clearly insisting on a greater measure of centralization, this impulse toward more-local decision making can provide what Morris calls "a tough balancing act" for individual pastors.

But walking a tightrope is often what leadership is all about. The changing character of the Catholic people, the new medical and scientific discoveries of a technological era, and the reconfiguration of the world since the collapse of the Soviet Union present exciting new challenges to the leaders of the Catholic Church as it moves into the twenty-first century. This is certainly something to which Cardinal Bernard Law is giving a great deal of serious thought. In looking ahead, he speaks with some confidence about what he calls the Boston Plan for Planning, a projection based on proposals for the future developed by clusters of parishes and worked out through building a consensus of pastors and other parish leaders. And future appointments of pastors, he indicates, will less and less be determined by age, and more by those qualities needed "for the new challenges which the office of pastor entails." The successful pastor in the future, the cardinal predicts, will be measured by "his ability to collaborate and delegate." The skill of Church leaders in determining the dividing line between respectful dissent and disobedient rebellion, between the wonders of modern science and the dangers of reckless experimentation, and between the interests of the universal Church and the concerns of individual national cultures may help shape the course and direction of the Catholic Church in the next hundred years. It certainly cannot fail to have a significant impact upon the type of religion practiced by Boston Catholics.

Index

Abenaki Indians, 7, 8

Abolition movement, xii, 98–99, 100

Abortion controversy, 314, 316, 317, 318, 322, 325–26

Academy of the Sacred Heart (Boston), 218, 221

Acre, the, 46

Act of Union, 17

Ad limina visit to Rome, 199

Adams, Charles Francis, 66

Adams, John, 11, 12, 24, 29, 30

Adams, John Quincy, 68

Adams, Samuel, 11

Addams, Jane, 175

African Americans, 145; Catholic, in Boston, 273–76; demands for equal rights, 288, 298–99

"Age of Big Business," 174

Alexis, Sister Ann, 49, 50 (illus.), 126–27

Algonquin Indians, 7

Alien and Sedition Acts, 30–31

Aloysia, Sister Ann, 126

American Baptist Home Missionary Society, 174

American Catholic (Morris), 312, 337

American Catholics (Hennesey), 4

American Ecclesiastical Review, 185

American Expeditionary Force (AEF), 225

American Federation of Labor, 186

American Freedom and Catholic Power (Blanshard), 255

American Hebrew Congregations, 258

American Lutheran Church, 253

American party, 93–96, 97, 98, 105, 113. *See also* Know-Nothing party

American Protective Association (APA), 151–53

American Revolution, 11, 17, 54, 70, 159

Americanist controversy, 183–85, 187–88

Americanist views, 183–84, 184–85, 187, 197, 223, 227

Amory, Rufus, 24

Amoskeag Manufacturing Company, 84

Ancestors and Immigrants (Solomon), 171

Andrew, John, 105–6

Andrew Square (Boston), 169

Anglican Church. *See* Church of England

Anglo-Saxon heritage, 147, 152, 215, 216, 221, 235

Ann Street, 56

Annulment, process of, 314–15

Anti-Mason movement, 57

Anti-priest law, 9

Anti-Semitism, in Boston during 1940s and 1950s, 256–58
Antietam, Battle of, 109
Appomattox Courthouse, 112
Arch Street (Boston), 245
Archbishop's Stewardship Appeal, 292
Archdiocesan Archives, 294
Aroostook County, Me., 72–74
Artificial insemination, 317
Assisi, Italy, 267
Association of Boston Urban Priests, 276
Atkins, Thomas, 276
Atlantic Monthly, 153
Augustinians, 126
Australia, 143
Austria-Hungary, 159
Ave Maria, 184
Awful Disclosures (Monk), 63
Azores, 164, 269

Back Bay (Boston), 121, 218
Balkans, 159
Ballimore, Ireland, 86
Ballina, Ireland, 86
Baltimore: Fifth Provincial Council, 74; First Plenary Council, 91; Second Plenary Council, 128, 132; Third Plenary Council, 133–34, 135, 137, 185
Baltimore Catechism, 135, 212, 324
Bangor, Me., 47, 84
Banks, Robert, 306
Bapst, John, 97n
Baptists, 56, 99, 273
Bardstown, Ky., 26
Bay of Pigs, Cuba, 277
Beacon Hill (Boston), xiii, 23, 55, 80, 138, 273
Beatty, Jack, 232n, 235
Beecher, Lyman, 63–64, 69
Beijing Conference on Women, 336
Belcher, Jonathan, 9
Belfast, Me., 21
Belgium, 108, 110, 149
Bells of St. Mary's (film), 246
Benedict XV, Pope, 207n, 227
Benedicta Community, 72–74, 130
Berkeley, Calif., 269

Berrigan, Daniel, 276, 289
Berrigan, Philip, 276, 289
Beverly, Mass., 202
Bible, King James version, controversy, 91, 92, 95, 97, 150
Bigelow, John, 90
Birth control controversy, 230, 289, 314
"Bishop John," 79, 115. *See also* Fitzpatrick, John
Bishops' Committee for Ecumenical and Interreligious Affairs, 304
Black Robes, 7
Blaine, James G., 151n
Blanshard, Paul, 255
Blenkinsop, William 127
Blessed Mother, 210, 211
Blessed Sacrament Church (Cambridge), 201
Blinstrub's Village, 259
Board of Aldermen, Boston, 139
Boggs, Lindy, 336
Bok, Derek, 294
Boles, John, 294
Bolivia, 244
Bolshevism, 225, 228
Bonaparte, Napoleon, 23, 31, 53, 55
Boston, 4, 6, 8; made a diocese, 24–25; made an archdiocese, 129; changing character of population, 310–12
Boston Associates, 46, 47
Boston Authors' Club, 145
Boston Central Council, 140
Boston City Council, 276
Boston City Hospital, 120, 121
Boston College, 97n, 121, 194, 207, 218, 220, 223, 224, 245, 249, 259, 266
Boston College High School, 241, 242
Boston Common, 6, 34, 70, 106, 305
Boston Common Council, 139
Boston Confronts Jim Crow (Schneider) 145
Boston Ecclesiastical Seminary, 130–32
Boston Edison Electric Company, 122, 244
Boston Elevated Railway, 240
Boston Fire Department, 244
Boston Gas Company, 122, 244
Boston Latin School, 71, 80
Boston Neck, 55

Boston Particular Council, 140
Boston Police Department, 244
Boston Post, 231
Boston Public Library, 145, 207
Boston Recorder, 57
Boston Redevelopment Authority (BRA), 296
Boston School Committee, 93, 139, 276
Boulard, A. Leon, 163
Bourget, Ignace, 162
Bowers, Henry F., 151
Boy Scouts, Catholic, 217
Boyle, John, 16
Boyle, Robert, 332, 333
Bradford, William, 8
Brady, John J., 199
Brady, Robert, 111
Brahmins, Boston, xiii
Braintree, Mass., 83, 202
Breen, John, 139
Bridgewater, Mass., 151, 202
Brighton, Mass., 121, 130, 132, 219, 220, 251
Brimmer, Martin, 58
Bristol, Me., 21
Broad Street (Boston), 55, 123; Broad Street riot, 67–68
Brockton, Mass., 104, 159, 170, 203
Brook Farm, 73
Brookline, Mass., 256
Brothers of Charity, 126, 177
Brown v. Board of Education of Topeka, 298
Brownsville, Tex., 283, 284, 285, 300
Bulfinch, Charles, 23, 55
Bullock, Alexander, 113
Bunker Hill Day, 301
Burlington, Vt., 83
Burns, Anthony, 100
Burns, Michael, 16, 23
Busing controversy, 298–304; decline of, 306–7
Byrne, Patrick, 46
Byrne, William, 199

Cabinet secretaries, under Cardinal Law, 306–7
Cabotville, Mass., 83

"Cafeteria Catholics," 317
Cagney, James, 246
Cahill, Mary (Cushing), 240
Callahan, Owen, 23
Calvert, Sir George, 42
Calvinism, xi
Cambodia, 288; immigrants from, 307, 310
Cambridge, East, Mass., 47, 72
Campbell, Patrick, 16, 23
Canada: French colony, 6; British possession of, 10, 11–12; American desire for friendship with, 12; in modern times, 162, 163
Cape Cod, 3
Cape Verde Islands, 164
Cardinal Cushing School (Hanover, Mass.), 259–60
Cardinal Medeiros Remembered, 303n
Cardinal O'Connell Seminary (Jamaica Plain), 270
Cardinal's Appeal, 307–8
Carew, Sister Jane, 294n
Caribbean, immigration from, 273
Caritas Christi, 307, 325–26
Carney, Andrew, 126–27, 180–81
Carney Hospital, 127, 178, 180–81, 225–26, 233, 325
Carroll, Charles, 12, 18
Carroll, John, 12, 18, 29, 52; bishop of Baltimore, 18, 21, 22, 23, 24, 51; archbishop, 25; first synod, 26; death of, 33
Carroll, John P., 320
Carroll, Thomas, 268
Carver, Mass., 22
Cass, Thomas, 105
Casserly, Ann, 150
Cassidy, James, 284
Castro, Fidel, 327
Catechism of the Catholic Church, 324
Cathedral High School, 333
Cathedral of the Holy Cross (Franklin Street), 23–24, 25 (illus.), 26, 34, 43, 45, 66–67, 75, 104, 123, 125, 130
Cathedral of the Holy Cross (South End), 64n, 129–30, 131 (illus.), 139, 182 (illus.), 188, 194, 199, 200, 218, 222, 223, 226, 267, 287, 294

Catholic education, 69, 91–92, 130, 135–38, 147–48
Catholic Festival, 141
Catholic Interracial Council (Boston), 275
Catholic Union, 141, 143
Catholic University, 134, 184, 188, 207, 284
Catholic World, 184, 187
Catholic Youth Ministry, 326
Catholic Youth Organization (CYO), 249, 320, 326
Catholics, in Boston, xii; excluded from liberty of conscience, 10; post-Revolutionary status, 14; numbers, 16–17; Irish character of, 23; population in 1940, 232–33; religious life during 1920s and 1930s, 208–14; during 1940s and 1950s, 246–48; activities, 249–50; population during 1940s and 1950s, 251–52
Celibacy, 215
Centennial of archdiocese, 217, 222
Central Burying Ground (Boston), 34
Chancery building, 219
Channing, William Ellery, 26
Chaplains, Catholic: in Civil War, 106; in World War I, 225; in World War II, 245, 249
Charitable Irish Society, 49
Charity, Catholic attitudes toward public forms of, 175–77
Charleston, S.C., 43, 51, 53
Charlestown, Mass., 45, 47, 63–66, 104, 121, 300, 302
Chavez, Cesar, 285
Chelmsford, Mass., 309
Chelsea, Mass., 83, 152, 256
Chestnut Hill, Mass., 220, 241
Cheverus, Jean-Louis de, 18, 19, 20 (illus.), 21–24, 51, 58, 123, 223; made first bishop, 25; activities in Boston, 26–28, 29, 30, 41, 45, 48, 52, 54, 160, 215; during War of 1812, 33, 46; St. Augustine's Cemetery, 34–36; return to France and death, 36
Chicopee, Mass., 104
Child labor controversy, 228–30; defeat of referendum, 230

Child Labor Amendment, 230
"Children's Day," 223
China, immigrants from, 307
Chmielinski, John, 169
Cholera epidemic of 1849, 87
Christian Spectator, 57
Christian Watchman, 57
Christmas, celebration of, 160; observances, 209, 247
Church of England, 3, 4, 5, 10–11, 16, 17
Cicognani, Amleto, 239, 262, 263
Civil Constitution of the Clergy (France), 19
Civil Rights movement, 269
Civil War, 105–12, 150; social effects on Boston Catholics, 119–20; economic effects, 120–22
Clergy, role in parish life, 212–14
Cobb, Samuel, 129
Cobh, Ireland, 240
Coffin ships, 86
Cogo, Joseph, 311
Cohasset, Mass., 83, 202
Cold War, 246, 255
College of the Sacred Heart (Newton), 221
Collins, John F., 277, 296
Collins, Joseph, 268
Colombia, immigrants from, 310
Columbian Artillery, 105
Committees of Correspondence, 12
Common Council, 122
Common Ground (Lukas), 276
Commonwealth Avenue (Boston), 218
Communism, 224, 244, 246, 327
Confederate States of America, 105
Confraternity of Christian Doctrine (CCD), 335
Congregation for the Doctrine of Faith, 317
Congregation of the Missionary Priests of St. Paul the Apostle. *See* Paulists
Congregational style of worship, xi, 4, 5, 16, 22
Congregationalists, 56
Connaught, Ireland, 46
Connecticut, 48, 74
Connell, Ellen, 49

Connolly, James, 284
Connolly, John, 52
Connor, Edmund, 23
Conscription Act, 109–10
Constitution on the Sacred Liturgy, 268
Continental Army, 12
Continental Congress, 12
Contraception, 317
Conway, Katherine, 143–45, 146 (illus.)
Conwell, Henry, 53
Coolidge, Joseph, 24
Copp's Hill Burying Ground, 34
Corn Laws, repeal of, 55
Cornell, Robert J., 290
Corrigan, Michael, 185
Cottrill, Matthew, 22
Coughlin, Charles E., 230, 256
Council of Trent, 263, 324
Covenant for Justice, Equity, and Har-
    mony, 299
Cromwell, Oliver, 5, 143
Cronin, Daniel, 279
Crosby, Bing, 246
Cuba, 221; immigrants from, 310; pope's
    visit to, 326–27
"Culture Factory," 148
Curley, James Michael, 139, 207, 228,
    231–32, 235, 261
Cushing, Patrick, 240, 241
Cushing, Richard J., 226, 319, 333; early
    life and education, 240–42; ordained,
    242–43; work in Propagation of the
    Faith, 243–44; named auxiliary bishop,
    243; made archbishop of Boston, 243;
    interest in foreign missions, 243–44;
    fundraising techniques, 244–45,
    291–92; opposition to Communism,
    246; radio apostolate, 248; management
    style, 250–51; parochial schools,
    252–53; ecumenical movement, 253–55,
    257 (illus.); opposition to anti-Semit-
    ism, 256–58; and Feeney Affair,
    258–59; work with disabled, 259–60 (il-
    lus.); local political associations,
    260–61; serious illnesses, 261, 276; ele-
    vated to cardinal, 262–63, 322n; speak-
    ing at Vatican Council, 264–65; liturgi-
    cal changes, 267–68; and seminarians'

strike, 269–71; problem of rising debt,
    271–72, 291; and racism, 273–75, 276;
    association with John F. Kennedy,
    277–78 (illus.); declining health, 277,
    279; possible successors, 279; Medeiros
    as successor, 283, 287; death of, 287,
    292

Daily, Thomas V., 294, 304
Daly, Patrick, 179
Daly, William J., 133
Daly Industrial School (Dorchester), 179
Damariscotta River (Maine), 22
Danvers, Mass., 201
D'Arcy, John M., 293, 294, 304
Daughters of Charity, St. Vincent de Paul,
    126, 181, 182 (illus.), 225, 295n
De facto segregation, 298
Dearden, John, 279
Death penalty, controversy over, 318
Debt, archdiocesan, 271–72, 291–93,
    307–9
Declaration of Independence, 12
Declaration of the Rights of Man
    (France), 28
Deer Island, 88; hospital, 90
Democratic party, 68, 69, 105, 152
Demographic changes in archdiocese,
    309–11
D'Estaing, Charles Henri, 13
Detroit, 279
Dever, Joseph, 244, 271
Devereux, Henry, 59
Devotional calendar, 208–11
Diaconate, 293–94
Dignitatis Humanae, 264
Diocesan Charitable Bureau, 234
Dissenters, English, 4
Divorce, 289, 295, 314–15
Donahoe, Patrick, 59, 60 (illus.), 105, 106,
    141–42, 178, 204
Donahoe Buildings (Boston), 142
Donovan, John J., 139
Dorchester (section of Boston), 139, 169,
    178, 179, 256, 275
Dorchester Heights (section of Boston),
    33
Dougherty, Dennis, 227

Douglas, Stephen, 100, 105
Dover, Me., 84
Dow Chemical Company, 289
Doyle, John, 310
Dozois, John, 162
Dracut, Mass., 202
Draft Riots: New York, 110; Boston,
 110–11
Dred Scott case, 100
Drinan, Robert F., 289
Driscoll, Arthur, 293
Drogheda, Ireland, 143
Druillettes, Gabriel, 8–9
Dublin, Ireland, 86
DuBois, Jean, 51
DuBourg, Louis, 51
Dudleian lectures, 10–11
Dudley, Thomas, 8, 9
Duggan, John, 16, 23
Duggan, Patrick, 16
Durfee High School (Fall River, Mass.),
 284
Dutch Reformed Church, 18
Duxbury, Mass., 202
Dwight, Thomas, 140

East Boston, 152, 166, 203
East Cambridge, Mass., 47, 72
Eastport, Me., 47, 84, 199
Eck, Gustavus, 161
Ecumenical movement, 253, 255, 259
Egan, Ann (Williams), 123
El Salvador, immigrants from, 310
Eliot, John, 9
Eliot, Samuel, 67
Eliot School, 92
Elizabeth I, Queen, 3, 5
Elliott, Walter, 187
Ellsworth, Me., 84, 97n
Emancipation Proclamation, 109, 274
Emerson, Ralph Waldo, xii
Emmanuel College, 221
Emmitsburg, Md., 48, 49
Encarnacao, João, 164
Enclosure Acts, 55
England, John, 51, 53
Episcopal Church, 17

Evacuation Day, xiii
Everett, Edward, 70, 86
Everett, Mass., 203
Exposé literature (anti-Catholic), 62–63
Expostulator, 61

Falconio, Diomede, 205, 222
Fall Muster, 1837, 70
Fall River, Mass., 83, 104, 253, 284
Famine, Irish potato, 84–86, 113; Boston
 response to, 86–87
Faneuil Hall, 153
Farley, John, 205, 226
Farrell, John, 294n
Farrington, Joshua, 15–16
Fascism, 225
Father Jim Hennessy Club, 244
Fatima, shrine at, 248
Fawkes, Guy, 5, 10
Federal Bureau of Investigation (FBI), 246
Federalist party, 28, 29, 30, 31
Feeney, Leonard, 258–59
Fellows, Nathan, 24
Female Charitable Society, 49
Fenton, John H., 252
Fenway Park, 259
Fenwick, Benedict, 41–43, 44 (illus.), 79,
 91, 123, 127, 160, 161, 177, 332; sec-
 ond bishop of Boston, 43; building
 more churches, 45, 80; and Catholics in
 Lowell, 46–47; working with Indians,
 47–48; conflicts over nationalities,
 50–51; lay trustee dispute, 51–54; and
 problem of nativism, 56–59; establishes
 the Pilot, 59–61, 141–42, 204; anti-
 Catholic attacks, 62–64, 66–67; burning
 of Ursuline convent, 64–66, 70; and
 Fitzpatrick, 71, 83, 113; creates Bene-
 dicta Community, 72–74; founds Holy
 Cross College, 74; death of, 75–76
Fenwick, Enoch, 42
Fenwick, George, 42
Field's Corner (Dorchester), 310
Fifty-Fourth Regiment, 273
Fighting Ninth, 105
Fillmore, Millard, 98
Finnegan, Thomas, 261

First Friday Devotions, 211, 234, 247

Fish Pier, 245

Fitton, James, 45, 74, 111

Fitzgerald, John F. ("Honey Fitz"), 139, 145, 215, 216 (illus.), 218

Fitzpatrick, John, 71, 72, 74–76, 81 (illus.), 106, 109, 111–12, 123, 125, 129, 130, 132, 142, 161, 180, 188, 189, 215, 220, 223, 332; third bishop of Boston, 79–80, 82–84, 114–15; and potato famine, 85; and Irish immigrants in Boston, 86–89; spending policies, 89–90; and cemetery problems, 90, 91; and education of Catholic children, 91–92, 135; and public school controversy, 92–93; and Know-Nothing movement, 93–98, 111; and slavery, 100; and Healy, 101, 103; receives Harvard degree, 108, 119; death of, 112–13

Flaget, Benedict, 51

Flanagan, Bernard, 279

Florida, 252

Flynn, Raymond L., 306, 336

Fontbonne Academy (Milton, Mass.), 269

Forbes, Robert Bennet, 86

Fort Hill district of Boston, 45, 49, 82, 123

Forty Hours' Devotion, 139

Foster, August John, 32

Foster, Susanna, 34

France, 13, 108, 159

Franciscan Sisters, 178, 179, 180, 182

Franciscans, 126; Italian, 165; Polish Conventual, 170

Franklin, Mass., 309

Franklin Street (Boston), 22, 24, 34, 36, 43–44, 67, 75, 76, 101, 104, 123

Free Silver movement, 151

Freemasonry, 57

French, in North America, 6, 7; colonial fears of, 9–10; English defeat of, 10; American friendship with, 12, 13–14, 54, 159–60

French and Indian War, 11. See also Seven Years' War

French immigrants, 159–60, 162–64; and French-speaking parishes, 202

French Revolution, 17, 28–29, 53

Fulton, Robert, 139

Galero, 263

"Gangplank Bill," 207. See also William Henry O'Connell

Gardner, Henry, 95

Garrison, William Lloyd, 66, 98–99

Garrity, W. Arthur, Jr., 298, 299

Gasson, Thomas I., 220

Gaston, William, 129

Gate of Heaven Church (South Boston), 165, 240

Georgetown College (D.C.), 42, 101

Gerbi, Emiliano, 165

Germany, immigrants from, 51, 160–62, 309

Gettysburg, 110, 112

Ghent, Treaty of, 33

Gibbons, James, 145, 184, 186, 197, 200, 223, 226

Gillette Razor Company, 244

Girl Scouts, Catholic, 217

Glanworth, Ireland, 240

Glendon, Mary Ann, 336

Gloucester, Mass., 83, 152, 164

Glover, Ann, 6

Going My Way (film), 246

Good Government Association, 230

Goodwin, Doris Kearns, 148

Gould, Abraham, 34

Graham, Billy, 245, 257 (illus.)

Granby Street, 204, 243

Grant, Ulysses S., 112

Great Boston Fire of 1872, 142, 162

Greek immigrants, 159, 171, 195

Greenback party, 175

Greene, Gardiner, 24

Greene, Henry, 61

Gregorian University (Rome), 284

Gregory XVI, Pope, 100

Grey Nuns, 126, 179

Gricius, Joseph, 170–71

Groppi, James, 289

Guerrini, Joachim, 166

Guild, Curtis, Jr., 222

Guild of the Blind, 268

Gunpowder Plot, 5
Guy Fawkes Day, 10

Haiti, immigrants from, 307, 310
Hale, Edward Everett, 87
Half-Acre, the, 46
Hallihan, Paul, 279
Hamilton, Alexander, 28, 29, 30
Hancock, John, 12
Hanly, Patrick, 22
Hanly, Roger, 22
Hanover, Mass., 260
Hanover Street Church (Boston), 63
Harkins, Matthew, 188, 199
Harper's Weekly, 151, 153
Harrington, Joseph, 15
Hart, Daniel, 303
Hartford, Conn., 75
Harvard College, 10, 11n, 85, 119, 207,
    217, 259, 277, 304, 317
Harvard Law School, 298
Harvard Medical School, 140
Harvard Stadium, 208
Haskins, George Foxcroft, 91, 101
Haverhill, Mass., 203
Hawthorne, Nathaniel, 73
Hay, Daniel, 15
Hayes, Patrick, 240
Healy, Alexander Sherwood, 101n, 127
Healy, Hugh, 101
Healy, James, 49, 101, 102 (illus.), 103,
    110–11, 127, 198
Healy, Michael, 101
Healy, Patrick, 101n
Hecker, Isaac, 187
Helmick, William, 288, 303n
Hennesey, James, 4, 128, 183, 226
Hennigan, James, 298n
Henry VIII, King, 3, 5
Hibbard, George A., 222
Hicks, Louise Day, 276, 298
Higginson, Stephen, 24
"Higher law," xii, 99
Hingham, Mass., 83
Hispanic immigrants, 285
History of the Archdiocese of Boston (Sexton), 12

Hogan, William, 53
Holmes, Oliver Wendell, 171
Holy Cross Church. *See* Cathedral of the
    Holy Cross (Franklin Street)
Holy Cross College, 74, 75, 82, 96, 97n,
    100, 101, 103, 298
Holy Cross Sisters, 108
Holy Family, 211
Holy Ghost Hospital (Cambridge), 233
Holy Hours, 211
Holy Name Church (Fall River), 284
Holy Name Church (West Roxbury),
    201
Holy Name of Jesus Church (Chicopee),
    109
Holy Name Society, 139, 211, 222, 223,
    249, 307
Holy Thursday, 209, 210
Holy Trinity Church (Boston), 82, 160,
    161, 162, 169
Holy Trinity Church (Lawrence), 170
Home for Destitute Children, 178
Home Missionary, 57
Honduras, immigrants from, 310
Hoover, J. Edgar, 246
Hôtel Dieu Nunnery (Montreal), 63
Houlton, Me., 84
House of the Angel Guardian (Boston),
    91, 101, 177, 233
House of the Good Shepherd (West End),
    177
"House seminary," Fenwick's, 45, 74, 75
Howe, Samuel Gridley, 86
Hughes, Alfred, 304
Hughes, Henry, 164
Hughes, John, 53, 108
Huguenot chapel (Boston), 14, 23
Hull, Mass., 202
Hull House (Chicago), 175
Human Rights Commission, 275, 299
Humanae Vitae (Paul VI), 316
Huron Indians, 7
Hyde Park, Mass., 274
Hynes, John B., 261, 298

Immaculate Conception Church (Lawrence), 170

Immaculate Conception Church (South End), 104, 121, 211, 218
Immigration Restriction League of Boston, 172
Imperial Wars (England and France), 7, 8, 10
Impressment of American sailors, 32
In vitro fertilization, 317
"Inculturation," 317
Independent Catholic Church of America, 51
Indiana, 149
Indians. *See* Native Americans; *individual tribes*
Infallibility, papal, 128
Influenza epidemic of 1918, 225
International bankers, 230
International Congress on Pastoral Unity, 267
Ipswich, Mass., 83, 203
Ireland, immigrants from, 4, 5, 6, 16n; living conditions in Boston, 45–46, 55; population, 1830, 55; harassment of, 56, 66–68; "famine Irish," 86–88, 98; reaction to, 88–89; and abolitionists, 98–99; involvement in Civil War, 104–12; social effects, 119–20; economic effects, 120–22; mobility, 122–23
Ireland, John, 184, 186, 197
Iroquois Indians, 7
Italy, immigrants from, 158, 159, 165–66, 167 (illus.), 168–69, 171, 309; and Italian-speaking parishes, 202–3
"*Iuravit Dominus,*" 195

Jackson, Andrew, 33, 51, 68–69
Jackson, Miss., 304
Jackson State College (Miss.), 288
Jacksonian democracy, 52, 73
Jamaica Plain, Mass., 274
Jamestown, U.S.S., 86
Jamestown, Va., 6
Japan, 199
Jefferson, Thomas, 28, 29, 30, 31, 67
Jesuit, The, 58–59
Jesuits, in Canada, 7, 8, 19; in United States, 42, 63, 104, 126, 151, 180, 199, 211, 218, 241
Jews, in Boston, 197, 230; violence against, 256; Cushing's relationship with, 256–58; Cushing speech at Vatican Council, 265
John XXIII, Pope, 262, 263; death of, 263
John Paul I, Pope, 295
John Paul II, Pope, 268, 296, 304, 313, 316–17, 322, 325; visit to Boston, 296, 297 (illus.); visit to Cuba, 327–28, 334
Johns Hopkins University, 226
Josephite priests, 274, 275n
Joyce, Robert Dwyer, 145

Kane, Paula, 218
Kansas-Nebraska Act, 97, 100
Kavanagh, James, 22
Keane, John, 184, 187–88
Keely, Patrick, 125, 129
Keith, Benjamin F., 219, 221
Kelly, Patrick, 51, 53
Kennebec River (Maine), 7
Kennedy, Edward ("Ted"), 302
Kennedy, John F., 277, 278 (illus.), 299, 333; assassination of, 278
Kennedy, Joseph, 315n
Kennedy, Joseph P., 277
Kennedy, Joseph P., Jr., 277
Kennedy, Robert F., 279
Kennedy, Rose Fitzgerald, 216 (illus.), 218
Kennedy Memorial Hospital, 277
Kensington, Pa., 97
Kent State University (Ohio), 288
Kentucky, 148
Kentucky and Virginia Resolutions, 30
Keys of the Kingdom (film), 246
Killala, Ireland, 86
King, Martin Luther, Jr., 275–76
King, Philip J., 268
King's Chapel, 13
Kingston, Mass., 202
Klein, Félix, 158
Knights of Columbus, 140, 225, 226, 249
Knights of Labor, 186–87

Know-Nothing party (American party), 93–95, 96, 97, 98, 105, 113, 120, 122, 150, 151
Kraemer, Mathias, 160
Kraemer, Melchior, 160
Kraemer, Sebastian, 160

Laity, rise of in Boston, 139–40; growing role after Vatican II, 312–13; increasing role under Cardinal Law, 318–19
Laity's Directory to Church Services, The, 42–43
Lally, Francis J., 275, 298
Lane Theological Seminary, 63
Laos, immigrants from, 307, 310
Lariscy, Philip, 34, 35
Larkin, John, 16
Latin America, 243, 244, 277, 304, 326, 327
Law, Bernard F., early life and education, 304, 308 (illus.), 313, 335, 338; bishop of Springfield–Cape Giradeau Diocese, 304; named archbishop of Boston, 304–6, 317; creation of Cabinet system, 306–7; closing of churches, 309, 312; and new Catholic immigrants, 309–11; official positions of 318, 334; assessment of, 318–21; elevated to cardinal, 322; conducts Eighth Synod, 322–23; role in creating new catechism, 324; and Catholic health-care system, 325–26; and Youth Ministry, 326; attends Vatican synod, 326–27; travels to Cuba, 327–28
Lawrence, Abbott, 66
Lawrence, Amos A., 108
Lawrence, Mass., 83, 103, 139, 159, 164, 170, 180, 202, 203
Lawrence, William, 221
Lay trustee disputes, 53–54, 79
League of Catholic Women, 145, 249, 250 (illus.)
League of the Sacred Heart, 139
Lee, Robert E., 112
Legion of Mary, 211, 307
"Lend-lease" program for priests, 252
Lenten devotions, 209, 213, 247

Leo XIII, Pope, 140–41, 187, 188
Leonard, William J., 245, 265, 266, 268
Liberator, 97
Liebman, Joshua, 245
Lincoln, Abraham, 104, 105, 106, 107, 108, 109, 112, 125; assassination of, 112
Lincoln, Frederic, 110, 111, 113
Literary and Catholic Sentinel, 59
Lithuania, immigrants from, 158, 159, 169, 170–71, 172 (illus.)
Little Red Schoolhouse, 153
Little Sisters of the Poor, 126, 180
Liturgical Conference, in Boston, 267
Liturgical reforms, post–Vatican II, efforts at, 266–69
Liturgical Weeks, 267, 268
Living Wage, A (Ryan), 227
Lobb, George, 15
Lobb, Mary, 15
Logan Airport, 244, 262
Lomasney, Martin, 177, 197, 230
Lord's Prayer, dispute over, 92–93
Los Angeles, 279
Louisiana, 252
Louisiana Purchase, 31, 35
Louisville, Ky., 97
Lourdes, shrine at, 248
Lowell, James Russell, 66
Lowell, Mass., 46, 47, 48, 83, 95, 104, 139, 159, 162, 163, 164, 169, 170, 179, 180, 187, 193, 202, 203, 205
Lowell High School, 194
Lubec, Me., 84
Lukas, J. Anthony, 276
Lusitania, sinking of, 242
Lutheran Church, 4, 18, 253
Lyman, Theodore, 24
Lyndon, Patrick, 130, 189
Lynn, Mass., 82, 152
Lynnfield, Mass., 201

Madison, James, 30–31, 32
Madonna de Soccorso, La, 168
Madonna delle Grazie, La, 168
Magennis, Thomas, 149
Magginis and Walsh, 132, 220

Magner, John, 15, 23, 34
Maguire, Joseph, 285, 287, 304
Mahew, Jonathan, 10, 11, 16
Mahoney, John, 46
Maine, 6, 19, 21n, 29, 70, 73, 83, 84, 103, 130
Malden, Mass., 90
"Man's Cities and God's Poor," 299
Manchester, N. H., 84, 279
Mann, A. Dudley, 108
Mansfield, Frederick W., 231
Manton, Joseph E., 247
Marblehead, Mass., 82, 172
Maréchal, Ambrose, 33, 43, 51
Marier, Theodore, 268
Marist Fathers, 163, 202
Married men, ordination of, 313, 314
Massachusetts Bar Association, 230
Massachusetts Bay Colony, 4, 5
Massachusetts bill of rights, 14
Massachusetts Catholic Order of Foresters, 140
Massachusetts Citizens Against the Death Penalty, 318n
Massachusetts Electric Company, 122
Massachusetts Emergency Public Health Committee, 226
Massachusetts General Court, 8, 9, 13
Massachusetts state constitution, 14
Mather, Cotton, 6
Matignon, François, 18, 19, 21–24, 28–29, 34, 41, 54, 159–60
May processions, 209, 234, 247
Mayo, Ireland, 86
McCarthy, Joseph, 246
McCloskey, John, 129, 205
McClure, Anna, 16
McCormack, John W., 256
McDonnell, Thomas, 299
McElroy, John, 82, 104
McGreevy, John, 208, 214, 250
McQuaid, Bernard, 185
Mead, Edwin D., 148
Medeiros, Antonio, 283
Medeiros, Humberto S., 165n, 286 (illus.), 297 (illus.), 305, 319; early life and education, 283–84; made bishop of

Brownsville, 284; installed as archbishop of Boston, 285; conditions in archdiocese, 287–90, 334; diocesan debt, 291–93; creates episcopal regions, 293, 335; permanent diaconate, 293–94; campus ministries, 294; elevated to cardinal, 295, 322n; and busing crisis, 298–303, 302 (illus.); death of, 303
Medeiros, Maria, 283
Medieval Institute (Toronto), 268
Medley, Margaret (Fenwick), 42
Mellony, Michael, 15
Melodeon Theater, 126
Melville, Annabelle, 19, 26
Merrimack River, 46, 83
Merrimack Valley, 162
Merry del Val, Raphael, 198
Merton, Thomas, 245
Messenger of the Sacred Heart, 185
Methodist Church, 17, 56, 99, 273
Mexican War, 82
Mexico, 304, 327
Middleboro, Mass., 202
Mill girls, 162
Milton, Mass., 82, 202
Minnihan, Jeremiah, 279
Miraculous Medal Novena, 211
Missions, 211
Mission Academia, 242
Mission Church (Roxbury), 211, 247
Mission Hill district (Boston), 231
Missionaries of St. Charles Borromeo ("Scalabriani"), 168
Missionary Sisters of the Sacred Heart, 168
Missions, foreign, 243, 244
Mississippi Valley, 69, 151
Mohawk Valley, 7
Monk, Maria, 63
Montagnais Indians, 8
Montgomery, Richard, 70n
Montgomery Guards, 69–70
Montreal, 6, 123, 126
Morgan, Tallulah, 298n
Morgan v. Hennigan, 298
Morris, Charles, 312, 337
Morris, Robert, 273

Morse, Samuel F. B., 69
Mother Teresa, 286 (illus.)
Mount Benedict, 43, 64
Mullen, John, 163
Mulligan, Francis, 15
Mundy, John, 136
Music Hall, Boston, 141
Mussio, John, 279

Nantucket, Mass., 82
Nantucket Sound, 19
Narragansett Bay, 70
Nast, Thomas, 151, 152 (illus.)
National Assembly (France), 19
National Association for the Advancement of Colored People (NAACP), 298
National Catholic War Council (NCWC), 227–28
National Catholic Welfare Conference (NCWC), 227–28
National Conference of Catholic Bishops, 327
National Council of Catholic Men, 268
National Council of Churches of Christ, 253
National Labor Union, 186
Native Americans: during colonial times, 7; in Maine, 19, 21, 22, 47, 145
Nativism, 56–57, 62, 68–69, 93, 94 (illus.), 150, 152 (illus.); response to "famine Irish," 87–88
Naval war, between Britain and France, 31
Nazism, 224
Neale, Leonard, 42
New Bedford, Mass., 48, 104, 164
"New Boston," 333
New Deal programs, 228
New England Telephone and Telegraph Company, 122
New France, 6, 7
New Hampshire, 6, 83, 103
New Harmony community, 73
New Jersey, 141, 158
New Orleans, 97
New Orleans, Battle of, 33, 51
New York, 6, 16, 41, 53, 125, 158, 240
New York Observer, 57

New York Times, 252
Newburyport, Mass., 22, 180, 201
Newcastle, Me., 21, 22
Nicaragua, immigrants from, 307
Nineteenth Amendment, 228
Ninth Regiment (Irish), 105, 106, 136
Nixon, Richard M., 288
Norfolk, Va., 53
North American College, Rome, 133, 194–95, 197, 198, 219, 240, 242, 262–63
North Andover, Mass., 202
North End (Boston), 10, 45, 71, 82, 90, 121, 122, 165–68, 202
Northampton, Mass., 82
Northeastern University, 294
Norwood, Mass., 170, 202
Notre Dame des Victoires Church (Boston), 163–64
Nova Scotia, 148
Novena of Grace, 211
Nunnery Committee, 96
Nuns: in Civil War, 107–8; teaching orders, 149–50; decline in numbers, 311–12

Oates, Sister Mary, 149, 150
O'Beirne, Patrick, 54, 71
Oblates of Mary Immaculate, 126, 162, 203, 211
O'Brien, Hugh, 139, 147
O'Brien, John, 137, 181
O'Brien, Michael, 180
O'Brien, Pat, 246
Observer, 142
Ockenga, Harold J., 255
O'Connell, Brigid, 193
O'Connell, Denis, 184, 187, 197
O'Connell, James, 206
O'Connell, John, 193
O'Connell, Joseph, 139, 215
O'Connell, William Henry, 133, 169, 170, 187, 188, 193–95, 196 (illus.), 197, 242, 243, 249, 251, 332; rector of North American College, 197–98; made bishop of Portland, 198; mission to Japan, 199; made archbishop of Boston,

200–201; growth of churches, 201–3; management style, 203–4, 205–6; made cardinal, 205, 322n; problem with nephew, 206; personal style, 207–8, 319; and religious vocations, 214; and parochial schools, 215; influence on archdiocese, 215–18, 219–23; silver jubilee, 223; golden jubilee, 223; sociopolitical views of, 224–25; during World War I, 225–26; postwar social views, 226–29 (illus.), 230–33, 234–36; death of, 239–40

O'Connor, Maurice, 274

Office of Spiritual Development, 295

O'Flaherty, Thomas, 54, 59, 71–72

O'Hara, John, 262, 263

Old Granary Burying Ground, 34

Old Hickory. *See* Andrew Jackson

Old Town, Me., 21, 47, 199

Oneida Community, 73

O'Neill, Thomas P. ("Tip"), 278 (illus.), 302

Orangemen, 152

Order of American Freedom, 150

Order of the American Union, 150

Order of the Star Spangled Banner, 93

Order of United Americans, 93

Ordination: of married men, 313, 314, 318; of women, 303, 314, 317, 318

O'Reilly, John Boyle, 142–43, 144 (illus.), 145, 147, 177

Ortega, Jaime, 328

Otis, Harrison Gray, 64, 66

O'Toole, James, 203, 207, 208

Our Lady of Czestochowa Church (South Boston), 169, 170

Our Lady of Fatima Church (Peabody, Mass.), 165n

Overseers of the Poor, 175

Owen, Robert, 73

Paddy Camps, 46

Papist conspiracy, rumors and fears of, 6, 7, 9, 10, 51, 57, 59, 62–63, 69

Papyrus Club, 143

Paris, 123, 132

Parish Boundaries (McGreevy), 214

Parishes: importance of, 208; religious observances in, 208–10; boundaries of, 234; demographic changes, 309; problem of foreign-language churches, 310

Park Street Church, 255

Parkman, Francis, 138

Parochial schools: difference of opinions on, 135–36, 138; establishment of, 147–49, 217, 218, 251, 252; declining numbers, 289–90; 305–6

Passamaquoddy Indians, 19, 22, 47, 84

Passionists, 211

Pastoral Plan for Mission, 323

Patriotic League of the Revolution, 150

Paul VI, Pope, 263, 268, 317

Paulist Press, 187

Paulists, 187

Pawtucket, R. I., 48

Peace of Mind (Liebman), 245

Peale, Norman Vincent, 245

Pedophiliac priests, problem of, 315–16

Pennsylvania, 51, 159

Penobscot Indians, 21, 22, 47, 84, 97n

Penobscot River, 19

Pentecostals, 273

Perfectionism, 72–73

Perkins, James, 24

Perry School (South Boston), 241

Peru, 244

Peters, Andrew J., 226

Peterson, John B., 220

Philadelphia, 26, 53

Philosophy House, St. John's Seminary, 132, 219

Physician-assisted suicides, 317

Pilot, Boston, 59–61, 75, 89, 96, 100, 105, 120, 139, 141–42, 143–45, 153, 177, 211, 275, 296; as archdiocesan newspaper, 204, 270

Pimentel, Antonio, 165

Pittsfield, Mass., 82

Pius VII, Pope, 25, 26

Pius IX, Pope, 113, 125, 128, 141, 194

Pius X, Pope, 145, 199, 205

Pius XI, Pope, 207n, 223

Pius XII, Pope, 207n, 240, 243, 261, 267

Pleasant Point, Me., 19

Plymouth, Mass., 6, 22, 83
Plymouth Plantation, 4, 8
Plymouth Rock, dedication of, 147
Poland, immigrants from, 159, 169;
    Polish-speaking parishes, 203, 309
Polish Catholic Independent Church, 170
Polish National Church, 170
Pontifical College Josephinum (Ohio), 304
Pope John XXIII National Seminary for
    Delayed Vocations, 271
"Pope's Night," 9, 12, 67
Populist movement, 151
Porter, James, 315
Portiuncula Chapel (Hanover, Mass.),
    260n
Portland, Me., 84, 101n, 198, 199, 206,
    273
Portuguese immigrants, 164–65, 166
Poterie, Claude de la, 14
Power of Positive Thinking (Peale), 245
Powers, John E., 277
Pregnancy Help, 325
Presbyterian Church, 17–18, 22, 56, 99
Priests, archdiocesan: decline in numbers,
    270, 289, 312; during busing contro-
    versy, 302–3
Primeau, Ernest, 279
Pro-Life movement, 317
Pro-Life Office, archdiocesan, 325
Project Rachel, 325–26
Proparvulis Club, 249
Protestant, 57
Protestant mission societies (American),
    56–57
Protestants, English, 3
Providence, R.I., 128, 188
Public housing, integration of, 306
Public school controversy, 91–93
Puritans, 3, 4, 5, 6, 7, 13
Puritanism, xi, 10
Pusey, Nathan, 278 (illus.)

Quakers, 73
Quasi-war, 30
Quebec, 6, 7, 9
Quincy, Josiah, Jr., 86, 90
Quincy, Mass., 202, 326

Race relations in Boston, 273. 296
Racial Imbalance Law, 300
Radcliffe College, 258
Raffeiner, John, 160–61
Randolph, Mass., 83, 202
Râle, Sebastian, 7
Ratzinger, Joseph, 316
Reardon, Cornelius, 163
Redemptorists, 126, 211
Reed, Rebecca, 63
Reformation, 263
Regional system, under Cardinal Med-
    eiros, 292–93
Regis, Mother Mary, 150
Regis College, 221
Reiter, Ernest, 161–62
Republican party (Jefferson), 28, 29, 30,
    31
Republican party (modern), 104, 224
Rerum Novarum (Leo XIII), 187
Retreats, 211, 247
Revere, Mass., 201, 202
Rhode Island, 48, 74, 79, 80
Richard, Gabriel, 289n
Richmond, Va., 51, 112
Riley, Lawrence, 248, 304
Riley, Thomas, 279, 304
Ring, Thomas, 140
Ripley, George, 73
Roberts, Sarah, school segregation case,
    273
Robin, Abbé, 13
Roche, David, 178
Roche, James Jeffrey, 143
Roddan, John, 100
Roe v. Wade, 325
Rolof, James, 161
Romanist views, 184, 185, 187, 197, 223
Rome, 127, 128, 263, 316
Roncalli, Angelo Giuseppe (Pope John
    XXIII), 262, 263
Roosevelt, Franklin Delano, 230
Roosevelt, Theodore, 222
Rosary, reciting of, 211, 248
Rosary Society, 212
Roslindale, Mass., 274
Rousselet, Louis de, 15, 17

Roxbury, Mass., 8, 90, 95, 121, 139, 180

Russia, immigration from, 159

Ryan, Bridget, 49

Ryan, J. Joseph, 268

Ryan, John A., 227, 228

Rynne, Paul, 275

Sacred Heart, image of, 211

Sacred Heart Church (East Cambridge), 137

Sacred Heart Church (North End), 168

Sacred Heart Review, 137

St. Anne's Church (Lawrence), 164

St. Anthony's Church (Cambridge), 165

St. Anthony's Church (Lowell), 165

St. Anthony's School (North End), 168

St. Anthony's Shrine (Boston), 244

St. Augustine's Cemetery, 34–35, 45, 90, 130

St. Benedict's Center (Cambridge), 259

St. Brigid's Church (Lexington), 275

St. Casimir's Church (Cambridge), 170

St. Cecilia's Church (Boston), 211

St. Charles College (Maryland), 194

St. Clement's Hall (seminary), 219

St. Coletta-by-the-Sea (Hanover, Mass.), 259–60

St. Elizabeth's Hospital (Boston), 181, 221, 233, 307, 325

St. Eulalia's Church (South Boston), 201, 241, 242

St. Francis de Sales Church (Charlestown), 104

St. Francis de Sales Church (Roxbury), 179

St. Francis Xavier Church (Weymouth, Mass.), 104

St. Helena House (Boston), 180

St. James Church (Arlington), 274

St. James Church (Boston), 101n, 123, 140

St. Jean-Baptiste Church (Lowell), 162

St. John Lateran (Rome), 195

St. John's Church (Cambridge), 72

St. John's Church (Quincy), 202

St. John of God Church (Fall River, Mass.), 284

St. John the Baptist Church (Fall River, Mass.), 72, 82

St. John the Baptist Church (North End), 164, 166

St. John's Hospital (Lowell), 181, 233, 307

St. John's Industrial School (Newton), 179

St. John's School (North End), 168

St. John's Seminary (Boston), 130–32, 170, 219, 220, 233, 240, 242, 252, 268, 332; strike at, 270–71

St. Joseph's Church (Lowell), 162

St. Joseph's Church (Medford), 195

St. Joseph's Church (Peabody, Mass.), 170

St. Joseph's Church (Roxbury), 80

St. Joseph's Church (South Boston), 171

St. Joseph's Church (West End), 133, 195

St. Joseph's Church (Westfield, Mass.), 133

St. Joseph's Hospital (Lowell), 234, 307

St. Joseph's Seminary (St. Benedict, La.), 304

St. Joseph's Seminary (Troy, N.Y.), 130

Saint Lawrence River, 6

St. Leonard's Church (North End), 166, 168

St. Louis, Mo., 97

St. Margaret's Church (Dorchester), 169

St. Margaret's Hospital (Dorchester), 233, 307

St. Mary's Church (Cambridge), 136–37

St. Mary's Church (Charlestown), 332, 333

St. Mary's Church (Lowell), 83

St. Mary's Church (North End), 54, 71–72, 82, 111

St. Mary's Church (Quincy), 72, 82

St. Mary's Church (Salem), 82

St. Mary's College, 145

St. Mary's Infant Asylum and Lying-in Hospital (Dorchester), 178, 233

St. Mary's Seminary (Baltimore), 42

St. Michael's Church (Bangor, Me.), 84

St. Michael's Church (Fall River, Mass.), 283

St. Michael's Church (Haverhill, Mass.), 170

St. Michael's Church (Hudson, Mass.), 163
St. Monica's Church (South Boston), 201
St. Nicholas Church (East Boston), 111
St. Patrick's Cemetery (Fall River, Mass.), 303n
St. Patrick's Church (Brockton, Mass.), 104, 202
St. Patrick's Church (Lowell), 47, 83, 180
St. Patrick's Church (Newcastle, Me.), 22
St. Patrick's Church (Providence, R.I.), 72
St. Patrick's Church (South End), 45
St. Patrick's Day Parade, xiii, 249, 256
St. Patrick's Home for Working Girls, 180
St. Paul's Church (Dorchester), 201
St. Peter's Basilica (Rome), 27 (illus.), 205, 263
St. Peter's Church (Burlington, Vt.), 72, 83
St. Peter's Church (Dorchester), 201
St. Peter's Church (Lowell), 72, 83
St. Peter's Church (New York), 42, 53
St. Peter's Church (South Boston), 171
St. Peter's Orphan Asylum, 233
St. Richard's Church (Roxbury), 274, 275
St. Sauveur, Chevalier de, 13
St. Stanislaus Church (Chelsea), 170
St. Sulpice seminary (Montreal), 71, 101, 162, 220
St. Sulpice seminary (Paris), 71, 101, 158, 220
St. Theresa's Church (Methuen, Mass.), 163
St. Thomas's Church (Jamaica Plain), 149
St. Vincent de Paul Society, 140–41, 212, 233
St. Vincent's Church (Fort Hill section), 82
St. Vincent's Orphan Asylum (South End), 49, 91, 177, 233
St. William's Church (Dorchester), 201
St. William's Hall (seminary), 219
SS. Peter and Paul Church (South Boston), 45, 127, 310
Salem, Mass., 22, 82, 169, 180, 203
Salvation Army, 174
Salvi, John, 321

San Marco Society, 168
San Sossio Baronia, Italy, 168
Sandwich, Mass., 48, 83, 104
Sanford, Henry, 109
Santa Susanna (Rome), 263
Satolli, Francesco, 198
Scapular Society, 212
Schneider, Mark, 145
School Street, 22
"Schoolmen," 136
Schurr, Dennis, 327
Scituate, Mass., 22
Scott, Dred, 100
Scully, Thomas, 136–37
Sears, David, 24
Secret societies, fear of, 185–86
Secretary for Pastoral Services, 307
Secretary for Social Services, 307
Segregation, in Boston public schools, 298
Selma, Ala., 275
Seminarians: during 1940s and 1950s, 252; decline in numbers, 271, 289–90, 310
Sen Fu Club, 244
Separation of church and state, 29, 52, 115, 264
"Separatist integration," under Cardinal O'Connell, 217, 235
Separatists, 4
"Servant Church," 275
Seton, Elizabeth Bayley, 24, 27 (illus.), 48
Settlement houses, 174
Seven Storey Mountain (Merton), 245
Seven Years' War, 10. See also French and Indian War
Seward, William, 108
Sex scandals, 315–16
Sexton, John E., 12
Shakers, 73
Shattuck, George C., 66
Shattuck, Lemuel, 87
Shawmut Avenue (Boston), 82, 161, 169
Shawmut Peninsula, 3, 4
Sheen, Fulton J., 245–46
Sheridan, Philip, 112
Sherman, William T., 112

Short Abridgment of the Christian Doctrine,
61–62
Simmons College (Boston), 294
Sioux Falls, S.D., 252
Sisters of Charity, 24, 27 (illus.), 48, 49,
108, 126, 178
Sisters of the Good Shepherd, 177
Sisters of Mercy, 108, 126
Sisters of Notre Dame de Namur, 149,
221
Sisters of St. Francis of Assissi of Milwau-
kee, 259
Sisters of St. Joseph, 149–50, 168, 179,
221, 268
Six Months in a Convent, 63
Slavery, 97; Irish attitude toward, 97–98;
Catholic Church position on, 100
Sligo, Ireland, 86
Smith, Jerome V. C., 95
Social Action Department, NCWC, 228
Social Justice, 230
Society for the Propagation of the Faith,
234, 243, 244, 254, 307
Society of St. James the Apostle, 244
Society of the Noctural Adoration of the
Blessed Sacrament, 139
Sodality of the Blessed Virgin Mary, 139
Solomon, Barbara, 171
Somerville, Mass., 152, 203
Song of Bernadette (film), 246
Sons of '76, 93
Sons of the Sires, 93
South Boston, 33, 90, 120, 121, 126, 127,
130, 165, 168, 170, 179, 225, 240–41,
242, 254, 256, 259, 276, 301
South Boston High School, 241
South Carolina, 51, 52; secession, 104
South End (Boston), 10, 55, 82, 104, 121,
125, 139, 177, 194, 211, 240, 241, 273;
deterioration of, 218–19, 220
South Station Railroad Terminal, 245
Southern European immigrants, 158–59,
172–73; living conditions of, 173–75
Soviet Union, 224, 246, 255
Spalding, John Lancaster, 184
Spalding, Martin, 127

Spanish Inquisition, 62, 63
Spellman, Francis J., 240, 243
Springfield, Mass., 82; made a diocese,
129
Stamp Act, 11
Stanwood, Jacob, 130
State House (Boston), 23, 55
Steubenville, Ohio, 279
Stoughton, Mass., 80
"Stranger's Vault," 13
Sulpicians, at St. John's Seminary: teach-
ers, 219; removed, 220
Sumner, Charles, 66
Sumter, Fort, 104, 125
Sundays, religious routines, 211–212
Symphony Hall, 223
Synod, archdiocesan, first, 24; second,
127; eighth, 322–23
Synod, Vatican, on America, 326

Taney, Roger B., 100
Taylor, William, 41
Television, impact of, 314
Templars of Liberty, 150
Testem Benevolentiae (Leo XII), 188
Tewksbury, Mass., 202, 309
Texas, 252
Thanksgiving, xiii
Thayer, John, 15, 17
Theology House, St. John's Seminary, 130,
132, 219
Third Order of Our Lady of Mount Car-
mel, 211
Third Order of St. Dominic, 164, 211
Third Order of St. Francis, 181, 211
Thursday Evening Club, 80
Tisserant, John, 24
Tobin, Maurice J., 231–32
Tocqueville, Alexis de, 29–30, 185
Tonnant (ship), 13
Torreón, Mexico, 304
Tottenham, England, 19
Tracy, Spencer, 246
Tralee, Ireland, 86
Transcendentalism, xii
Trinity Church, (Georgetown, D.C.), 42

Tuberculosis, 87
Tuckerman, Samuel, 24
Twenty-Eighth Regiment (Irish), 106
Twenty-One-Year Law, 95
Twomey, Mortimer F., 240, 241, 242
Tyler, William, 45, 75

Ulster, Ireland, 15
Unitarian-Universalist Association, 253
Unitarians, xi, 56
United Church of Christ, 253
United Fruit Workers, 284
United Prebyterian Church, 253
United States Catholic Intelligencer, 59
United States Naval Academy, 256
Universalists, 56
Urban renewal in Boston, 295
Ursuline convent, 62, 64; burning of, 64–
    66, 65 (illus.), 72, 73, 88
Ursuline nuns, 34, 35, 43, 63–64
Utah, 252
Utopian communities, 72–73

V-E Day, 239, 249
V-J Day, 239
Vatican Council, First, 128, 132, 133, 164
Vatican Council, Second: proceedings of,
    263–65; impact of, 265–67, 314, 316–
    17, 324, 334, 335; disputes about, 268–
    69, 290
Venice, Italy, 261
Vermont, 83, 84, 103
Vernacular, use of at Mass, 265
Vicksburg, Miss., 112
Vietnam, immigrants from, 307, 310
Vietnam War, reaction to, 269, 272, 276,
    288, 333
Virginia, 51, 52
Visitation of parishes, 323–24
Vocations, in Boston, during 1930s,
    213–15

WIHS-TV, 248
Wall, Thomas, 92
Walpole State Prison, 259
Walsh, David I., 215, 228
Walsh, Louis S., 200

Walsh, Michael P., 278 (illus.)
Waltham, Mass., 173
Walton, Susan, 182
Wangler, Thomas, 210
"War Hawks," 31
War of 1812, 32, 35, 46, 51
Ward Eight, 197
Wareham, Mass., 86
Washington, George, 11, 28
Waterford, Ireland, 86
Wayman, Dorothy, 133, 203
Weigel, Gustav, 314
Weld, William F., 322
Wellesley College, 217, 294
West Church, 10
West End, 121, 143, 177, 195, 230, 296;
    slum conditions in, 195–96
West Indies, immigration from, 273
West Machias, Me., 84
West Roxbury, Mass., 72
Western Canal, Lowell, 46, 47
Westport, Me., 82
Weymouth, Mass., 82, 202
"Whatever God Wants" (Medeiros), 295n
Whelan, Eleanor, 49
White, Kevin H., 276, 298
Whitman, Mass., 202
Whittier, John Greenleaf, 66
Wightman, Joseph, 112
Wiley, William, 43
Williams, John, 103, 113, 124 (illus.),
    186, 188, 193, 194, 198, 200, 212–13,
    215, 223, 319; fourth bishop of Boston,
    123, 125, 154, 158; schools and
    churches, 125–26; and Carney Hospi-
    tal, 126–27, 180; second synod, 127; at-
    tends First Vatican Council, 128; made
    archbishop, 129; constructs cathedral,
    129–30; builds seminary, 130–32, 219;
    style of dress, 133; management style,
    134, 203, 205; controversy over Catho-
    lic schools, 135–37, 137–38, 147–48;
    rise of Catholic laity, 139–40; charitable
    activities, 140–41, 177–80, 182; forma-
    tion of the Catholic Union, 141; involve-
    ment with *Pilot,* 141–42; increase of
    teaching orders of nuns, 149–50; and

new immigrants, 162–65, 168, 169–71, 173; and Catholic hospitals, 180, 181; death of, 188–89, 202
Williams, Michael, 123
Willis, John W., 153
Winthrop, John, 3, 4
Winthrop, Mass., 201
Winthrop, Robert C., 112
Wojtyla, Karol (Pope John Paul II), 316
Women suffrage movement, 228
Women in Boston, Catholic, 48, 120; members of religious orders, 233; during 1940s and 1950s, 249; entering religious life, 252; controversy over ordination, 292, 313, 317
Women's Christian Temperance Union (WCTU), 175
Women's Rights movement, 269
Worcester, Mass., 74, 75, 80, 82, 95, 100, 278
Working Boys' Home, 178–79
Working Girls' Home, 179

World Trade Center (Boston), 312
World War I, 225–27
World War II, 235, 239, 243, 245, 246; impact on postwar generation, 253–54, 255, 273
Wrentham, Mass., 22
Wyoming, 252

Xavier, St. Francis, 210

Yellow fever (in Boston), 22
Young Catholic, 187
Young Catholic's Friend, 61
Young Men's Catholic Association of Boston, 176 (illus.)
Young Men's Catholic Association of Boston College, 140
Young Men's Christian Association (YMCA), 174, 217
Young Women's Christian Association (YWCA), 174, 217
Yugoslavia, 256n